Kerala's Demographic Future

Kerala's Demographic Future

Issues and Policy Options

Editors

S. IRUDAYA RAJAN
K.C. ZACHARIAH

ACADEMIC FOUNDATION
NEW DELHI

First published in 2012
by

ACADEMIC FOUNDATION
4772-73 / 23 Bharat Ram Road, (23 Ansari Road),
Darya Ganj, New Delhi - 110 002 (India).
Phones : 23245001 / 02 / 03 / 04.
Fax : +91-11-23245005.
E-mail : books@academicfoundation.com
www. academicfoundation.com

Cataloging in Publication Data--DK
Courtesy: D.K. Agencies (P) Ltd. <docinfo@dkagencies.com>

Kerala's demographic future : issues and policy options / editors, S. Irudaya Rajan, K.C. Zachariah.
p. cm.
Contributed articles.
ISBN 13: 9788171887866
ISBN 10: 8171887864

1. Kerala (India)--Emigration and immigration. 2. Population aging--India--Kerala. 3. Public health--India--Kerala. 4. Kerala (India)--Population policy. I. Irudaya Rajan, S. (Sebastian), 1959- II. Zachariah, K. C. (Kunniparampil Curien), 1924-.

DDC 304.61095483 22

Typeset by Italics India, New Delhi.
Printed and bound in India.

In the memory of Dr C.R. Soman

Contents

Section III: Unemployment

Section IV: Ageing

Section V: Other Emerging Issues

List of Tables and Figures

Tables

Figures

About the Editors/Contributors

Editors:

S. Irudaya Rajan holds a Ph.D in Demography from the International Institute for Population Sciences, Mumbai, and is currently a Chair Professor of Research Unit on International Migration (set up by the Ministry of Indian Overseas Affairs) at Centre for Development Studies, Thiruvananthapuram, Kerala. He has more than two decades of experience of research into demographic issues in Kerala, published extensively, and has contributed seminally to debates on the demographic aspects of the 'Kerala Model' of development in national and international forums. He has worked on issues relating to sex ratio, migration and ageing and has been involved in four major surveys, the Kerala Fertility Survey, the Kerala Migration Survey, Kerala Mental Health Survey and Kerala Ageing Survey. His work has been frequently used in public debate on health, population, sex-selective abortion, and issues of senior persons in Kerala. He is the co-ordinator of Kerala State Development Report prepared for the Planning Commission, Government of India.

K.C. Zachariah holds a Ph.D in Sociology from the University of Pennsylvania, United States of America, and is currently Honorary Professor at Centre for Development Studies, Thiruvananthapuram, Kerala. He was a senior demographer at the World Bank, Washington D.C. (1971-1987) the UN Expert on Demography at the Cairo Demographic Centre (1966-1970) and Deputy Director, International Institute of Population Sciences, Mumbai (1957-1966). He has worked extensively on migration and co-ordinated four large-scale migration surveys (1998, 2003, 2007 and 2008) in Kerala along with Prof. S. Irudaya Rajan.

Contributors:

Sabu Aliyar, Post Doctoral Fellow, CANADA-HOPE Scholarship, Acadia University, Halifax, Canada.

Manja Bomhoff, Doctoral Scholar, Leiden University, The Netherlands.

J. Devika, Associate Professor at Centre for Development Studies, Thiruvananthapuram, India.

Prabhu Dass G. is Doctoral Scholar at Centre for Development Studies, Thiruvananthapuram, India.

K.S. James is Professor at the Institute of Social and Economic Change, Bangalore, India.

Shanthi Johnson, Professor, Acadia University, Halifax, Canada.

K. Ajithkumar, Assistant Professor, Trichur Medical College, Trichur, Kerala, India.

K. Anil Kumar is Clinical Psychologist at the Ansar Institute of Psychological Medicine and Rehabilitation, Ansar Hospital, Perumbilavu, Trichur, Kerala, India.

Aju Mathew, a former intern at Karolinska Institute (Stockholm, Sweden), is currently associated with Health Action by People, Thiruvananthapuram, India.

Udaya S. Mishra is Associate Professor at Centre for Development Studies, Thiruvananthapuram, India.

E. Mohamed is Director at the Ansar Institute of Psychological Medicine and Rehabilitation, Ansar Hospital, Perumbilavu, Trichur, Kerala, India.

P.M. Saidu Mohammed is Clinical Psychologist at the Ansar Institute of Psychological Medicine and Rehabilitation, Ansar Hospital, Perumbilavu, Trichur, Kerala, India.

K. Navaneetham is Professor at Centre for Development Studies, Thiruvananthapuram, India.

Remya Prabha is Doctoral Scholar at Centre for Development Studies, Thiruvananthapuram, India.

Mytri Prasad is Doctoral Scholar at Centre for Development Studies, Thiruvananthapuram, India.

Syam Prasad is Doctoral Scholar at Centre for Development Studies, Thiruvananthapuram, India.

Priyajit Samaiyar is Doctoral Scholar at Centre for Development Studies, Thiruvananthapuram, India.

Alice Sebastian is Doctoral Scholar at Centre for Development Studies, Thiruvananthapuram, India.

C.R. Soman, Chairman, Health Action by People, Thiruvananthapuram, Kerala, India.

Sreerupa is Doctoral Scholar at Centre for Development Studies, Thiruvananthapuram, India.

Rakkee Thimothy is Doctoral Scholar at the Jawaharlal Nehru University, New Delhi, India.

Sajan Thomas is a M.Phil Scholar in Department of Social Anthropology at University of Bergen, Norway.

M. Vijayanunni is former Registrar General and Census Commissioner of India and former Chief Secretary, Government of Kerala.

Foreword

Kerala has achieved international fame for its record in human development, particularly in the field of education and health. This is clearly on account of the vision of the first Communist government that came into power in 1957 that the development activities should be based on human development. Though this track of development has been widely applauded, there are criticisms as well. It is worth noting that in spite of the alternate governments that came into power in the state, this trail could not be done away with. Now it is widely accepted that development is nothing but to be assessed on the basis of human development index.

In key indicators used to calculate the human poverty index, India registers declining performance. The latest Human Development Report released by the UNDP in India recently serves to confront and challenge the tall claims with the rude realities of India's poor human development performance. UNDP and the Planning Commission suggest that the continuously declining performance in human development indicators should serve as a call for an immediate course correction on the part of the Indian government to take comprehensive measures to make universal access to food, jobs, health and education. It was as part of this approach that the State Planning Board had prepared its human development report in 2005. Further studies are needed in matters relating to the changes in life indices, psychological and social issues in the modern era and the like.

In this edited volume entitled *Kerala's Demographic Future: Issues and Policy Options*, the editors choose to present three emerging demographic issues of Kerala in the 21st century—'International Migration', 'Population Ageing' and 'Educated Unemployment'—and discuss various policy options on the subjects by eminent scholars in Kerala. With Kerala celebrating its Golden Jubilee decade since November 1, 2006, I congratulate Drs. S. Irudaya Rajan and K.C. Zachariah, the editors of this volume, for their excellent efforts to take stock of the Kerala demographic scenario during the first 50 years since the formation of the state on 1st November 1956 and predict Kerala's demographic future during the next 50 years of the 21st century.

— V.S. Achuthanandan

Chief Minister of Kerala

Section I

Overview

1

Kerala's Demographic Future

S. IRUDAYA RAJAN and K.C. ZACHARIAH

The demographic transition in Kerala has reached its final stage with low levels of fertility and mortality. The levels of replacement fertility hovering over the past 15 years are comparable to those of any part of the developing world. Similarly, infant mortality has been brought down to nearly 10 per thousand live births by 2003, thus enabling an average Keralite to live beyond 70 years, at birth. The principal components of the population growth—birth and death rates—have declined rapidly over the past 30 years and this decline has led to the achievement of Kerala of the lowest population growth rate in the country during 1991-2001. It is expected that the decline would continue to reach a negative growth rate by around 2041.

As per the 2001 Census, Kerala is ahead of most other states in India in the matter of population density with 819 persons per sq.km. The growth rate of population is below 1 per cent as against 2 per cent for the country as a whole. Kerala's sex ratio is unique among the states of India (without considering the predominant male emigration to Gulf countries), being the only state which has a population of females in excess of the population of males, with 1058 females per 1000 males (Zachariah *et al.*, 2003). Kerala achieved universal literacy by as early as in 1991. However, its worker participation rates for both men and women are lower than those of all-India.

The vital rates of Kerala such as of mortality and fertility are the lowest in India, the crude birth and death rates being 15.0 and 6.2 in 2005. All the different components of the infant mortality rates are also the lowest in the state. The infant mortality rate stood at 14 in 2005. The child-woman ratio is also the lowest in Kerala among all the states in India. According to our estimates based on the 2001 Census, Malappuram was the only district in Kerala with a total fertility rate above the replacement level (Guilmoto and Rajan, 2002).

Exactly 10 years ago, the editors of this volume brought out a volume on patterns and determinants of Kerala's demographic transition and its implications for the future (Zachariah and Rajan, 1997). That volume was partly an outcome of the papers presented at the International Congress on Kerala Studies (ICKS) organised by the AKG Centre for Research and Studies at Thiruvananthapuram, during 27-29 August 1994 in which the editors of this volume organised the session on demographic transition. E.M.S. Namboodiripad, Chairman of the ICKS not only wrote the foreword for the volume but also released it in the AKG Centre in 1997.

As Kerala has reached an advanced stage in its demographic transition, migration is emerging as a major component of its population growth—internal, international and replacement migration. Continuous decline in the number of births and of children is compensated by the increase in the proportion of the working population and of the elderly. In 2001, Kerala has reported 45 per cent of its population in the working ages of 25-59 years. Thus, unemployment among the educated youth is an emerging issue which will plague the Kerala society for several years to come. Continued low fertility has its undesirable effects too, the most important of which is the rapidly increasing number of elderly persons. As of 2007, 15 per cent of the population in Kerala has come under the age group of 60 years and above. Kerala needs to work out a policy framework to deal effectively with the social, economic, psychological and physical health problems associated with the elderly.

In his inaugural address at the International Congress on Kerala Studies in 1994, E.M.S. Namboodiripad had said, "We need to take fresh stock of our present situation and draw up a new agenda. This is not a task of any one political party or of political parties alone. It is a national task, in which the academic community and scientific professionals have an important role to play." He further stated, "When we set out to draw agenda for a democratic Kerala half a century ago, there were hardly any academic community and few modern professional experts. We activists took up the challenge. The problems of today are different and, perhaps, more complex. We need urgently a dialogue between academics and professionals in various disciplines and political activists and between various political parties—both on the Left and the Right—on how the development process in our state can be sustained. Political differences will remain, but a consensus on a broad platform of measures to overcome the crisis can be achieved." (Thomas, 2005).

Again, on December 9-11, 2005, the AKG Centre for Research and Studies organised the second International Congress on Kerala Studies on the theme "Agenda for Kerala Development—2006-2016." West Bengal Chief Minister, Buddhadeb Bhattacharjee inaugurated the conference in the presence of V.S. Achuthanandan, the then Opposition Leader in the Kerala Assembly. In his address, then Chief Minister, Oommen Chandy said, "Kerala is being victimised by the Finance Commission for the advances made in the field of public health, education and other social sectors. We have seen 2.5 million Keralites leaving the state in search of job opportunities and another four million seeking job" (*Deepikaglobal.com*, 2005). The editors of this volume organised two technical sessions—Demography and Migration—in the Congress. This book is an outcome of some of the papers presented in those sessions. Later, S. Irudaya Rajan organised the Twenty-eighth Annual Conference of the Indian Association for the Study of Population during 7-9 June 2006 in which he devoted a special session to Emerging Demographic Issues in Kerala in the 21st century. Some papers presented in this session also form part of this book.

The main themes discussed in the two seminars were: (1) the economic implications of low fertility and mortality and (2) the emerging issues in internal, international and replacement migration. In the discussion, the following questions were raised: Could Kerala reap benefits from the demographic windows of opportunities? What are the emerging health threats? Is Kerala able to provide pensions and social security for the growing number of elderly?

On November 1, 2006, Kerala's golden jubilee or the 50th anniversary of the State formation day in 1956, began. At 50 years, it is time for celebration and self-congratulation but also is an occasion for introspection and self-criticism. At the 50th anniversary celebrations of *Kerala Piravi* on November 1, 2006, the Prime Minister Manmohan Singh stated, "The people of Kerala have made India proud. Kerala has achieved international fame for its record in human development particularly in the field of health and education" (Government of Kerala, 2006).

This book is expected to take stock of the demographic situation during the past 50 years and to predict the demographic future for the next 50 years, with focus on three emerging demographic-induced issues which will continue to occupy the debate in Kerala economy and society in the coming years—migration, unemployment and ageing—along with a few other issues worthy of investigation.

The projections made of the population growth in Kerala indicate that the population size would not exceed 37.0 million by 2051 and that significant changes are likely to come about in the age structure, a factor which has significant implications for educational planning, employment opportunities, labour force composition, marriage prospects for women and problems of the elderly population. Kerala is likely to achieve zero population growth (ZPG) in 25 to 30 years from now. The school-age population would decrease, the proportion of the labour force would come down after two decades from 2001, the proportion of unemployed persons in the higher age groups of the labour force would rise, the number of males in the age group 25-29 years would become smaller than the number of females in the age group 20-24 years (who would marry males in the age group of 25-29 years) thus, creating an atmosphere favourable for marriageable market for females, and the problem of the elderly in general and the elderly in the oldest-old age group in particular, would become acute.

Kerala's demographic trends in the first half of the 21st century would be dramatically different from those of the second half of the 20th century. Whereas the total population of the state increased by 135 per cent during the second half of the 20th century (from 13,549 thousand in 1951 to 31,838 thousand in 2001), the growth, if at all, in the population during the next half century would be negligible. The crude death rate declined from about 20 per thousand to about 6 per thousand in the past half century, but it is likely to increase to 13 per thousand during the first half of 21st century. The crude birth rate decreased from 40 per thousand to about 16 per thousand in the last half of the 20th century, but it is likely to remain more or less stable in the next half century. While Kerala experienced varying degrees of net out migration and net emigration in the second half of the 20th century, the migration trends in the first half of the 21st century remain uncertain. However, they would depend more on socio-economic developments in the country and abroad than on demographic trends.

The socio-economic implications of the reversal of the demographic trends would be far-reaching. Mainly, the pressure on schools and colleges for admission of students would become a thing of the past, giving ample opportunities for the educational system to concentrate on the quality of education rather than on increasing numbers of students. This feature holds good also for hospitals and health care personnel catering to the health needs of children. It would be easier in the years ahead to bring about needed improvements in the quality of services in both education and health so as to consolidate the gains made in the human development scenario during the past 50 years (State Planning Board, 2005; Planning Commission, 2007).

Other things being equal on the economic front, the rate of unemployment among Kerala's young working age population would decline in the coming decades and educated young workers will be able virtually to pick and choose the jobs they want. However, unemployment would constitute an issue, which haunts the planners and policy makers for another 10 to 20 years. However, this will be the case with older workers. The older working age population is expected almost to double in number in the 20 years during 2001 to 2021, thus creating an atmosphere of unemployment more among the older age groups than among the youths in the foreseeable future.

During the past half century, the major socio-economic problems faced by Kerala were related to schooling, maintenance of health and nutrition, and employment for its youths. During the first half of the 21st century, the major socio-economic problems would be of finding gainful employment for both the young and the old working age population, maintenance of health and nutrition of the elderly, providing the elderly with subsistence through social security measures, pensions and other support programmes, and also effectively managing both internal and international migration in the era of globalisation.

The book is divided into four broad sections. The first section documents the current trends in both internal (from census data) and international migration (from the second Kerala Migration Survey), replacement migration to Kerala from other parts of India to undertake major infrastructure and other construction activities, macro and micro impact of remittances on the economy, society and households, and demographic expansion and its role in pushing migration from Kerala. The second section overviews the trends in unemployment in Kerala, particularly among women and examines the determinants of unemployment based on two primary surveys conducted at the Centre for Development Studies: The Second Kerala Migration Survey (2003) and The Employment and Unemployment Survey (2003). The third section focuses on population ageing and its pressure on public pensions, and role of welfare funds in providing social security for the informal sector workers, as well as a case study of vulnerability among widows. This section also has a chapter on emerging health concerns among the elderly, prepared on the basis of the large scale Kerala Ageing Survey conducted in 2004. The last section reports various other issues which have emerged in the recent past and are likely to engage research attention during the coming years in Kerala, such as lifestyle diseases, mental health, community palliative care, urbanisation and the growing menace of HIV/AIDS.

Migration

We have included five chapters in this section. The first chapter is by K.C. Zachariah and S. Irudaya Rajan on internal migration from Kerala to other states of India based on the five decennial censuses conducted since the formation of the state of Kerala. This chapter analyses the dynamics of migration between Kerala and the other states in India and attempts to relate it to demographic transition and the recent resurgence of external migration. Migration has been one of the means by which Kerala population coped with the ill effects of the rapid demographic transition in the second half of the 20th century. It was, and still is, one of the prime movers in the social transformation of Kerala over the past half-century. While international migration, especially Gulf migration, has been instrumental in the socio-economic transformation of many a relatively poorer working class family in Kerala in the 1980s and the 1990s, the money sent by internal migrants over the past 50 years had not only provided sustenance to a very large number of middle-class families back home, but also helped to finance higher education of children from these families to ensure their upward social-economic mobility. Thus, migration, both internal and external, played a major role in making of the Kerala society to what it is today, the state with the highest rank in India in terms of social development. Will such development continue in the years to come? Will migration from the state continue at high rates in the years to come?

Until about the middle of the last century, Kerala had remained basically an area of net in-migration. More persons had moved into Kerala than Keralites who had moved out. There had been during those days, little economic necessity for Keralites to migrate to other parts of the country. The situation changed during the second half of the 20th century. With the integration of the erstwhile Travancore and Cochin states to the Indian Union, the youths of Kerala began to move out in increasing numbers to other states in search of economic opportunities. The era of migration out of Kerala began and continued at an accelerated rate during much of the second half of the last century. With the maturing of the demographic transition, and the consequent decline in the rate of population growth and the onset of a period of emigration to the Gulf region and other foreign countries, out-migration began to slow down. At the end of the century, conditions were ripe enough for a reversal of the role of the migration trend in Kerala. There was empirical support to conclude that out-migration from Kerala decelerated. But in the last decade of the last century, some revival was in evidence of the increasing trend in out-migration from the state. Out-migration during 1991-2001 was larger than that during 1981-1991. Some plausible reasons for the reversal is also spelt out in the chapter.

This chapter also argues that out-migration from the state was a response to demographic transition and the consequent explosive (compared to the conditions in the other states of the country) population growth. The deceleration in out-migration after the 1980s could also be considered a response to the rapid decline in population growth that had set in since the early 1960s. The recent onset of replacement migration (a case study on contract workers to Kerala is provided in Chapter 5) to the state is explained on similar lines. The replacement migration is basically a response to the rapid decline in the number of workers in the young working ages caused by fertility decline to below replacement level, emigration of a large number of young persons to the Gulf region and other destinations abroad and economic improvements in the state economy which have fostered an aversion to low paid and unskilled jobs on the part of the youths in the state.

Migration begets migration. This is a basic fact about migration. Kerala has already passed the critical mass with respect to the number of out migrants and emigrants needed to sustain migration from the state at a reasonably high level. The rapid expansion in secondary level education, the lack of adequate gainful employment opportunities for Kerala's educated youths and the attainment of a critical mass of Kerala migrants living outside the state, would most probably ensure a continuation of the migration phenomenon at a relatively high rate even under the emerging unfavourable demographic and socio-economic trends. It may not be the demographic checks, but a very rapid expansion of service-related employment opportunities in Kerala that could put a break to the acceleration in the migration flows from the state.

The next chapter by K.C. Zachariah and S. Irudaya Rajan on international migration is based on the Second Kerala Migration Survey conducted by the authors in 2003 among 10000 households in Kerala (more details about the survey, see Zachariah and Rajan, 2004; 2005). In the first Kerala Migration Survey, Zachariah *et al.* (2001) concluded, "Migration has provided the single most dynamic factor in the otherwise dismal scenario of Kerala in the last quarter of the twentieth century. It is one of the positive outcomes of the Kerala Model of Development. Kerala is approaching the end of the millennium with a little cheer in many of its homes, thanks to migration and the economic returns that it brings. In Kerala, migration must have contributed more to poverty alleviation than any other factor including agrarian reforms, trade union activities and social welfare legislation."

During the five-year period 1999-2004, the number of emigrants increased from 13.6 lakh to 18.4 lakh, and the number of non-resident Keralites (emigrants plus return emigrants) increased from 21.0 lakh to 27.3 lakh. The Gulf region has not been the only, although a very dominant, destination of Kerala emigrants of 2004. Kerala emigrants have spread their wings over a larger number of countries during 1999-2004, including countries in Europe, America and South East Asia. Within the Gulf region itself, significant realignments have taken place. Saudi Arabia has lost some of its charm and United Arab Emirates has emerged, as the preferred destination.

Remittances to Kerala from abroad increased from Rs. 13.65 thousand crore in 1999 to Rs. 18.46 thousand crore in 2004. As a result of remittances, the per capita state income in Kerala increased by Rs. 5,678. Foreign remittances to the state have been 7 times of what the state received from the

Government of India as budget support, 15 times the receipts from cashew export and 19 times the receipt from marine exports. They have formed 1.8 times the annual budget of the state. However, the proportion of remittances to state domestic product showed a slight decrease from 25 per cent in 1999 to 22 per cent in 2004.

The chapter emphasised the beneficial effects of emigration on per capita income, education, employment, housing, household amenities and consumer durables. In the early stages of Kerala emigration, the beneficial effects overshadowed the adverse effects. Now that Kerala emigration has come of age, secondary effects, which are not so beneficial, are beginning to appear. The authors have emphasised the emerging negative impacts of emigration more than the positive impacts.

The first and the foremost among the negative impacts of emigration is that on the unemployment rate (Chapter 7 is on migration and unemployment). It gives an unorthodox view of the relationship between emigration and unemployment. Another point of view this chapter emphasises is that, emigration is a causative factor in the high unemployment rate prevailing in the state.

An equally important "adverse" consequence is the emergence of "replacement migration". Emigrants from Kerala have converted Kerala itself into a "Gulf" for many a migrant worker from other states in India. By accepting low wages and poor living conditions, these outside workers are taking away a lot of work, which otherwise could have gone to Kerala workers. Replacement migration is a consequence of emigration, and is having significant effect on unemployment and wage rates in Kerala. It is nullifying some of the potentially positive spin-off effects of emigration (see Chapter 5 on contract migration).

The greatly increased disposable income in the Kerala households had its effect on the consumption patterns. Higher levels of consumption, however, have not helped industrialisation in Kerala, as most of the goods Kerala consume come from outside. The potential spin-off effects of remittances on employment are benefiting workers outside Kerala more than workers in Kerala. Consumerism is draining the state of the development potential of its remittance receipts. It is leading many a Kerala family to financial ruin and even to suicide. Consumerism, brought about by emigration, has gone amok in the state with minimum positive impact on its employment situation.

The increasing economic and political clout of the "new rich", who became rich because of emigration and the Gulf connection, is creating a climate of resentment against them among some communities in Kerala. Mr A.K. Antony, former Chief Minister of Kerala was accused of anti-minority mentality for his alleged observation that minority communities were cornering undue benefits, using their newly acquired wealth power and high level connections, both being the consequences of emigration. This study has shown that minority communities have indeed undoubtedly benefited much more than the majority communities have, from emigration. Justified or not, such expression of resentment against the "new rich" of the minority communities by the "old rich" is another of the adverse effects of emigration.

Five years ago, we thought that Kerala's Gulf connection was a passing phase in its history (Zachariah *et al.*, 2002). Today, we think otherwise. Not only has Gulf emigration become well entrenched, some of the second-generation emigrants are settling in the host country on a permanent basis too, and others are spreading their wings to a much wider spectrum of countries. Migration is here to stay for a long time to come. The process of demographic contraction at work in Kerala would be the only major obstacle to Kerala emigration taking off to higher orbits. It is important that Kerala takes policy measures to see that emigration is kept at a sustainable level, and too much of its brain power is not drained off to other countries, and too much of its remittances are not drained off to other states. A policy for moderating brain drain and better and more productive utilisation of remittances for Kerala's development is essential.

While the significance of migration in shaping Kerala's economy is undeniable, the emerging migration market raises concern about the situation in which every individual does not have the same opportunity as others to migrate as it used to be the case in the past. In this context, Udaya S. Mishra and Priyajit Samaiyar point out that international migration is playing a divided role rather than a role of leveling off incomes in Kerala. The international migration market is getting selective day by day and the future migration potential needs to be assessed in terms of quality and not of quantity. These quality-quantity terms would relate to skilled/unskilled differentiations and the kinds of wages and labour conditions offered. In that regard, a migration-dependent economy like that of Kerala has to prepare to attune itself to the emerging demand of the international migration market. In a migration-driven economy, the macro-level advantages of remittance need to translate into micro-level welfare and to see that migration does not give rise to undesirable disparities at the micro-level. Given that the selectivity of migration is expected to grow, the migration divide at the households level is ought to grow further. Hence, micro-level adversities of migration in the state need to be recognised.

Using the second Kerala Migration Survey, 2003, the authors denote migration as the single most powerful agent inducing inequity in the supposedly egalitarian state of Kerala. In that sense, changing potentials and opportunities for migration should not be allowed to become selective so as intensify this inequality further. On the contrary, an effort towards universal migration opportunities may be the need of the hour. The state has an opportunity in hand with the availability of the best type of human capital and the capacity to tune it to the type of demand for labour force to make migration choice available to every Keralite. If today migration is selective or is the differentiating factor in determining economic status, tomorrow management of migration well may be worthwhile in restoring the unique character of a welfare state. On the whole, encouraging and universalising of migration remains the key to reap the most from the migration and migratory character of the Keralite. Such a management would result in a situation in which a migrant is no longer found as a distinct and superior class in society which creates divide as is observed at present.

Replacement migration to Kerala occurs in several ways to replace the work once managed by Keralites by other workers. Mythri Prasad maps the role of contract migration to Kerala in making urban public infrastructure, focusing on the road construction sites of the multinational Punj Lloyd Ltd. in the Thiruvananthapuram city of Kerala in the fifth chapter. If one assesses the historical development of Gulf countries, especially in its early stages of infrastructural development, the role of Keralite unskilled and semi-skilled workers is obvious; the same phenomenon is evinced in Kerala, workers from other states of India taking up the type of work that Keralites used to do. This chapter explores an emergent economy that connects these urban sites with villages in north and north–eastern India and the emergence of a fluid, multinational corporate space. It also documents the process of recruitment and deployment of labour through a chain of sub-contractors and investigates the process of sub-contracting in practice as a spatial strategy. It also traces the trajectories and patterns of relocations of workers by highlighting the element of journey involved in these relocations, based on the field work done by the author in the receiving state of Kerala and some of the sending states of Bihar and West Bengal.

An attempt is made to understand the processes of recruitment and relocation by looking at the ecology and economy of the villages the workers come from, their occupations and livelihoods and the reordering of lives which entail migration and encounters with travel and the city. Sub contracting of procurement of materials and of labour recruitment is a spatial strategy employed by capital in its process of accumulation. The spatial strategy of capital makes use of geographical differentiation and uneven development, particularly in the case of labour sub-contracting, recruiting new ethnic groups to minimise conflicts between labour and capital.

Geographical inequalities have been exacerbated by interventions in riverine ecology by the state without reforming the agrarian structure of the regions, particularly in the case of district Saharsa in Bihar. Caste and kinship play a crucial role in the recruitment process, though in a contingent manner. For example, in Malda, commissions or contractors are invariably Muslims. *Dafadars* who recruit workers from the villages are usually Muslims too, though occasionally, men from other communities also become *dafadars*. *Meths,* who negotiate on behalf of the workers, would belong to the same community to which the workers belong; i.e., if the majority of the workers were *Adivasis*, then the *meth* also would be an *Adivasi*. In Banma, Bihar, the *musahars,* who are traditional agricultural labourers of the village who come to Thiruvananthapuram to work in the road construction undertaken by Punj Lloyd travel together for work, often choosing their headman as *meth*. Interestingly, if one or two workers from other communities, say *yadavs* or *malekaars*, accompany them, the *meth* continues to be the headman of *musaharas* who are considered to be below the *yadavs* and *malekaars* in terms of the caste hierarchy.

The absence of women in the workers' journeys to work sites is viewed by men in terms of women's 'inability' to work in hazardous conditions and the need for their participation in agricultural work to ensure subsistence, often with a gendered disdain and disapproval of women who dare to move and work. It signals to an economy of space which rests on all-male labour camps, subsistence activity in the villages and a temporality which circulates these spaces ensuring subsistence and reproduction of labour power.

Accounts of workers bring to the fore a map of the city as a 'labour market' and the experiences of everyday life of the worker in the city. These accounts also call for an understanding of migration as a journey for these workers bringing out the element of unfreedom perpetuated by the recruitment process fraught with cheating and inadequate information.

The last chapter in this section is by S. Irudaya Rajan and K.S. James on demographic dividend and migration. It makes an attempt to examine the pace of the age structure transition and its likely impact on the Kerala economy. It also discusses the plausible mechanism through which the working age group boom creates a favourable economic outcome. The chapter argues that the age structure transition in the form of the bulging working age group population, has resulted in a serious crisis at the employment front. However, the opening up of Gulf countries to labour from Kerala has come as a boom for the Kerala economy. The huge unemployed population of the state largely took advantage of the Gulf boom and the economy of Kerala in general and the people of Kerala in particular, have flourished in the course of the age structure transition. As per the 2001 census data, the working age population (15-59 years) of Kerala constitutes about 64 per cent of the total population, the highest among the Indian states. The short-term and the long term implications of higher growth rates among the working population in Kerala are hardly studied nor understood. Further, the strategy adopted by the Keralite to overcome the hurdle of increasing working population remains largely unknown and undocumented.

This chapter attempts to understand some of the emanating changes in Kerala, which the authors believe, are primarily the result of demographic transition and the consequent age structural change. The story of demographic change in Kerala, which happened in an environment of poor economic growth is well known and needs no further description. But the rapid demographic transition has led to a significant change in the age structure of the population with a bulge in the working age group and a decline in the growth rate in the younger age groups. The dependency ratio, as a result, has come down drastically. This stage of demographic transition is generally found to be the boom period for any economy.

The study found that since the 1980s, Kerala has been experiencing a boom in the size of the population in the working age group and a resultant decline in the dependency ratio. In a population of high literacy rate, a high growth rate of population in the working age group would have serious adverse impact, other things being equal, on the unemployment problem. However, the migration opportunities to the Gulf region came as a boom for the ailing employment scenario of Kerala. The demographic factors have created a peculiar type of supply-demand problem in the labour market. While on the one hand, there had been an abundance of educated labour seeking job but unable to find them, there also existed scarcity of labour within the state for doing manual work. The scarcity of labour to do manual work resulted in in migration of manual labourers from different parts of the country.

At the general level, the economic revival of Kerala from the mid-1980s coincides with the period of the age structure transition. Although this chapter made no attempt to seriously test this relationship using econometric tools, it appears that, the demographic factors played a crucial role in the revival of the economy. For instance, the important change that occurs in an economy with low dependency ratio is the improvement in the saving rate. It is so because with small number of children per couple, parents are able to save more than earlier. The available data also suggest significant enhancement in the saving rate of the state, particularly in the 1990s.

On the whole, demographic transition seems to hold different types of impact in different societies and to take different types of turns and shapes according to the opportunities available in each society. In the case of Kerala, it presents some interesting features in terms of changes in the labour market composition, and emigration coupled with in-migration of different segments of the population. Perhaps, an integrated framework is necessary to understand all these mechanisms simultaneously.

Unemployment

The most tragic development failure in the state is manifested in the chronic rates of unemployment of both men and women. Reckoned in terms of all the three measures of unemployment—usual status, current weekly status and current daily status—used by National Sample Survey, Kerala has the highest incidence of unemployment both for males and females and both in rural and urban areas, in India. Unemployment has been a burning problem in Kerala for quite some time now. About 40 lakh of persons, out of a total about 240 lakh of adults, are currently registered with the Employment Exchanges in the state seeking employment. Not all of them are, however, unemployed; quite a large proportion of them are indeed employed. We have two chapters devoted to this subject in the volume.

The first chapter is by K.C. Zachariah and S. Irudaya Rajan on migration and unemployment based on the data gathered from 10,000 households as a part of the second Kerala Migration Survey. The chapter focuses on the dynamics of unemployment and the geographic, social, economic and demographic characteristics of the unemployed. What are the factors underlying the acute levels and peculiar patterns of unemployment in Kerala?

Although emigration and remittances are given as factors for the increase in the proportion of the population with higher levels of education, they should be taken by no means as the only (or the major) factor. Increase in the number of persons opting for higher levels of education should be viewed in the context of the larger macroeconomic changes taking place in Kerala. The economic value of education has been on the increase in the state even much before the era of Gulf emigration began. The importance of agriculture and other primary sector activities in the economy has been on the decline in Kerala for quite some time. In the light of this persistent trend, there were not many alternatives for aspiring youngsters in Kerala, but to try to get good education and get into the non-agricultural sectors of activity. Thus, irrespective of Gulf migration, the rising demand for higher education would have manifested itself. What this chapter suggests is that the shift to higher education was accelerated by the increased demand for higher education (triggered by the possibility of emigration) and through the supply of funds for education that became available through remittances, which followed emigration.

Is unemployment as much an economic catastrophe as it is often portrayed to be? Unemployment is, no doubt, a major problem in Kerala. About 4 million (about 15 per cent of the adult population of Kerala) were registered with Employment Exchange in the state seeking jobs. About 2.3 million or 19.2 per cent of the labour force, 41 per cent of the female labour force or 35 per cent of the labour force in Thiruvananthapuram district, and about 50 per cent of labour force in the 15-24 age groups were unemployed. These figures certainly indicate the seriousness of the unemployment problem. At the same time, they should be read along with other statistics indicating that the unemployment problem in the state is not very much an acute economic problem. First of all, nearly 75 per cent of the unemployed get a job within five years of waiting; and hardcore unemployment is confined to about 5 per cent (25 per cent of 19.2) of the labour force. Second, there is no geographical area that remains a high employment area for long periods of time. Areas of high unemployment rate undergo rapid transitions to lower rates and vice versa. The unemployment rate of a *taluk* in 2003 was found to be not correlated with its unemployment rate in 1998; the correlation coefficient between the two was not statistically significant. Third, the unemployment rate among persons of 30 years of age or above was only 6 per cent. Fourth, many of the unemployed come from well-to-do households possessing good houses and expensive household gadgets and equipment. Fifth, the unemployed are rarely the heads of households (breadwinners). They are mostly unmarried sons or daughters, or married females whose husbands are the breadwinners of the family.

Regarding policies to reduce unemployment, creation of new jobs is, of course, the direct route to reduce unemployment. There is, undoubtedly, plenty of scope for this line of approach in the state as most of the goods consumed in the state are produced outside the state. But there is only a small chance that any effort in this direction would yield positive results in the near future. A prior condition for such efforts to succeed is that our educated youths are "employable". A policy for tackling the unemployment problem has to do with educational reform to make education relevant for employment. Educational reforms must be the number one priority. This is not a finding of this study, but it merits reiteration, in the context of policy suggestions to reduce unemployment.

To cite a finding from the study: in 1998, the unemployment rate in the state was higher among degree holders than among persons with secondary school certificates: 31.4 per cent among degree holders and 23.1 among secondary school certificate holders. In 2003, the relationship was reversed. The unemployment rate was higher among persons with secondary school education (38.5 per cent) than among degree holders (36.4 per cent). The increase in the number of unemployed persons during 1998-2003 was 100 per cent for persons with secondary school education, but only 60 per cent for degree holders. One possible reason for this shift could be that by 2003, degrees holders in Kerala became more "employable" than they had been in 1998. The proportion of persons with technical degrees among all degree holders has increased in recent years, from 4.0 per cent in 1998 to 11.8 per cent in 2003. Could this increase in the relative share of technical graduates be the reason for the increase in the unemployment rate among degree holders being lower than that among the secondary school educated persons? Does it suggest that a cure for the unemployment problem lies in making the secondary school educated persons more employable by establishing some sort of match between education and the job market?

The second chapter in this section, by Alice Sebastian and K. Navaneetham assess the determinants of female unemployment. It is important in the Kerala context because labour force participation rate among females is much lower than among males. Similarly, unemployment among women is much higher than among males. The study situates women's education and employment in the specific case of Kerala. In the context of female work participation, it has been generally hypothesised that economic growth and education increases female workforce participation rates. Kerala, where economic growth is higher than in all-India and where women are relatively more educated, experiences the lowest female work participation and the highest unemployment rates among the major states in India, especially among the educated. In the light of this contradiction, the chapter attempts to identify the factors that cause unemployment among the educated women in the state. The study tries to investigate how unemployment is related to educational achievements of women, conditioning on individual, household and demographic characteristics.

Analysis of macro-level data on employment and unemployment shows that wide divergence exists between male and female participation rates in economic activities. In Kerala, while the male work participation rates improved in the past two decades, female work participation rates declined and formed only half the male work participation rate. This is contrary to the general trend observed in other Indian states. Changes in the sectoral distribution of female workforce in Kerala clearly shows that structural transformation of women's economic activity has indeed taken place in the state with the primary sector losing its importance and the tertiary sector taking up its place.

Using the 2003 employment/unemployment survey data conducted by the Centre for Development Studies, the study finds that 74 per cent of the educated women remained unemployed in the sample. Women are found to be more educated than men across all educational categories except diploma and secondary education. But this advantage is not translated into gainful employment opportunities for them.

The study uses multivariate logistic regression analysis to determine the factors that influence female work participation. The study uses both individual characteristics—level of education, age, marital status, religion, place of residence—and household characteristics—economic status, husband's education and employment—to examine the likelihood of women being in the workforce. The results show that education, age, marital status, place of residence, economic status and husband's employment turned out to be significant in determining women's entry into the workforce. Within education, diploma and professional education shows the maximum odds ratio where women with diploma and professional education have 6 and 18 times more probability, respectively to be employed compared to women with higher secondary or secondary education. It shows the importance of skill-oriented education rather than general education in improving the employability of women.

Age and marital status turned out to be the major factors determining the employment status of educated women. It has been found that work participation is higher for women in higher age groups. Odds ratio of marital status shows that single women have two times more probability to work than married women. The relationship between economic status and work participation shows that women from low economic status are more likely to work than those from high economic status. Further, it has been found that women whose husbands are employed at medium or low status work are less likely to enter the labour market. Also, there exists considerable spatial variation in women's employment. The study shows that individual and household characteristics can go a long way in explaining women's entry into the labour market. Education alone does not enable women to acquire gender equity in economic participation. Women's education has not played the transformative role so generally expected of it. Low levels of female employment and persistence of a gendered work structure have limited women's claims to independent sources income.

Ageing

The ageing scenario of Kerala is unique among the states of India. This section includes six papers on this subject looking at various issues relating to the elderly in Kerala. The introductory chapter is by S. Irudaya Rajan and Sabu Aliyar. Kerala had 10.5 per cent of its population in the age group of 60 years and above as against only 7.5 per cent in all India in 2001. Among the elderly in Kerala, there are 1028 females per 1000 males. The size of the elderly population in the state is expected to increase from 33 lakh in 2001 to 57 lakh in 2021 and to 120 lakh in 2061. In 2061, the proportion of the elderly would constitute 40 per cent of the total population: 6.7 per cent in the age group 60-69 years; 23.8 per cent in the age group 70-79 years and 9.1 per cent in the age group of 80 years and above. While the young dependency ratio (the number of persons aged 0-14 years per 100 persons of the working age group of 15 to 59 years) has been declining, the old age dependency ratio (the number of persons above 60 years of age per 100 persons in the working age group of 15 to 59 years) has been increasing. During the period 2001-2061, the young dependency ratio is expected to decline from 41 to 16; the aged dependency ratio would, on the other hand, increase from 17 to 76. In the old age group, women would be more numerous than men. The cost of the dependency burden of households would be rising quite rapidly in the future. Kerala is ahead of all the states in India in all the indices of ageing.

The Centre for Development Studies has completed two large-scale migration surveys in Kerala in 1998 and 2003, covering 10,000 households throughout the state. The surveys indicate that the proportion of households that do not have old persons has been decreasing. As of now, only half of the households in Kerala have at least one elderly person to take care. Inter-district variations are observed in the proportion of the elderly to total population, with 21 per cent in Pathanamthitta, followed by Alappuzha, Kottayam, Ernakulam and Thiruvananthapuram.

Kerala has introduced the largest number of social security and welfare schemes among the states in India. It spends almost 3 per cent of its annual budget on these schemes. Among the schemes for the elderly, the ones which have the largest number of beneficiaries are Agricultural Workers Pension Scheme, Widow/Destitute Pension Scheme, Pension Schemes for Persons with Disabilities and the National Old Age Pension Scheme. Nearly 12 lakh out of 32 lakh elderly persons in the state receive financial assistance from the government.

Can Kerala afford to provide social security or assistance or financial security for the growing number of the elderly? According to the 2001 census, the number of elderly persons in Kerala in 2001 was 33 lakh. Kerala has approximately 4 lakh pensioners (retired from the Kerala government services plus retired from other state governments outside Kerala and returned to Kerala after retirement plus the military, railways, post and telegraph pensioners). In other words, close to 15 per cent of the elderly in Kerala belong to the creamy layers of senior citizens. They are not looking for any assistance from the Kerala government.

If the government can implement all the schemes very seriously and provide assistance to the really needy among the elderly (the senior author filed observations which indicate starvation among Kerala elderly), Kerala can continue to run the social assistance schemes without much financial constraints. The annual budget for social welfare could be enhanced by allocating funds from family planning and primary education. We hope that the government, through *panchayat* level institutions, will be able not only to identify the needy (real) beneficiaries but also to enhance financial assistance to them from the current level of Rs. 110 to Rs. 300 per month (Incidentally, West Bengal pays Rs. 300 as old age pension). For this, a bold step in the right direction is needed.

As Kerala leads other states of India, Syam Prasad's chapter highlights the fiscal pressure on the formal pension system in Kerala. It examines how demographic and health phenomenon of 'living longer' could result in a grave fiscal dilemma. Long-term stability and the fiscal constraints of the state-run pensions in an ageing society of Kerala are the major focus of the chapter.

The pension liability on the part of the government through civil service pensions has been going up drastically upward in India, both at the Centre and the states, during the last two decades. The total pension liability of both the Centre and the states went up from Rs. 6870 crore in 1990-91 to Rs. 55712 crore in 2001-02. The fiscal strain is very high in states such as Tamil Nadu, Kerala, West Bengal, Andhra Pradesh where life expectancy and the formal pension coverage rates are high. At the national level, the expenditure on pensions as a per cent of revenue expenditure, accounts for 12 per cent and at the state level, the corresponding figure is 17.6 per cent.

During the last two decades, the pension expenditure of the government of Kerala went up from Rs. 33 crore in 1980-81 to Rs. 1990 crore in 2003-2004. The pension liability has been hovering around 4.5 to 5 per cent of the state domestic product in the recent years. The pension expenditure accounted for almost one-fourth of the revenue expenditure and nearly 30 per cent of the own revenue of the state, which had added extra pressure to the already strained financial burden. The pension system in Kerala that drains huge fiscal resources of the state, covers only 10 per cent of the aged. It is difficult to sustain the present pension system in the long run as the system dependency ratio is much higher than the demographic dependency ratio. This shows a structural crisis in the pension system with huge fiscal stress on the government treasury. The financial projections reveal increase to unsustainable levels of the pension payment system in future.

As stated earlier, nearly 12 lakh elderly persons receive social assistance in terms of means tested monthly pension directly from the government.

However, Kerala has another unique experience of forming 24 welfare fund boards based on occupation groups, for providing collective social security. The funds offer various benefits to their members such as old age pension, provident fund, gratuity, retirement benefits, ex-gratia payments, disability allowance, funeral expenses, educational allowances (scholarships and cash awards for children of the members), medical allowances, marriage grant, maternity benefits, unemployment benefits and housing loans. S. Irudaya Rajan provides an overview of all the 24 welfare fund boards in terms of their years of establishment, the number of workers covered, the membership eligibility and the pattern of their financing.

As of 2003, 44 lakh unorganised labourers in Kerala were registered with one or the other types of welfare fund boards and received various welfare benefits including old age pensions. The highest number of workers was registered with the agricultural workers welfare fund (17 lakh), followed by construction workers (9 lakh) and labour welfare funds (5 lakh). Most of the welfare funds receive income from government, employers and employees. However, six welfare fund boards receive no grants from government and another five receive no income from employers. The Kerala government contributes Rs. 30 million for pension payments and another 17 million for insurance premiums per year, to the Kerala fishermen welfare fund.

Out of the 24 welfare fund boards, 14 (58 per cent) offer old age pensions to their members. The first such old age pensions was the one implemented for Kerala agricultural workers in 1980; currently they are paid Rs. 120 per month and the total number of beneficiaries is around 5 lakh. Among them, half are women. All eligible agricultural labourers can avail the old age pension without being members of the Kerala Agricultural Workers Welfare Fund Board. It is one of the most popular schemes of cash transfers in Kerala. During 1987, the Fishermen Welfare Fund Board offered pension to its members and another three boards (handloom, cashew and *khadi* workers welfare funds) joined the group in 1989. Though the toddy worker welfare fund came into existence as a pioneer welfare fund model in Kerala, it began to offer old age pension to its members only in 1997, after 28 years since its inception. The monthly pension varies from the minimum of Rs. 100 person to a maximum of Rs. 200 per person. The national old age pension initiated by the Government of India offers only Rs. 75 per month. A few welfare funds are seem to have failed in the proper maintenance of data on pension payments. As of 2002, around 7 lakh senior citizen received old age pension through different welfare fund boards and the coverage is likely to be around 25 per cent of the old population in Kerala.

An emphatic feature of the demographic profile of the aged women is the higher proportion of widowhood. More than half of all the aged women in India are widows compared with only less than 10 per cent of old men in India. The higher female life expectancy at ages 60 and 70, the universal tendency for women to marry men older than themselves and the social restrictions on the remarriage of widows have led to a high incidence of widowhood among aged females (Gulati and Rajan, 1999). The incidence of widowhood is slightly more than three times that widowerhood at the national level. Seventy-one per cent of women are widowed as against only 29 per cent of men among the oldest—those 80 years and above of age. It may be seen that at any given age, there are more widows than widowers and as age advances, the prevalence of widowhood also increases. In this context, Sreerupa analyses the health vulnerability among widows using the unit level data of the 52nd round of the National Sample Survey, carried out by the National Sample Survey Organisation throughout India.

The analysis of the unit level data revealed the presence of disparities in the health status of the aged by gender and by marital status. Being an aged widow/widower was a risk factor for poor health status. Widows were particularly vulnerable to poor general health status and disability. The results provide strong support to the contention that the state of widowhood will be very different for men and women due to structural disadvantages associated with gender and marital status. A comparison revealed that widowhood is a much greater risk factor for aged women than for aged men.

Sreerupa also explores possible explanations for health vulnerability of aged widows in their differential access to material and care resources as widows represent not only a higher proportion among the elderly but also among women. It was found that economic dependency was a risk factor for poor health outcomes (i.e., self-reported health status, prevalence of at least one disability and prevalence of at least one chronic illness) for all the aged women and widows among them. These results compliment the literature on health, which have shown that even at old ages the health of a person is related to her/his socio-economic condition. They have also revealed how gender and marital status structures affect access to resources even among the aged.

The next chapter in this section presents fresh observations on the health of the elderly, based on the Kerala Ageing Survey conducted in 2005. S. Irudaya Rajan, along with Shanthi Johnson and Sabu Aliyar, profiles the marital status and living arrangements among the elderly in addition to their health behaviour and health care utilisation patterns. In Kerala, 4 per cent of the elderly females live alone and most likely, all of them are widows. Another 8 per cent live as elderly couples. Three-fourths of the elderly males live with their spouses, children and grandchildren, compared to 50 per cent in the case of females. On the other hand, almost 40 per cent of females live in Kerala without spouses but with their children and grandchildren as against just 11 per cent in the case of males. One-fourth of the elderly who live in households of their sons or daughters, are almost entirely widows or widowers.

The Kerala Ageing Survey results have shown that the age of participants ranged from 60 years to over 100 years of age, with 54 per cent of them women. The study showed that joint pains were the most often reported morbidity condition among the elderly, with the percentage of women reporting being higher (54) than men (43). Other common health problems include: loss of memory, fatigue, chest pain and stomach problems. Common chronic illnesses among the elderly in Kerala are hypertension/blood pressure, diabetes, arthritis, asthma, emphysema or bronchitis and heart problems. Osteoporosis, an emerging chronic disease was reported less often. This was perhaps related to the silent nature of this disease. Prevalence of disabilities was high with over 75 per cent reporting vision problems. For medical needs, close to 40 per cent accessed public hospitals and 56 per cent used private hospitals. The reasons for accessing private hospitals and public hospitals varied. Most of them accessed public hospitals for the free service they provided whereas those private hospitals were accessed for the availability of better services, good care and attention.

In the survey, only about 30 per cent were found to undergo routine medical check-up; but over 50 per cent were taking medications on a regular basis. Gender difference was clearly evident in the matter of behavioural factors with men smoking cigarettes and drinking alcohol and women chewing betel leaf more often than men did. Self-reported participation in physical activity decreased with age. Approximately 60 per cent of the young-old participated in physical activities mostly in the form of household activities; such participation reduced to 35 per cent among the oldest-old—80 years and above. Dietary patterns showed that most consume three meals a day with a greater tendency for the old-old and the oldest-old age groups to skip or miss meals. Also, the type of food changed from non-vegetarian to vegetarian, as people grew older. Approximately 30 per cent were on special diet such as diabetic diet or low salt diet. The study also showed that prevalence of falls and fracture rates was high among the elderly resulting in further disablement.

The last chapter in this section explores the discourses on ageing and the social lives of urban living, well-educated and financially privileged seniors from Thiruvananthapuram district of Kerala state. Using qualitative research methods, the various discourses that exist on ageing and one on the living arrangements of seniors has been explored. Manja also found that a definition of 'old' based on the number of years lived was not the most representative description, rather definitions based on matters such as experience, retirement, the birth of grandchildren and health. Moving away from giving an account of how 'the average Keralite elderly' lives and with whom, the chapter illustrates how the elderly feel about their living arrangements, how they see the role of their children and the actual practicalities of living 'independently' or with family.

Other Emerging Issues

The first chapter in this series by J. Devika draws upon the insights that have been generated in recent historical and anthropological work on twentieth century Kerala to reflect on emergent research challenges for demographers. It highlights the changing vicissitudes of marriage, family and childcare patterns in Kerala in the last century to argue that post-demographic transition issues of children deserve to be counted as a major focus of research. The demographic shifts of the early and mid-twentieth century in Kerala have been well-studied and their social ramifications have also been explored, though to a limited degree only. The chapter argues that several fresh questions that have emerged in the late twentieth century context have, however, remained completely unexplored. Identifying the late twentieth century to be an important conjuncture of several emergent historical forces and social phenomena, such as the early appearance of certain features of globalisation in the Malayali society, the rising educational levels of mothers among the Malayali elite, increasing aspirations towards upward mobility through migration and widening inequalities within the Malayali society, the chapter suggests several hypotheses regarding changes in childcare practices within homes and in schools. These are often discussed actively by the Kerala's public but have hardly received careful attention from researchers. Also, the chapter proposes a shift in methodology to tackle second-generation issues for demographic research that takes full advantage of the interdisciplinary turn in demography. This, it is argued, may not diminish the status of demography as a policy science. It may, however, completely alter our notion of what 'policy' ought to be.

The state of Kerala has had a relatively slow but consistent growth in the urban population till 1981; however, since then, the state has witnessed a spectacular growth in its urban population. Remya Prabha analyses the trends and patterns of urbanisation in Kerala over the past 50 years. The latest 2001 census data indicate that Kerala could not keep its pace of urbanisation and that there has been a significant decline in the urban growth process. The assessment indicates that the exceptional increase in the degree of urbanisation during 1981-1991 was mainly due to the creation of new towns in the state, while the slowdown in the pace of urbanisation throughout 1991-2001 was due to the extensive declassification of towns. The declassification of erstwhile towns into villages has resulted in a loss of urban population which is much higher than the increase in urban population due to addition of new towns.

The availability of better infrastructural facilities, education and health services and the prevalence of high rates of wages without any rural-urban locational differences, have resulted in a peculiar pattern of inter-district migration in Kerala with little preference for urban areas. The peculiar pattern in urban growth during the decades 1961-2001 is explained mainly in terms of reclassification of urban areas and migration. The emergence of large number of towns along with increased volume of urban migrants explains the high degree of urbanisation found during 1981-1991.

Over the past 50 years, Kerala has witnessed an amazing transformation in its health status, the values of all its health and allied indicators showing tremendous decline. Over the same period, new chronic diseases also emerged. C.R. Soman did his epidemiological study covering seven *panchayats* in Varkala with a total population of 1,62,753 persons, for a long period. Out of 1,62,753 persons, 79,877 were males and 82,876 females. During the first five years of follow-up, the survey lost 3973 persons on account of death.

Heart attack remains the single highest contributor to mortality in Kerala, followed by stroke and cancer. About two generations ago, all chronic diseases together contributed to less than 25 per cent of mortality while the contribution of infectious diseases to death was more than 60 per cent. Today, all infectious diseases together are responsible for only 5 per cent of the deaths in Kerala. Suicides and accidents also contribute its share for deaths. The detailed analysis by Soman indicates that death due to coronary heart disease in Kerala is far higher than in the United States of America and the United Kingdom, the affluent economies of today.

The prevalence of overweight and obesity in Kerala is alarmingly high. The irony is that the high prevalence co-exist with an energy intake still below the recommended dietary allowances. The paradox is understood in the context of massive unemployment and/or under-employment in Kerala. The prevalence of overweight and obesity was about 50 per cent among women and 40 per cent among men. A peculiar feature of the problem of obesity in Kerala is the dominant deposition of fat in and around the abdomen. Abdominal obesity, marked by an increase in waist circumference poses considerably higher risk of diabetes and coronary disease. A body mass index (BMI) of 25 or above is considered the cut-off point for defining overweight. However, the studies carried out by Soman suggests that when the BMI exceeds 23, the people of Kerala invites a three-fold risk of developing diabetes and hypertension.

The burden of non-communicable diseases in Kerala threatens development in more than one way. When struck by these diseases, the quality of life suffers and the attendant's loss of productivity affects economic development. These lifelong diseases impose a heavy economic burden for primary treatment. Complications, when they occur inflict still higher expenditure. Premature mortality results in heavy economic losses to the family and to the nation. Preventive strategies, with emphasis on exercise from childhood, eating grains and more of green leafy vegetables and fruits and avoiding tobacco and alcohol consumption are among the principal successful interventions practiced in the West. It is time that we wake up to the unpleasant realities and meet the challenges head-on.

With high morbidity, emerging lifestyle diseases and an ageing population, Kerala is expected to enter a health care crisis sometime in the present century. In this context, Sajan Thomas, Aju Mathew and Prabhu Dass G. explore the unexplored area of community-based palliative care experiment by using the 2005 field survey data of palliative care clinics in northern Kerala.

Experience across the world shows that for meaningful palliative care a combination of socio-economic, cultural and medical solutions is required: the northern Kerala experiment has proved that the community is able to take the responsibility of its chronically and terminally ill. It also demonstrates the ascendancy of a community-based initiative as a preferred alternative to the hospice approach or the institutionalised medical approach, for purposes of palliative care. Given the coincidence of demographic and health transitions, decline of public-financed systems of health care and escalation of medical expenditure, this initiative from northern Kerala is found to be an appropriate and well-timed one.

This community-based experiment has special relevance, in the context of the crisis, to the Kerala model of health. First, it showed that comprehensive and integrated palliative care programmes can be implemented at no additional cost to the existing health care system. The emerging partnerships with the local government institutions and their positive outcome with regard to the utilisation of funds and existing health care infrastructure; incorporation of more diseases/patients and the transition of Neighbourhood Networks in Palliative Care (NNPC) to Neighbourhood Networks in Health Care (NNHC); the physical and financial self-sufficiency of palliative care units in the state; the promising role of religious and social actors, especially their role as volunteers; and the rehabilitation support provided to patients and families point to the importance of this community-driven experiment. Given its sizeable infrastructure and firm enmeshment in local settings, the palliative care movement has immense potential as a facilitating institutional base for improving the health care system of the state. Its continuing success urges the need for framing policies for utilising human, physical and financial resources of this community-based movement for addressing the health care crisis in Kerala. This community experience may also be replicated in other parts of India.

Internal and international migration from Kerala to other parts of India and outside India is likely to persist in the present century. Kerala is also witnessing large-scale in-migration from other parts of the country, especially from the high HIV prevalence states, to replace migrants who left the shores of Kerala. In this context, K. Ajithkumar and Rakkee Thimothy illustrate emerging issues with respect to HIV prevention and control. Their study has also a section on various dimensions of HIV infection and control activities in India with a critical evaluation of the HIV programmes in Kerala.

Though the state of Kerala continues to be a low HIV-prevalent state in India, it has many features, which increase the risk of high HIV prevalence. Despite having better awareness and knowledge on HIV transmission and prevention, there exists intense public stigma and discrimination against persons infected by and affected with HIV. Increased attention is required to reach the general population and the high-risk population, effectively and to monitor the ART (Anti-retroviral Therapy) programme closely.

As of now, Kerala stands ahead of all states in India, in the matter of suicides, with 32 suicides per lakh population as against 8 per lakh population for the country as a whole. Though Kerala has achieved the highest measurable social and human development among states in India, the mental health scenario of the state needs great attention. However, no data exist on this subject. To fill the gap, the first Kerala Mental Health Household Survey was conducted in a randomly selected sample of 1000 households, eliciting information from among all the members of the age group 15-59 years, and among responding persons between the ages of 60 and 69 years. The authors of the study, E. Mohamed, S. Irudaya Rajan, K. Anil Kumar and P.M. Saidu Mohammed, report their salient findings.

The major aim of the study was to elucidate gender-related issues in mental health, human well-being and stress experience of the Keralites. Men, in general, were found to have relatively a better sense of well-being and mental health than women. Women reported more stress than men in most of the areas concerned. However, there is indication that gender differences have been converging over the generations; especially, women seem to be changing more in a positive direction in most of the selected indices. The overall impact of a woman being the head of the family, is positive on men living in the same household. But the same does not hold good in the case of women.

The younger generation, the better educated and the unmarried scored better on most of the indices irrespective of gender. Marriage seems to have a negative impact, in terms of both well-being and mental health of people. Migration status exerts a positive influence on the well-being of people but not necessarily on mental health. Working in the public sector is found good for men and women on all counts but men are definitely better off than women in public sector jobs. Farmers in Kerala suffer the most compared to persons in any other walk of life. Well-being and mental health of men steadily increase as one moves from the north to the southern regions of Kerala, while the reverse is true for women.

In the concluding chapter, M. Vijayanunni takes us to the concept of 'ecological footprint', which connotes the extent of land needed to maintain a given population at its present level of consumption. The current population of the world of 630 crore, is already 'over the limit' and hence, the present level of consumption cannot be expected to be sustained.

References

Deepikaglobal.com (2005). "Open to FDI for Kerala Development: Karat", December 11.

Government of Kerala (2006). "Next Century Kerala's: PM", *Kerala Calling*. pp. 8-11.

Guilmoto, Christophe Z. and S. Irudaya Rajan (2002). "District Level Estimates of Fertility from India's 2001 Census", *Economic and Political Weekly* XXXVII(7): 665-72.

Gulati, Leela and S. Irudaya Rajan (1999). "The Added Years: Elderly in India and Kerala", *Economic and Political Weekly* XXXIV(44): WS-46-51.

Planning Commission (2007). *Kerala State Development Report*. New Delhi: Academic Foundation.

State Planning Board (2005). *Kerala Human Development Report 2005*.

Thomas, Issac (2005). "International Congress on Kerala Studies", *People's Democracy* XXIX(51) (Weekly Organ of the Communist Part of India (Marxist), December 18.

Zachariah, K.C. and S. Irudaya Rajan (eds.) (1997). *Kerala's Demographic Transition: Determinants and Consequences*. New Delhi: Thousand Oaks; London: Sage Publications.

———. (2004). "Gulf Revisited: Economic Conseguences of Emigration from Kerala: Emigration and Unemployment", *Working Paper* No. 363. Thiruvananthapuram: Centre for Development Studies. *www.cds.edu*

———. (2005). "Unemployment in Kerala at the Turn of the Century: Insights from CDS Gulf Migration Studies", *Working Paper* No. 374. Thiruvananthapuram: Centre for Development Studies. *www.cds.edu*

Zachariah, K.C., E.T. Mathew and S. Irudaya Rajan (2001). "Social, Economic and Demographic Consequences of Migration on Kerala", *International Migration* 39(2): 43-71.

———. (2003). *Dynamics of Migration in Kerala. Dimensions, Determinants and Consequences*. Hyderabad: Orient Longman Pvt. Limited.

Zachariah, K.C., K.P. Kannan and S. Irudaya Rajan (2002). *Kerala's Gulf Connection: CDS Studies on International Labour Migration from Kerala State in India*. Monograph Series. Thiruvananthapuram: Centre for Development Studies.

Section II
Migration

2

Internal Migration

K.C. ZACHARIAH and S. IRUDAYA RAJAN

Introduction

This chapter analyses the dynamics of migration between Kerala and other states in India and attempts to relate it to the demographic transition in the state and to the recent resurgence of external migration. Migration has been one of the means by which Kerala population coped with the ill effects of the rapid demographic transition in the second half of the 20th century. It was and still is one of the prime movers in the social transformation of Kerala over the past half-century. While international migration, especially Gulf migration, has been instrumental in the socio-economic transformation of many a relatively poorer working class family in Kerala in the 1980s and the 1990s, the money orders sent back by the internal migrants over the past 50 years had not only provided sustenance to a very large number of middle class families back home, but also helped to finance higher education of children from these families ensuring their upward social mobility. Thus, migration, both internal and external, played a major role in making the Kerala society what it is today, the state with the highest rank in India in social development. Will such development continue in the years to come? Will migration from the state continue at high rates in the years to come? Some of such questions are addressed in this study.

Data Sources

The main source of data on internal migration in India is the periodic censuses taken every 10 years since 1881. These data on internal migration have several deficiencies: conceptual as well as those caused by frequent boundary changes.

The concept of migration has both a temporal and an areal dimension. While the Indian census data on migration have an areal dimension, most of them lack precise temporal dimension. For example, the birthplace data are vague with respect to the time interval during which migration took place.

Since not much can be done to correct such conceptual problems, they are largely ignored in this analysis. It is maintained that most of the broad conclusions reached in this chapter would remain valid in spite of the conceptual problems.

Non-comparability of data from one census to another due to boundary changes is a serious problem, for which adjustment is rather difficult. Fortunately, Kerala did not undergo any external boundary changes after 1956. Therefore, no adjustment is called for in this respect.

The Malayali Psyche

Malayalis, in general, have an excessive attachment to their own *nadu*. They used to be quite contended with the living conditions in the state. Consequently, very few of them ventured out of the state to make a living. The number of Keralites living outside state was very small; in any case their number was much smaller than the number of out-of-state persons living in Kerala. Net migration to the state remained positive for a long time, in particular in the first half of the last century.

This pattern, however, is history, the situation which had prevailed when Maharajas were ruling the state, not at all since India became a Republic.

Keralites' attitude towards moving out of the state began to change with World War II. This change of attitude coincided with the demographic expansion in the state caused by high and stable fertility rate and declining mortality rate. An additional factor was the explosive growth in secondary level education in the state and lack of similar developments in most other states in the country. The proportion of population with higher levels of education was much higher in Kerala than in most other states in India. Integration of the erstwhile Travancore and Cochin states with the rest of India in 1947, and the opening up of a large number of independence-related employment opportunities in the metropolitan cities of India also helped this transition. The educated Malayalis could find plenty of employment opportunities in the metropolitan cities of independent India.

What began as trickle soon reached the dimensions of torrent. How long has this trend in migration from the state continued? How is it related to the recent emigration flows to the Gulf region? Which are the states to which migrants from Kerala used to go and from which states did migrants come to Kerala? What are the demographic and social characteristics of these migration streams? What is going to be future of migration to and from the state? These are some of the specific questions addressed in the present chapter.

DYNAMICS OF MIGRATION

Population Mobility in Kerala

Kerala enumerated about 31.8 million persons in the 2001 census. Among them, about 9.2 million were migrants in the sense that they had lived elsewhere before moving into the place of enumeration in the state at the time of the census. Their place of last residence (POLR) was different from the place of enumeration. In that respect, they were migrants. They constituted about 29 per cent of the total population of the state. This is an overall measure of the mobility of the Kerala population in 2001 (Table 2.1).

Table 2.1

Population Mobility in Kerala, 1971-2001

(Migrants as Per cent of Total Population)

Year	*Total*	*Males*	*Females*
2001	28.9	21.9	35.5
1991	28.2	20.7	35.4
1981	27.3	21.1	33.3
1971	22.3	17.5	27.1

Between 1971 and 2001, there was considerable increase in the population mobility in Kerala, but much of the increase occurred between 1971 and 1981. After 1981, the increase in population mobility in Kerala was marginal.

Population mobility was always larger among females than among males. The differential was maintained in all the decades.

Inter-state Out-migration from Kerala

Out-migration has been the dominant migration stream affecting Kerala during the second half of the last century. However, as mentioned earlier, in much of its history Kerala had remained essentially a net in-migrating state, a place where the unemployed in the neighbouring states could make living. Table 2.2 and Figure 2.1 give the broad trend in out-migration from the state since 1901.

Kerala had relatively negligible out-migration during much of the first half of the last century. It is only after 1951 that out-migration started acclerating. The acceleration continued for a few decades but slowed down after 1981. In fact, there was some decline in the number of lifetime migrants in 1991 over the corresponding number for 1981. Out-migrants as a proportion to the total population also started declining from 1981 (Figure 2.2).

Table 2.2

Lifetime Out-migrants from Kerala based on Birthplace Data, 1901-2001

	Year	Total	Males	Females
Travancore-Cochin	1901	16172	8515	7657
	1911	21498	11917	9581
	1921	21347	12780	8567
	1931	42095	23378	18717
	1941	124524	71933	52591
	1951	206952	120487	86465
Kerala	1961	617743	401662	216081
	1971	942639	586314	356325
	1981	1131598	639309	492289
	1991	1123006	589500	533506
	2001	1221861	630912	590949

Note: Figures for 1941 are rough estimates made by the authors.

Figure 2.1

Lifetime Out-migrants, Kerala, 1901-2001

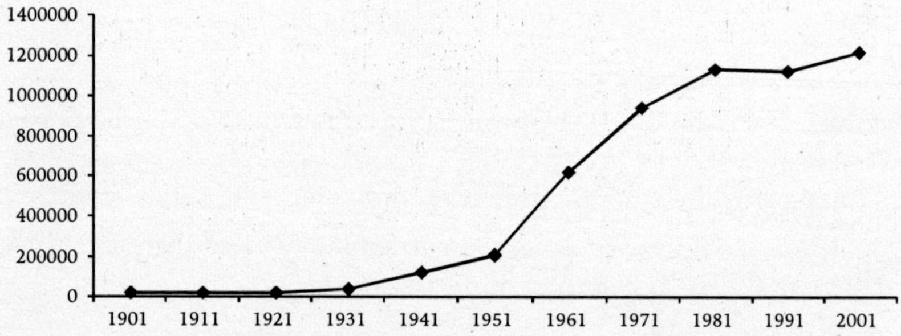

Figure 2.2

Out-migrants per 100 Total Population

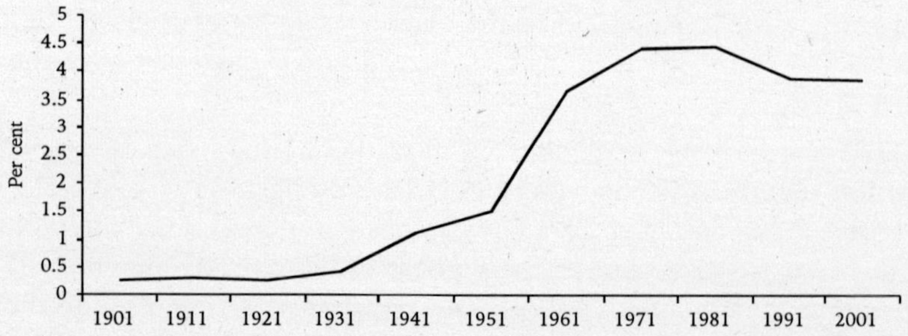

A confirmation of the trend shown by the birthplace data is also rendered by the migration data obtained from the census question on place of last residence. Although the figures are not identical, the overall trend in both seems to hold good (Figure 2.3).

Figure 2.3

Out-migrants from POB and DOR Data

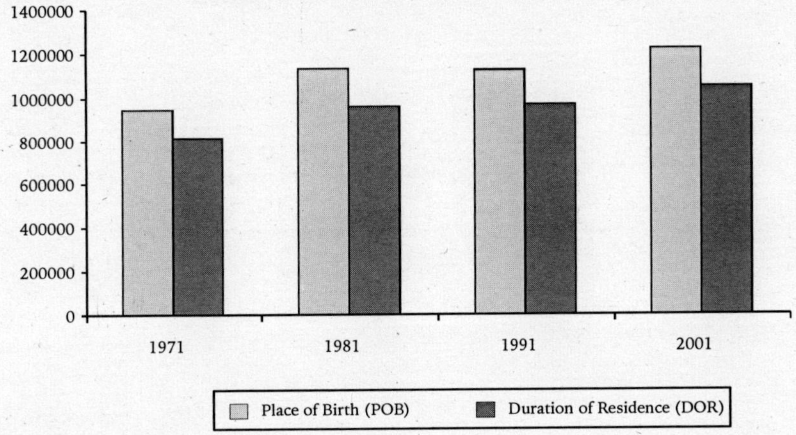

Inter-state In-migration to Kerala

Although Kerala is not basically an in-migrating state, in-migration to the state also continued at an accelerated rate throughout the last century. Unlike in out-migration, however, there was no notable deceleration or decline in the number of in-migrants. One reason for the acceleration in in-migration was that in-migration was partly caused by out-migration. Where there is out migration, there would be some return-migration also (Table 2.3 and Figure 2.4). The number of in-migrants to Kerala was merely 2.3 lakh in 1961, and the number increased to 4.1 lakh in 2001.

Inter-state Net Lifetime Migration

During pre-Independence years, net migration to Kerala had been positive, more migrants coming to Kerala than migrants going out from Kerala. However, after 1941, net migration became negative and it has remained negative in every decade since then. More people left the state than people who came to Kerala. The loss in number to the state continued at an accelerated rate. There was a short pause during 1981-1991 decade, but the decrease during this decade was made up fully in the following decade (Table 2.4 and Figure 2.5).

Table 2.3

Lifetime In-migration to Kerala based on Place of Birth Data, 1901-2001

		Total	*Males*	*Females*
Travancore-Cochin				
	1901	81069	42927	38142
	1911	82248	41824	40824
	1921	86681	42501	44180
	1931	161683	79763	81920
	1941	71152	57792	13360
Kerala				
	1951	194106	92383	101723
	1961	233245	122706	110539
	1971	248775	129075	119700
	1981	341160	170237	170928
	1991	398470	197970	200500
	2001	412849	210219	202630

Figure 2.4

Lifetime In-migrants to Kerala, 1901-2001

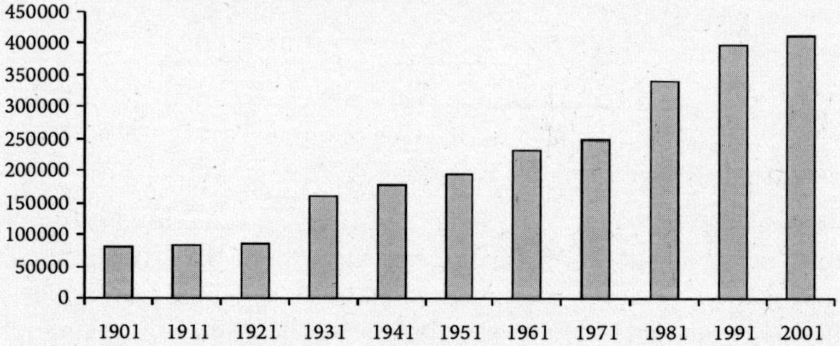

Table 2.4

Net Lifetime Migrants based on Place of Birth Data, 1901-2001

	Year	*Total*	*Males*	*Females*
Travancore-Cochin	1901	64897	34412	30485
	1911	60750	29907	31243
	1921	65274	29721	35613
	1931	119588	56385	63203
	1941	53371	14141	39231
	1951	-12846	-28104	15258
Kerala	1961	-384498	-278956	-105542
	1971	-693864	-457239	-236625
	1981	-790438	-469072	-321361
	1991	-724536	-391530	-333006
	2001	-809012	-420693	-388319

Note: Figures for 1941 are rough estimates.

Figure 2.5

Net Lifetime Migrants, 1901-2001

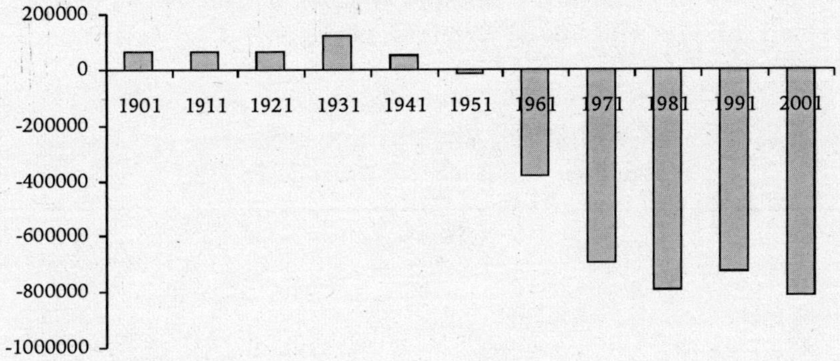

Inter-census Migration

One problem with the migration data discussed above is that the required time-dimension of migration is missing. The deficiency is partly filled by period-specific migration data. Measures of migration between two censuses are obtained from duration of residence data of the censuses. How many persons who had been living in Kerala during 1991-2001 were enumerated outside the state in the 2001 census? How many persons who had been living outside the Kerala during 1991-2001 were enumerated in Kerala in the 2001 census? The former gives the period-specific out-migration from Kerala during 1991-2001. The latter gives the period-specific in-migration to Kerala during 1991-2001. These data are given in Table 2.5 for the past four decades.

These data confirm that there was indeed some decline in out-migration from Kerala during 1991-2001. However, in-migration was higher during this decade. Net migration showed continuous decline since the 1961-1971 inter census period. The loss to the state by way of migration during 1991-2001 was about 100,000 persons less than that in the 1961-1971 decade. Both males and females shared this decline but the decline was more among males. Net migration among females was fairly constant, merely 109 thousand in 1961-1971 and about 107 thousand in 1991-2001.

A more reliable picture of inter-census net migration is provided by the balancing equation method. Calculations for the 1991-2001 decade are given in Table 2.6. Kerala had net loss of a million persons during 1991-2001. Of them, two-thirds were males and the balance females.

Another source of data is the census age distribution. Net migration during an intercensal period is calculated by age and sex by subtracting the expected survivors in the end of the decade from the enumerated number of persons. One advantage of this method is that it provides net migration by age and sex (Table 2.7 and Figure 2.6). Net migration was positive among 60-69 years indicating that many Keralites working outside Kerala during their working ages, are returning to Kerala in old ages.

Table 2.5

Inter-census Migration based on Duration of Residence Less than 10 Years, 1961-2001

	Total	Males	Females
Out-migration			
1961-1971	467665	284470	183195
1971-1981	498655	279281	219374
1981-1991	439285	228684	210601
1991-2001	431821	216129	215692
In-migration			
1961-1971	169550	94985	74565
1971-1981	220831	117861	102970
1981-1991	225336	120403	104933
1991-2001	235087	126669	108418
Net Migration			
1961-1971	-298115	-189485	-108630
1971-1981	-277824	-161420	-116404
1981-1991	-213949	-108281	-105668
1991-2001	-196734	-89460	-107274

Table 2.6

Net Migrants by Balancing Equation, 1991-2001

	Males	Females	Total
Population 2001	15622771	16209194	31831965
Population 1991	14315171	14758882	29074053
Growth 1991-2001	1307600	1450312	2757912
Births 1991-2001	2991730	2822386	5814116
Deaths 1991-2001	1069667	955060	2024727
Natural increase 1991-2001	1922062	1867327	3789389
Net migration 1991-2001	-614462	-417015	-1031477

Table 2.7

Net Migrants by Age and Sex based on Survival Ratio Method, Kerala, 1991-2001

Age	*Population*	*Males*	*Females*
0-4	-232419	-113064	-119355
5-9	-209660	-99645	-110015
10-14	227899	123728	104171
15-19	-39608	-44142	4534
20-24	-20778	-71388	50610
25-29	-265252	-186866	-78386
30-34	-473153	-227154	-246000
35-39	-135258	-80285	-54973
40-44	-206656	-91425	-115231
45-49	52977	23939	29038
50-54	-75169	-27065	-48104
55-59	-74330	-43198	-31132
60-64	38944	17399	21544
65-69	72011	27763	44247
70-74	-66355	-18091	-48263
75+	339081	149142	189939
Total	-1067728	-660352	-407375

Figure 2.6

Net Migrants by Age and Sex, Survival Ratio Method

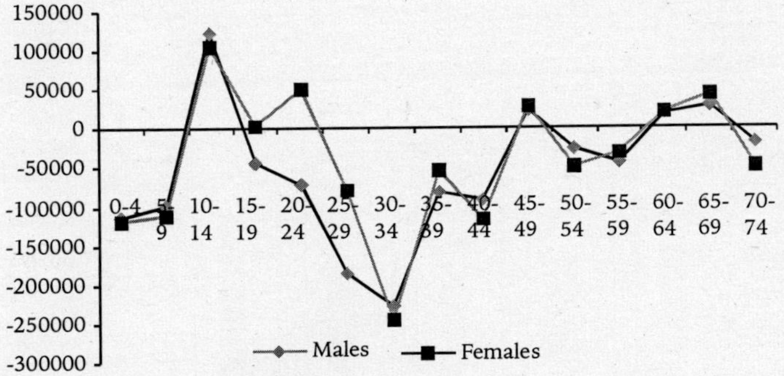

Geographic Aspect of Internal Migration in Kerala

One strong point about census data on migration is the information they provide on the spatial aspects of migration: the number of persons who migrated from each state and the state to which they moved. Information on both the birthplace and the place of last residence provides data on the spatial aspect. In this section, data on the place of last residence (POLR) are used for analysis.

Three states account for most of the migration to and from Kerala. These are: Tamil Nadu, Karnataka and Maharashtra (Table 2.8 and Figure 2.7).

Table 2.8

In-migration to Kerala based on Place of Residence, 1961-2001

State	*1961*	*1981*	*2001*
Karnataka	9.2	11.5	13.4
Maharashtra	2.4	6.0	6.0
Tamil Nadu	82.4	69.5	67.3
Delhi	0.2	0.8	1.0
Andhra Pradesh	0.8	2.1	2.1
Gujarat	1.3	1.3	1.3
Madhya Pradesh	0.3	0.9	1.1
Rajasthan	0.1	0.3	0.5
Uttar Pradesh	0.4	1.4	0.9
Pondicherry	1.1	2.2	2.4
Other states	1.6	4.0	4.1
Total	100.0	100.0	100.0

Figure 2.7

Per cent of Out-migrants from Kerala to Selected States

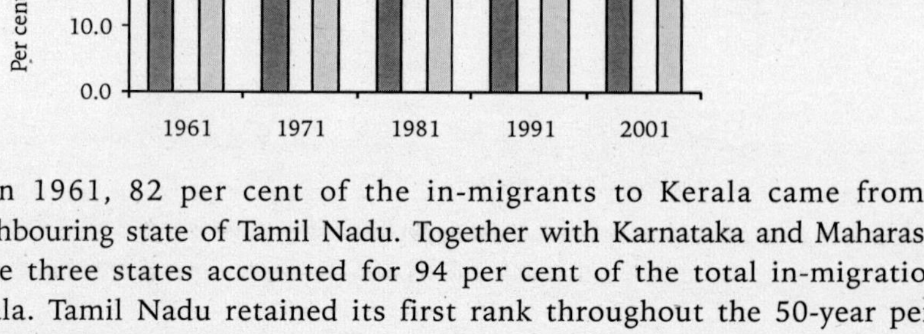

In 1961, 82 per cent of the in-migrants to Kerala came from the neighbouring state of Tamil Nadu. Together with Karnataka and Maharashtra, these three states accounted for 94 per cent of the total in-migration to Kerala. Tamil Nadu retained its first rank throughout the 50-year period, although its share declined to 67 per cent by 2001. On the other hand, Karnataka and Maharashtra increased their shares during this period, from 9 per cent to 14 per cent in the case of Karnataka and from 2 to 7 per cent in the case of Maharashtra.

In the case of out-migration from Kerala also, the three states of Tamil Nadu, Karnataka and Maharashtra accounted for 82 per cent in 1961. In 1961, 44 per cent of Kerala out-migrants had gone to Tamil Nadu, 22 per cent to Karnataka and 16 per cent to Maharashtra. However, their ranks did not change considerably by 2001. Karnataka became the number two destination of Kerala migrants in 2001. Maharashtra came third. Tamil Nadu continues to be the largest destination. Their total share in 2001 was only 78 per cent (Table 2.9 and Figure 2.8). The share of Delhi increased from 1.6 per cent in 1961 to 2.7 per cent in 2001. Gujarat also showed considerable increase.

Table 2.9

Out-migration from Kerala based on Place of Residence, 1961-2001

State	*1961*	*1981*	*2001*
Karnataka	22.0	19.3	21.1
Maharashtra	15.7	19.1	20.2
Tamil Nadu	44.3	42.3	36.7
Delhi	1.6	1.7	2.7
Andhra Pradesh	4.0	3.2	3.6
Gujarat	1.3	1.6	2.5
Madhya Pradesh	2.9	3.5	4.1
Rajasthan	0.3	0.7	1.1
Uttar Pradesh	0.9	1.5	1.1
Pondicherry	0.9	0.9	1.0
Other states	6.1	6.3	5.9
Total	100.0	100.0	100.0

These data indicate that over the years, out-migration from Kerala has spread to a much larger circle of states, covering almost all the states in the country by the year 2001. However, in-migration remain concentrated to the neighbouring states.

Based on this geographic configuration of out-migrants from Kerala, the Railway Minister in Delhi should have started new trains from Kerala to Karnataka and not to Tamil Nadu. The proportion of Kerala migrants going to Karnataka has increased from 19 per cent in 1971 to 25 per cent in 2001. At the same time, the proportion going to Tamil Nadu has halved from 42 per cent in 1971 to 21 per cent in 2001. The proportion going to Delhi has increased from a mere 2 per cent to 6 per cent.

Figure 2.8

Per cent of Out-migrants from Kerala to Selected States

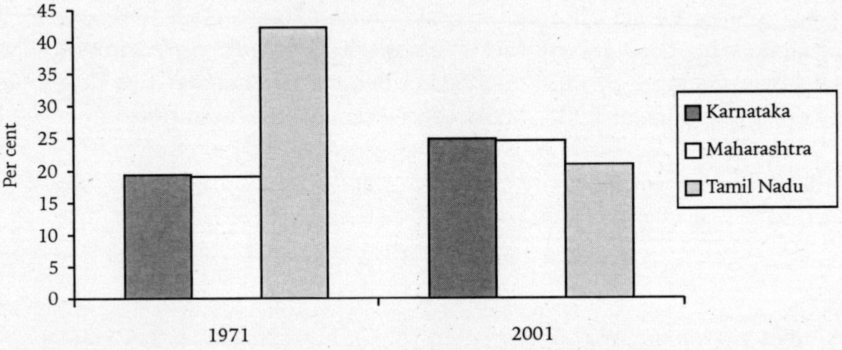

The proportion of in-migrants to Kerala from Tamil Nadu has also shown a significant decline from 70 per cent to 62 per cent, a decrease of 8 percentage points. On the other hand, the corresponding proportion from Karnataka has increased by 2.5 percentage points.

A more relevant criterion for allocating new trains from Kerala should be the increase in absolute numbers of Kerala out-migrants to the various states. According to this, both Karnataka and Maharashtra share the same rank, each showing an increase of 105,000 migrants from Kerala during 1971-2001. They together received 210,000 migrants out of an all-India total of 245,000 out-migrants from Kerala.

At the same time, Tamil Nadu had experienced a decline of 123,000 out migrants from Kerala during the same period. The other states that should be considered for new trains from Kerala should be Delhi (+56,000 persons) and Gujarat (+30,000 persons). There was absolutely no statistical justification to introduce new trains from Kerala to Chennai.

Demographic Composition of the Kerala Migrants

Sex Composition

Internal migration of Kerala has been fairly balanced with respect to sex composition. This was particularly true with respect to in-migration. In fact, in several years, lifetime in-migrants included more females than males. Although males dominate in employment-related migration, females dominate in marriage-related migration.

The overall proportion of women among Kerala migrants was 49.1 per cent among in-migrants and 48.8 per cent among out-migrants. Over the years, out-migration from Kerala consisted of an increasing proportion of women, from a mere 35 per cent in 1961 to 48.4 per cent in 2001. However, there was no such trend among the in-migrants to the state (Tables 2.10 and 2.11).

Table 2.10

Percentage of Female Migrants to and from Kerala, 1901-2001

	Year	*% of Female In-migrants*
Travancore-Cochin	1901	47.0
	1911	49.6
	1921	51.0
	1931	50.7
	1941	51.6
	1951	52.4
Kerala	1961	47.4
	1971	48.1
	1981	50.1
	1991	50.3
	2001	49.1

Table 2.11

Per cent of Females among Migrants to and from Kerala based on Duration of Residence Less than 10 Years, 1961-2001

	Out-migrants
1961-1971	39.2
1971-1981	44.0
1981-1991	47.9
1991-2001	49.9

Inter-state migrants include a high proportion of persons who cross state boundaries for reasons of marriage. Such migrants are mostly females. Nearly 97 per cent of out-migrants from Kerala who left Kerala because of marriage were females. The corresponding proportion among in-migrants was 87 per cent. Thus, one reason why migrants in India have a high proportion of females is the existence of a large proportion of marriage-induced migration. If marriage-related migration is excluded and migration caused by other reasons included, the proportion of females would only be 36.3 per cent (Table 2.12).

Table 2.12

Reasons for Migration among Female Migrants, Kerala

Reason	*Out-migration*	*In-migration*
Employment	16.7	20.2
Business	10.2	13.7
Education	51.1	32.7
Marriage	97.0	86.8
After birth	45.9	46.0
With household	63.2	57.6
Others	48.0	29.8
Total	48.7	48.0

The proportion of females among in-migrants from Kerala varies with the destination state. In 2001, the highest proportion of females among in-migrants from Kerala was in Andhra Pradesh (93 per cent) and the lowest was in Uttar Pradesh, 39 per cent. Over the years the proportion of females has increased in all the in-migration streams from Kerala (Table 2.13).

Table 2.13

Per cent of Women among Migrants to and from Kerala based on the Place of Birth

State	*In-migrants*	
	% Women 1971	*% Women 2001*
Karnataka	51.6	57.7
Maharashtra	36.3	48.1
Tamil Nadu	47.8	47
Delhi	36.4	50.2
Andhra Pradesh	37.3	93.4
Gujarat	40.8	47.9
Madhya Pradesh	43.3	49.3
Rajasthan	36.7	41.3
Uttar Pradesh	27.3	38.6
Pondicherry	57.4	59.2
Other states	31.5	35.3
Total	46.3	48.5

On the basis of these pieces of evidence, it is in order to conclude that Kerala migrants include a relatively high proportion of females and that over the decades their share has kept on increasing. The age profile of female migrants to and from Kerala shows that the highest flow of out-migrants from among them occurs between 15-29 years of age, partly due to marriage (Table 2.14).

Table 2.14

Per cent of Women Migrants to and from Kerala based on Duration of Residence, 2001

Age	*In-migrants*	*Out-migrants*
0-4	49.5	48.6
5-9	48.8	48.9
10-14	46.7	46.9
15-19	41.6	50.4
20-24	49.3	53.2
25-29	55.7	56.0
30-34	47.2	49.3
35-39	39.9	41.1
40-44	36.0	37.0
45-49	36.7	38.4
50-54	39.8	41.1
55-59	37.5	43.8
60-64	33.9	54.5
65-69	33.6	56.8
70-74	40.4	59.4
75-79	43.0	61.5
80+	49.8	58.2
Not stated	41.9	46.3
Total	46.1	49.9

Age Distribution

The largest proportion of migrants to and from Kerala belonged to the 25-29 year age group. There is relatively higher concentration among the out migrants than among the in-migrants, in this age group.

Reasons for Migration

The main objective of migration is employment. Most migrants move out from their native state seeking a job. This is true not only for migrants from Kerala but also migrants from other states.

Figure 2.9

Age Distribution of In- and Out-migrants, Kerala, 2001

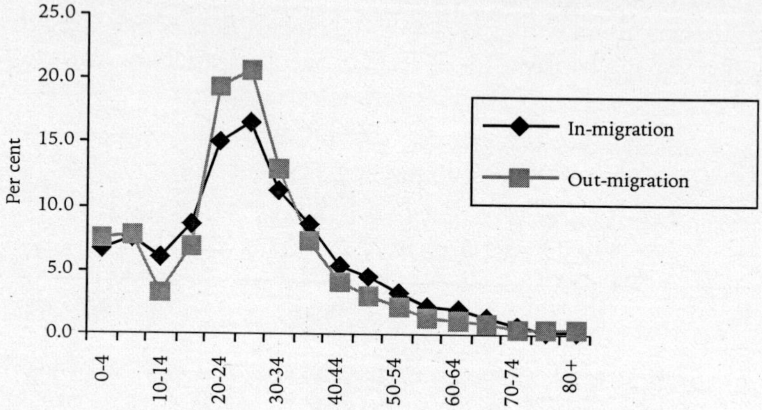

Table 2.15

Age Distribution of Inter-Census Migrants based on Duration of Residence Less than 10 Years, Kerala, 2001

Age	*In-migrants*	*Out-migrants*
0-4	6.8	7.5
5-9	7.5	7.7
10-14	6.1	3.3
15-19	8.7	7.0
20-24	15.0	19.5
25-29	16.5	20.6
30-34	11.2	12.9
35-39	8.6	7.4
40-44	5.4	4.2
45-49	4.4	3.1
50-54	3.1	2.1
55-59	2.2	1.4
60-64	2.0	1.1
65-69	1.2	0.8
70-74	0.6	0.5
75-79	0.3	0.3
80+	0.3	0.4
Not stated	0.1	0.2
Total	100.0	100.0

Table 2.16

Reason for Migration to and from Kerala, 2001

Reason	*In-migration*	*Out-migration*
Work/Employment	27.4	33.5
Business	1.9	2.0
Education	1.3	4.1
Marriage	19.5	18.2
By birth	5.1	7.2
With family	27.8	19.6
Others	17.1	15.3
Total	100.0	100.0

Nearly a third of the migrants from Kerala migrated to other states in search of job. In this respect, the proportion of migrants moving out in search of job is higher among Kerala out-migrants than among in-migrants to Kerala.

There are two other important reasons for migration to and from Kerala. These are marriage and shifting of the household. Neither of them is economically very significant.

Education as a reason for migration is relatively more frequent among the Keralites who move out of the state than for outsiders coming to Kerala. Kerala is not as attractive a place for out-state persons to move in for education as other states are for Kerala youths to move out to.

Conclusions

This chapter is about migration from Kerala to other states in India and from other states to Kerala, that is, internal migration in Kerala. Censuses of India are the main source of data. Conceptual and other inadequacies of census data for migration analysis are well documented in other sources, especially in UN Manual IV and therefore, are not dealt here. A point of view taken in this chapter is that, in spite of these inadequacies, because of the abundance of comparable data extending over half a century, the major conclusions of this study are unlikely to be disputed. Some of the conclusions about the dynamics of internal migration in Kerala are summarised below:

1 Until about the middle of the last century, Kerala had remained basically an area of in-migration. More persons had moved into Kerala than Keralites who had moved out of the state. There had been during those days, little economic necessity for Keralites to migrate to other states.

2 The situation changed during the second half of the last century. With the integration of the erstwhile Travancore and Cochin states to the Indian Union, the youths of Kerala began to move out to other states in search of economic opportunities. The era of migration out of Kerala began and continued at an accelerated rate during much of the second half of the last century. With the maturing of the demographic transition, and consequent decline in the rate of population growth and the onset of a period of emigration to the Gulf region and other foreign countries, out-migration began to slow down. At the end of the century, conditions were very ripe for a reversal of the migration trend in Kerala. There was empirical support to conclude that out-migration from Kerala decelerated. But in the last decade of the last century, there was some revival of the increasing trend in out-migration from the state. Out-migration during 1991-2001 was larger than that during 1981-1991.

3 This chapter takes the view that out-migration from the state was a response to demographic transition and the consequent explosive (compared to the conditions in the other states of the country) population growth. The deceleration in migration after the 1980s could also be considered a response to the rapid decline in population growth that had set in since the early 1960s.

4 The recent onset of replacement migration to the state is explained on similar lines. The replacement migration is basically a response to the rapid decline in the number of workers in the young working ages caused by fertility decline to below replacement level, by the emigration of a large number of young persons to the Gulf region and other destinations abroad, and the economic improvements in the state economy which has fostered an aversion to low-paid and unskilled jobs on the part of the youths in the state.

5 With all such favourable conditions for a decrease in the migration from the state, a perplexing question remains: why did during the most recent decade, 1991-2001 end up with an increase in out migration and emigration from the state? A few possible reasons are suggested below:

(i) Kerala out-migrants used to return to the state when they pass the working age. Living conditions in the state were attractive enough to entice them back. This may not be the situation any longer. With the large-scale emigration to the Gulf countries, the cost of living in Kerala has gone up very much in comparison with that of the host states. With limited retirement benefits, Kerala out-migrants could live more comfortably in their host state than in their mother state.

(ii) Many of the out-migrants who came from one-child or two-child households may not have any family back home to return to. The change in family demography could be another reason for the slowing down of return migration from other states.

(iii) In the past, educational opportunities were much better in Kerala than in other states in India. This again may not true any longer. Host states could now offer better educational opportunities.

(iv) Migration begets migration. This is a basic fact about migration. Kerala has already passed the critical mass with respect to the number of out-migrants and emigrants needed to sustain migration from the state at a reasonably high level. The rapid expansion in secondary level education, the lack of adequate employment opportunities for Kerala's educated youths, and the attainment of a critical mass of Kerala migrants living outside the state, would most probably ensure a continuation of the migration phenomenon at a relatively high rate even under the emerging unfavourable demographic and socio-economic trends.

(v) It may not be the demographic checks, but a very rapid expansion of service-related employment opportunities in Kerala that could put a break to the acceleration in the migration flows from the state. The expertise brought by the return emigrants and the very large flow of workers' remittances could offer conditions necessary for the development of a viable service-oriented economic sector in the state. This could ensure a slowing down of the out-migration process and stimulate return of earlier migrants.

3

International Migration

K.C. ZACHARIAH and S. IRUDAYA RAJAN

Introduction

In our earlier study (Kerala Migration Study, KMS), we concluded thus:

> Migration has provided the single most dynamic factor in the otherwise dismal scenario of Kerala in the last quarter of the twentieth century. It is one of the positive outcomes of the Kerala Model of Development. Kerala is approaching the end of the millennium with a little cheer in many of its homes, thanks to migration and the economic returns that it brings. In Kerala, migration must have contributed more to poverty alleviation than any other factor including agrarian reforms, trade union activities and social welfare legislation (Zachariah, Mathew and Irudaya Rajan, May 2000, *CDS Working Paper* No. 303)

KMS speculated that the era of large-scale emigration from Kerala to the Gulf countries was largely over, that in the coming years emigration trend would decelerate, that a larger number of emigrants would return to Kerala and that the return emigrants could outnumber fresh emigrants in the early twenty-first century. The rationale for this speculation was the fact that the early emigrants from Kerala to the Gulf had been mostly persons with less than secondary level of education and employed in low-level jobs in the construction sector in the host countries. By the end of the last century, the construction phase of the Gulf reconstruction was by and large, over. The glamour of the local workers for a larger share of the job market was getting increasingly loud. Governments in the Gulf region were being forced to take restrictive measures in the employment of foreign workers. More and more economic and commercial sectors in the Gulf countries were getting closed to workers from foreign countries. And, declining emigration and increasing return emigration were thought to be the logical outcomes of these developments.

If these expectations had materialised, remittances from abroad would have declined with all its adverse impacts on the socio-economic situation in the state. The study, therefore, placed several policy options before the Government to ensure continued emigration, the chief among them being the suggestion to give special attention to the general and technical education, and to provide special training to potential emigrants so as to enable them to compete successfully with their counterparts from other countries.

The study also recommended that the state should have a migration monitoring system (MMS). Unlike fertility and mortality trends, migration trends are highly volatile depending, as they do, not only on conditions within the state, but also, and to a much higher degree, on conditions in the destination countries and the policies taken by them. Outbreak of a war (like the Kuwait war of 1991) or the appearance of some natural calamity could upset all calculations about emigration prospects. For the Kerala population, depending as they do heavily on remittances, a continuous monitoring of emigration and return emigration should be part of its development planning strategy.

Pending the development of a formal MMS, the CDS has decided to undertake periodic assessment of the international migration situation. The CDS-SANEI (South Asia Migration Study or SMS for brevity) study was undertaken in that spirit and with that objective. Being a "revisit", the scope of this study is limited to the basic information needed to assess the economic consequences of emigration.

Design of SMS: The SMS of 2004 was designed after the KMS of 1999. The basic data used in both the studies were of the same order: primary data collected from 10,000 households from 225 localities (200 localities in KMS) selected at random from the 14 districts of the state. The questionnaire used in the two studies was the same; the data-collecting agency was also the same. The methodology of analysis followed in both the studies was quite similar, but the objectives were slightly different. In the KMS, the main concern had been the assessment of the migration situation in 1998-99. In SMS, the concern was not only assessment of the situation in 2003-04, but also a review of changes (dynamics) during 1999-2004. The findings of the two studies are quite comparable.

Dimensions of Emigration

Demographic Dimensions

Contrary to expectations, emigration from Kerala continued unabated during 1999-2004. The number of emigrants in 2004 was 18.4 lakh persons, roughly 27 emigrants per 100 households. The comparable figure in 1999 (KMS) was 13.6 lakh persons, roughly 21 emigrants per 100 households. There has taken place relatively large increase of about 35 per cent, in the number of emigrants from Kerala during the last five years. This is one of the unexpected results of SMS.

The number of return emigrants was 8.9 lakh persons in 2004 as against 7.4 lakh persons in 1999. They represented 13.0 persons per 100 households in 2004 and 11.6 persons per 100 household in 1999. The return emigration showed a slower rate of growth, about 21 per cent in the 5-year period. This finding also was contrary to expectation.

The number of non-resident Keralites (NRKs), defined as the sum of emigrants and return emigrants, was 27.3 lakh in 2004 and 21.0 lakh in 1999, indicating an increase of 30 per cent during 1999-2004. There were about 40 NRKs per 100 households in 2004 but only 33 in 1999. The number of NRKs per 100 households increased by 7 persons during the period.

Although there were 40 NRKs per 100 households in 2004, only about 26 per cent of the households were direct beneficiaries of emigration; 74 per cent were not. The proportion of households with at least one emigrant or one return emigrant (NRK > 0) was 24 per cent in 1999 as against 26 per cent in 2004. There was thus, a slight increase in the spread of emigration among the households in Kerala. At the same time, the total number of households without an NRK has actually increased by about 2.7 lakh during the 5-year period, from 48.39 lakh in 1999 to 51.08 lakh in 2004.

This analysis provides a good reminder of the fact that direct beneficiaries of emigration are a relatively small minority in Kerala; that the vast majority of the households in the state are exposed to the ill effects of emigration such as price increase without having been in receipt of any direct benefits at all. Contrary to the common belief, Kerala is not flooded with NRKs and NRK households, even today. The Muslims and the Mar Thoma Syrian Christians are somewhat of an exception (see later).

Although emigration has not decreased, the rate of increase has declined significantly in recent years, from 74.7 per cent during 1993-1998 to 39.9 per cent during 1998-2003. The same pattern holds for return emigrants and non-resident Keralites also, but the rates of growth have been higher. The decline in the rate of increase is higher for emigrants than for return emigrants.

Though not unexpected, between 1999 and 2004, women, especially married women, have increased their presence significantly among the emigrants. On the contrary, married men lost out to unmarried men. The new emigrants included a relatively larger share of unmarried men and married women.

The increase in the number of "Gulf wives" (married women whose husbands are away in the Gulf), has not kept up with the increase in the number of emigrants. The number of "Gulf wives" has remained almost unchanged at about 1 million between 1999 and 2004. The increase in the proportion of married women among the emigrants could have compensated for the increase in the total number of emigrants.

Geographic Dimensions

In the past five years, Kerala emigrants have spread their wings over a much wider spectrum of countries in the world: North America, Europe and South East Asia. Within the Gulf region itself, there were some significant realignments, some countries gaining ground at the expense of others. Within Kerala there were signs of realignment as far as the district of origin is concerned, some districts gaining ground at the expense of some traditionally important districts of emigration.

In 1999, about 95 per cent of Kerala emigrants went to the Gulf countries; and the other 5 per cent went mainly to the USA and Africa. By 2004, the share of the Kerala emigrants in the Gulf has declined to about 90 per cent and that in countries other than the Gulf has increased to 10 per cent. The principal destinations of Kerala emigrants outside the Gulf were the United States of America, England, Singapore and Maldives Islands. Within the Gulf region, the principal destinations were the United Arab Emirates and Saudi Arabia, which together accounted for more than two-thirds of all emigrants in the Gulf. In 2004, the share of the UAE increased to 36.5 per cent, up from 31.0 per cent in 1999. On the contrary, the share of Saudi Arabia declined to 26.7 per cent from 37.5 per cent in 1999. There was thus, a significant realignment between these two countries in recent years.

Along with the change in the destinations, there were also changes in the relative importance of districts as the places of origin of Kerala emigrants. Although Malappuram district continued to send out the largest number of emigrants, it has lost some ground to other northern districts. Between 1999 and 2004, there was a slight northward shift in the centre of location of emigrants from Kerala.

Social and Cultural Dimensions

The principal destinations of emigrants from Kerala were Muslim countries. A natural consequence of it was that, the majority of the emigrants were also Muslims. Among the emigrants, the proportion of the Muslims was 43.7 per cent in 2004 and 41.9 in 1999. Their share in the sample population was only 25.9 per cent in 2004 as against 27.1 per cent in 1999. Hindus constituted 31.2 per cent of the total number of emigrants and Christians, 25.1 per cent. Over the 5-year period, while Muslims have increased their share, Hindus have decreased theirs.

For every 100 households there were 82 NRKs among Muslims, but only 22 among Hindus. However, the largest percentage increase (during 1999-2004) in the number of NRKs was not among Muslims (17.3 per cent) but among Christians (53.9 per cent).

Figure 3.1

Per cent Distribution of Emigrants by Country of Residence and Religion

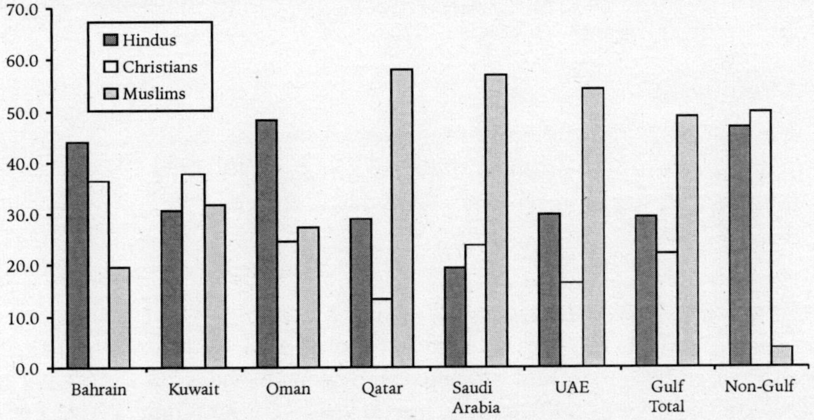

Muslims also stand apart with respect to the proportion of households with an NRK. Among them, one in two households has an NRK. This is also true of Mar Thoma Syrian Christians. Among the Scheduled Castes, only less than 5 per cent of the households have an NRK.

Thus, the picture which emerges from this analysis of the dimensions of emigration is one of sustained rapid emigration and significant return emigration, and significant realignment both in the country of destination and the districts of origin, portending considerable enlargement in the spectrum of the emigrant's destinations. In spite of the relatively long period of emigration from the state to ever-enlarging destinations, only a minority of households in the state are direct beneficiaries of emigration—just about a quarter of the total.

Remittances

Remittances are the principal means by which emigration impacts upon the economy. There are of course other ways such as on-the-job development of technical and management skills, change in lifestyle and work culture, exposure to better and more modern tools and equipments. However, in this study the focus is on the consequences brought out through remittances and their disposition. How much money comes to Kerala as workers' remittances in a year? The data collected in this study are not sufficient to answer this question.

We have made a distinction between total remittances and household remittances. Secondary data from official statistics of the Reserve Bank of

India (RBI) and other sources are used to arrive at an estimate of the total remittances. On the other hand, data from this study were used to estimate household remittances, that is, remittances received by households in Kerala directly from emigrants abroad.

Total Remittances

Our best estimate of the total remittances for 2004 was Rs. 18,465 crore. This compares with the estimate of Rs. 13,652 crore for 1999. Thus, the total remittances that Kerala receives annually has increased by 35 per cent during 1999-2004.

The infusion of Rs. 18,465 crore a year to Kerala via remittances should have had considerable impact on the Kerala economy. Rs. 18,465 crore per year distributed among the 32.5 million persons of Kerala would give each person in Kerala, young and old, men and women about Rs. 5,680 per year or Rs. 473 per month sufficient to buy at least one kilogram of rice per day per person. This calculation clearly indicates how important remittances are for the Kerala economy.

The net state domestic product (NSDP) for Kerala was Rs. 83,782 crore for 2002-03. The remittances (Rs. 18,465 crore) come to about 22 per cent of the NSDP of Kerala. The past five years experienced a general decrease in the ratio of remittances to NSDP, from about 25 per cent in 1999 to 22 per cent in 2003.

The per capita domestic income for Kerala was about Rs. 25,764 in 2003. This estimate does not include remittances. The modified state domestic income, including remittances, would be Rs. 102,248 crore and the modified per capita income, including remittances, would be Rs. 31,442. The effect of remittances on Kerala's per capita annual income in 2003 was an increase of Rs. 5678.

The importance of remittances in Kerala's economy becomes more evident from a few other comparisons. The remittances were 1.74 times the revenue receipts of the state, 1.8 times the annual expenditure of the Kerala government and 7 times of what the state received from the Central government. Remittances were sufficient to wipe out 60 per cent the state's debt in 2003.

Export of cashew kernels and marine products are two important earners of foreign exchange in Kerala. The remittances in 2003 was 15 times the export earnings from cashew and 18 times that from marine products.

At the district level, remittances were the highest in Thrissur district with Rs. 3,234 crore. Malappuram district came next with Rs. 2892 crore. As expected, Idukki and Wayanad received the lowest.

Remittances were 22 per cent of the state's NSDP. However, considerable variations are observed among districts. In Malappuram district, remittances formed about 46 per cent of the district domestic income. It was a meagre 1 per cent in Idukki district. Thrissur (38.2 per cent), Pathanamthitta (28.6 per cent) and Kollam (26.9 per cent) received relatively high proportions of their domestic income from remittances.

Figure 3.2

SDP Per Capita and Remittances Per Capita

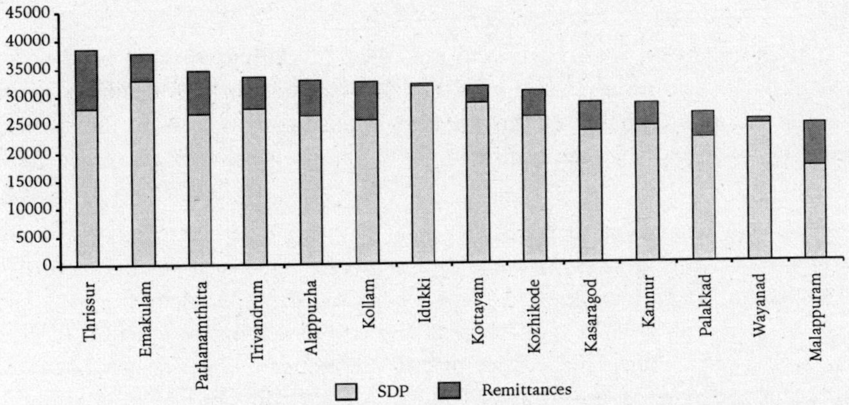

The impact of remittances on district level per capita income is the highest in Thrissur where remittances raised per capita income to Rs. 38,525 or by Rs. 10,654. Six districts where the impact is more than the state average are Thrissur, Malappuram, Pathanamthitta, Kollam, Alappuzha and Thiruvananthapuram. Remittances contributed more than Rs. 10 a day on the average income of persons in 11 districts, more than Rs. 20 a day in 3 districts and about Rs. 30 a day in Thrissur district.

Household Remittances

A part of the total remittances to Kerala is received by members of their households. This is what we call household remittances.

Not all households received remittances. Only 17.6 per cent of the households had emigrants, and only 16.7 per cent of the households received remittances in cash. About 17.1 per cent of households have received remittances in one form or another. Thus, most of the households which had emigrants from them, have received remittances. At the same time, it is important to underline the point that 83 per cent of the Kerala households were not direct beneficiaries of workers remittances from abroad.

An estimate of the total household remittances (cash, commodities and funds received for buying land, houses, scooter etc.) received by Kerala households for various purposes was Rs. 7,965 crore. Of this total, cash remittances were Rs. 5,509 crore. The corresponding figure for 1999 had been Rs. 3,530 crore indicating an increase of 56 per cent during the 5-year period. Increase in the number of emigrants during the period was only 34 per cent. Thus, the increase in household remittances was more than that in the number of emigrants by 22 percentage points. Obviously, remittance per emigrant has increased considerably during the past five years. The increase could have been due to structural changes among the emigrants, and their spread to developed countries in the West.

"In the eighties, we mostly had unskilled or skilled workers heading for west Asia. In the nineties, we have had knowledge workers heading for the more salubrious climates of the western hemisphere, driven by the demand from the booming services sector in the US and elsewhere" *(Economic Times,* 8/4/2004).

The total cash value of goods (clothes, electrical and electronic good, etc.) received from emigrants was Rs. 562 crore in 2004 and Rs. 541 crore in 1999, indicating an increase of a mere 4 per cent. In 1999, remittances in kind were 15 per cent of cash remittances. The corresponding proportion in 2004 was 10 per cent. Thus, the practice of bringing household goods, gold, clothes, etc., for the use of members of their households has not kept up in proportions with the increase in the number of emigrants. Increase in the local availability of goods, which used to be imported, could have been the reason behind this slowdown.

In addition to cash and commodities, households received Rs. 1,575 crore by way of funds for investment in land and buildings. Of this amount, 87 per cent (Rs. 1367 crore) was used for the purchase of land and the balance Rs. 208 crore on construction/purchase of home buildings.

An amount of Rs. 319 crore was received by households for the purpose of buying cars, motor cycles, for starting small scale industries and for paying dowry etc. Much of this amount (90 per cent) was spent on dowry payments and meeting other miscellaneous expenses. Only less than half of one per cent of these 319 crore was spent on starting small-scale industries. About 10 per cent (Rs. 32 crore) was spent for buying cars, scooters, etc.

Much of the cash value of commodities bought by the emigrants (about Rs. 562 crore) was the value of clothing bought by the emigrants on their home visits. Next in importance was gold ornaments brought in. Another equally important item brought in by emigrants was electrical and electronic goods.

Household remittances were meant mainly for the subsistence of the emigrant's relatives back home. About 50 per cent of the cash remittances was indeed used for subsistence. About half of that amount (25 per cent or 1,400 crore) was used for educational purpose.

Geographical Aspect of Remittances

Out of the total household remittances of Rs. 7,965 crore to Kerala in 2004, Rs.1,368 crore (or 17.1 per cent) was received by households in Thrissur district. This is the largest among the 14 districts of the state. Households in Malappuram district received 1,257 crore (15.8 per cent of the total). The other districts which received substantial share of the remittances were Kollam (10.6 per cent) and Thiruvananthapuram (10.2 per cent).

In 1999, the district which received the largest amount by way of household remittances had been Malappuram, which received Rs. 766 crore or 18.8 per cent of the total. The share of Malappuram district decreased to 15.6 per cent in 2004, compared to 18.8 per cent in 1999. On the other hand, Thrissur's share increased from 14.0 per cent in 1999 to 17.1 per cent in 2004. The other districts, which experienced a significant increase in their shares, are Kollam and Thiruvananthapuram. On the other hand, some districts have experienced decline in their shares: from 11.9 per cent to 7.7 per cent in Ernakulam, from 6.6 per cent to 5.0 per cent in Pathanamthitta and from 8.7 per cent to 6.6 per cent in Palakkad.

All the 14 districts had experienced increases in the amounts received by households by way of remittances. The largest increase was in Thrissur district (Rs. 826 crore). The other districts of importance in this respect are Malappuram (Rs. 481 crore), Kollam (Rs. 467 crore) and Thiruvananthapuram (Rs. 456 crore).

Remittances per emigrant were the highest in Thrissur district, Rs. 51,750. Idukki district came close with Rs. 50,000 per emigrant. Ernakulam and Kollam are next in importance with about Rs. 40,000 per emigrant. Per emigrant remittances were the lowest in Kannur, only Rs. 15,000.

It was mentioned earlier that remittances in any form were received only by 17 per cent of the households in Kerala. The remaining 83 per cent were not direct beneficiaries of remittances. The distribution of emigrants per household differed widely among the districts. At one extreme is Idukki district where only 1.5 per cent of the households received remittances from emigrants in any form. On the other hand, in Malappuram district as much as a third of all households were direct beneficiaries of remittances from abroad. Pathanamthitta and Kasaragod were the other two districts, which had relatively larger proportions of households receiving remittances from abroad.

Remittances by Religion

The total remittance of Rs. 7,977 crore consists of Rs. 2,365 crore received by Hindu households, Rs. 2,021 crore by Christian households and Rs. 3,590 crore received by Muslim households. The average remittances per emigrant were Rs. 43,220. There was not much variation in this respect across communities. On the other hand, average remittances per household vary considerably by religion. The Muslim households have an average remittance of Rs. 24,000 (Muslim households have larger number of emigrants per household) while Hindu households have an average of only Rs. 6,134 per household.

Figure 3.3

Per cent of Households Directly Benefitted from Remittances

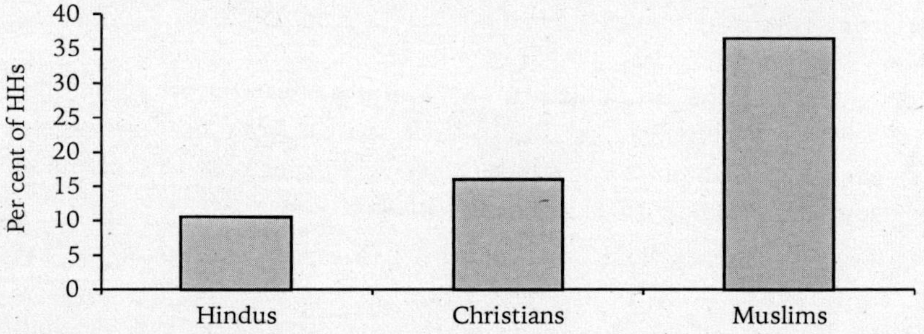

Remittances by Community

We have seen that the amount of remittance per household was the highest among Muslims. But Mar Thoma Christian households had received even larger amounts. An average Mar Thoma Christian household received Rs. 26,098 as remittances in 2003-04, which was higher than the average for Muslims, Rs. 24,350.

In the order of remittances per household, the Mar Thoma community comes first followed by Muslims, Jacobite/Orthodox Christians, Latin Catholics, Roman Catholics, Nairs and followers of the Church of South India. The SC/ST group comes last with only Rs. 725 per household.

Emigration and Possession of Consumer Durables

One of the inevitable consequences of emigration is the substantial increase in the disposable funds at the household level. This increase has had considerable impact on the consumption pattern of Kerala households. After paying back money borrowed for meeting the cost of emigration, remittances are used to acquire a variety of consumer goods as well as land and houses, vehicles and household accessories. We have indicated earlier, how the remittances are used for housing, purchase of land, paying back debts, education of dependents, dowry of children and other relatives. Here we discuss the effect of remittances' on acquisition of housing amenities, possession of household goods and other consumer durables.

Housing

A major sector in which emigration seems to have had a very significant effect is housing. About 22 per cent of the houses in the sample were categorised as, "luxurious" or "very good" in 2004. The corresponding percentage in 1999 had been 14.5 per cent. Thus, during the 5-year period, the housing quality improved considerably. However, there were large differences in the quality of houses occupied by the three religious groups. The proportion of luxurious or very good houses was 18.3 per cent among the Hindus, 25.8 per cent among the Christians and as much as 28.7 per cent among Muslims. This is one area in which Muslims stand much ahead of other religious groups.

Figure 3.4

Per cent of Houses that are Luxurious or Very Good by Community

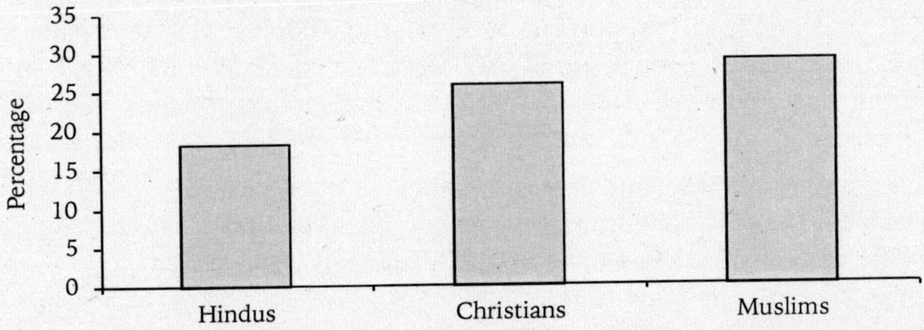

Emigration has had considerable impact on the quality of housing. Perhaps housing has been the very first requirement to receive emigrants' attention. About 58.3 per cent of the houses of the NRKs in 2004 were either "luxurious" or "very good". Among the non-NRKs, the corresponding proportion was only 17.1. The difference is as high as 41.2 percentage points. The corresponding difference had been only 13.1 percentage points in 1999. Thus, the effect of emigration on housing has become much stronger in recent years.

Comparison between the situation in 2004 and 1999 is very revealing. In 1999 only 2.4 per cent of the NRK houses had been luxurious, but by 2004 as much as 17.2 per cent of them became luxurious. Similarly, only 22 per cent of the NRK houses had been "very good" in 1999. But by 2004, as much as 41 per cent of the houses of NRKs became "very good".

Even among the non-migrant households, some improvements have been observed in the quality of houses. Among them, 11.3 per cent of the houses had been "luxurious" or "very good" in 1999. The corresponding percentage was 17.1 in 2004. But unlike the case of electrification and use of LPG gas, the improvement in the quality of houses during 1999-2004 is seen to have been much stronger among emigrant households than among non-emigrant households. Emigration has had indeed an independent positive effect on housing quality. This positive effect of emigration on housing quality is independent of the district of origin of the emigrants or their religious affiliation. It is pervasive.

Possession of Consumer Durables

Remittances sent back by the emigrants, and money brought back by them on return increase the amount of disposable income of the NRK households. These households are, therefore, in a position to acquire durable consumer goods much more than their non-NRK counterparts.

In 2004, 60 per cent of the Kerala households possessed television sets, 45 per cent had telephone connection and 30 per cent had refrigerators. All the corresponding proportions had been much smaller in 1999. Between 1999 and 2004, the proportion of Kerala households with television sets increased from 38 per cent to 60 per cent. The corresponding change in the case of telephones was from 15 per cent to 44 per cent, and in the case of refrigerators from 19 per cent to 30 per cent.

In terms of actual numbers, the increases between 1999 and 2004 were 2,048 thousand telephone connections, 1,720 thousand television sets, 852 thousand refrigerators, 548 thousand VCRs, 509 thousand scooters/motor cycles and 330 thousand motor cars.

The effect of emigration on the possession of the consumer durables could be understood better by comparing the increases during 1999-2004 as between emigrant households and non-emigrant households. The increase in the percentage of households with telephones among emigrants was by 40.9 points but only by 24.1 points among non-migrant households. In the case of television sets, the increases were 31.4 percentage points among emigrant households, but only by 21.1 percentage points among non-emigrants households. In all other items of consumer durables also, the increases were markedly higher among the migrant households. Emigration has indeed contributed significantly to the possession of consumer durables.

On the whole, the vast majority of Christian households own most of these consumer durables more than the other two communities. Seventy per cent of the Christian households have television sets compared with only 60 per cent of Hindu households and 51 per cent of Muslim households. Hindus have the lowest proportion in the case of ownership of cars, scooters, telephones, cell phones, VCRs and refrigerators. Muslims come last with respect to the possession of television sets and cars. But they lead others with respect to the ownership of taxis.

As shown earlier, emigration has significant effect on the possession of consumer durables. The effect is significant among all the three communities; but is the highest among Christians with respect to possession of telephones and refrigerators. In the case of television sets, the largest impact of emigration has been on the Muslim community. The difference between migrant and non-migrant households in the matter of possession of television is as much as 35 percentage points.

Economic Consequences of Emigration

Income Redistribution

It was mentioned earlier that the direct beneficiaries of emigration were only 26 per cent of the total number of households in the state, the ones with NRKs. The balance 74 per cent received any benefit from emigration, if at all, only indirectly. If 26 per cent have received direct benefits and 74 per cent have not, what has been the impact of remittances on income or wealth redistribution in the state? The answer would depend on who the 26 per cent are. If they are of the bottom stratum of the income ladder, as had been the case in the early nineties, probably emigration would have contributed to reducing inequalities in the income distribution of the Kerala economy. On the other hand, if the 26 per cent were from the top stratum of the society, emigration would have contributed to greater concentration of income. We don't have any information on the income level of the Kerala emigrants. The best approximations that could be gathered from our survey were the educational level of the emigrants, the type of houses they live in, the type of fuels they use for cooking, etc.

One evidence is provided by the relative amount of remittances received by the well-educated (secondary level or degree) *versus* the less-educated (below secondary level). In 1999, households with well-educated emigrants had received 54.8 per cent of the total "household cash remittances". By 2004, the share of the well-educated emigrant households increased to 64.2 per cent. Thus, more of the remittances received by the Kerala households sent in recent years have gone to households with well-educated emigrants (assumed to be from wealthy households). Similarly, in 1999, households with "luxurious" or "very good" houses had received only 39.5 per cent of the remittances. By 2004, the corresponding proportion was 56.4 per cent, an increase of 17 percentage points in five years. Another statistics supporting this conclusion is the increase in the share of remittances, received by households with LPG connection (presumably the richer households). In 1999, LPG-households received 42.1 per cent of the total remittances. By 2004, more than 60 per cent of the remittances went to LPG-households, an increase of 18 percentage points.

All these indirect evidences point to the conclusion that in recent years, emigration and remittances were not helping to reduce inequalities in the society of Kerala.

The New Rich versus the Old Rich Controversy

An adverse impact of Gulf emigration, which has received considerable public attention in recent days, is the emergence of social and political problems arising from the class of the "new rich" (*puthan panakkar*). Gulf money has played a major role in restructuring the Kerala society, at a rate never before experienced in the state. From the bottom five per cent of the income ladder, some of the Gulf NRKs have gone up all the way to the top five per cent, transcending family background, caste or creed. In fact, most of the transformation took place among the minority communities. Such overstepping of the traditional hierarchy is not liked by the "old rich" and has resulted in some resentment and social tension.

Sometime back, the former Chief Minister of Kerala, Sri A.K. Antony was "accused" of being "anti-minority" when he is alleged to have observed that minority communities in Kerala were cornering "undue benefits" using their political and economic clout gained through Gulf remittances and influential Gulf emigrants.

Emigration brings money; and money brings power and the appetite for power, resulting in conflicts between the new rich and the old rich, between the traditional centres of power and the aspiring centres of power. This is one of the inevitable consequences of emigration taking place not only in state politics but also in local politics, religious organisations, etc. It is instructive at this juncture, to recall what we have learned in this study about the community factor in Gulf migration. According to SMS, more than half the population of Kerala is Hindu, about 56 per cent. However, among the emigrants from Kerala, only 31 per cent were Hindus. Muslims constitute less than 25 per cent of the total, but as much as 44 per cent of the emigrants were Muslims. About 20 per cent of the population was Christian, but as much as 25 per cent of the emigrants belong to this community.

Within the Hindu and the Christian religious groups themselves, there exist vast differences with respect to emigration and remittances. For example, among Hindus, emigration rate (emigrants per 100 household) varied from 36.1 among the Brahmins to 3.1 among the Scheduled Castes. Among Christians, the Mar Thoma Syrian sect has an emigration rate of 70 per 100 households while for the Latin Catholics and the followers of the Church of South India, the emigration rate was only 22 per 100 households.

What we have described above about emigration is also true of remittances. Hindu households received only 30 per cent of the total remittances. On the other hand, Muslim households received 45 per cent and Christian households received 25 per cent. Within the Hindu group, remittances per household varied from Rs. 725 among the Scheduled Castes to Rs. 9,225 among the Nairs. Within the Christian group, remittances per household varied from Rs. 9,198 among households belonging to the followers of Church of South India to Rs. 26,098 among the Mar Thoma Syrians.

Thus, according to SMS, remittances from emigrants are certainly benefiting the minority communities much more than the majority communities.

The accusation of exerting undue pressure by the minorities should be viewed in the light of their current status in the society and their inherent aspiration to better their socio-economic status. Muslims are the most backward community in Kerala with respect to human resources. While 29 per cent of the Hindus and 36 per cent of the Christians are educated up to the secondary or higher levels, only 15 per cent of the Muslims had received secondary or higher levels of education.

In the 1999 KMS we observed,

"Nearly 51 per cent of the emigrants were from Muslim households; and Muslim households have received nearly 50 per cent of the remittances from abroad. At the same time, Muslims have the highest illiteracy rate, and the lowest proportion of persons with a secondary school certificate."

"Of all the districts in Kerala, Malappuram sent out the largest number of emigrants (270,000) and received the largest amount (Rs. 6,295 million) as remittances from abroad. Malappuram has the highest birth rate, the highest rate of population growth, the highest average family size, the highest proportion of illiterates and the lowest proportion of persons with a secondary school certificate or a degree."

"These facts establish a very strong case for development of public policies, which would enhance this educationally backward population to use part of the remittances it receives for improvement of its educational level."

There was a time (more than 100 years ago), when personal achievements in terms of education or wealth were not as important as the situation into which a person was born or the community he/she belonged to. It was not acquired factors such as education or remittances from abroad or contacts with prominent emigrants, but ascribed characteristics such as religion, caste or family background, over which a person has no control, that mattered most for achieving positions of influence. But now money power has become more important. Is there much of a difference? Is there anything basically wrong if a backward community asserts itself with its newly acquired money power and connections for its betterment in social and political terms?

Replacement Migration

In the early phase of Gulf emigration from Kerala, the emigrants were mostly non-agricultural labourer with low levels of educational qualification. They also included some skilled workers like carpenters, masons and electricians. The emigration of the unemployed unskilled workers helped to reduce unemployment. The money they sent back accelerated the construction industry and thus, helped further to reduce unemployment.

Initially, emigration of skilled labour did not create any major bottleneck back home, but their continued emigration resulted in significant scarcity of skilled workers in the state. It is often said that it is easy to find a plastic surgeon in Kerala than a good carpenter. The scarcity was followed inevitably by increases in wage rates.

At present, Kerala has the highest wage rates among the states in India. The increasing wages in agriculture along with stagnant or declining prices of agricultural products in Kerala have resulted in decreasing employment opportunities in agriculture. Money spent on high wages could not be recovered from the sale proceeds of agricultural products because of their falling prices. It was cheaper to buy imported rice from Andhra Pradesh or imported bananas from Tamil Nadu than to produce them locally. The result is shrinkage in the agricultural activities and employment opportunities in agriculture.

The differentials in wage rates between Kerala and the neighbouring states received the attention of workers in other states. And they began to move into Kerala and to take up work, which had used to be done by Kerala workers, especially in the construction sector. What started as a trickle soon assumed the dimensions of a torrent in the course of a few years. Thus, started the era of replacement migration to Kerala.

After a lapse of about 60 years, Kerala is again becoming an in-migrating state. As soon as a contractor takes up a contract for any construction or road work, he appoints an agent to recruit workers not only from neighbouring states but also from states as far away as Uttar Pradesh, Bihar and West Bengal. In many construction sites in Kerala, the *lingua franca* is not Malayalam but Hindi, Bengali or Tamil. Emigration of workers from Kerala, demographic contraction of the supply of young workers brought about by the rapid demographic transition in the state, the higher wages charged by Kerala workers, the ability of Kerala workers to sustain themselves with remittances from relatives even without work for long periods, the reluctance on the part of Kerala workers to do hard physical work—all these have engendered the era of replacement migration in Kerala. For the in-migrant workers from other states, Kerala is, for all practical purpose, their promised land, the "Gulf". The way Kerala workers have penetrated into every economic sector in the Gulf, the replacement workers from other states have started penetrating into most economic sectors in Kerala. Are they to blame? Or is it an unwelcome development in our federal economy?

It is true that remittances from the Gulf kept up economic activity in the construction and the service sectors in Kerala. Normally, the additional jobs thus created should have gone to the Kerala workers. But given the large differences existing between the current wage rates in Kerala and the rest of the states in India, and the unwillingness of Kerala workers to do certain types of hard physical work, workers from other states have grabbed the unfilled employment opportunities in Kerala. Thus, replacement migrants have taken the places which Kerala workers could have filled.

The so-called spin-off effects benefited outside workers more than Kerala workers. Thus, emigration, which initially helped reduce unemployment in Kerala, has in fact, become a significant factor for the higher unemployment situation in the state at present.

References

Zachariah, K.C. and S. Irudaya Rajan (2001a). "Gender Dimensions of Migration in Kerala: Macro and Micro Evidence", *Asia Pacific Population Journal* 16(3): 47-70.

———. (2001b). "Migration Mosaic in Kerala. Trends and Determinants", *Demography India* 30(1): 137-165.

Zachariah, K.C., B.A. Prakash and S. Irudaya Rajan (2002). "Gulf Migration Study: Employment Wages and Working Conditions of Kerala Emigrants in United Arab Emirates", *Working Paper* No.326. Thiruvananthapuram: Centre for Development Studies. *www.cds.edu*

———. (2003). "The Impact of Immigration Policy on Indian Contract Migrants: The Case of the United Arab Emirates", *International Migration* 41(4): 161-172.

———. (2004). "Indian Workers in UAE: Employment, Wages and Working Conditions", *Economic and Political Weekly* XXXIX(22): 2227-34. May 29.

Zachariah, K.C., E.T. Mathew and S. Irudaya Rajan (2001a). "Impact of Migration on Kerala's Economy and Society", *International Migration* 39(1): 63-88. (first published as a *CDS Working Paper* No. 297. *www.cds.edu*)

———. (2001b). "Social, Economic and Demographic Consequences of Migration on Kerala", *International Migration* 39(2): 43-71. 88 (first published as a *CDS Working Paper* No. 303. *www.cds.edu*)

———. (2003). *Dynamics of Migration in Kerala. Dimensions, Determinants and Consequences*. Hyderabad: Orient Longman Pvt. Limited.

Zachariah, K.C., K.P. Kannan and S. Irudaya Rajan (2002). "Kerala's Gulf Connection: CDS Studies on International Labour Migration from Kerala State in India", *Monograph* Series. Thiruvananthapuram: Centre for Development Studies.

Zachariah, K.C., P.R. Gopinathan Nair and S. Irudaya Rajan (2001). "Return Emigrants in Kerala: Rehabilitation Problems and Development Potential", *Working Paper* No.319. Thiruvananthapuram: Centre for Development Studies. *www.cds.edu*

Table 3.1

Migration Trend, Kerala, 1982-2003

Year	*Emigrants*	*Return Emigrants*	*Non-Resident Keralites*
1982	230740	39408	270148
1983	274804	51853	326657
1984	273342	67754	341096
1985	313980	85039	399019
1986	329083	99557	428640
1987	364909	120298	485207
1988	405513	151410	556923
1989	449611	163855	613466
1990	510214	197732	707946
1991	566668	219856	786524
1992	637103	253733	890836
1993	754544	287610	1042154
1994	819025	331166	1150191
1995	957388	379562	1336950
1996	1062376	433489	1495865
1997	1178589	486033	1664622
1998	1318489	553096	1871585
1999	1412649	620851	2033500
2000	1501917	684457	2186374
2001	1600465	739766	2340231
2002	1717695	794385	2512080
2003	1844023	893942	2737965

Table 3.2

Emigrants (EMI), Emigrants per 100 Households and Percentage Distribution by Districts, 2004

Districts	Emigrants		EMI Per 100 HHs		Percentage to Total	
	2004	1999	2004	1999	2004	1999
Thiruvananthapuram	168046	130705	21.5	19.9	9.1	9.6
Kollam	148457	102977	24.4	18.4	8.1	7.6
Pathanamthitta	133720	97505	44.3	33.1	7.3	7.2
Alappuzha	75036	62870	15.2	13.2	4.1	4.6
Kottayam	106569	35494	24.0	9.1	5.8	2.6
Idukki	7880	7390	2.9	2.9	0.4	0.5
Ernakulam	121237	103750	16.9	17.0	6.6	7.6
Thrissur	178867	161102	27.2	25.6	9.7	11.8
Palakkad	177876	116026	32.6	21.8	9.7	8.5
Malappuram	271787	296710	45.0	49.2	14.8	21.8
Kozhikode	167436	116026	28.6	22.0	9.1	8.5
Wayanand	7704	4552	4.4	2.9	0.4	0.3
Kannur	202414	88065	43.2	19.0	11.0	6.5
Kasaragod	71449	38747	30.6	19.1	3.9	2.8
KERALA	1838478	1361955	26.7	21.4	100.0	100.0

Table 3.3

Return Emigrants (REM), Return Emigrants per 100 Households and Percentage Distribution by Districts, 2004

Districts	Return Emigrants		REM Per 100 HHs		Percentage to Total	
	2004	1999	2004	1999	2004	1999
Thiruvananthapuram	103059	118878	13.2	18.1	11.5	16.1
Kollam	69314	74106	11.4	13.2	7.8	10.0
Pathanamthitta	83502	54537	27.7	18.5	9.3	7.4
Alappuzha	43109	34572	8.7	7.2	4.8	4.7
Kottayam	28368	18164	6.4	4.6	3.2	2.5
Idukki	3766	5017	1.4	2.0	0.4	0.7
Ernakulam	74435	45028	10.4	7.4	8.3	6.1
Thrissur	86029	116788	13.1	18.6	9.6	15.8
Palakkad	55008	39238	10.1	7.4	6.2	5.3
Malappuram	141537	123750	23.5	20.5	15.8	16.7
Kozhikode	109101	60910	18.6	11.5	12.2	8.2
Wayanand	3852	3327	2.2	2.1	0.4	0.5
Kannur	45394	28263	9.7	6.1	5.1	3.8
Kasaragod	47468	16667	20.3	8.2	5.3	2.3
KERALA	893942	739245	13.0	11.6	100	100

Table 3.4

Distribution of Non-Resident Keralites (NRK) by Districts, 2004

Districts	*Non-Resident Keralites (NRK)*			*NRK per 100 HHs*		*Percentage to Total*	
	2004	*1999*	*Percentage Increase*	*2004*	*1999*	*2004*	*1999*
Thiruvananthapuram	271105	249583	8.6	34.6	38.0	9.9	11.9
Kollam	217771	177083	23.0	35.8	31.6	8.0	8.4
Pathanamthitta	217222	152042	42.9	72.0	51.6	7.9	7.2
Alappuzha	118145	97442	21.2	24.0	20.4	4.3	4.6
Kottayam	134937	53658	151.5	30.4	13.7	4.9	2.6
Idukki	11646	12407	-6.1	4.3	4.9	0.4	0.6
Ernakulam	195672	148778	31.5	27.4	24.4	7.2	7.1
Thrissur	264896	277890	-4.7	40.3	44.2	9.7	13.2
Palakkad	232884	155300	50.0	42.6	29.2	8.5	7.4
Malappuram	413324	420460	-1.7	68.5	69.7	15.1	20.0
Kozhikode	276537	176936	56.3	47.3	33.5	10.1	8.4
Wayanand	11556	7879	46.7	6.6	5.0	0.4	0.4
Kannur	247808	116328	113.0	52.9	25.1	9.1	5.5
Kasaragod	118917	55414	114.6	50.9	27.3	4.4	2.6
KERALA	2732420	2101200	30.0	39.7	33.0	100	100

Table 3.5

Emigrants, Return Emigrants and Non-Resident Keralites per 100 Households, by Community

Community	*EMI*	*REM*	*NRK*
SC/ST	3.1	2.5	5.6
Nairs	20.7	8.3	29.0
Ezhavas	16.2	9.6	25.8
Brahmins	36.1	5.4	41.5
Other Hindus	12.4	7.1	19.5
Roman Catholics	24.0	9.7	33.7
Latin Catholics	22.4	19.2	41.6
Jacobite/Orthodox	36.0	15.0	51.6
Mar Thoma	69.5	29.6	99.0
CSI	22.6	15.1	37.7
Muslims	54.7	26.5	81.3
KERALA	26.8	13.1	39.0

Table 3.6

Remittances, NSDP, Remittances as Per cent of NSDP, Per Capita Income, and Modified Per Capita Income, by Districts, 2004

Districts	(1)	(2)	(3)	(4)	(5)	(6)
Thiruvananthapuram	1927	9153	21.1	27686	33514	5828
Kollam	1813	6737	26.9	25646	32548	6902
Pathanamthitta	954	3341	28.6	26901	34582	7681
Alappuzha	1339	5638	23.8	26459	32746	6287
Kottayam	580	5676	10.2	28622	31545	2923
Idukki	39	3617	1.1	31697	32041	344
Ernakulam	1515	10428	14.5	32918	37702	4784
Thrissur	3234	8459	38.2	27871	38525	10654
Palakkad	1148	5920	19.4	22132	26425	4293
Malappuram	2892	6316	45.8	16766	24443	7677
Kozhikode	1357	7639	17.8	25964	30576	4612
Wayanand	68	1994	3.4	24432	25260	828
Kannur	976	5973	16.3	24369	28350	3981
Kasaragod	623	2894	21.5	23414	28457	5043
KERALA	18465	83783	22.0	25764	31442	5678

Note: (1) Total State Remittances of 18,465 crore is distributed among the districts on the basis of the per cent distribution of total household remittances by districts given later in this Chapter.

(2) District-wise Net Domestic Product (NDDP), *Planning Board Economic Review, 2003, Table 3.7.*

(3) Remittances as per cent NDDP = (1)/(2).

(4) District-wise income per capita, *Planning Board Economic Review, 2003, Table 3.8.*

(5) Adjusted NDDP: Estimated using data from (1), (2) and (4): 5=(1+2)*(4/2)

(6) Increase in NDDP due to remittances: (6)=(5)-(4)

Table 3.7

Macroeconomic Impact of Remittances, 1999-2003

(In crores)

Indicators	*1999*	*2000*	*2001*	*2002*	*2003*
Remittances	13652	14438	15732	17362	18465
Net state domestic product (NSDP)	53552	62557	63715	73049	83783
Per capita income (in rupees)	16062	18262	19951	22668	25764
Modified NSDP	67204	76995	79447	90411	102248
Revenue receipt of government	7198	7942	8731	9056	10634
Transfer from Central government	1991	2218	2202	2590	2653
Government expenditure	5855	8263	8679	8528	10029
Value added in manufacturing	558175	612334	603075	682150	689145
State debt	15700	20178	23919	26950	31060
Receipt from cashew export	1317	1878	1153	965	1217
Receipt from marine product export	817	1142	1046	951	995
Modified per capita income (Rs.)	20157	22477	24877	28056	31442
Remittances as per cent of NSDP (%)	25.49	23.08	24.69	23.77	22.04
Remittances as ratio of revenue receipt	1.9	1.82	1.8	1.92	1.74
Remittances as ratio of transfer from central government	6.86	6.51	7.14	6.7	6.96
Remittances as ratio of govt. expenditure	2.33	1.75	1.81	2.04	1.84
Remittances as ratio of state debt	0.87	0.72	0.66	0.64	0.59
Remittances as ratio of receipts from cashew	10.37	7.69	13.64	17.99	15.17
Remittances as ratio of receipts from marine products	16.71	12.64	15.04	18.26	18.56

Note: Except remittances, all other data are compiled from *Economic Review* published by the State Planning Board, Thiruvananthapuram.

Table 3.8

Household Remittances by Districts (in Millions of Rs.)

Districts	*2004*	*1999*	*Actual Increase (1999-2004)*	*Percentage Increase (1999-2004)*	*Per cent of HHs which received Remittances 2004*
Thiruvananthapuram	8312	3750	4562	121.6	18.1
Kollam	7821	3152	4669	148.1	15.0
Pathanamthitta	4115	2705	1410	52.1	23.3
Alappuzha	5777	2558	3219	125.8	15.5
Kottayam	2501	1374	1127	82.0	7.6
Idukki	169	129	40	31.1	1.5
Ernakulam	6537	4852	1685	34.7	13.2
Thrissur	13949	5685	8264	145.4	16.5
Palakkad	4953	3526	1427	40.5	16.1
Malappuram	12476	7661	4815	62.9	32.0
Kozhikode	5854	2495	3359	134.6	20.7
Wayanand	292	78	214	273.9	3.6
Kannur	4209	2118	2091	98.7	19.7
Kasaragod	2687	632	2057	324.4	22.9
KERALA	79654	40715	38939	95.6	17.1

4

Migration the Divider

UDAYA S. MISHRA and PRIYAJIT SAMAIYAR

Introduction

International labour movement and its impact on economic development and international trade are well known and discussed in economic literature. Human mobility also induces movement of all means of production. The historical movement of population in the course of the development process is well documented and has a prominent role in many development strategies. For Brazil, internal migration leading to urban population growth has been a positive factor in distribution of national product in the post-war period (Yap, 1976). Economic studies of labour migration in less developed countries (LDCs) focus on the potential contributions that migration could make in absolute terms to the size of the relevant migration unit (the individual, the family or the household). Stark (1991) has hypothesised that the main reason behind rural-to-urban migration is to improve an individual's or a household's comparative income position with respect to that of other individuals or households. It has also been hypothesised that migration redistributes through remittances sent back home by migrants and also contributing towards poverty alleviation. Migration is always regarded as a positive phenomenon for development by various studies focusing on its macro bearing.

Discussion regarding impact of migration on overall economic inequality is marginal. Such inequality primarily arises due to the remittances sent by the migrants. Remittances are defined as money and goods that are received by native households back home from individuals working away from their origin communities.[1] They are usually termed as household transfers motivated by altruism, either as an implicit intra-family contractual arrangement or as an implicit family loan. Over time, it is observed that remittances serve as a significant source of external financing for developing

1. For a taxonomy, see Wahba (1991).

countries, and by the year 2004, they have emerged as the second largest source of net financial flow to these countries following foreign direct investment. They are not only greater than official development assistance but have also proved to be one of the least volatile source of foreign exchange earnings since the 1990s (Maimbo and Ratha, 2005). Remittances have a direct implication on poverty because it increases and broadens the opportunities for earning by the recipient. Evidences from household survey show that remittances increase savings and asset accumulation (liquid and non liquid assets), help to smooth income and consumption (Kannan and Hari, 2002) and act as an insurance mechanism by responding positively to adverse shocks[2] (Lucas and Stark, 1985, Yang and Jung, 2005). The other promising face of remittances relates to the increase of household expenditures in areas considered vital for development, particularly education, health and entrepreneurship (World Bank, 2006). They help to ease working capital constraints on farms and small scale enterprises. Stark (1991) initiating the "New Economics of Labour Migration" hypothesised that migrants play the role of financial intermediaries, enabling rural household to overcome credit and risk constraints on their ability to achieve the transition from familial to commercial production. Orozco (2002) also pointed out that remittances can increase social capital and ability to participate in social groups and activities, savings clubs, money rounds or reciprocal labour pools. At the community level, they help to improve local physical infrastructure and generate local employment opportunities.

On account of adversities due to remittances, one of the most often mentioned is an increased dependence on remittances among recipients, making them more vulnerable to migration cycles. It is also emphasised that a disproportionate share of remittances result in non-productive investment and short-term consumption gains, and households tend to adopt patterns of conspicuous consumption.[3] Remittances might also create distortions in local factor markets, especially land and labour (Maimbo and Ratha, 2005: Chapter 3).

The most recent studies have focused on three poverty indicators: the headcount index to measure the percentage of the population living beneath the poverty line at the time of the survey, the poverty gap index to measure

---

2. Yang and Jung (2005) found that in the Philippines, in households with overseas migrants, exogenous changes in income lead to changes in remittances of the opposite sign, consistent with an insurance motivation for remittances. In such households, roughly 60 per cent of exogenous decrease in income are replaced by remittances inflows from overseas.

3. This is often a major concern at the national level because the potential multiplier effect of remittances may decrease and the import demand and inflation may simultaneously increase if remittances earnings are spent primarily on imported consumer goods.

the "depth of poverty" and the square poverty index which indicates the severity of poverty. To give an example, Adams (2004) compared the poverty headcount, poverty gap and squared poverty gap of Guatemalan households that received remittances from international and/or internal migrants, with those of households that did not receive remittance income. He found that both internal and international remittances reduced poverty. Remittances had a quantitatively larger effect on the severity of poverty (the poverty gap) than on the poverty rate (headcount). In other words, they served positively for the poorest of the poor. Maimbo *et al.* (2005) using the basic growth-poverty[4] model suggested by Ravallion (1997), estimate the variations in poverty as a function of mean per capita income, income distribution and level of official and unofficial remittances for a large set of countries. They find that a 10 per cent increase in total remittances will lead to a 0.9 per cent decline in the level of poverty. While first using the official remittance data in their model, they do not find a statistical impact of remittances on the level and depth of poverty. Hence, the suggestion made thereof lies in estimating the size of unofficial remittance flows to correctly understand the impact of international remittances.

The literature surveyed above does highlight the role of remittance in shaping poverty. In particular, the long-term impacts of remittances on poverty are highly sensitive to the expenditure pattern of families and to the local economic conditions of the recipient area.

Given the positives of remittances in shaping the economy at macro level, the inequality concerns at micro level remains overshadowed. But remittances as earning to the state do induce an imbalance in the purchasing power at individual level as well.

However, the literature offers conflicting results on the impact of remittances on inequality. Lipton (1980) has argued that migrant's absence from rural areas generates negative externalities of various types and these externalities are responsible for a worsening distribution. In his view, migrant's remittances do not sufficiently compensate for this adverse impact because, in net terms, the remittances are either small or benefit

4. The growth-poverty model can be written as:

$$\text{Log } P_{it} = \alpha i + \beta_1 \log(\mu_{it}) + \beta_2 \log(g_{it}) + \beta_3 \log(x_{it}) + \varepsilon$$

Where P is the measure of poverty in country *i* at time *t*, β_1 is the "growth elasticity of poverty" with respect to mean per capita income given by μ, β_2 is the elasticity of poverty with respect to income distribution given by *g*. β_3 is the elasticity of poverty with respect to variable x (such as official international remittances) and ε is an error term that includes errors in the poverty measure.

One of the main assumptions of this model are that the level of income inequality affects poverty reduction, and that countries receiving more international remittances will have less poverty.

disproportionately to those better off. Conversely, Stark and Yitzhaki (1982) find that migration can enhance equality by diversifying risks and alleviating credit constraints. They also point out that an increase in income inequalities does not necessarily lead to a social welfare loss and can be consistent with a situation that is preferred under both general social welfare and Pareto criteria.

Stark *et al.* (1986) provide a helpful theoretical framework linking migration, poverty and inequality that reconcile the opposite views. Following Stark and Bloom (1985), they conceive migration as a diffusion process. The impact of migrant remittances on the rural income distribution by size depends on a village's migration history and on the degree to which migration opportunities are diffused across village household. At the initial stage of the migration process, few households have established contacts at the migration destination. Information being costly and scarce, migration constitutes a high-risk, high return "investment" that is more likely to be assumed by the households from the upper end of the village income distribution. Thus, they found that remittances from international migrants generate inequality in the income distribution in a Mexican village that recently had begun to send migrants to the United States, but an equalising effect on another village that had a long history of participating in international migration

Three specific case studies on rural Mexico, Pakistan and Egypt clearly illustrate the relevance of the diffusion hypothesis. Indeed, the findings about the impact of remittances on inequality vary accordingly to the stage of the studied village in the migration process—initial, medium or final—and the type of migration involved—internal or external migration. Thus, the impact of remittances on inequality is neither automatic nor inevitable. In a study on rural Egypt, Adams (1989) found that the remittances earnings from migrants abroad had a negative impact on income distribution, because households in the top income quintile benefited the most from remittances. Adams and Richard's (1996) findings in a study on rural Pakistan also suggest that while internal remittances have an equalising impact on rural income distribution, external remittances have just the opposite effect. Finally, Taylor *et al.* (2005) using data from the Mexico National Rural Household Survey, together with inequality and poverty decomposition techniques obtained results consistent with the previous case studies: while remittances from migrants abroad slightly increase rural income inequalities, remittances from internal migrants are income equalisers in areas where migration is a recent phenomenon. However, they also found that both types of remittances have an equalising effect on incomes in high-migration areas.

Finally, the most recent studies based on calculations of Gini coefficient did not find any increase in inequality, even after controlling for the counterfactual income loss from migration. For instance, Adams (2005a) found that in Ghana, the inclusion of international remittances in households expenditures led only to a slight increase in income inequality, but that the Gini coefficient remained relatively stable, between 0.38 and 0.40. De and Ratha (2005) found that in Sri Lanka, the Gini coefficient falls from 0.46 to 0.40 as a result of remittances. Once again, it is necessary to be careful when comparing the empirical evidence from various studies. For instance, the Gini coefficient does not adequately capture income mobility and it remains unchanged if one person moves up and another moves down the income ladder.

The conclusions emerging from these papers are the following: despite their positive effect on inequality at the initial stage of the community migration's history, international migrant remittances reduce poverty by a greater amount than internal remittances. As economies become more integrated with migrant labour markets, the ameliorative effect of remittances on poverty increases.

The Kerala Case

In India, the state of Kerala is well known for its achievement in the spheres of social development with an unmatched level of economic development. This has always made the state distinct from other Indian states and its experience has been prescribed by many scholars and ideologues as a "model of development" for other developing countries. The point of distinction in Kerala's experience and the "Kerala model" of development exemplify the capability of a society with relatively low income and in conditions of low-production growth to achieve high quality of living levels. For instance, life expectancy at birth in Kerala for the period 1992-1996 was 73 years which was the highest at the national level, and the state has the lowest birth and death rates in India. Kerala has also achieved the highest literacy rate in the country, a rate of 90.92 per cent as against the all India rate of 65.38 per cent (2001 census). Another feature of Kerala's development performance is the very minimal disparities between achievements in the urban and rural regions of Kerala. The regional imbalance too across regions of the state is less sharp when compared with other parts of the country. The percentage of poor in rural areas declined from 50 per cent in 1973-74 to 12.7 per cent in 1999-2000 (Radhakrishna, 2005). Kerala's record of overcoming poverty even with moderate economic growth has been attributed to its effective implementation of land reforms, comprehensive social and food security coverage, and public action of democratically elected state governments, decentralised system of governance and a highly conscious civil society. However, the poor growth performance of commodity producing sectors like agriculture and industry has led to the slowdown of the growth rate of employment and income generation within the state. It has also reduced the rate of growth in government revenue and thereby, investment in economic sectors and expenditure on welfare programmes. The employment scenario in the formal sector is quite bleak and Kerala continues to have the highest rate of unemployment at 20.77 per cent. The persistence of the crisis has raised concerns about the sustainability of the achievements already made in health, education and other human development spheres, and the further efforts to improve the quality of life and capability of the people.

Migration flows from Kerala is always viewed within this framework of high unemployment and high social achievements. These particular socio-economic characteristics must be taken into account when assessing the impact of remittances on Keralite's living standard and consumption pattern, since these latter variables are highly sensitive to the level of education, the health condition and the political consciousness of the recipients.

Remittances from migrants in case of Kerala by no means remain negligible (see Figure 4.1). Zachariah and Rajan (2006), estimating the remittances to Kerala under two headings, total remittances and household remittances, obtained a figure of Rs. 18.5 thousand crore[5] as remittances for 2003 and this number itself is likely to be an underestimate. The per capita domestic income for Kerala was about Rs. 25,764 and the modified per capita income, including remittances would have been Rs. 31,442. The effect of remittances on Kerala's per capita annual income in 2003 recorded an increase of Rs. 5678.

Figure 4.1

Remittances Flow to Kerala in Rs. Crore

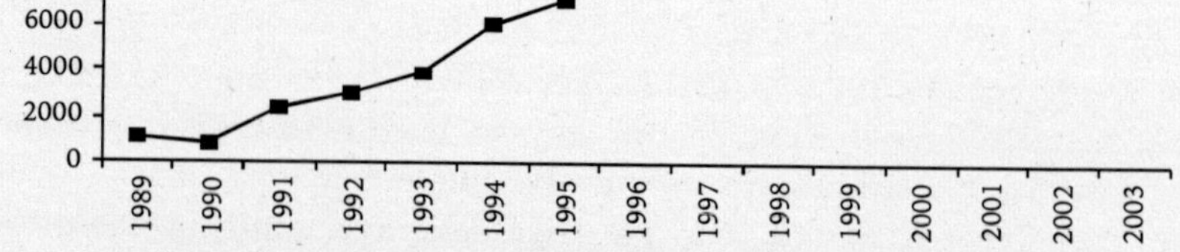

Source: Zachariah and Rajan (2006) based on SMS 2003 data and banking data.

5. In 2003, 1$=Rs.48; a crore=10 million.

The remittances represented 22 per cent of the net state domestic product (NSDP). The importance of remittances to Kerala economy is evidenced by comparisons with other relevant economic indicators. They were reported to be 1.74 times the revenue receipts of the state, 7 times the transfers to the state from the Central government and were sufficient to wipe out 60 per cent of the state's debt in 2003. Compared to the two most important export products, the cashew kernels and the marine products, remittances were 15 times of the export earnings from cashew and 18 times those from marine products. So the increasing levels of remittance justify the debate on migration and inequality at household level.

In the light of above argument, the objective of the chapter is to examine the economic inequality at the micro level among in-migrant, immigrant and non-migrant households in Kerala.

Data and Methods

The following empirical analysis is based on migration survey conducted in the state of Kerala in 2003 (SMS 2003 by Zachariah and Irudaya Rajan, 2003). SMS 2003 collected migration related information only on Kerala migrants, that is, those emigrants and out migrants who have their families living in Kerala and are included in the registers of local bodies in Kerala. Information about the migrants were collected from the families in Kerala. This survey was specifically designed to examine migration and remittances issues. Non-Keralite migrants and Keralites who migrated out long ago and are living abroad with all their family members in areas such as Mumbai, Delhi and the United States of America were not included.

The following four types of migrants are identified:

1. Return Migrants (REM), that is, members of the household who, in the past, had emigrated out of India, but had returned to Kerala and were now members of the household.
2. Emigrants (EMI), that is, persons who had moved out of Kerala after 1980 and were living outside India at the time of the survey.
3. Return out-migrants (ROM), that is, members of a household who had moved out of Kerala after 1980 and were living outside India at the time of the survey.
4. Out-migrants (OMI), that is, persons who had moved out of Kerala after 1980 and were living outside Kerala but within India.

Based on the above definition of migrants, households have been classified in five different categories which are:

1. Households having either of the four type of migrants categorised as 'Migrant households'.
2. Households not having either of these migrants as 'Non-migrant households'.
3. Households having at least one EMI or REM as 'Emigrant households'.
4. Households having at least one OMI or ROM as 'Immigrant households'.
5. Households having either both EMI & OMI, or REM & ROM, or EMI & ROM, or REM & OMI as 'Both Migrant households'.

Apart from categorising households based on migration criterion, they were also classified according to economic status defined in terms of an 'economic index'. Such an index comprised of the household assets, electricity availability, type of house and type of fuel used for cooking by the household. Household assets and availability of electricity were dichotomous variables reported as 'Yes' or 'No'. 'Type of fuel used' and 'type of house' were made dichotomous clubbing households using LPG as good and households not using LPG as poor. Similarly, luxury and very good houses are clubbed as good households and other households as poor. Complementary weighing scheme for all the variables were adopted in combining them into a single value index i.e., maximum weight is assigned to the variable less commonly possessed and minimum weight to the variable frequently possessed to get a score for each household. Further, five quintile groups are made by dividing the maximum and minimum value of the index into equal parts to comment on the inequality among different types of households within and among the quintiles.

Results

Before presenting the primary data analysis, we present some of the inequality observed in type of school attended, type of college attended, type of medical facilities availed, type of hospital preferred, type of private hospital preferred and in possession of consumer durables among Non-Resident Keralites (NRK) and non-NRK borrowed from the SMS report. This is shown with the help of bar graph in which the bar represents the distance of NRKs and non-NRKs from the prevailing average level in the surveyed households as a whole. Such a depiction provides the degree of advantage/disadvantage enjoyed by the NRK/non-NRK households in relation to any specific indicator.

In case of all the variables, there is clear inequality among Keralites and non-resident Keralites (Figure 4.2). Government services utilisation, which is cheaper than private in terms of school, college and medical facilities among NRK is well below the prevailing level of use in general. Government/public services are less preferred by NRKs which is indicative of the disproportionate purchasing power they have as most of the private services are to be bought with a price. Secondly, this purchasing power for certain services by a segment of households is giving way to the sustained presence of private players in the market and threatening the public presence in the long run. Possession of consumer durables too is reported to be high among NRK households, clearly indicating towards their better standard of living when compared with non NRK households.

The economic index computed to comprehend the relative economic status of households is analysed here across different type of households. The type of households defined according to the migration criterion is used to understand the distribution of economic index values within and between households of different types (Table 4.1).

Table 4.1

Mean and Median Value of Economic Index for Different Types of Households

Type of Household	*Mean*	*Median*
Non-migrant	0.165	0.070
Migrant	0.288	0.246
Emigrant	0.292	0.259
In-migrant	0.253	0.222
Both migrants	0.391	0.409
Total	0.214	0.141

Source: Calculated from unit level data of SMS, 2003.

Table 4.1 reports the mean and median index values for the households having different types of migrants along with households without migrants. Non-migrant households have the least mean and median score for the index and the households with in-migrant as well as emigrant household reported as both migrant households here, have the highest mean and median index value. The distance of these index value in contrast with the prevailing average index value of the surveyed households is presented in Figure 4.3 which reiterates the kind of disparity observed in the earlier analysis.

Figure 4.2

Relative Disparities among NRKs and Non-NRKs in Terms of Distance from the Level of Total Population

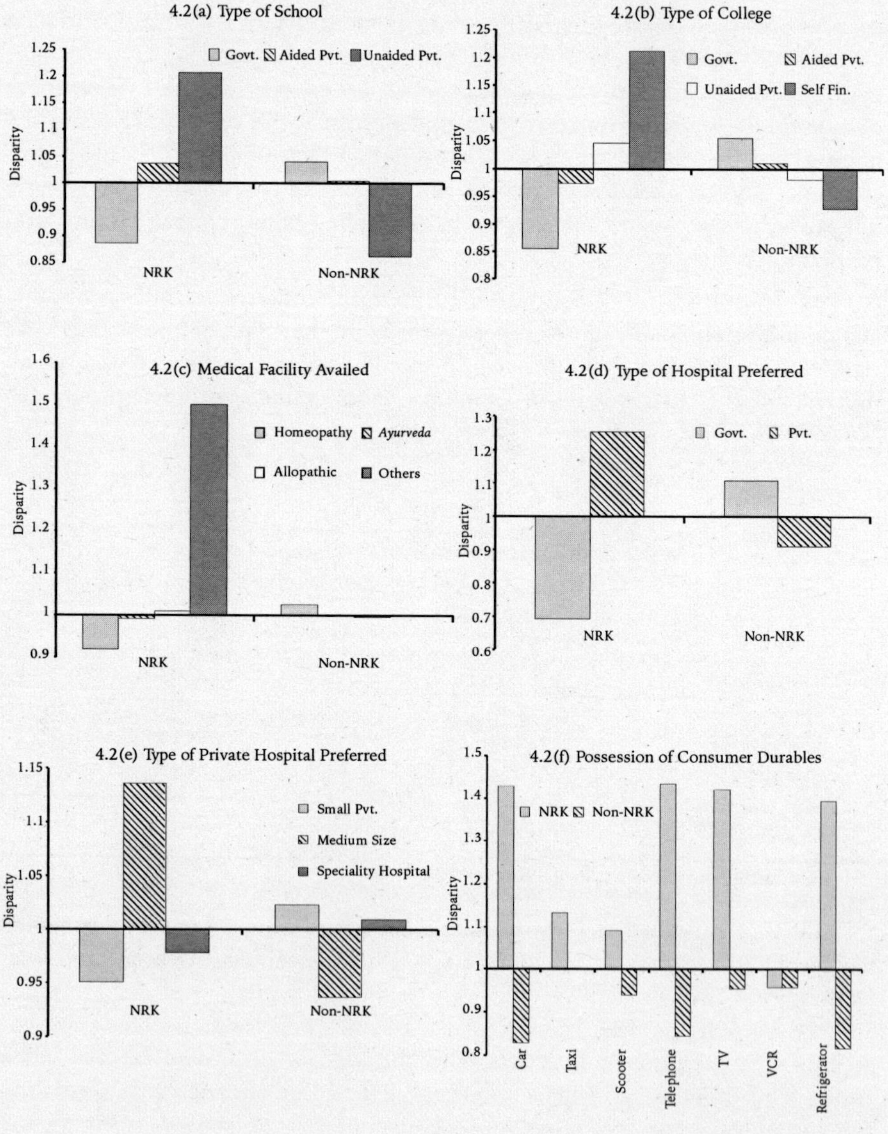

Figure 4.3

Overall Economic Index Value for Different Migrant Groups

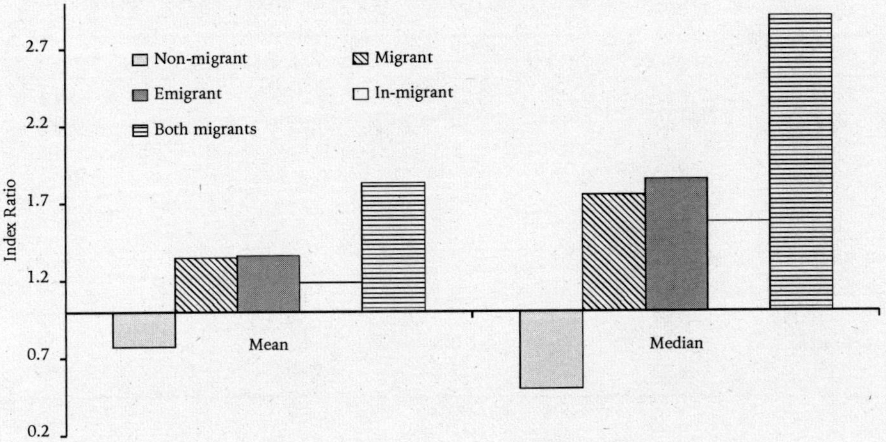

Source: Drawn from Table 4.1.

The economic index value is further seen in disaggregation across its quintiles. Dividing the index range into five equal ranges, the variation in the index value is examined across different type of households. The purpose of such an exercise is primarily to locate the inequality beyond, stating that there is inequality between different type of households according to migration status. Given the fact that this economic index value presents a skewed distribution across households, the inequality across quintiles is viewed in terms of both mean and median values of the index among all types of households (Table 4.2). The economic index value is aggregated (both in terms of mean as well as median) for each of the quintile ranges and such an aggregated value is compared with a similar aggregated parameter across households of different types within the quintile ranges. As can be seen from Table 4.2, based on the mean aggregate measure, there is not much of difference across household types (defined according to migration status) within quintile groups when compared against the overall aggregate index value for all households. If one conceives inequality as the maximum difference between these aggregate values across household types, then the difference is visibly the most in the lowest quintile group of the economic index (Table 4.2). A similar description of inequality based on the median aggregate measure demonstrates inequality in a relatively better manner across all quintile groups of economic status. These inequalities assessed against the prevailing aggregate of the quintile category (given in the last column of Table 4.2) are minimal for all quintile categories but for the lowest quintile.

Table 4.2

Quintile-wise Mean and Median Economic Status Index Values for Different Types of Household

Quintiles	*Non-migrant*	*Migrant*	*Emigrant*	*In-migrant*	*Both Migrants*	*Total Pop.*
First	0.063	0.083	0.087	0.075	0.097	0.068
Second	0.283	0.284	0.288	0.279	0.280	0.284
Third	0.467	0.470	0.471	0.469	0.466	0.469
Fourth	0.679	0.671	0.667	0.680	0.669	0.674
Fifth	0.872	0.870	0.869	0.867	0.876	0.871
Median						
First	0.038	0.070	0.070	0.070	0.100	0.038
Second	0.277	0.289	0.310	0.265	0.277	0.285
Third	0.448	0.451	0.457	0.441	0.431	0.449
Fourth	0.646	0.639	0.634	0.652	0.634	0.639
Fifth	0.857	0.857	0.857	0.857	0.857	0.857

Source: Calculated from unit levels data of SMS, 2003.

Such an exposition otherwise could perhaps be due to the migration potential being different between the rich and the poor. However, if one observes this inequality in terms of the differences observed between household types, then the aggregated median measure exposes inequality till the second quintile group and such inequality seem to reduce and becomes even in the richest quintile group. Figures 4.4(a) and 4.4(b) explain it pictorially.

Following this observation of inequality associated with migration identity, an attempt is made as to whether these inequalities translate themselves into inequalities in human capital dimension, namely health and education. In this regard, a description of expenditure incurred in health and education is made across household types according to migration status. Table 4.3 reports mean per capita expenditure on health and education for different households. Only non-migrant households report a level below the level estimated for the entire surveyed households. There is also a clear distinction in this expenditure between non-migrant households and households with any migration identity. Further, there is difference between different migrant category households with emigrant and both migrant category households spending disproportionately higher on health and education compared with other households (Figures 4.5(a) and (b)).

Figure 4.4(a)

Quintile-wise Inequality in Mean Index Value according to Different Migrant Status of Households

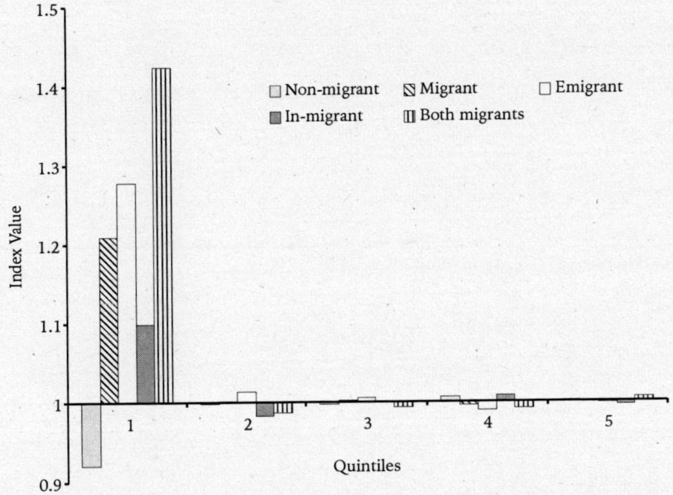

Figure 4.4(b)

Quintile-wise Inequality in Median Index Value according to Different Migrant Status of Households

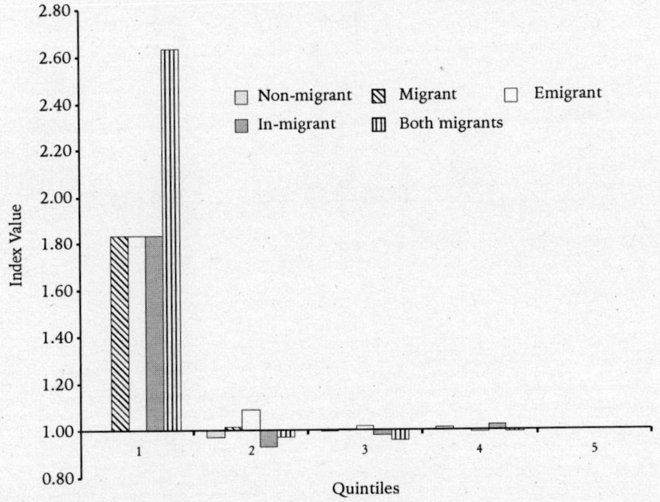

Source: Drawn from Table 4.2.

Table 4.3

Disparity in Expenditure Per Capita among Different Types of Households

Type of Household	*Health Expenditure*		*Education Expenditure*	
	Mean	*Median*	*Mean*	*Median*
Non-migrant	867	333	1717	650
Migrant	1634	417	3241	925
Emigrant	1643	400	2444	925
In-migrant	1245	375	4039	847
Both migrants	2959	600	5759	1000
Total	1171	357	2315	750

Source: Calculated from unit level data of SMS, 2003.

Figure 4.5(a)

Inequality in Average Per Capita Expenditure on Health according to Migrant Status of Households

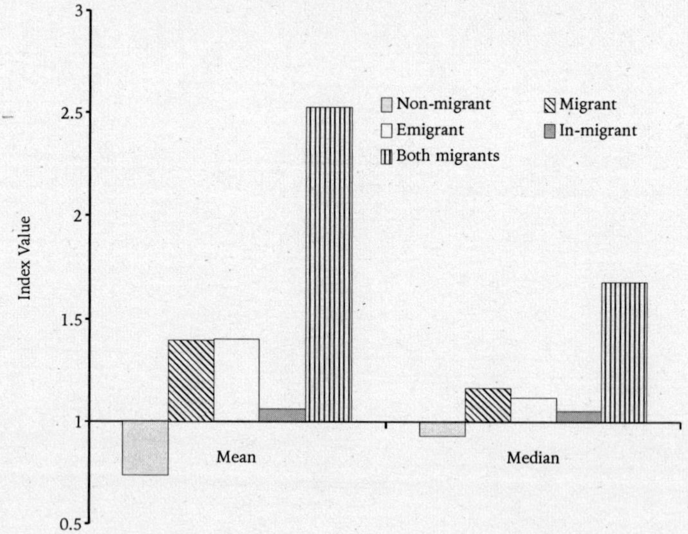

Figure 4.5(b)

Inequality in Per Capita Expenditure on Education according to Migrant Status of Households

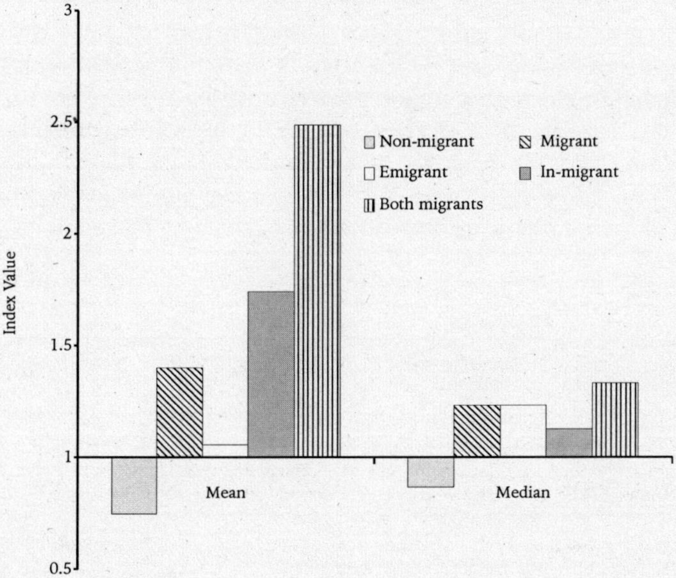

Source: Drawn from Table 4.2.

Conclusions

While significance of migration in shaping Kerala's economy is undeniable, the emerging migration market raises one concern where every individual does not have the same opportunity as the other to migrate as it used to be in the past. The international migration market in particular is getting selective day by day and future migration potential need to be assessed in terms of quality and not in quantity terms. These quality-quantity terms will be more relating to skilled/unskilled and the kind of wages and labour conditions offered. In that regard, a migration-dependent economy like that of Kerala has to prepare itself in tune with the emerging demand of the international migration market. Having said that, in a migration-driven economy, the macro-level advantages of remittance need to translate into micro-level welfare and migration does not give rise to an undesirable disparity at the micro-level. Given the selectivity of migration expected to grow, the migration divide at the households level is ought to grow further. Hence, micro-level adversities of migration in the state need to be recognised.

The present analysis clearly denotes migration as the single most powerful agent inducing inequity in the egalitarian state of Kerala. In that sense, changing potential and opportunities for migration need not be selective to intensify this inequality further. On the contrary, an effort towards universal migration opportunities may be the need of the hour. The state has an opportunity in hand with the best human capital to tune it to the demand for labour force and make migration a choice for every Keralite. If today migration is selective or the differentiating factor in determining economic status, tomorrow managing migration well may be worthwhile in restoring the unique character of a welfare state. On the whole, encouraging and universalising migration remains the key to deriving the most from migration and migratory character of the state. Thus, we may no longer find migrant as a class in the society and create a divide observed at present.

References

Adams, Jr. and H. Richard (2005). "International Remittances and the Household: Analysis and Review of Global Evidence", Paper Presented at the Plenary Session of the African Economic Research Consortium, May 29, Nairobi.

———. (1989). "Worker Remittances and Inequality in Rural Egypt", *Economic Development and Cultural Change* 38(1): 45-71.

———. (1996). "Remittances, Inequality and Asset Accumulation: The Case of Rural Pakistan", in O'Connar, David, Farsakh, Leila (ed.), *Development Strategy, Employment and Migration, Country Experiences*. Paris: OCDE. p.259.

———. (2004). "Remittances and Poverty in Guatemala", World Bank Policy Research *Working Paper* 3418, September, Washington D.C.: World Bank.

Adams, R.H. (1989). "Worker's Remittances and Inequality in Rural Egypt", *Economic Development and Cultural Change* 38(1): 47-71.

———. (2004). "Remittance and Poverty in Guatemala", *Policy Research Working Paper* no. 3418. Washington DC: World Bank.

———. (2005). "Remittances and Poverty in Ghana", *World Bank Policy Research Working Paper* 3838. Washington DC: World Bank.

De, P. and D. Ratha (2005). "Remittance Income and Household Welfare: Evidence from Srilanka Integrated Household Survey". Unpublished paper.

Harris, J. and M. Todaro (1970). "Migration, Unemployment and Development: A Two Sector Analysis", *American Economic Review* 60(1): 126-42.

Kannan, K. and K. Hari (2002). "Kerala's Gulf Connection: Emigration, Remittances and Their Macroeconomic Impact, 1972-2000", CDS *Working Paper* 328. Thiruvananthapuram: Centre for Development Studies.

Kapur, D. (2005). "Remittances: The New Development Mantra", in Munzele Maimbo, Samuel, Ratha, Dilip (ed.), *Remittances, Development Impacts and Future Prospects*. Washington D.C.: The World Bank. pp.331-360.

Lipton, M. (1980). "Migration from Rural Areas of Poor Countries: The Impact on Rural Productivity and Income Distribution", *World Development* 8: 1-24.

Lucas, Robert and Oded Stark (1985). "Motivations to Remit: Evidence from Botswana", *Journal of Political Economy* 93(5): 901-17.

Maimbo S.M. and D. Ratha (2005). *Remittances, Development Impacts and Future Prospects*. Washington DC: World Bank.

Maimbo, S.M. *et al.* (2005). *Migrant Labour Remittances in South Asia*. Washington DC: World Bank.

Orozco, Manuel (2002). "Worker Remittances in an International Scope", *Working Paper* Commissioned by the Multilateral Investment Fund of the Inter-American Development Bank, Inter-American Dialogue and the Tomás Rivera Policy Institute. *www.thedialogue.org/publications*

Radhakrishna, R. (2005). "Food and Nutrition Security of the Poor: Emerging Perspectives and Policy Issues", *Economic and Political Weekly*, April 30.

Radhakrishna, R. and Shovan Ray (ed.) (2005). *Handbook of Poverty in India, Perspectives, Policies and Programmes*. Oxford: Oxford University Press. p.185.

Ravallion, M. (1997). "Can High-inequality Developing Countries Escape Absolute Poverty", *Economic Letters* 56: 51-57.

Registrar General of India (2001). *Socio Cultural Tables*. Census of India.

Stark, Oded (1991). *The Migration of Labour*. Cambridge: Blackwell.

Stark, Oded and D. Bloom (1985). "The New Economics of Labour Migration", *American Economic Review* 25: 173-80.

Stark, Oded, Edward J. Taylor and Shlomo Yitzhaki (1986). "Remittances and Inequality", *The Economic Journal* 96: 722-40.

Stark, Oded and Edward, J. Taylor (1991). "Migration Incentives, Migration Types: The Role of Relative Deprivation", *The Economic Journal* 101(408): 1163-78.

Stark, Oded and S. Yitzhaki (1982). "Migration, Growth, Distribution and Welfare", *Economic Letters* 10(3-4): 243-249.

Taylor, J.E., J. Mora, R. Adams and A. Lopez-Fieldman (2005). "Remittances, Inequality and Poverty: Evidence from Rural Mexico", *ARE Working Papers* 05-003, Davis CA: University of California, Davis, Dept. of Agriculture and Resource Economics.

Wahba, S. (1991). "What Determines Worker's Remittances?", *Finance and Development* 18: 59-83.

World Bank (2006). *Economic Implications of Remittances and Migration*. Washington D.C.: World Bank. p.157.

Yang, D. Choi and Hwa-Jung (2005). "Are Remittances Insurance? Evidence from Rainfall Shocks in the Philippines", Ford School of Public Policy *Working Paper*, No. 05-004, July.

Yap, L. (1976). "Internal Migration and Economic Development in Brazil", *The Quartely Journal of Economics* 90(1): 119-127.

Zachariah, K.C. and S. Irudaya Rajan (2003). *South Asia Migration Survey (SMS)*. Thiruvananthapuram: Centre for Development Studies.

———. (2006). "Gulf Revisited", CDS *Working Paper*. Thiruvananthapuram: Centre for Development Studies. p.231.

———. (2006). *Gulf Revisited, Project Report*. CDS *Mimeograph*.

Zachariah, K.C., K.P. Kannan and S. Irudaya Rajan (ed.) (2002). "Kerala's Gulf Connection, CDS Studies on International Labour Migration from Kerala State in India". Thiruvananthapuram: Centre for Development Studies. p.230.

Zachariah, K.C., E.T. Mathew and S. Irudaya Rajan (2003). *Dynamics of Migration in Kerala Dimensions*. New Delhi: Orient Longman. p.476.

5

Contract Migration

MYTHRI PRASAD

This chapter maps the making of urban public infrastructure in Kerala by focusing on the road construction sites of the multinational Punj Lloyd Ltd. (PLL) in Trivandrum city. It explores an emergent economy of space that connects these urban sites, villages in north and north–eastern India and a fluid multinational corporate space. I present the process of recruitment and deployment of labour through a chain of sub-contractors. Towards this, I investigate sub-contracting as a spatial strategy employed by capital in the process of accumulation. Second, I try to trace the trajectories and patterns of relocations of workers by highlighting the element of journey involved in these relocations. I trace the role of ecology and interventions by the state in taming ecological processes in creating a footloose workforce in the context of near-feudal agrarian structure. I attempt an understanding of the processes of recruitment and relocation by looking at the ecology and economy of the villages the workers come from, their occupations and livelihoods and the reordering of lives which entail migration and their encounters with travel and the city.

Spatial Strategy of Accumulation

Massey (1995) observes that spatial form and strategy can be an active element of accumulation and calls these spatial structures of production. There are many different ways in which the fact of distance and geographical variation can be actively used in the process of production and accumulation of capital. She, therefore, interprets spatial distribution of employment as the outcome of the way in which production is organised. She further states that precisely because geographical form can influence the rate of accumulation, it may well be that one of the conditions for the development of particular kinds of division of labour within production in the first place is the existence of particular kinds of geographical differentiation.

Construction, where production has to be invariably at the site of demand, is different from other forms of industry where production and sale/use occur in different sites. At the risk of stating the obvious, a road has to be made where it is needed; it cannot be made somewhere and fixed or assembled elsewhere—at least at the level of technology currently available. Even if this were available, the assemblage or fixing, which is integral to the production of a road, would still have to be done at the site of demand. The fixity in terms of location is quickly undermined when we consider road making as a site of production and work.

Construction, seen merely as a service sector activity, tends to ignore its specificities as a produced commodity, a commodity produced with "men, materials and machines" as any other industrial product. This commonality with the classic factory is lost once we consider the spatiality of its production, particularly in the case of road making. While roads do not move, road making does! This lack of fixity as a site of production manifests itself not only in terms of this physical movement of the site but also in terms of the changing workforce, 'undefined' employer and the period of employment.

The distinctiveness of road works—that is, production has to necessarily take place at the site of demand/consumption—necessarily rules out the possibility of sub-contracting as it happens in commodity manufacturing with parts or components made in various countries and assembled in still another country or a similar division of labour within a country with uneven regional development. The spatial strategy of accumulation involved in sub-contracting appears in a different form in road making as fragmenting production (distributing it across centres where labour and materials are cheap and across different organisational segments as small scale units or household production) is not possible, capital reaps the benefit of geographical/spatial differential through other means—by drawing labour from various centres where it is cheap, even drawing them over long distances. With labour contractors and sub-contractors controlling their set of labour at the work site, it is like sub-contracting occurring right on the site of final commodity production. Viewed thus, a site of roadwork is a complex site of production as this section and the next would elaborate.

Allies in Accumulation

The entry of Punj Lloyd had rendered local capital vulnerable and resulted in their displacement from infrastructure building in Kerala. Rivalry and competition, however, constitutes only one aspect of the relationship of Punj Lloyd with local/regional capital. There is also a realm of close cooperation between the two. This section explores the strategic alliances PLL has formed with local or regional capital to procure materials and at times to carry out construction itself.

The stones to build the roads and flyovers as part of the Thiruvanathapuram City Roads Improvement Project come from a quarry situated in Mookkunnimala in the south-eastern region of Trivandrum district. The quarry is operated by Mr. K.K. Verghese who is a retired assistant manager of Catholic Syrian bank. His visiting card tells us that he is the state vice president of the All Kerala Crusher Owners' Association. He was an administrative council member of the Archdiocese of Trivandrum and has held posts in the Y's men's club and Lion's club. He runs the K.K. Rocks and Granite India Pvt. Ltd. and the Kottakkal Granite and Earthmovers. The latter owns the vehicles and the equipment like excavator, earthmovers and tipper lorries while the former company owns the crushing unit and the crushing area and operates the quarry.

A chat with Verghese during my visit to the quarry revealed his economic position and the nature of the contract with Punj Lloyd Ltd. An extract from my field journal dated 30.08.2005:

> He owns around 51 acres in the area. He says the area and equipments are worth 6 crore. He has leased the crushing unit from Punj Lloyd worth Rs. 6 crore, which the PLL might give him when they leave. His contract with PLL is to supply 9 inch soling (aggregates) for 30 months. The land was given to freedom fighters from Kuttanad by the government. Each of them had 3.5 acres. He bought the land from them. He says that he allows the local people to collect firewood etc., that is, "sharing but not everything". There was a massive crusher which produced aggregates of different sizes which was collected directly into tipper lorries. One could also see the excavators and JCBs (loader backhoes) and other machines transporting the gouged out stone pieces to the crusher. The place was full of the sound and dust of the crusher. Massive conveyor belts were all over the place. It was gigantic in size than anything I have seen ever. A little distance away, the hill stood showing the white of its rock.
>
> Apart from the trajectory of the transactions which had taken place on the land, i.e., from the government to freedom fighters in Kuttanad and finally to the owner of a quarry, what struck me was the everyday life of this businessman.
>
> Then he started talking about the daily chores he performs. He claimed that he gets only a profit of Re.1 per load of aggregates he delivers to Punj Lloyd. A while ago he had told me that he doles out Rs. 10000 a month on an average as bribe or as contribution to local organisations and religious groups. The output per day was around 150 loads on an average. Annually he pays Rs. 3 lakh as electricity tariff. That left me clueless about his turnover. He had to go to the *panchayat* office to get the water pipe removed which passes through the site. He had already paid bribe to the previous officer-in-charge, but he got transferred. Now probably he would have to pay the new guy again. He said that going the political line was useless, Mani (Minister of Revenue) and all he knew, but no point. "To get things done, we have to find our own means."

Sub-contracting the procurement of materials involved striking deals with local capital which was in a better position to negotiate local bureaucracy as quarrying involves obtaining environmental clearances and getting around bureaucracy and local population. Sub-contracting, seen in this context, is a strategy employed over space and influences the process of capital accumulation.

Punj Lloyd realised while doing the piling work for a flyover in Trivandrum as part of the project that the hydraulic rig it uses for piling cannot handle the hard rock characteristic of the sub-soil in many parts of Trivandrum, which begins to show up after 10 metres or so. It therefore, contracted out the piling work to a company called Raman Dayar & Sons (RDS). Excerpts from my field journal dated 30.07.2005:

> RDS does the work with a chain rig which is a heavy metal shaft propped up on three metal poles. It is operated by a worker by rotating a chain which results in the shaft hitting the ground and slowly pounding the surface beneath. When we were looking on, three workers were repairing the machine with a welder helping them.
>
> A chain rig is slower than a hydraulic one, but is more efficient in handling hard rock. As the chain rigs PLL possesses are engaged elsewhere in the country, it had to sub-contract the work.

Labour Farmers: The Recruitment Process

Sub-contracting of labour recruitment and employment presents an altogether different element of space in the production of roads where the fact of spatiality appears not as a passive surface on to which relations of production are mapped or as distance to be crossed, but as an active element and strategy in the production of roads. Structures of dominance and subordination between economic activities in different places mirror the way in which the relations of production are organised over space (Massey, 1995). Recruiting labour from multiple sources constitute a spatial strategy of capital to bring in new social groups in to the labour force, to manage and control labour process which helps to minimise the conflict between capital and labour. Viewed in this context, the mobility of labour, geographical differentiation and uneven development which triggers off these movements becomes more intelligible.

The construction boom as a result of the increased remittances due to Malayali migration to the Gulf in the 1970s resulted in large-scale in migration of Tamil workers to Kerala (Anand, 1986). 1990s witnessed in migration from north and north-eastern India into Kerala's construction industry as Tamil workers learned to negotiate the labour market better. More careful research, however, is required to map these changes in the source of labour for Kerala's construction industry. The present case, however, marks a qualitatively new phase where the movements are being orchestrated by global capital deploying uneven development and ethno-social differences as strategies of accumulation.

Labour migrations are often perceived through the 'push and pull' framework that emphasises the specific, local conditions in the places of origin and employment. Taking into account the spatial forms of production and employment might be helpful in circumventing the orthodoxy of 'push and pull' framework.

The workers are drawn from the villages in Bihar, Jharkhand, West Bengal, Orissa and Karnataka. The workers, particularly the 'unskilled' workers come for 52 days involving a work day of 12 hours. The fieldwork was carried out in village Banma of district Saharsa in Bihar and in Kaliachak in district Malda in West Bengal.

The workers from Malda are recruited through a chain of intermediaries. Contractors known as commissions are at the top of the hierarchy. A professor in a local college remembered a certain 'Chihir commission' who once had 30,000 workers under him. The commissions also run economic societies/saving pools which award the savings to the workers in advance on a lottery basis. Commissions recruit workers through *dafadars*. *Dafadars* move around in the countryside, talk to workers about the work, distribute advance which he gets from the commission, buy tickets depending on the number of workers he has mobilised and sometimes travel with the workers to the worksites. The commissions provide the finances. The next in this hierarchy are *meths* who negotiate with the commissions and *dafadars* on behalf of the workers on wages, on the amount of work if it is piece rate work and on working hours. At the work site, the *meth* has to work like an ordinary worker though he occasionally supervises them. *Dafadar,* if at all he stays back in the work site, will only engage in supervisory work.

The recruitment process in Malda, West Bengal has evolved over a longer period of time and is more nuanced and is entwined with caste and kinship systems. In Malda, commissions are invariably Muslims. *Dafadars* are usually Muslims, though occasionally, men from other communities become *dafadars* as well. *Meths* would belong to the same community as the workers do i.e., if the majority of the workers were *Adivasis*, then the *meth* also would be an *Adivasi*.

The workers of Punj Lloyd were mobilised through a commission named Sayed Ali whose *dafadars* recruited workers from the district Sahibganj in Jharkhand as well on the west of district Malda, on the banks of river Mahananda, a tributary of river Ganga.

In Banma (Bihar), the chain of intermediaries did not include *dafadar* as the negotiations were carried out between the *meth* and the contractor who is called *dhekkedar*. The *dhekkedar* for Punj Lloyd was A.K. Singh from district

Siwan[1] in Bihar who had been recruiting workers from the village for the past five years to road projects in Gujarat and parts of Bihar. As in Malda, caste and kinship ties play an active role in the recruitment process. The *musahars,* who are traditional agricultural labourers of the village, who had come to Trivandrum to work in the road construction undertaken by Punj Lloyd go together for work, often choosing their headman as *meth.* Interestingly, if one or two workers from other communities, say *yadavs* or *malekaars* accompany them, the *meth* continues to be the headman of *musaharas* who are below the *yadavs* and *malekars* in terms of caste hierarchy. This shows that caste and kinship play a crucial role in the recruitment process, though in a contingent manner.

Migration as Journey

The UN Multi-lingual Demographic Dictionary defines migration as a form of geographical mobility between one geographical unit and another, generally involving a change of residence from the place of origin to place of destination or place of arrival. But there is a general lack of unanimity in employing specific time and space criteria while defining migration and migrants.[2] As the workers stay only for a few months in these sites, the temporality of their relocation makes one wary of applying any criteria on to them. Journeys, rather than settlement, characterise the life of these workers. In this section, I attempt to trace the migration of workers to the sites of infrastructure building by focusing on the element of journey.

In Saharsa district, 1 or 1½ kg of grain, actually 2 *ser,* was the wage rate, for agricultural work. This was in the year 1978. Nobody went out in search of work those days. The workers were organised by the Communist Party of India. There was a one-day *hartal* demanding 4 kg of rice as wage. There was *lathi* charge against workers. The workers were in bondage to their masters—the *kisans*. But the demand was granted and the wages increased to 4 kilograms of rice. The workers' strength increased. In 1984, there was a *juloos* to Delhi and 200-300 workers went in that rally. From 1984-85 onward, workers started going for *juloos* to Delhi 2-3 times a year. There were at least 4-5 *juloos* every year. So after the *juloos,* some people started to stay back in the city. They got used to journeys and the city. They found work in the city. After some years, contractors started coming here in search of workers, take workers and bring them back. The workers also thought, 'how long will we sit without work, let us go out to work'. Some of them became *meths* and started getting commission too.

1. Another worker told me he is not from Siwan, but from Bhagalpur.
2. Varghese, Preethi Saro (2004). *Migration: A Bibliographic Study on Kerala.*

This account is by Jaykishore Mahasay, the local committee secretary of CPI, Banma-Itarhi, who was instrumental in this struggle for better wages by agricultural workers in the area. It signals to the possibility that getting acquainted with the city and travelling long distances was an unintended outcome of the workers' movement and the *juloos* to Delhi (also called *Dilli Chalo*) to demand from the state their rights.

Ravaged by Rivers: Ecology and History of Migration

The struggle for the rights of the agricultural workers occurred in the context of widening inequalities in the Kosi area, comprising of the districts of Saharsa and Purnea, after the introduction of flood control mechanisms and irrigation in the absence of land reforms (Appu, 1973). Kosi area is prone to floods and change of course caused by relentless riverine activity. It has, therefore, been the target of projects to tame the river and use the water for irrigation purposes from the colonial era. The giant Kosi project which started in 1955, benefited the area through protection from flood and improved irrigation facilities. Appu (1973) observes that the salient features of agrarian structure of the Kosi area were extreme concentration in the ownership of land, absentee landlordism with all its accompanying evils, widespread sharecropping characterised by insecurities of tenure as well as a multitudinous population of landless agricultural labourers eking out a precarious livelihood under the extant near-feudal relations of production in agriculture. The project resulted in enhanced land values and increased productivity of land which had given incentive to landowners to oust sharecroppers who were mostly members of the Scheduled Castes and Scheduled Tribes. Coupled with the lack of institutional reform in the agrarian sector, this resulted in the increase of the number of landless workers who formed 53.39 per cent of the population in the district Saharsa as against 47.31 per cent for the state of Bihar according to the 1971 census. In North Bihar, migration has a longer history, dating back to 18th century and the destinations were often as far away as Mauritius, Fiji, Suriname, British Guiana and Uganda which were European colonies. The Bidesia genre of Bhojpuri folk songs is an articulation of the experience and culture of migration. They often reflect the loneliness and waiting of the worker and his family and the hard work in an alien setting.[3]

Railiya na bairi se jaha jawa no bairi se paisawa bairi na

mor saiyan ke bilmawe se paiswa bairi na

3. Das, Arvind N. (1992). *The State of Bihar: An Economic History without Footnotes.*

(It is neither the train nor the ship that is our enemy but rather the money that compels our husbands to migrate to other lands).[4]

Songs like these poignantly capture the agony and pain of separation caused by migration and recognises the compulsions which underpin these journeys. Ships and trains appear not as mere conveyance, but seem to have a life of their own, and form an integral part of the experience of migration.

Though similar information is not available on Malda district in West Bengal, labour migration from the district also seems to have a long history and at least some of this is entwined with the zigzag ways of river Ganges which has forced people to move constantly in search of shelter and livelihood. *The District Gazetteer of Malda* (1918) attributes "emigration to the constant changes of jurisdiction caused by variation in the course of the Ganges and to the settlement of the surplus *diara*[5] population in the vacant *chars*[6] of Purnea and in the *dubas* in Dinajpur". The phenomenon of migration to the construction sites in various cities of India, however, is a fairly recent one, catching up only in the late 1980s and early 1990s.

Occupations and Livelihoods

The 11 workers who came to work in Trivandrum from Banma (Bihar) belong to different communities. My field experience is based on a short stay with Mukhilal Sada, a worker whom I met in Trivandrum and who later on became a friend. During the stay, I interviewed some of the workers who had come to Trivandrum. Out of the 11 workers who came to Trivandrum from Banma, four were *musahars,* three were *machcuas,* two were *yadavs* and the rest two belonged to *kumbhar* and *malekar* castes. The wages for agricultural work is around Rs. 40 while for construction work it is around Rs. 50-60. Most of the workers cited lack of employment rather than a wage differential as the main consideration in their decision to travel in search of work. The wages offered when they went to Trivandrum was Rs. 2700 for 52 days of work which means around Rs. 52 per day. The wages for roadwork in Kerala for a Malayali worker can be as high as Rs. 350 per day or even more.

Musahars are largely landless agricultural workers and belong to Scheduled Castes. According to Risley (1891), *musahars* are an offshoot of the Bhuiya tribe of Chota Nagpur and the name *musahar* means 'rat-catcher' or 'rat-eater', following a popular etymology in an apparent reference to their "fondness for eating field-mice". The *musahar* hamlet in which I stayed consists of around

4. Tiwary, B.N. (2003). "Migration, Change and Folk Culture".
5. A strip of alluvial area formed as a result of the centuries of fluvial action by river Ganges.
6. Island formed as result of fluvial action of river Ganges.

24 families and Mukhilal Sada is the headman of the hamlet. An extract from my field journal dated 20.03.2006:

> I learned that two of Mukhilal's two sons and three brothers are in Delhi working in the Delhi Metro. Mukhilal's house is a concrete one room with a veranda and a cooking place in the front. His sons and brothers also have concrete houses made with Indira Awaas Yojana (Central government scheme to build houses for the poor) funds. Their wives and children live there. Mukhilal and his sons' and brothers' families are a close-knit group but cook separately. The other houses in the *tola* (hamlet) were not as good as Mukhilal's. Each had their own stove made of mud and storage places for grain called *kothis* made of mud which looked like earthen almirahs. Each family has to fend for their needs but gets support from Mukhilal at times of great need. Apart from Mukhilal and Mukhilal's son Rajkumar, two others, Bindasree Sada and Jalo Sada came to Trivandrum from the *tola*. At the time of my visit, Rajkumar and Bindasree were away in Delhi though the latter turned up towards the end of my stay.
>
> During my journey to the village from Patna, I met an advocate in the train, practising in Saharsa, coming back after meeting his brother in Jawaharlal Nehru University, New Delhi. He questioned me thoroughly about my plans and intentions. He showed me Kosi and Bhagmati and told me about their zigzag ways wreaking havoc on the banks. A washed away bridge was being reconstructed. The train moved through a makeshift wooden bridge. He told me that the title 'Sada' belongs to a caste called *Musahar*, and that it means one who eats rats and gave an extremely sarcastic smile. But he did not quite explain and quickly brushed away the topic as co-passengers protested saying that his remarks were quite out of context and unnecessary. *Musahars* are often the targets of caste violence and massacres carried out by *Bhumihars* and *Yadavs* in Bihar.
>
> Bindasree Sahni and his son, Mangal Sahni came to Trivandrum and belong to *machhua* community who are traditional fish workers. Bindasree had to go out in search of work because of a decline in the amount of fish in river Kosi which according to him is due to the excessive use of chemicals by fish workers to catch fish. Sudo Pandit who died of malaria in Trivandrum was a potter whereas Surendar Sarma belongs to the *malekar* community which makes garlands and other items of decoration for *pooja* and marriage. But Surendar never engaged in the traditional occupation, as he had learned carpentry at a young age. He has to go out and do construction work since in his village, he is usually unemployed. *"Do roz kam milta hain toh char roz baidhtha hain"* (If I get work for two days, then I sit (at home) for (the next) four days). He has one and a half acres of agricultural land and he cultivates maize, *daal* and rice. Pappu and Bijendar, *yadavs*, owned some land but not enough to support them and their families throughout the year. *Yadavs* are traditionally cowherds and milkmen, but were the beneficiaries of *zamindari* abolition along with *bhumihars* and *kurmis*.[7] The *musahar* workers borrowed money for their travelling and other expenses from their *yadav* landowners who are their employers. The recruitment process to the sites of global capital, paradoxically, is facilitated by the same relationship of bondage with the landowning castes in an agrarian setting.

---

7. Das, A.N. (1992) notes that land reforms in Bihar was limited to the abolition of *zamindari* and never touched those at the bottom of agrarian hierarchy—Dalits and *Adivasis*. *Zamindari* abolition substantially benefited the rich and middle peasants who replaced the relatively weak among the upper layers of the agrarian order. In caste terms, this meant the replacement of the landed power of most *kayasthas* and many *rajputs* by *bhumihars*, *yadavs* and *kurmis* etc. Following the consolidation of the new rich peasantry, conflicts manifested themselves between the powerful new elements in the countryside and the rural poor.

The workers who came to the worksites in Trivandrum from Malda, West Bengal, are predominantly Muslims and are mostly skilled masons, drivers and helpers of masons. They belong to the Shershabadiya community who are descendants of the army of Sher Shah[8] and the name is derived from Shershabad Pargana of Murshidabad district, from where they were forced to migrate, owing to the erosion of Ganges.[9] Carter describes them as "good agriculturists who spend much time and labour on the reclamation of land which the ordinary cultivator would not attempt to clear". *The District Gazetteer of Malda* (1918) reports that Shershabadi Muslims were immigrating facilitated by the construction of the railway in those regions. Though this signals to possibilities of skill formation as a result of their engagement in the army of Shershah who was also a road builder and later in the construction of railway by the British, more detailed research is required to confirm this.

Reordering Lives in the Village

As had already been pointed out by authors researching migration, lives of women are reorganised to cope with the absence of the men. Gulati (1993) profiles wives of men who have migrated from Kerala to West Asia and observes that the lives of those who are left behind are radically transformed in many ways. She notes that women start performing tasks that traditionally men excluded them, which increases their mobility.

In Banma, the experience of women left behind are reflected in numerous songs which recount the 'loneliness at nights, though the days are bearable'. The ways in which days are made bearable constitute the theme of the present section. The workers I met never take their families during their sojourns though there are a few workers in the vicinity who have taken their women and children with them. In most agricultural households, women do not migrate, as there are tasks to be performed during the agriculture season. Kakhridevi, Mukhilal Sada's co-sister hires a motor pump and irrigates the land she has taken on rent when her husband is away.

The villages in the area lie submerged in flood water for three months (*Savan, Bhadro* and *Asin)* beginning from August which is the time when men usually migrate though migration during other times is not uncommon. The water dries up in *Karthik*. After water recedes, they cultivate rice. After harvesting rice, maize, wheat and sunflower are cultivated followed by green

8. Sher Shah Suri (1472-1545) was the Shah of Delhi during 1540-1545 after defeating Mughal King Humayun and was known for his administrative abilities. He built the Grand Trunk Road, introduced a land revenue system and undertook extensive repairs of major roads.

9. Carter, M.O. (1938). *Final Report on the Survey & Settlement Operations in the District of Malda*. p.45.

gram. There is a second crop of rice, during which varieties which stand in flood water are sowed. When I went in March, it was the beginning of the harvest of wheat exclusively carried out by women. Sunflowers were in full bloom.

Mukhilal told me that they had stopped raising cows because it was difficult for women to get grass from far off places or take them for grazing. Only goats are raised in the *musahar* hamlet, as they are easier to manage. The reordering of lives for women takes shape in the context of gendered roles and norms of mobility as much as in the context of pressures to carry out chores of subsistence and agricultural routine, stretching further their role as subsidisers.

In Malda, women engage in rolling *bidis* alongside, carrying out their role as agricultural workers during the harvesting season. Though this might not be consequent to migration, it is an important way of ensuring the subsistence of the family. Through an arrangement that resembles the putting-out system, they manage Rs. 35 or 40 for 1000 *bidis*. The contractor provides *tendu* leaves and tobacco; rolling is done in homes or in sheds rented in by workers themselves.

In most agricultural households, women do not migrate. This is particularly true of workers who own small amounts of land who use a part of their wages to finance agriculture. Surendar Malekar, who owns 1½ acres of land, ploughs back the income into agriculture. *Adivasis*, who practice low capital, low productivity shifting agriculture, do migrate with their families. An extract from my field journal dated 19.03.2006:

> Ramvilas Ram thinks that women could not work in the construction work sites. They work in the fields of others in the village, mainly during harvest season for which they get *anaaj* (grains) in return. This is very useful during the time when their men go out. If they do not remain in the village, this income will be lost. Second, they will not be able to do hard work of loading and unloading stones and bricks. Only those who stay there permanently in the city as family, those women, do *labour ka kaam*. Haven't you seen Chhattisgarhis (reference to *Adivasi* migrants from Chhattisgarh) who make huts in the sites and live with their families? They will tie a swing for their children in the site or they will make the child lie on the floor. We have seen children dying in the site. Sometimes, a stone falls or an iron rod breaks loose. We know how these work sites are. That is why we do not take our families. Even if we are hungry or thirsty, we will not let our women do work outside. "We will go out. You sit and eat and drink at home."

The nuances of the passage above raises a host of questions but defies inferences on the nature of agency of the non-migrant women and their role in the process of migration. The absence of women in the men's journeys to work sites is viewed by men in terms of their 'inability' to work in hazardous conditions, the need for participating in agricultural work to ensure subsistence, and with a gendered disdain and disapproval of women who move and work. The narrative oscillates between these explanations. One could argue that basic subsistence is ensured by labour of women in the village fields when men migrate for work. This would, however, require a more nuanced documentation of the agricultural routine during the absence of men and when they are around. It would also necessitate a closer look at the ways of perceiving and valuing cash as against grain or any other payment in kind in terms of subsistence. Another layer of the narrative contains understanding of work sites as a dangerous terrain which is anti-thetical to family life and domesticity practiced in their households. This aspect becomes more complex due to the reference to *Adivasi* migrants who move with their families which perhaps hints at the relatively better position of the workers from Banma.

The passage also raises questions about the recruitment practices in terms of a tacit preference for male workers. It signals to an economy of space which rests on all male labour camps, subsistence activity in the villages and a temporality which circulates these spaces ensuring subsistence and reproduction of labour power. It might, however be noted that, these observations are intended as areas of possible research than as inferences.

The migration also made telephone a part of every day life of the workers and their families. A clear evidence to this is the public call offices mushrooming all over the region. An extract from my field journal dated 19.03.2006:

> At night, there were a lot of phone calls from the brothers and sons of Mukhilal who are in Delhi. They talked to me. When Dinesh, one of the sons called, he started scolding his wife, Renju, saying that she picked up the phone always. His brother (Rajkukar) apparently complained to him that Dinesh's wife was too eager to pick up calls. Then Mukhilal intervened and scolded and told him to behave properly to his wife.

Telephone etiquettes practised in the house mirror relations of power and proprieties followed among the members of family. Another instance represented how telephone is used to deal with erring contractors and to negotiate better wages for the family members working in the city.

> Mukhilal and Bijendar (Sada) came by 9 o'clock and the moment they heard that Gorelal (the contractor) had called, they started shouting. Both of them were drunk. At first I thought it had to do something with me. My heartbeats steadied only when I came to know that the target of their wrath was Gorelal. Both of them wanted to speak to him. Bijendar, who is generally very gentle and soft-spoken, looked very angry. He said if Gorelal cheated Mukhilal's sons and brothers, he would not be pardoned. A short while later Gorelal called again and Mukhilal gave him a good scolding and asked him to pay wages immediately. Two-and-a-half months of wages were pending. Gorelal said the company was not paying. But Mukhilal was unrelenting and threatened him.

Telephone plays an important role in the recruitment process and constitutes one of the limited resources with which the workers have to negotiate and manoeuvre the spaces of infrastructure building managed by global capital.

Cities and Journeys

In this section, I attempt a sketch of the journeys, the workers of Banma, Bihar have undertaken in their search for work and their experience of the city. The account is by Bindasree Sahni who brings to fore a map of cityspaces as 'labour markets' as well as the everyday life as worker in the city.

He was 17-18 years old when he went out first for work in Guwahati which was in the late 1980s. He used to load and unload coal in a *godam* near the railway station. It was on piecework basis. Three-four workers used to join together and take *dhekka* (contract) of a particular load of coal. If it was a good day, they can make up to Rs. 300, but there used to be days when they made only Rs.100 or even less. He was there for only a month. In Delhi, he went without the aid of a contractor. He used to search for work on a daily basis. There used to be places where labourers used to assemble and where employers or their agents came to pick up labourers as many as they want. These were called '*labour chowks*'. These are there everywhere in Delhi according to him. He did building construction work being a helper to a *mesthri*. He lived with two others from his village renting a room and cooking on their own, in Baroula in UP near Noida. He got Rs. 40 which was very less and was not making any 'profit' after paying for rent and food. He came back after three months. He came back alone. He was not scared. Somebody commented "*Bihari mein dar to nahin hota* (there is no fear in a Bihari)."

Bindasree's son, 18 year old Mangal, went out for work in Delhi when he was just 12 with his *chacha* (paternal uncle). Children are recruited for diverse tasks and under inhuman conditions of work. The older relatives who accompany the children see to it that they are not given heavy work for which they negotiate with the contractor and later with the supervisors at the work site.

Mangal worked in a wedding card factory. He worked from 8 o'clock in the morning to 5 in the evening, delivering the wedding card to those who had placed orders. There was no break for lunch. He used to get Rs. 500 per month for working 30 days. He never went to school. He used to play *kancha* (marbles). His friends went there first and told him about the work. His friends were getting get Rs.1500 per month. They were trained in card printing and he was told that he would also become *karigaar* after getting some work experience. After coming back from Delhi, he went to Noida. He was the helper of a *mesthri* at a building site. He went with his younger brother. He used to cook for himself and his brother during the 'free time'. The wage rate agreed upon was Rs. 80. The contractor went away without paying their wages when the work got over. His name was Purushottam and was from Munghyr district in Bihar. They could not locate him. Nobody got their wages.

Ramvilas Ram, a worker who is trained to repair machines, including road building equipments, had roamed around all over Delhi. The city and its delights are treated with care and caution.

"Under the Jama *masjid* I have seen the *chor bazaar jahan pe doh number ka kaam hote hain.* Suppose I see a walkman for Rs.2000 and bargained down to Rs.1000. Even if we buy it, we might be robbed of our money and the *samaan.* That is the kind of place. But if you are lucky you get nice stuff there. They sell *chori ka saman* (stolen goods) there."

Surendar Malekar, who is a district committee member of the Communist Party of India, went out first 10 years ago when he was 18.

He lived in Sant Nagar in Delhi near Buradi *gaav* in a room rented out by a lawyer. He did loading and unloading sand (*mathi*) and used to get Rs. 50 per trip. He used to load the sand from the banks of Yamuna to Sant Nagar where the construction of a building was taking place. Three or four men would take up a truckload of sand and they used to make 10-15 trips. A worker would get something between Rs. 100 to Rs. 200. He met Mukhilal in Delhi accidentally one day when he was buying paan at a shop. Mukhilal was also working in the same area. He was with another 10-12 men. The contractor was from Siwan. They had given Rs. 900 for their expenses on food to him. He disappeared with that without paying them anything. They lost the wages of two months. He said this person must have been doing the same thing by shifting his recruiting base to other areas.

Cheating contractors are penalised by spreading the word about their practices among workers. Surendar recounts how he was tricked into doing agricultural work when he was taken to Ludhiana where they were told by the contractor that the work was to lay telephone cables. But when they reached there, they were asked to do harvesting work. Surendar had never done harvesting in his life. He was never into agricultural work, particularly harvesting. But he had no choice but do it; otherwise, how would he find food in a place where he knew no one? His hands got swollen and it pained a lot. He used to wash his hands everyday with hot water to ease pain. All the 12 people from the village went because Surendar was going. *Ham ko kya idea tha yeh dhan katvaenge?* (How can we have the idea that these people will make us do harvesting?) Such instances underline the lack of informed choice in the recruitment process and the element of unfreedom involved in these forms of labour it perpetuates.

Ramkhilon Sada went to Delhi, when he was very young and spent six months there. He went when Indira Gandhi was assassinated. He had to come back from Khagariah railway station after hearing the news and he postponed the journey. He went after 10 days. The riots were still going on in the city. He was helping a *mesthri* in a building site. The wages were as low as Rs. 11 a day. He used to sleep in a park near Subhash Nagar in Delhi. During those days, very few people went out to work from these areas. Earlier, he used to go to Haryana and Ludhiana for sowing and harvesting. Now he is 45-50 year old. He went out for the first time when he was quite young. It was to Nepal for the construction of a bridge and he stayed there for 2½ months. He used to get 75 Nepali rupees which are around Rs. 35 according to him.

Ramkhilon added that when he used to go in 1980s, the train fares were as low as Rs. 80-95 for Saharsa–Delhi, now it has become Rs. 250. They go in general compartment. Sometimes they used to enter first class but then the police picked them up; they had to shell out 10 or 15 rupees. They say, "*kai chada first class mein?* (Why did you get in to first class, compartment)? Then, give us something too, *khane pine ke liye*...(to eat and drink)." General compartment will be very crowded. Those who are travelling alone would be thrown out of the train by bigger groups of workers.

Workers from a nearby village Salkua in Saharsa district told me that the Railway Protection Force harassed them. They asked for identity card even if they had shown the ticket and would often tell the workers that they have boarded the wrong train. Workers are often picked up and thrown out of the train.

These accounts urge for an understanding of the experience of migration in the light of journeys undertaken, the spaces they inhabit in the cities and towns they move to, and the conditions under which they embark on these journeys.

Summary

Sub-contracting of procurement of materials and labour recruitment is a spatial strategy employed by capital in its process of accumulation. The spatial strategy of capital makes use of geographical differentiation and uneven development, particularly in the case of labour sub-contracting, recruiting new ethnic groups to minimise conflicts between labour and capital.

These geographical inequalities have been exacerbated by interventions in riverine ecology by the state without reforming the agrarian structure of the regions, particularly in the case of district Saharsa in Bihar. Caste and kinship play a crucial role in the recruitment process, though in a contingent manner. For example, in Malda, commissions or contractors are invariably Muslims. *Dafadars* who recruit workers from the villages are usually Muslims, though occasionally, men from other communities become *dafadars* as well. *Meths,* who negotiate on behalf of the workers, would belong to the same community as the workers do i.e., if the majority of the workers were *Adivasis,* then the *meth* also would be an *Adivasi*. In Banma, Bihar, the *musahars,* who are traditional agricultural labourers of the village, who had come to Trivandrum to work in the road construction undertaken by Punj Lloyd go together for work often choosing their headman as *meth*. Interestingly, if one or two workers from other communities say *yadavs* or *malekaars,* accompany them, the *meth* continues to be the headman of *musaharas* who are below the *yadavs* and *malekars* in terms of caste hierarchy.

The absence of women in the men's journeys to work sites is viewed by men in terms of their 'inability' to work in hazardous conditions, the need for participating in agricultural work to ensure subsistence, and with a gendered disdain and disapproval of women who move and work. It signals to an economy of space which rests on all male labour camps, subsistence activity in the villages and a temporality which circulates these spaces ensuring subsistence and reproduction of labour power.

Accounts of the workers bring to fore a map of the city as a 'labour market' and experiences of everyday life of the worker in the city. These accounts also call for an understanding of migration as a journey for these workers bringing out the element of unfreedom perpetuated by the recruitment process fraught with cheating and inadequate information.

References

Anand, S. (1986). *Migrant Construction Workers: A Case Study of Tamil Workers in Kerala.* Unpublished M.Phil Dissertation, Centre for Development Studies.

Appu, P.S. (1973). "Unequal Benefits from Kosi Development: Cost of Bypassed Institutional Reform", *Economic and Political Weekly* VIII(24). June 16.

Carter, M.O. (1938). *Final Report on the Survey & Settlement Operations in the District of Malda 1928-1935.* Suptt. Government Printing. Alipore, Bengal.

Das, Arvind N. (1992). *The State of Bihar: An Economic History without Footnotes.* VU University Press: Amsterdam.

Gulati, Leela (1993). *In the Absence of their Men: The Impact of Male Migration on Women.* Delhi: Sage Publications Pvt. Ltd.

Lambourn, G.E. (1918). *The District Gazetteer of Malda.* Calcutta: The Bengal Secretariat Book Depot.

Massey, Doreen (1995). *Spatial Divisions of Labour: Social Structures and the Geography of Production*. London: Macmillan.

Risley, H.H. (1981)(1891). *Tribes and Castes of Bengal: Ethnographic Glossary* Volume II. Calcutta: Firma K.L. Mukhopadhyay.

Tiwary, B.N. (2003). "Migration, Change and Folk Culture", *The International Institute of Asian Studies News Letter* 30 *http://www.iias.nl/iiasn/newslet.html* (accessed 23.05.06).

Varghese, Preethi Saro (2004). *Migration: A Bibliographic Study on Kerala*, Unpublished M.Phil Dissertation. School of Social Sciences, Mahatma Gandhi University, Kerala.

6

Demographic Dividend and Migration

S. IRUDAYA RAJAN and K.S. JAMES

Introduction

Among the Indian states, Kerala state has an impressive demographic performance well recognised world over. The state has pioneered in mortality and fertility transition in the developing world. The mortality transition in the state is traced back to the beginning of the 20th century and the onset of fertility transition dates back to the 1950s with unfavourable economic background. The current demographic indicators of Kerala are far ahead of India by at least 25 years. The state has also achieved all the Millennium Development Goals (MDG), at least a decade earlier.

In the process, Kerala is experiencing a negative growth rate of children (aged less than 10 years). The working age population, however, registered a phenomenal growth of around 4 per cent per annum in recent years. As per the 2001 census data, the working age population (15-59 years) of Kerala constitutes about 64 per cent of the total population, the highest among Indian states. The short-term and long-term implications of higher growth rates among working population in Kerala are less studied and understood. Further, the strategy adopted by the Keralite to overcome the increasing working population is largely unknown and documented.

There has been evidence of positive effect of demographic transition on the society in general and economy in particular from several countries (Bloom and Williamson, 1998; Bloom *et al.*, 2000; Mason, 2001; Navaneetham, 2002). The impact of demographic transition on economy is primarily due to positive changes in the age structure of the population from young to the adult working age group. Perhaps, this may be true in the case of Kerala where demographic transition has, of late, led to significant change in the age structure of the population towards bulging adult age groups. However, the economy enhancing power of the age structure transition observed commonly from elsewhere has not been adequately explored in the case of Kerala.

Age structural transition is a process of shifting age structure from young aged population to old aged population. During the process, there will be a short period in which proportion of working population will be significantly higher compared to young or old people. The dependency rate will be the lowest during this period. This period provides a 'demographic bonus' to the countries by way of several favourable economic growth inducing conditions such as high saving rate and enhanced productive investment. This had been established from the experience of East Asian countries, where the economic transformation since the 1980s is attributed to the demographic regime (Asian Development Bank, 1997; Bloom and Williamson, 1998; Cyrus Chu and Lee, 2000; Mason, 1988). As a result, it is universally accepted that the increase in working age population will lead to rapid economic growth for any countries. However, the mechanisms by which, such a relationship operates in the context of developing countries are scarcely understood.

This chapter makes a modest attempt to examine the pace of age structure transition and its likely impact on Kerala economy. It also discusses the plausible mechanism through which the working age group boom creates favourable economic outcome in the context of Kerala. The chapter argues that the age structure transition in the form of bulging working age group population has resulted in serious crisis at the employment front. However, the opening up of Gulf countries accepting labour from Kerala has come as a boom for Kerala economy. The huge unemployed population of the state largely took advantage of the Gulf boom and the economy of Kerala in general, and Keralites in particular, have flourished in the course of age structure transition.

The chapter is divided into four sections. The first section discusses the theoretical underpinning of the concept of age structure transition and its impact on economic performance. The empirical aspect of age structure transition in Kerala is discussed in section two. Section three provides a description on the unemployment crisis in Kerala and the magnitude of out migration from the state in the course of age structure change. The impact of age structure transition on the Kerala economy is presented in section four. Finally, the study provides the major conclusions from the analysis.

The Theoretical Underpinnings of Age Structure Transition

Age structure transition, as pointed out earlier, is simply a process of shifting age structure from a young to old population. This is primarily the result of falling fertility and mortality. However, in the course of age structure transition from young to old, there will be a short period of rapid growth of adult population in the working age group (15-59 years). This short period is manifested by low dependency ratio and increase in the working age population. Economic demographers call this as the period of "demographic bonus" or "window of opportunity" brought out by the demographic transition (Bloom and Williamson, 1998). The concept of demographic bonus is based on the assumption that with change in the relative size of age groups, the relative intensity of economic behaviour also changes (Bloom *et al.*, 2003). As a result, each age group of population behaves differently with distinct economic consequences. Hence, as the size of one age group increases relative to other age groups, it will have favourable or negative impact on the economy as well.

The age structure transition has different stages depending upon the level of demographic transition. In the first stage, mortality declines, particularly in the younger ages resulting in sharp increase in young population and young dependency ratio. In this stage, there are too many children compared to adults and elderly. This stage involves considerable investment in children's health and education and is expected to reduce savings at household level. Hence, this period is not conducive for investment and economic growth. In the second stage, the fertility decline results in a bulge in the working ages producing lowest dependency ratio. As the dependency ratio for both young and old are at the lowest level, this stage is believed to be highly conducive for economic growth. Third stage records an old age dependency increase with ageing. However, there is no evidence yet to suggest that there will be period of deceleration in economic growth during this stage.

Demographic Bonus Stage

The second stage of the age structure transition is expected to have the following characteristics:

- Growth in labour force at the macro level.
- Decline of young and old dependency ratios at the macro level.
- Increase in the saving rate among households.
- Spurt in government saving and investment.
- Spurt in economic growth.

The empirical evidence from countries shows a significant positive impact of labour force growth in the second stage of the age structure transition on the economy. For instance, the studies from South East Asian countries revealed that around 30-40 per cent of economic growth in that region could be accounted for age structure transition (Bloom and Williamson, 1998). Bloom *et al.* (2003) has also provided evidence of significant economic boom in Ireland as a consequence of age structure transition or demographic dividend. Similar evidences are also gathered in the case of several other countries. The growth spurt in India and China since 1980 is also attributed to the increasing share of working age group population (Bloom *et al.*, 2006). Deaton and Paxson (1997) showed a strong positive impact on saving as a result of age structure transition whereas Navaneetham (2002), on the contrary, concluded that the South Asian countries benefited little from the age structure transition. According to him, the South Asian countries did not perform well in terms of economic growth relative to South East Asian countries at the onset of their age structure transition.

Although the positive link between age structure transition and economic growth are evident in many instances, it is also often argued that there is nothing automatic in this linkage (Bloom *et al.*, 2006). Age structure transition only gives certain advantages, but the ability of the economy to make use of this depends solely on the policies adopted by each government. Age structure transition also creates a glut in the employment market. It is suggested that economic growth inducing effect of age structure transition depend upon the quality of governmental institutions, openness to trade, labour legislation, macroeconomic management and educational policy of the respective governments (Bloom *et al.*, 2006).

Age Structure Transition in Kerala

An important effect of demographic transition in the state is the change in the age structure of the population. There has been a shift in the age structure of the population in the state from young to adults. The bulge in the working age group population is clearly evident in recent years. Figure 6.1 outlines the population growth for Kerala and India over the last 100 years. Though India had a negative growth rate during the period 1911-1921, the growth rates in Kerala remained positive. Kerala registered a growth rate of above 2 per cent during 1941-1971 whereas the same pattern was true for India during 1961-1991. Until 1971, Kerala's growth rate was always higher than India's and India only overtook Kerala in terms of the growth rate during 1971-1981. Over the last century, Kerala's population doubled five times (6 million in 1901 to 32 million in 2001) whereas India's population grew slightly more than three times (238 million in 1901 to 1027 million in 2001). Kerala has also registered the lowest growth rate during 1991-2001 among the states and union territories in India.

Mortality Transition

Reliable data on mortality and fertility trends of Kerala are available only with the introduction of the Sample Registration System (SRS) from the early

1970s (Zachariah and Rajan, 2007). According to the available estimates, the crude death rate (CDR) in Kerala hovered around six during the last 10 years (Figure 6.2). The life expectancy at birth in Kerala is 68 years for males and 74 years for females with a gender gap of six years in favour of females.

Figure 6.1

Population Growth Rates for Kerala and India, 1901-2001

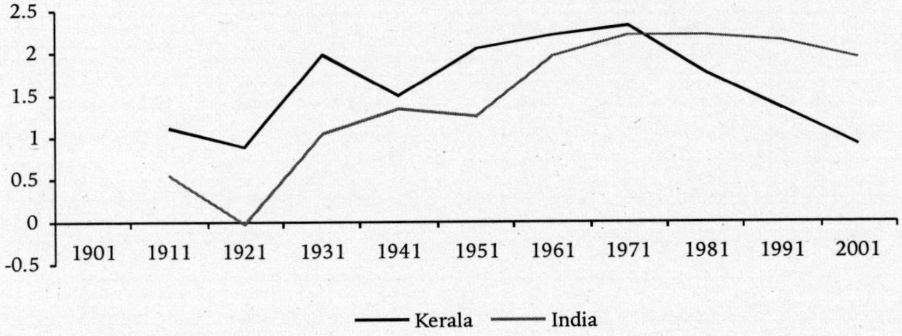

Source: Census of India, various issues.

Figure 6.2

Crude Death Rates for Kerala and India, 1971-2001

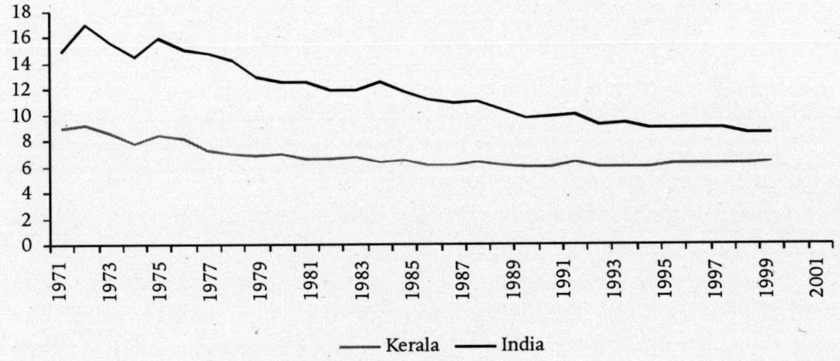

Source: Sample Registration System, various issues.

The fertility has also shown a significant declining trend in Kerala particularly since the 1970s. Figure 6.3 presents the trend in total fertility rate in Kerala and India since 1951. The first three decadal figures are drawn from census and other data are from Sample Registration System (SRS). According to the estimates, the TFR declined from 5.8 to 1.7 by 1991 and then stabilised at that point. However, at all India level the TFR is still far higher than the replacement level of 2 children per women.

Figure 6.3

Trends in Total Fertility Rate: Kerala and India

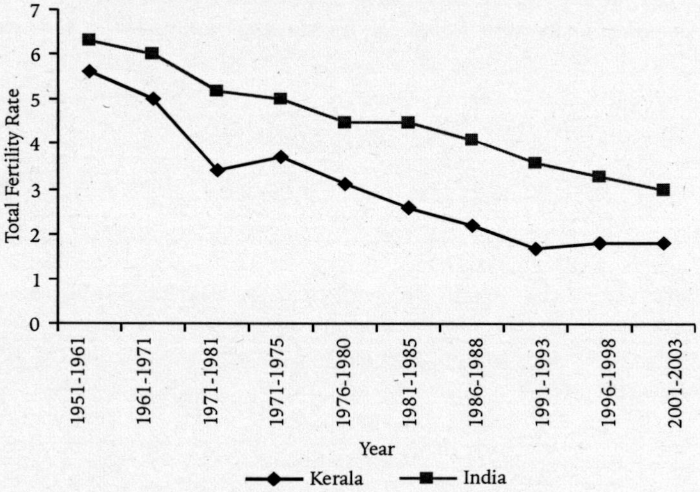

Source: Bhat and Rajan (1990) and Sample Registration System, various issues.

As a result of early demographic transition, Kerala is experiencing a fast change in the age structure of the population. Table 6.1 presents the age distribution of population by broad age groups for major states in India for the year 1961 and 2001. It can be observed that there has been a drastic change in the age structure of population in ages 0-14, 15-59 and 60 and above among Indian states over the last four decades. There are significant inter-state variations in age structure of the population in line with the pace of demographic transition. For instance, states like Gujarat, Karnataka, Kerala, Punjab and Tamil Nadu recorded a decline of more than 10 percentage points among children of 0-14 years. On the other hand, states such as Bihar, Madhya Pradesh and Rajasthan have registered a decline of only less than three percentage points.

In the prime working ages of 25-59 years, a phenomenal increase of 10 percentage points is registered by Kerala during the last four decades. In fact, among the major states under investigation, Kerala is leading with the highest proportion of working age population (about 45 per cent). An increase of five percentage points is observed for states such as Gujarat, Karnataka, Punjab and Tamil Nadu.

Table 6.1

Percentage Distribution of Population by Broad Age Groups for Major States, 1961 and 2001

State	*0-14*		*15-24*		*25-59*		*60+*	
	1961	*2001*	*1961*	*2001*	*1961*	*2001*	*1961*	*2001*
Andhra Pradesh	39.54	32.07	16.67	19.08	37.56	41.24	6.23	7.61
Bihar	42.32	41.54	15.70	16.55	36.37	35.46	5.62	6.45
Gujarat	42.89	32.84	17.34	19.80	34.83	40.45	4.94	6.91
Haryana	N.A	35.99	N.A	20.00	N.A	36.49	N.A	7.52
Karnataka	42.16	31.91	16.51	19.45	35.60	40.95	5.73	7.69
Kerala	42.64	26.08	16.96	18.76	34.57	44.68	5.84	10.48
Madhya Pradesh	40.82	38.21	16.54	17.86	37.48	36.80	5.16	7.14
Maharashtra	40.67	32.14	16.97	19.04	37.10	40.08	5.27	8.74
Orissa	39.10	33.23	16.55	18.29	38.68	40.21	5.67	8.27
Punjab	43.57	31.39	17.05	20.17	32.82	39.40	6.56	9.03
Rajasthan	42.66	40.10	16.72	18.21	35.47	34.91	5.14	6.78
Tamil Nadu	37.61	26.96	17.29	19.34	39.50	44.81	5.60	8.89
Uttar Pradesh	40.50	40.83	16.32	17.84	36.90	34.26	6.29	7.07
West Bengal	40.93	33.28	17.15	18.36	36.91	41.24	5.01	7.12

Source: Estimated by authors from various census reports.

The growth rate of population by broad age groups among Indian states is presented in Table 6.2. It can be seen that those in younger ages of 0-14, Kerala had the lowest growth rate of 1.76 per cent in 1961-1971 and reached a negative growth rate during the last two decades. On the other hand, Bihar and Uttar Pradesh have recorded an increase in the growth rate of population during the same period. Similarly, Kerala had also recorded a significant decline in the growth of population among ages 15-24 years compared to the rest of the states.

Unlike the age groups 0-14 and 15-24, which witnessed a negative growth rates, the prime working age group growth rate reveals an opposite trend in Kerala. For instance, the growth rate of prime working age groups (25-59) worked out to be 2.0 per cent during 1961-1971, reached a peak of 2.6 in 1981-1991 and reached the same level of 2.0 in 1991-2001. India's general population is growing at 2 per cent per annum today whereas Kerala's working age group follows a similar pattern of growth.

Table 6.2

Growth Rate of Population by Broad Age Groups in Major States of India, 1961-1971 and 1991-2001

States	*0-14*		*15-24*		*25-59*		*60+*	
	1961-1971	*1991-2001*	*1961-1971*	*1991-2001*	*1961-1971*	*1991-2001*	*1961-1971*	*1991-2001*
Andhra Pradesh	2.13	0.21	1.70	1.80	1.70	1.96	2.11	2.49
Bihar	2.00	2.56	1.87	2.50	1.81	2.37	2.44	2.69
Gujarat	2.62	1.22	2.83	2.12	2.31	2.70	3.20	2.83
Haryana	N.A	1.60	N.A	2.78	N.A	3.28	N.A	2.23
Karnataka	2.24	0.39	2.57	1.90	1.79	2.47	2.79	2.57
Kerala	1.76	-0.41	4.12	-0.27	1.95	1.96	2.97	2.62
Madhya Pradesh	3.21	1.83	1.65	2.12	1.94	2.29	3.67	2.76
Maharashtra	2.59	1.01	2.22	2.46	2.21	2.37	3.25	4.28
Orissa	3.04	0.76	1.33	1.41	1.66	2.02	2.85	2.87
Punjab	N.A	0.80	N.A	1.95	N.A	2.39	N.a	3.21
Rajasthan	2.81	2.28	2.12	2.70	2.09	2.47	3.16	3.20
Tamil Nadu	2.06	-0.29	2.02	0.98	1.93	1.69	2.26	2.80
Uttar Pradesh	2.14	2.36	1.31	2.43	1.52	2.13	2.54	2.54
West Bengal	2.85	0.67	2.22	1.53	1.79	2.38	2.95	3.26

Source: Estimated by authors from various census reports.

The percentage share of population in each age group in Kerala over the period 1961-2001 is presented in Figure 6.4.

Figure 6.4

Percentage Distribution of Population by Different Age Group, Kerala, 1961-2001

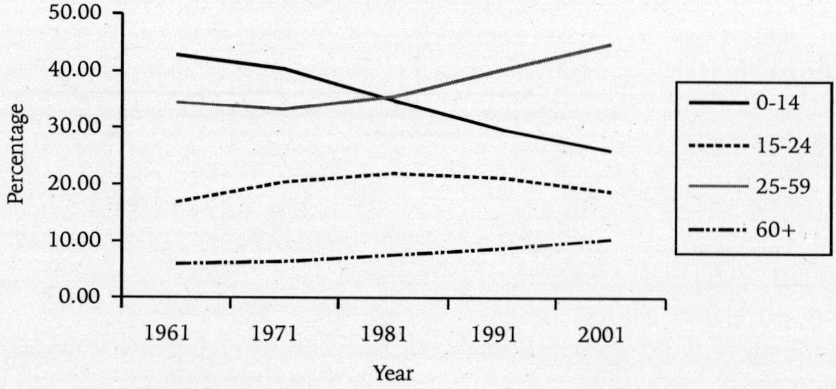

Source: Census of India, various years.

The figure shows drastic increase in the share of 25-59 age group population—the increase was marginal during 1971-1981, but accelerated thereafter. On the contrary, the proportion of population in the 0-14 and 15-24 age groups recorded a steep decline. The increase in the 60 and above age group is marginal although accelerated in recent years. The trend in population growth rate by broad age group in Kerala is presented in Figure 6.5. Over a period of last four decades, the gap between growth rates of children and prime working age groups widened significantly, indicating the windows of opportunities in Kerala. The gap also indicates another dimension of lowering of young dependency in Kerala in which parents have an opportunity to diversify their income from investment on children to more productive areas.

Figure 6.5

Growth Rate of Population by Different Age Group, Kerala, 1961-2001

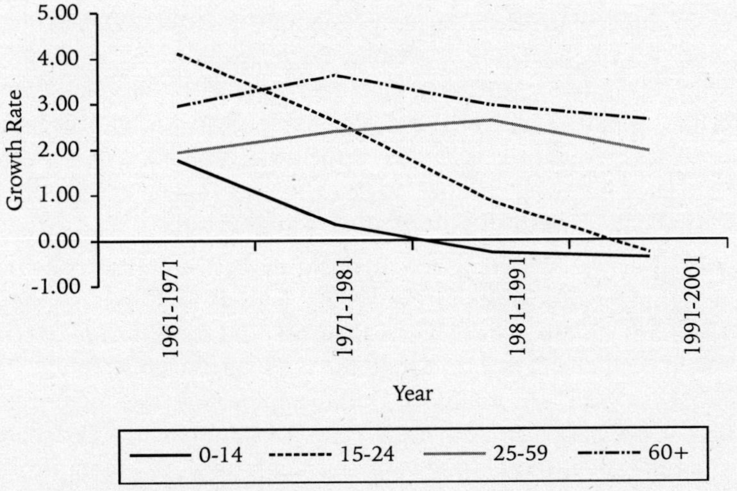

Source: Census of India, various years.

To understand the growth of working population in the state in recent years, growth rate of population by five year age group between 1991 and 2001 is presented in Figure 6.6.

The figure also confirms rapid growth of working age group population in the state. On the contrary, a negative growth rate of population is recorded till age 25. As have already pointed out, the boom in the working age group will be a short term phenomenon and is expected to vanish within the next two to three decades.

Figure 6.6

Age-specific Growth Rate for Kerala, 1991-2001

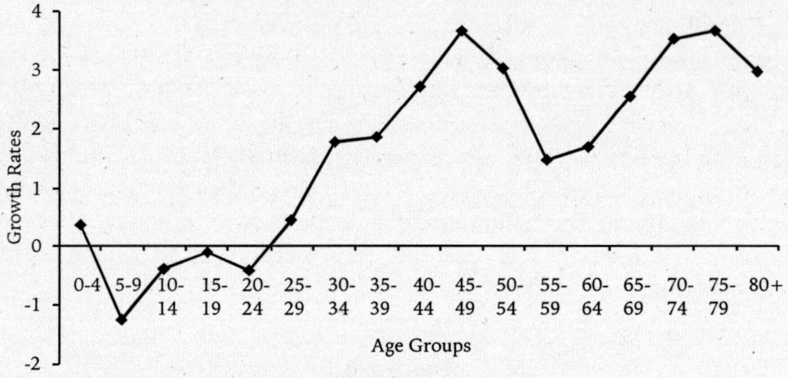

Source: Computed from Census data 1991 and 2001, Kerala.

As a whole, the demographic transition in Kerala has led to significant changes in the age structure of the population, particularly since the 1980s. The proportion of population as well as the growth rate in the prime working age group 25-59 is significantly higher in Kerala leading to a 'window of opportunity' for the state as far as economic growth is concerned. However, it is yet to see how far the economy of the state responded to such a change.

Age Structure, Unemployment and Emigration

The high levels of literacy accompanied by age structure transition have created significant turnover in the labour market in Kerala. Although the labour market changes have been documented in different context, its relationship with demographic change and consequent age structure transition has never been paid any attention. The unemployment was merely attributed to the economic backwardness of the state. Despite remarkable achievements in social and demographic front, the high rate of unemployment is highlighted as a major development issue in the state even earlier.

The work participation rate (proportion of workers to the total population) in Kerala for the three census decades is presented in Table 6.3. Kerala has the lowest work participation rate in the country, despite being the region with cent per cent literacy.

Not only that the work participation is poor in Kerala but it has also not recorded any significant increase over the period. This has to be attributed to the influx of working age group population in the state particularly since 1981 as a result of age structure transition. The work participation remained nearly stagnant, particularly of females in the last three decades. The above trends holds also true for inter-years as given by the NSS data. The work participation rate of females in Kerala is the lowest in the country and the literature points out that women were voluntarily withdrawn from the labour force despite having a high literacy rate (Eapen, 2004).

Table 6.3

Work Participation Rate in Kerala (%)

Year	*Kerala*		
	P	*M*	*F*
1981	30.5	44.9	16.6
1991	31.4	47.6	15.9
2001	32.3	50.4	15.3

Source: Census of India, 2001.

Due to the demographic transition and consequent shift in the age structure of the population, there has been a significant increase in labour force in the working age group and most of them were educated, irrespective of gender. However, the boom in the working age group has also sparked a huge outflow of migration from the state in search of job. Thus, the lack of opportunities within the state boundaries was partly addressed with the migration stream, particularly to the Gulf region.

Migration as a Strategy

Almost at the same phase of demographic transition, Kerala state has turned from in-migrating state to out-migrating state. Table 6.4 presents the population size, its growth and net migration rate in the state since 1901. Kerala has turned into a net out-migrating state from 1941. But the pace of out-migration has quickened since 1961. The rate of out-migration (both internal and international) has considerably gone up from decade to decade, particularly since 1961.

Thus, the strategy adopted to overcome the booming working population and severe pressure on land (Kerala has one of the highest population density in India) has been migration to other states in the first instance and later emigration to other countries in the world, particularly to the Gulf. Although the per capita income calculated for the state could not capture the role of remittances, it has certainly made huge impact in the consumption behaviour as reflected in the per capita consumption expenditure. Thus, the state could overcome poverty and malnutrition to a major extent using migration as a strategy. One of the recent studies concluded, "Migration has provided the single most dynamic factor in the otherwise dismal scenario of Kerala in the last quarter of the twentieth century. Kerala is approaching the end of the millennium with a little cheer in many of its homes, thanks to migration and the economic returns that it brings. In Kerala, migration must have contributed more to poverty alleviation than any other factor including agrarian reforms, trade union activities and social welfare legislation" (Zachariah *et al.*, 2003).

Table 6.4

Population Growth and Migration in Kerala, 1901-2001

Year	*Total Population (in '000)*	*Annual Growth Rate*	*Net Migration Rate*
1901	6,396		
1911	7,148	1.11	0.03
1921	7,802	0.88	0.04
1931	9,507	1.98	0.12
1941	11,032	1.49	-0.01
1951	13,549	2.06	-0.11
1961	16,904	2.21	-0.20
1971	21,347	2.31	-0.16
1981	25,454	1.75	-0.22
1991	29,011	1.32	-0.31
2001	31,839	0.91	-0.27

Source: Bhat and Rajan (1990); Zachariah *et al.*, 2003.

Emigration from Kerala continued to be unabated during the recent decades. The number of emigrants in 2004 was 18.4 lakh persons, roughly 27 emigrants per 100 households. The comparable figure in 1999 was 13.6 lakh persons, roughly 21 emigrants per 100 households (Zachariah and Rajan, 2004). There was relatively large increase of about 35 per cent, in the number of emigrants from Kerala during the last five years. In a recent study conducted at the Centre for Development Studies, the estimated total amount of remittances from abroad comes to around a quarter of state domestic product (Zachariah and Rajan, 2004). The magnitude of emigration from the states estimated through these two surveys is presented in Table 6.5.

It is interesting that while large number of people is emigrating from Kerala in search of job, there occurred a scarcity of labour within the state, particularly for manual work. Consequently, the wage rate of manual labour has considerably gone up and it is one of the highest in India. The scarcity of labour coupled with high wage rate attracted the migrants from other states in India to fill the gap in some segments of labour market, leading to a new era of 'replacement migration'. Thus, Kerala is again becoming an in-migrating state after a gap of 60 years.

Table 6.5

Estimates on the Magnitude of Emigration from Kerala, 1999 and 2004

Emigrants	*1999*	*2004*
No. of emigrants	1361955	1838478
Emigrants per 100 households	21.4	26.4
No. of return emigrants	739245	893942
Return emigrants per 100 households	11.6	13.0
Total (emigrants and return emigrants)	2101200	2732420
Total per 100 households (emigrants and return emigrants)	33.0	39.7

Source: Zachariah and Rajan (2005).

Remittances are the principal means by which emigration impacts upon the economy. In addition, the emigration from the state has important implications for reducing population pressure, unemployment and in general, changing the lifestyle of the people within the state. Table 6.6 presents the distribution of remittances, net state domestic product, remittances as percentage of NSDP, per capita income and the modified per capita income accounting the remittances in the state.

Table 6.6

Remittances, NSDP, Remittances as Per cent of NSDP, Per Capita Income and Modified Per Capita Income, by Districts, 2004

Net state domestic product (NSDP) (in million)	837830
Remittances as percentage of NSDP, 2003	22.0
Per capita income, 2003	25764
Adjusted per capita income	31442
Increase in per capita income due to remittances	5678

Source: Zachariah and Rajan, 2005.

The infusion of Rs. 18,4650 million in a year to Kerala via remittances is a significant amount considering its size of population of 32.5 million. For instance, distributing Rs. 18,4650 million among the 32.5 million persons of Kerala would give each person in Kerala about Rs. 5,680 per year. The remittances (Rs.18,4650 million) come to about 22 per cent of the NSDP of Kerala. The per capita domestic income for Kerala was about Rs. 25,764 in 2003. This estimate does not include remittances. The modified state per capita income including the remittances would work out to be around Rs. 31442, an increase of Rs. 5678. The importance of remittances in Kerala's economy becomes more evident from a few other comparisons. The remittances were 1.74 times the revenue receipts of the state, 1.8 times the annual expenditure of the Kerala government and 7 times of what the state received from the Central government. Remittances were sufficient to wipe out 60 per cent of the state's debt in 2003.

Implication of Age Structural Growth on Economy

Kerala is well known for its remarkable achievements in social development accompanied by economic backwardness. Thus, the Kerala model of development received considerable attention from many scholars and policy makers. At the same time, the low economic growth and consequent public finance crisis faced by the state was a grave concern for many scholars, who feared would 'limit the Kerala model of development' (George, 1998) and to some the very ingredients of the model carried elements of its self-destruction (Tharamangalam, 1998a and 1998b).

Recent studies has pointed out that the economic growth in Kerala cannot be considered to be very low, especially between 1987-88 to 2002-03 (Ahluwalia, 2002; Kannan, 2005; Chakraborty, 2005), which invalidates the long held criticism on the development process in Kerala. Among different sectors in the state, at present the teritory sector, leads the economic growth followed by secondary sector, while the performance of primary sector is far from impressive.

NSS data show that Kerala which was eighth in terms of per capita consumer expenditure in 1972-73 (27th round) rose to third position in 1983 (38th round), to the second position in 1993-94 (50th round) and to the top position in 1999-2000 (55th round) pushing down Punjab, the richest state (in per capita income terms) which consistently enjoyed the highest rank in all the previous years (Oommen, 2005). The GDP growth rate in the Kerala economy for three time periods is presented in Table 6.7.

Table 6.7

Trends in GDP Growth Rate in Kerala

Period	*Growth of GDP*
1965-1975	3.21
1975-1987	1.99
1987-1997	6.00

Source: Harilal and Joseph (2003).

It is clear that there has been a significant revival in the economic growth in the state, especially from later 1980s. While there is a general consensus on the turnaround in growth, the role of demographic factors are seldom considered seriously. It may be noted from the earlier analysis that adult age group population in the state had become significantly higher from the 1980s (Figure 6.4). As a result, young dependency burden has also systematically come down over the period. The economic revival of the state also coincides with the age structure transition. It is also clear that the remittances also played an important role in the economic revival of the state. Studies have shown that the growth of remittances in Kerala has exceeded the growth in SDP by a wide margin throughout the period (Kannan and Hari, 2002).

However, remittances are a function of the large scale emigration primarily induced by the demographic change in the state. Hence, it is necessary to understand more clearly the link between demographic and consequent age structural change on the economic revival of the state. Although this study is not in a position to statistically prove this relationship, our attempt will be primarily to generate certain hypothesis based on the available data. Table 6.8 presents the state NSDP growth rate, growth rate after modifying for the remittances, saving rate and the dependency ratio in Kerala.

Table 6.8

Net State Domestic Product, Modified State Income and Dependency Ratio for the Five Year Period since 1972, Kerala

Period	*NSDP*	*Modified State Income*	*Saving Rate*	*Dependency Ratio (%)*
1972-1975	0.29	0.62	24.67	86.9
1975-1980	2.00	3.34	15.00	73.8
1980-1985	1.44	1.83	12.80	73.8
1985-1990	4.60	5.24	10.00	63.0
1990-1995	7.18	10.64	27.00	63.0
1995-2000	5.03	7.85	47.60	57.6

Note: The dependency ratio of 1972-1975, 1980-1985 and 1990-1995 are for the census year 1971, 1981 and 1991 respectively and for 1975-1980, 1985-1990 and 1995-2000 are for the census years 1981, 1991 and 2001 respectively.

Source: Kannan and Hari (2002).

It is interesting to observe the drastic fall in the dependency ratio along with change in the economic pattern since 1971. It is, however, not clear how far these factors are interlinked. This part of the study is primarily meant to hypothesise that perhaps such a relationship exist which were never considered in the analysis of economic revival. This relationship is also mediated by labour market changes as well as the volume of emigration due to the labour market. Hence, we will discuss both these aspects.

On the whole, it is clear that Kerala had experienced a drastic change in the age structure of the population with a boom in the working age group, especially during the last 2-3 decades. This has brought about a drastic reduction in the dependency ratio and resultant favourable impact on economy in terms of saving and economic growth. As already pointed out, the age structure transition also had its repressions on labour market.

Summary

This study attempted to understand some of the emanating changes in Kerala which, we believe, is primarily the result of demographic transition and consequent age structure change. The demographic change in Kerala with poor economic growth is well known and needs no further description. But the faster demographic transition has led to a significant change in the age structure of the population with a bulge in the working age group and a negative growth in younger age groups. The dependency ratio, as a result, has come down drastically. This period is generally found to be the boom period for any economy. The aim of this study was to find out the impact of age structure transition on the Kerala economy and the pathways through which such a change could, if any, come through.

The study found that since the 1980s, Kerala is experiencing a boom in the working age group and resultant decline in the dependency ratio. Coupled with high literacy rate, high growth in the working age group has serious adverse impact on the unemployment problem. However, the migration opportunities to the Gulf region came as a boom for the ailing employment scenario. The demographic factors have created a peculiar supply-demand problem in the labour market in the state. While on the one hand, there had been an abundance of educated labour seeking job but unable to find them, there also existed a scarcity of labour within the state for manual work. The scarcity of manual labour resulted in in-migration of manual labourers from different parts of the country.

At the general level, the economic revival of Kerala from the mid 1980s coincides with the age structure transition. Although this chapter made no attempt to seriously test this relationship using econometric tools, it appears that the demographic factors played crucial role in the revival of the economy. For instance, the important change that occurs in an economy with low dependency ratio is the improvement in the saving rate. This is because, with the fewer number of children, parents are able to save more than earlier. The available data also suggest significant enhancement in the saving rate of the state, particularly in the 1990s.

On the whole, it looks like that the demographic transition will have different impact in different societies and take various turns and shapes according to the opportunities available in each of these societies. In the case of Kerala, it presents some interesting picture in terms of changes in labour market, emigration coupled with in-migration of different segment of population etc. Perhaps, an integrated framework is necessary to understand all these mechanisms in tandem. This chapter makes a modest attempt to document these changes rather than analyse them in a coherent theoretical framework.

References

Ahluwalia, M.S. (2000). "Economic Performance of the States in the Post Reform Period", *Economic and Political Weekly* 36(17): 1637-1648. 6 May.

———. (2002). "Economic Reforms in India since 1991: Has Graduation Worked?", *Journal of Economic Perspectives* 16(3): 67-88.

Asian Development Bank (1997). *Emerging Asia: Changes and Challenges*. Manila: Asian Development Bank.

Bhat, P.N. Mari, and S. Irudaya Rajan (1990). "Demographic Transition in Kerala Revisited", *Economic and Political Weekly* 25(35-36): 1957-80.

Bloom, David E. and J.G. Williamson (1998). "Demographic Transitions an Economic Miracles in Emerging Asia", *World Bank Economic Review* 12(3): 419-456.

Bloom, David E., David Canning and Pia Malaney (2000). "Demographic Change and Economic Growth in Asia", *Population and Development Review* 26: 257-290.

Bloom, David E., David Canning, and Jaypee Sevilla (2003). *The Demographic Dividend: A New Perspective on the Economic Consequences of Population Change*. Santa Monica, California: RAND.

Bloom, David E., David Canning, Linlin Wu, Yuanli Liu, Ajay Mahal and Winnie Yip (2006). *Demographic Change and Economic Growth: Comparing India and China*. Harvard University: Harvard School of Public Health (Unpublished).

Chakraborty, Achin (2005). "Kerala's Changing Development Narratives", *Economic and Political Weekly*, February 5, pp.541-547.

Cyrus Chu, C.Y. and Ronald Lee (2000). (eds.) "Population and Economic Change in East Asia", *Supplement to Population and Development Review* 26.

Deaton, Angus S. and C.H. Paxson (1997). "The Effects of Economic and Population Growth on National Saving and Inequality", *Demography* 34(1): 97-114.

Eapen, Mridul (2004). "Women and Work Mobility Some Disquieting Evidences From the Indian Data", *Working Paper: 358*. Thiruvanathapuram: CDS.

George, K.K. (1998). "Historical Roots of Kerala Model and its Present Crisis", *Bulletin of Concerned Asian Scholars* 30(4): 35-40.

Harilal, K.N. and K.J. Joseph (2003). "Stagnation and Revival of Kerala Economy: An Open Economy Perspective", *Economic and Political Weekly*, June 7.

Irudaya Rajan, S. and K.C. Zachariah (1998). "Long Term Implications of Low Fertility in Kerala, India", *Asia Pacific Population Journal* 13(3): 41-65.

Kannan, K.P. (2005). "Kerala's Turnaround in Growth: Role of Social Development, Remittances and Reform", *Economic and Political Weekly*, February 5, pp.548-554.

Kannan, K.P. and K.S. Hari (2002). "Kerala's Gulf Connection: Remittances and their Macroeconomic

Impact", in K.C. Zachariah, K.P. Kannan and S. Irudaya Rajan (eds.) *Kerala's Gulf Connection: CDS Studies on International Labour Migration from Kerala State in India.* Thiruvanathapuram: Centre for Development Studies.

Lee, Ronald, Andrew Mason and Timothy Miller (2000). "Life Cycle Saving and Demographic Transition: The Case of Taiwan", in C.Y. Cyrus Chu and Ronald Lee (eds.) "Population and Economic Change in East Asia", *Supplement to Population and Development Review* 26: 194-222.

Mason, A. (1988). "Savings, Economic Growth and Demographic Change", *Population and Development Review* 14(1): 113-144.

———. (ed.) (2001). *Population Change and Economic Development in East Asia: Challenges Met, Opportunities Seized.* California: Stanford University Press.

Navaneetham, K. (2002). "Age Structural Transition and Economic Growth: Evidence from South and Southeast Asia", *Working Paper* No. 337. Thiruvananthapuram: Centre for Development Studies, August.

Oommen, M.A. (2005). "Is Kerala Changing a Crisis to a Turnaround", *Economic and Political Weekly*, April 30.

Tharamangalam, Joseph (1998a). "The Perils of Social Development without Economic Growth: The Development Debacle of Kerala, India", *Bulletin of Concerned Asian Scholars* 30(1): 23-34.

———. (1998b). "A Rejoinder", *Bulletin of Concerned Asian Scholars* 30(4): 47-52.

Zachariah, K.C., E.T. Mathew and S. Irudaya Rajan (2003). *Dynamics of Migration in Kerala: Dimensions, Differentials and Consequences*. Hyderabad: Orient Longman Private Limited.

Zachariah, K.C. and S. Irudaya Rajan (eds.) (1997). *Kerala's Demographic Transition: Determinants and Consequences*. New Delhi: Sage Publications.

———. (2004). "Gulf Revisited", *Working Paper* No. 363, September. Thiruvananthapuram: Centre for Development Studies (*www.cds.edu*)

———. (2005). "Unemployment in Kerala at the Turn of the Century: Insight form CDS Gulf Migration Studies", *Working Paper* No. 374. Thiruvananthapuram: CDS.

Section III

Unemployment

7

Unemployment and Migration

K.C. ZACHARIAH and S. IRUDAYA RAJAN

Unemployment has been a burning problem in Kerala for quite some time now. About 40 lakh of persons, out of a total about 240 lakh of adults, are currently registered with the Employment Exchanges in the state seeking employment. Not all of them are, however, unemployed; quite a large proportion of them are indeed employed.

According to the National Sample Survey, unemployment rate (unemployed as a per cent of the labour force) was 21 per cent in Kerala in 1999-2000. The South Asian Migration Survey (SMS) came with an unemployment rate of more or less the same order of magnitude. In that respect, the study does not add anything new to the understanding of the overall unemployment situation. It, however, adds several new dimensions to our knowledge of the unemployment situation and proposes a few hypotheses, some very unorthodox, about the factors associated with the high unemployment rate. These dimensions, hypotheses and conclusions are the special contributions of this chapter.

Objectives

This chapter is concerned with several aspects of the unemployment situation in Kerala.

First, it is concerned with the dynamics of the unemployment rate, the current level of unemployment and the extent of its increase/decrease in recent years.

Second, it is concerned with the geographical aspect of unemployment, the variations of the unemployment rate from region to region, from district to district and from *taluk* to *taluk*.

Third, it raises questions about the demographic, social and economic characteristics of the unemployed: How do the unemployment rates vary between males and females, by age, marital status, education, religion, community etc.

In all the above aspects, an important point of enquiry is the dynamic aspect, the changes that took place in the unemployment rate among the various social and economic groups during the last five years.

Lastly, it is concerned with factors underlying the recent changes in the level and pattern of unemployment in the state.

Source of Data

This chapter is concerned with the analysis of the unemployment problem in Kerala on the basis of data obtained from the two Gulf migration studies conducted by the authors in recent years. The first of the two, conducted in 1998, was known as Kerala Migration Study (KMS). The second, conducted in 2003, was known as South Asia Migration Study (SMS). In both these surveys, a sample of 10,000 households, selected at random from all the 62 *taluks* in the state provided the needed data. In SMS, about 5,000 of the 10,000 sample households were the same as those selected in KMS in 1998. Thus, for these 5000 households, similar data are available at two points of time at a 5-year interval.

UNEMPLOYMENT

Unemployment Rate

The unemployment rate, defined as a proportion of the number unemployed to the number in the labour force, was 19.2 per cent in 2003 and 11.2 per cent in 1998.[1] The five-year period saw an increase of 1 million in the number of the unemployed, an 8 percentage points increase in the unemployment rate.

Panel data (household) give an unemployment rate of 12.0 per cent for 1998 and 18.6 per cent for 2003. The increase is 6.6 percentage points, slightly lower than what the full data showed (8.0 per cent). That there was a substantial increase in unemployment rate is confirmed by both the sets of data.

Unemployment by Districts

One noteworthy feature of the unemployment situation in Kerala is that the rates differed widely across the different parts of the state. In 2003, the

1. The National Sample Survey indicated a slightly higher unemployment rate of 21 per cent for 1999-2000. SMS and KMS did not include persons who are members of any household not listed in a *panchayat*/municipal ward Thus, the estimated total number of the unemployed in SMS and KMS could be an underestimate to that extent.

rate varied from 34.3 per cent in Thiruvananthapuram district to 9.6 per cent in Idukki district. At the time when the unemployment rate increased substantially at the state level and in most of the districts, there were other districts that experienced decrease. They are Idukki, Palakkad, Malappuram, Kozhikode and Thrissur. The districts, which experienced large increases in the unemployment rates, are Thiruvananthapuram, Kasaragod, Pathanamthitta, Kottayam, Ernakulam and Kannur. It will be instructive to see what factors were underlying the high rates and the large increases in some districts and the low rates and the low increases in some other districts.

Table 7.1

Unemployment Rate by District, 1998 and 2003

District	*1998*	*2003*	*Increase*	*Rate among Persons 20-29 Years*
Trivandrum	8.8	34.3	25.5	52.3
Kollam	7.0	15.0	8.0	39.9
Pathanamthitta	12.9	22.9	10.0	54.5
Alappuzha	14.5	21.7	7.2	50.5
Kottayam	6.8	16.5	9.7	44.6
Idukki	12.1	9.6	-2.5	25.7
Ernakulam	14.8	24.5	9.7	44.4
Thrissur	10.8	10.4	-0.4	20.5
Palakkad	14.1	11.2	-2.9	22.1
Malappuram	10.1	12.3	2.2	18.7
Kozhikode	13.1	13.1	0.0	25.1
Wayanad	12.0	13.2	1.2	31.5
Kannur	16.1	25.5	9.4	46.6
Kasaragod	5.8	27.7	21.9	42.4
Kerala	11.2	19.2	8.0	37.2

Unemployment by *Taluks*

Neither the KMS nor the SMS was designed to provide estimates at the *taluk* level. The sample size at the *taluk* level was not large enough for this purpose. However, the unemployment rate, being a ratio, is likely to be fairly reliable even with a small sample. The error in the numerator would be partly offset by error in the denominator. If the number of unemployed in a *taluk* is underestimated by 10 per cent, and the labour force is also under estimated by 10 per cent, the unemployment rate obtained would be the accurate one. The rate varies from 1.6 per cent in Devikulam *taluk* in Idukki district to 40.9 in Nedumangad *taluk* in Thiruvananthapuram district. The 10 *taluks* with the highest unemployment rates and the 10 *taluks* with the lowest unemployment rates are given in Tables 7.2 and 7.3. Eight of the *taluks* with high unemployment rates are located in South Kerala, in the former Travancore state.

Table 7.2

Ten Taluks with the Highest Unemployment Rate (From Highest to Lowest)

Sl. No.	*Taluks*	*% Unemployed*
1	Nedumangad	40.9
2	Kozhencherry	39.7
3	Trivandrum	36.3
4	Kunnathunadu	32.5
5	Neyyattinkara	31.9
6	Muvattupuzha	31.3
7	Hosdurg	29.7
8	Ranni	29.6
9	Karthikappally	28.8
10	Kannur	28.6

Table 7.3

Ten Taluks with the Lowest Unemployment Rate (From Lowest to Highest)

Sl. No.	*Taluks*	*% Unemployed*
1	Devikulam	1.6
2	Kunnathur	5.4
3	Mukundapuram	6.9
4	Palakkad	7.6
5	Thrissur	8.1
6	Chavakkad	8.2
7	Udumbanchola	8.9
8	Tirur	9.0
9	Manathawadi	9.4
10	Perunthanmannu	9.4

The 10 *taluks* with the lowest unemployment rates have their rates all below 10 per cent, the lowest being only 1.6 per cent in the Devikulam *taluk*. Three of the *taluks* are in the Malabar area, 5 of them in the former Cochin state area and 2 of them in the Idukki district of the former Travancore state area. It will be of interest to probe into the factors that caused such low unemployment rates.

Unemployment by Sex

The unemployment rate is different among males from that among females. In 2003, the number of unemployed males was 979,000 as against the number of unemployed females at 1,292,000. However in 1998, there was not as much difference between the two sexes with respect to the number unemployed.

Table 7.4

Unemployment Rates by Sex, 1998 and 2003

	Males	*Females*	*Total*
1998	7.46	23.09	11.14
2003	11.23	41.21	19.15
Increase, 1998-2003	+3.77	+18.12	+8.01

Sex differentials are large with respect to unemployment rate. In 2003, while the rate among males was only 11.2 per cent, that among females was almost four times higher, 41.2 per cent. There were similar large differences in 1998 also, 7.5 among males and 23.1 among females. Increase in the unemployment rate was only 3.8 percentage points among males but it was as much as 18.1 percentage points among females. In absolute terms, while the number of the unemployed males increased by 332,000, the number of the unemployed females increased by 676,000, double the figure for males. Thus, females contributed two-thirds of the increase in unemployment in Kerala during 1998-2003. This is a noteworthy development in the unemployment scenario in Kerala.

Unemployment by Age

Unemployment rate varies considerably by age. They are very high (above 50 per cent) among females at ages below 30 years of age. They are slightly lower among males but are as much as 46 per cent in the 15-19 ages and 32 per cent in the 20-24 ages. At higher ages, the rates are in general lower among both males and females. Sex differentials are maintained at all ages with females showing higher rates.

Table 7.5

Unemployment Rate by Age and Sex, 1998 and 2003

	1998		2003		
	Males	Females	Males	Females	Total
15-19	50.0	50.0	46.0	77.5	55.9
20-24	30.0	50.0	31.8	70.8	44.5
25-29	20.0	55.0	15.3	60.5	29.7
30-34	8.0	35.0	7.2	38.6	15.4
35-39	3.0	15.0	3.9	32.9	12.0
40-44	2.0	5.0	2.7	14.7	5.9
45-49	0.6 (M&F)		1.1	11.3	3.5
50-54	0.4 (M&F)		1.0	8.0	2.5
55-59	0.4 (M&F)		1.6	5.1	2.2

Table 7.5 is based on panel data in which the effect of sampling on relative increase in unemployment rate during 1998 to 2003 could not be very significant. It shows that unemployment rates in 2003 are consistently higher than in 1998 in all age groups.

Unemployment Rate by Marital Status

Unmarried females have a very high unemployment rate, almost 60 per cent. On the other hand, married males have a very low rate, only 2 per cent. One possible inference from these rates is that unemployment is not common among the heads of household, usually married males. The rate is relatively high (40 per cent) among married females, but then their husbands are likely to be the breadwinners of these households.

Table 7.6

Unemployment Rate by Marital Status, 2003

	Males	Females	Total
Single	30.4	59.1	37.4
Married	2.1	39.7	11.4
Others	2.0	4.6	3.9
Total	11.1	41.1	19.1

Unemployment by Religion and Community

Unemployment rates vary by religious groups within a narrow range, between 18.4 per cent and 20.7 per cent. Within this narrow margin, a very noteworthy feature of unemployment rate by religion is the shift in the differentials. In 2003, the Muslims had the lowest rate, but in 1998 they had the highest. The Christians had the highest unemployment rate in 2003, 20.7 per cent, but they had the lowest rate in 1998, 10.1 per cent. The Hindus had the same ranks in both the years. However, their rate increased from 11.3 per cent to 18.9 per cent.

Table 7.7

Unemployment Rate by Religion

	1998	*2003*
Hindus	11.3	18.9
Christians	10.1	20.7
Muslims	12.0	18.4
Total	11.2	19.2

The percentage increase in the number unemployed was close to the overall average for Hindus, very much below the average for Muslims and highest for Christians. The transition of the Muslim community from being the community with highest unemployment rate to one with the lowest rate is a significant aspect of the employment situation in Kerala in the last five years. It is also worth recalling that the increase in the unemployment rate in Muslim-dominated districts like Malappuram was very small.

Community classification within religious groups in KMS was different from that in SMS. Therefore, an exact comparison of 2003 unemployment rate with that for 1998 is not possible for all communities. Available details are given in Table 7.8.

Table 7.8

Unemployment Rate by Community, 1998 and 2003

Community	*1998*	*2003*
SC/ST	7.1	11.1
Nairs	16.8	25.1
Ezhavas	11.4	19.7
Brahmins	—	16.3
Syrian Christians	12.6	19.6
Catholic Christians	—	18.2
Orthodox/Jacobite	—	23.7
Mar Thoma Christians	—	29.2
CSI Christians	—	23.1
Muslims	12.3	18.4
Kerala	11.5	19.1

Among the Hindus, the Nair community had the highest unemployment rate and the Scheduled Castes had the lowest in 2003. Among the Christian groups, the Mar Thoma community had the highest unemployment rate and the Catholics had the lowest in that year. The Mar Thoma community among Christians and the Nair community among Hindus are the worst sufferers of the unemployment problem in the state.

Unemployment by Education

Education is an important factor in determining the level of unemployment in Kerala, as most of the unemployed are educated. This is evident from the unemployment rate by educational level given in Table 7.9.

In 2003, the highest unemployment rate was among persons with the secondary level of education, almost 40 per cent. The rate among the degree holders was not far lower, 36 per cent. In 1998, the situation was slightly different. Unemployment rate had been the highest among the degree holders, 31 per cent. There was hardly any unemployment among those with below primary level education either in 1998 or in 2003. Over the 5-year period 1998-2003, unemployment rate had increased by 8 percentage points, but the increase among the secondary certificate holders was almost double, as much as by 15 percentage points.

Table 7.9

Unemployment Rate by Educational Level, 1998 and 2003

	1998	*2003*	*Increase, 1998-2003*
Illiterate	0.1	1.2	+1.1
Literate	0.3	1.4	+1.1
Primary incomplete	1.1	1.3	+0.2
Primary	1.2	1.7	+0.5
Secondary incomplete	8.2	12.1	+3.8
Secondary	23.1	38.5	+15.4
Degree	31.4	36.4	+5.1
Total	11.2	19.2	+8.1

Unemployment and Household Economic Indicators

The earlier analysis had indicated that the unemployed in Kerala are mostly young, unmarried and educated, and that they were rarely the breadwinners of the households. The implication was that, the family of the unemployed was not necessarily deprived of its subsistence. Unemployment in Kerala is not likely to cause any major economic hardship to most of the households to which the unemployed belong. Unemployment is more a social problem than an economic problem in Kerala today. More data supporting this conclusion are given in Table 7.10.

Table 7.10

Percentage Distribution of the Unemployed by Relationship to the Head of the Household

	Per cent
Head	2.7
Spouse	8.4
Unmarried children	53.4
Married children	8.3
Son/daughter-in-law	18.6
Others	8.6
Total	100

Table 7.11 indicates that the unemployed in a household rarely happens to be its breadwinner. Heads of households were unemployed in only 2.7 per cent of the cases. More than half the unemployed were unmarried children of the heads of households. Nearly 90 per cent of the male unemployed and 13 per cent of the female unemployed were unmarried. Nearly 60 per cent of the unemployed females were currently married and their husbands would in all possibility be employed persons. Thus, the number of cases of real economic hardship among the households with unemployed, are likely to be relatively few. Further, support to this conclusion is given in Table 7.11.

Table 7.11 gives economic indicators separately for households without unemployed persons and for those with unemployed persons. Most of the households with unemployed persons have high quality houses and use LPG for cooking, possess cars, scooters, telephones, televisions, VCRs and refrigerators. In 1998, households with unemployed had received more money by way of workers' remittance than households without unemployed. But the relation did not hold in 2003. At the same time, it is important to note that households with unemployed received, in 2003, on an average Rs. 7,200 by way of workers remittances. Other than in this single aspect, the unemployed came from economically better-off households. Lack of contribution to the family income by the unemployed could not have caused real economic hardship to their families. Thus, the conclusion that unemployment is more a social problem than an economic problem is strongly supported by KMS and SMS data.

Table 7.11

Economic Indicators of Households with/without Unemployed Persons

Indicators	1998		2003	
	Without Unemployed	With Unemployed	Without Unemployed	With Unemployed
Remittances per household	Rs. 4957	Rs. 7056	Rs. 8303	Rs. 7163
Proportion of households with high quality houses	13.2	17.2	21.5	24.2
Proportion of households using LPG for cooking	17.3	22.2	21.9	25.5
Proportion of households possessing				
Automobile	2.5	2.5	2.7	3.0
Scooter	8.6	11.8	14.1	20.2
Telephone	14.1	19.3	41.1	50.4
Television	35.9	48.2	57.0	67.7
VCR	9.3	12.9	15.7	21.0
Refrigerator	18.6	22.7	28.7	34.3

DETERMINANTS OF UNEMPLOYMENT

Factors Associated with Unemployment

This section sets out the following four hypotheses as the reasons for the increase in unemployment in Kerala during 1998-2003.

- Influx of females in to the labour market
- Ageing
- Educational expansion
- Emigration

Ageing and emigration are not in the usual list of factors for unemployment. They are the ones that were referred to as "unorthodox" earlier in this chapter. This chapter describes how ageing and emigration could have contributed to the increase in the unemployment rate in Kerala in recent years. It gives considerable empirical support to these hypotheses.

Influx of Females into Labour Market

The earlier analysis indicated that the unemployment rate among females in Kerala was 41.2 per cent in 2003, 18.1 percentage points higher than the rate in 1998. The corresponding increase among males was only 3.8 percentage points. Thus, females contributed to a significant proportion of the increase in the unemployment rate during 1998-2003.

The proportion of females in the labour force increased from 23.5 per cent in 1998 to 26.4 per cent in 2003. The share of females in the increase in the labour force during 1998-2003, however, was as much as 68.1 per cent, twice the rate of increase among males. These figures indicate that the influx of women into Kerala's labour force in recent years could have been a factor underlying increased unemployment rate in the state.

Two factors related to this influx may be pointed out—increasing importance of the service sector and the increased educational level of women. The rapidly increasing share of the service sector in the Kerala economy, a sector in which women could compete on an equal footing with their male counterparts for most of the jobs, would be one of the reasons why more and more of them are trying to enter the job market. The increase in number of women opting for higher education, especially technical education, could also be a factor.

There was hardly any change in the proportion of educated men in the labour force, but among women with secondary education, the increase was very large, from 23.5 per cent to 36.6 per cent. Among male degree holders, there was actually a decline.

Table 7.12

Per cent of Men and Women in the Labour Force with Higher Education Levels, 1998 and 2003

		1998	*2003*	*Increase, 1998-2003*
	Secondary	68.9	70.0	1.1
Males	Degree	83.4	77.2	-6.2
	Combined	72.0	71.9	-0.1
	Secondary	23.5	36.6	13.1
Females	Degree	63.3	63.3	0.0
	Combined	32.2	43.9	11.7

Whatever is the reason, women are entering the labour market in larger numbers, and in the context of a relatively stagnant employment sector, they remain unemployed causing the unemployment rate in the state to increase.

Ageing as a Factor in Increasing Unemployment

Unemployment rates are higher at younger ages than at older ages. This was true in 1998 and also in 2003. But within each age group, the rates were consistently higher in 2003 than in 1998. Thus, the overall increase in unemployment rate during 1998-2003 was shared by all ages.

Demographic transition entails a decrease in the proportion of the population in younger ages. The decrease in the proportion of population at younger ages should contribute to a decrease in the overall unemployment rate. A five-year period is too short an interval for any significant change in age composition to take place; therefore, the decrease in the proportion of the population at the younger ages in the past five years was relatively small. As a consequence, decrease in the unemployment rate should also have been small. Calculations show that the possible decrease in unemployment rate due to demographic transition should be only about 1 per 1000 persons in the labour force. But the effect is in the direction of a decrease in unemployment rate and not an increase in it. From this point of view, ageing cannot explain the observed increase in the unemployment rate.

But there is another side to the story that could show that ageing could be a factor in the increase in unemployment rate. Demographic transition causes not only decrease in the population in the younger ages, but also increase in the older ages. As an increasing number of persons live beyond age 55 (the retirement age in Kerala) years, the number of gainfully employed persons at older ages would increase. If more and more persons continue to retain their job after ages 50 or 55 years, fewer and fewer employment opportunities would be open to the younger generation. As employed persons tend to remain employed for longer periods, unemployed persons remain unemployed for longer periods too. Thus, ageing process, which is taking place rapidly in Kerala, could have been a factor in the increased unemployment rate in the state during 1998-2003. A few calculations, based on data from KMS and SMS, are given below to support this conclusion.

Table 7.13

Proportion of Gainfully Employed Persons at Ages 50+ (55+, 60+) to Gainfully Employed at Ages 15-49 (15-54 Years, 15-59 Years) in 1998 and 2003

Ages	*1998*	*2003*
50+ to 15-49	28.0	34.7
55+ to 15-54	16.2	18.8
60+ to 15-59	9.2	15.8

These figures indicate that the proportion of gainfully employed persons at the older age groups increased during 1998-2003: from 28 per cent in 1998 to 35 per cent in 2003 for those at ages 50+ years, from 16 per cent to 19 per cent for those at ages 55+ years and from 9 per cent to 16 per cent for those at ages 60+ years.

Table 7.14

Proportion of Gainfully Employed Persons at Ages 50+, (55+, 60+) to Total Population 50+, (55+, 60+) Years in 1998 and 2003

Ages	*1998*	*2003*
50+ years	38.7	47.3
55+ years	32.1	39.7
60+ years	27.3	37.0

The overall conclusion is that with ageing, the employed persons remain employed for longer periods causing fewer new employment openings at younger ages. Thus, ageing could have been one of the factors in the increased unemployment rate in the state during 1998-2003.

Education as a Factor in Increase in Unemployment

Education is an important factor in determining the level of unemployment in Kerala, as most of the unemployed are educated as is evident from the unemployment rate by educational level given earlier in this chapter. In 2003, the highest unemployment rate was among secondary level educated persons, almost 40 per cent. The rate among the degree holders was not much lower, 36 per cent. In 1998, the situation was slightly different. Unemployment rate was the highest among degree holders, 31 per cent. There was hardly any unemployment among those with below primary level education either in 1998 or in 2003. Over the 5-year period 1998-2003, unemployment rate increased by 8 percentage points, but the increase among the secondary certificate holders was almost double, as much as by 15 percentage points.

Part of the increase in the unemployment rate during 1998-2003 was due to change in educational composition (increase in the proportion of population with higher levels of education). Had there been no change in educational composition between 1998 and 2003, the increase in unemployment rate would have been from 11.2 to 16.6 or just by 5.4 percentage points, instead of the observed 8.1 percentage points. Thus, 67 per cent of the increase in unemployment rate was real (due to changes in the unemployment rate within educational categories) and the balance 33 per cent was due to change in educational composition. Thus, education alone cannot explain the entire increase in unemployment rate during 1998-2003. There must be other factors too.

Although education alone cannot account for the entire increase in the unemployment rate, it is definitely an important factor as it explains almost a third of the total increase. The extent of the increase in the number of persons with higher levels of education is evident from detailed analysis. In 2003, 576,000 students appeared for SSLC examination and 311,000 appeared for the higher secondary examination. Five years ago, the corresponding numbers were 550,000 and 21,000 students respectively. The increase was 316,000 or 55 per cent in the number of students who took the SSLC or the higher secondary school examination.

District Level Analysis

It was shown earlier that unemployment rates varied considerably by district. The rate in 2003 was 35.2 per cent in Thiruvananthapuram district but only 13.5 per cent in Malappuram district. To what extent is the variation by district due to variation in educational level?

Two graphs are given below using district as the unit of analysis. One of them (Figure 7.1) relates unemployment rate in a district with the proportion of persons with high educational levels. The second one (Figure 7.2) relates the increase in the proportion unemployed in a district with increase in the proportion with high levels of education. Both the graphs show some degree of positive association between education and unemployment, but the association is not very close. However, statistical analysis (excluding data from Wayanad district) indicated that nearly two-thirds of the change in the unemployment rate could be explained by change in the proportion with high levels of education. R-square was 66.6 per cent, product moment correlation coefficient 0.6 which was statistically significant for 12 degrees of freedom.

Figure 7.1

Proportion Unemployed and Proportion with Higher Levels of Education, by Districts, 2003

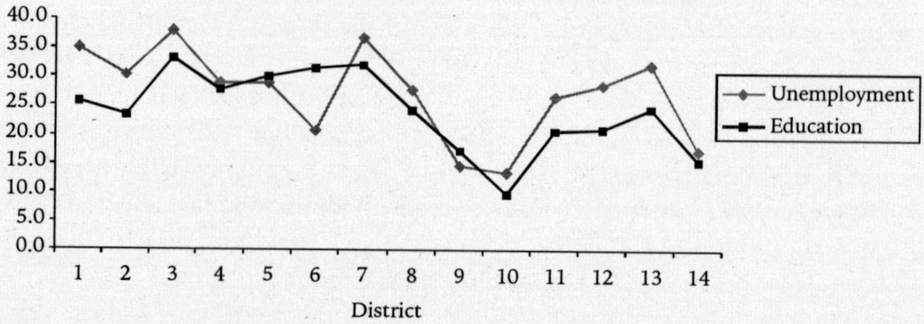

A potentially important variable that is missing in this analysis is the district of birth of the unemployed. How many of those who were unemployed in Thiruvananthapuram district (for example) were Thiruvananthapuram-born persons and how many were Idukki-born persons (for example) who migrated to Thiruvananthapuram in search of jobs? The high unemployment rate in Thiruvananthapuram could be a reflection of in-migration of unemployed from other districts.

Figure 7.2

Increase in the Proportion Unemployed and Increase in the Proportion with Higher Levels of Education, by Districts, 2003

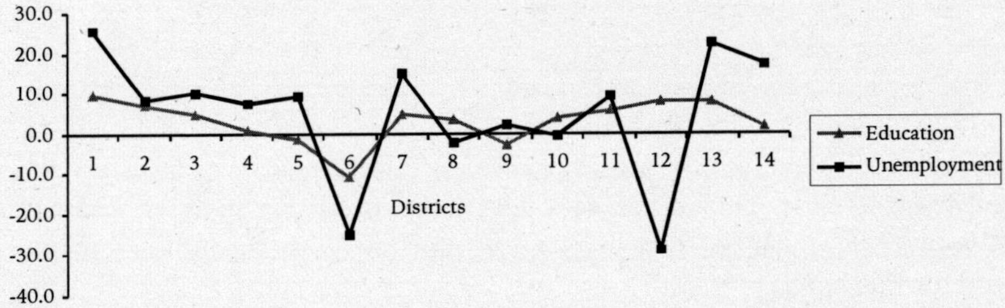

Taluk Level Analysis

The 63 *taluks* of 2003 were cross-classified by unemployment rate and the proportion of persons with secondary or higher levels of education in Table 7.15.

Table 7.15

Distribution of Taluks by Unemployment Rate and Per cent with Higher Levels of Education, 2003

Unemployment Rate	*Per cent with Higher Levels of Education*				
	36-45	*26-35*	*16-25*	*Below 16*	*Total*
Above 30%	2	3	1	0	6
20% to 30%	3	11	2	2	18
10% to 20%	0	0	13	14	27
Below 10%	1	4	4	3	12
Total	6	18	20	19	63

Chi-square = 36, d.f. = 9

Figure 7.3

Unemployment Rate: Actual and Expected

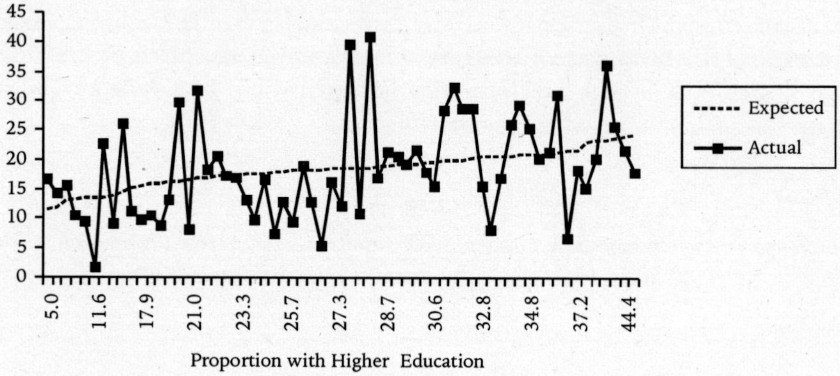

The Chi-square calculated from the contingency table was 36.0, which, for 9 degrees of freedom is statistically significant at 1 per cent level of significance. Thus, *taluk* level data also indicate strong positive association between unemployment rate and the proportion with secondary and higher levels of education.

However, there are many exceptions to a close association between education and unemployment rate at *taluk* level. The lowest unemployment rate was for Devikulam *taluk*, 1.6 per cent. Educational level in this *taluk* was also relatively very low, 11.6 per cent. This is mostly in line with the conclusion drawn above. At the same time, there are other *taluks* like Mukundapuram in which the unemployment rate was only 6.9 per cent but the educational level was 37.2 per cent, very much above the state average. Figure 7.3 gives the actual unemployment rate of *taluks* and the expected rate on the basis of their level of education. It shows that there are large deviations (both plus and minus) from the expected values.

Additional insights on the unemployment situation in Kerala are obtained by comparing the unemployment rate in 2003 with that in 1998, by *taluks*. The comparison shows that:

- The list of 10 *taluks* with the highest unemployment rate in 2003 has only one *taluk* common (Karthikappally) with the list of the 10 *taluks* with the highest rates in 1998.
- The list of 10 *taluks* with the lowest unemployment rate in 2003 has only one *taluk* common (Tirur) with the list of 10 *taluks* with the lowest rates in 1998.

The comparison also showed that there are many *taluks* in which the unemployment rates increased significantly and there are others in which the unemployment rates decreased substantially. These results point to an important conclusion about the unemployment situation in Kerala: the unemployment problem in an area is not a permanent phenomenon, but a transitory one. A *taluk* may have high unemployment rate today, but would have low rate in a couple years from today. The reverse is also true.

The relation between unemployment rate and education is examined further by comparing increases in unemployment rates of *taluks* during 1998-2003 with the corresponding increase in the proportions with higher levels of education in Figure 7.4. On the whole, the figures indicate a close relationship between changes in the educational levels with changes in the unemployment rates.

Figure 7.4

Increase in Per cent Unemployed and Per cent with Higher Education, by Taluk, 1998-2003

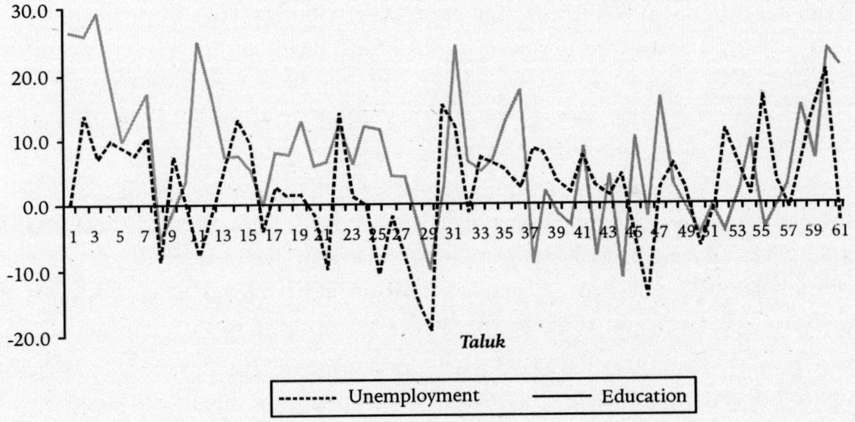

A more detailed analysis of the employment situation in *taluks* in which the unemployment rate is much larger than the rate expected (*taluks* like Nedumangad) on the basis of the level of education and of *taluks* in which the unemployment rate is much lower than the rate expected (*taluks* like Mukundapuram) could provide additional information on the factors associated with unemployment in Kerala.

Emigration and Unemployment

Emigration has direct as well as indirect effects on unemployment. The direct effect is through the relatively high rate of emigration from among the unemployed persons in Kerala. The indirect effect could either reduce unemployment or increase it. Emigration reduces unemployment through employment creation, following the utilisation of remittances sent home by emigrants and the money and expertise brought back by return emigrants. These effects would reduce unemployment, not increase it.

This chapter maintains that emigration could affect unemployment indirectly also, through educational expansion and replacement migration. These effects would be to increase unemployment. Thus, emigration could have both positive and negative effects on the unemployment rate. These effects are analysed further in the following sections.

Direct Effect

In the KMS, it was argued that emigration contributed to a decline in the unemployment rate in Kerala. Had there been no emigration, the unemployment rate in Kerala in 1998 would have been 14 per cent instead of the recorded (in KMS) 11 per cent. Thus, emigration contributed to a reduction of the unemployment rate. This is the direct effect, or effect contributed by the departure of a large number of the unemployed persons. In 2003 also, there was this direct effect of emigration. As in 1998, this effect was also to reduce the unemployment rate.

Had there been no emigration, the unemployment rate would have been 21.4 per cent instead of the observed 19.2 per cent. Because of the emigration of 621,354 unemployed persons from Kerala, the unemployment rate declined to 19.2 per cent. Thus, emigration contributed to a reduction in unemployment rate in 2003 by about 2.2 percentage points.[2]

Although emigration was 33 per cent larger in 2003 than in 1998, the impact on unemployment was lower, 2.2 percentage points in place of 2.6 points. The reason seems to be the much larger number of unemployed in the general population in 2003. A relatively smaller per cent of them only emigrated.

The number of unemployed persons was 2,292,392 in 2003 and 1,246,414 in 1998. The 2003 figure is higher by 84 per cent. The number of unemployed persons among the emigrants was 621,354 in 2003 and 360,917

2. The reported reduction of 3 percentage points in 1998 took into consideration not only emigration but also internal out-migration to other states in India. If internal migration were excluded, the decline would have been only 2.6 percentage points.

in 1998. The 2003 figure is higher by 72 per cent. The impact of emigration of the unemployed was thus lower in 2003, on the level of unemployment.

Indirect Effects

The indirect effects or spin-off effects of emigration on employment and unemployment would have, however, been much larger. As mentioned above, these effects work through the remittances that emigrants send home, and the money and expertise brought by return emigrants. These effects would be to decrease the unemployment rate, not to increase it. To understand the increase in unemployment rate, we have to look for other factors. A major avenue for such an impact is education. Emigration helps to increase the proportion of the population with higher levels of education and through this increase, to raise the unemployment rate. The impact of emigration on education works through at least two channels discussed below under: (a) the demand factor and (b) the income factor (Figure 7.5).

Demand Factor

A common aspiration among the youth in Kerala is to migrate to the Gulf countries, earn a lot of money, get married and settle down comfortably in Kerala. A high proportion of the Kerala emigrants are unmarried youth. In recent years, many governments in the Gulf region have made the secondary level of education mandatory to be eligible for becoming an emigrant to their countries. For instance, the United Arab Emirates made it mandatory that emigrants to that country should have a minimum of secondary level of education. This requirement, which has been introduced only recently, has indirectly encouraged Kerala youth to try to secure a secondary level education certificate.[3] Most of those who secured the certificate, however, would not get a chance to emigrate and, therefore, would remain unemployed in Kerala or they might go for higher education. Some of the recent increases in the number of the educated unemployed could be attributed to the large increase in the number of this category of youth.

Income Factor

Education is costly. Without some source of funds, many of the Kerala youth would not be able to pursue higher education. The required fund primarily came from emigrants' remittances. In this sense, emigration has fuelled the demand for higher education, supplied the means to meet the demand and indirectly contributed to Kerala's unemployment problem.

3. This restriction was removed by the UAE government in June 2005.

SMS estimated that the average cost of education of a household was about Rs. 6,540. It also showed that 24 per cent of the cash remittance received by Kerala households was used for educational purposes. Thus, emigration through remittances played an important role in increasing the proportion of Kerala's population with high levels of formal education. This increase in turn played an important role in increasing the unemployment rate in the state in recent years.

It must, however, be emphasised that the increase in the number of persons with higher levels of education was not solely due to the receipt of funds from emigrants by way of remittances. There are many other factors involved in the rapid expansion of education in Kerala in recent years. For instance, the stagnant and sometimes declining and uncertain economic returns from agriculture could have been a major factor for the heavy investment in higher education.

Figure 7.5

Emigration and Unemployment in Kerala

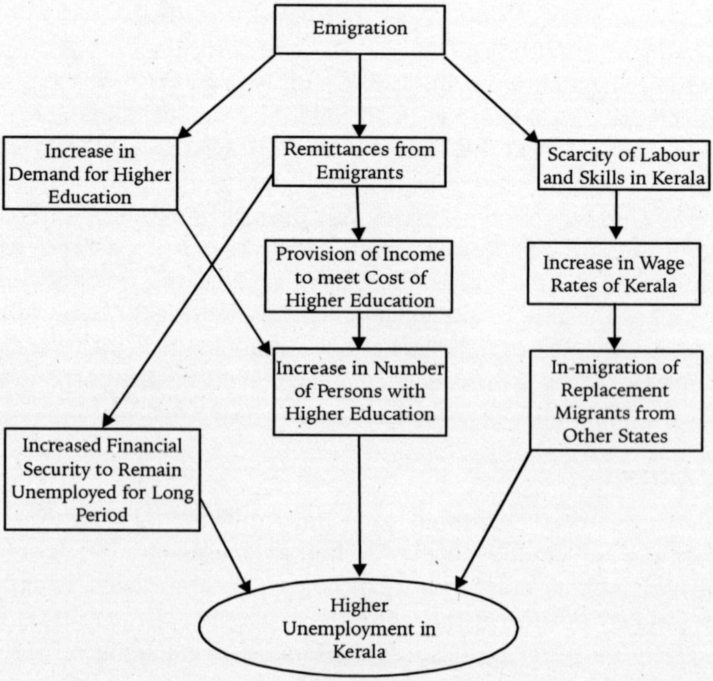

Source: Zachariah, K.C. and S. Irudaya Rajan (2004). "Gulf Revisited", Draft *Working Paper* I, CDS-SANEI, South Asian Migration Study (SMS), July.

The income factor works on increasing the unemployment rate in other ways too. If a person gets money from relatives abroad, he/she may be able to remain unemployed for an extended period. Why should the unemployed youth work when they can live comfortably from the money received from abroad? This is a question, which many people ask in Kerala in connection with the high unemployment rate in the state. In other words, remittances have reinforced and raised the reserve price of the labour.

Emigration could have contributed to increase in the unemployment rate for these reasons. But no statistical evidence has been supplied to support such an association. We attempt to do this here (Table 7.16).

It is evident from Table 7.16 that the unemployment rate among persons in households with emigrants is higher than among persons in households without emigrants. Unemployment increases steadily with the number of emigrants in households.

Such a relationship is observed in 1998 as well as in 2003. In both the years, unemployment is higher in households with emigrants than in households without emigrants. The rate is higher in households with 2 emigrants than in households with 1 emigrant. It is higher among households with 1 emigrant than in households without any emigrant.

Table 7.16

Unemployment Rate by Number of Emigrants in a Household Full Data: All Households

No. of Emigrants in the Household	*Unemployment Rate Among the Total Population*		*Unemployment Rate Among the Secondary Educated*	
	1998	*2003*	*1998*	*2003*
0	10.3	18.0	24.2	36.2
1	16.6	28.6	33.8	48.1
2	21.6	29.3	38.8	50.3
All households	11.20	19.2	25.6	37.8

The overall pattern of the relationship between emigration and unemployment rate is the same in both. One possible criticism of this conclusion could be the spurious effect of education. Emigration is higher among higher educated persons. Unemployment rate is also higher among higher educated persons. Therefore, the positive relation between unemployment and emigration could be actually a positive relation between unemployment and education. To verify this question, we calculated the relationship between unemployment and emigration for secondary educated persons only. These estimates are also given in Table 7.16. It shows that the high positive association between emigration and unemployment rate is observed strongly when education factor is controlled, that is, by carrying out the analysis among secondary educated persons alone.

Regression Analysis

The relationship between the unemployment rate (as dependent variable) and the levels of education and emigration and a few economic indicators (as independent variables) is analysed further with the help of multivariate regressions. This exercise was done with *taluk*-level as well as with household level data.

Taluk Level Analysis

This was a limited exercise using only two independent variables—education and emigration. The result indicated a positive and statistically significant association with education, but not with emigration. In 1998 also, the correlation between the unemployment rate and the proportion with higher education was statically significant (For details see Annex A-7.1).

Some of the other results of the analysis were the following:

- The unemployment rate in 2003 had no statistically significant correlation with the unemployment rate in 1998;
- The unemployment rate in 2003 had a statistically significant correlation with the increase in the proportion of persons with high levels of education during 1998-2003.
- Improvement in the higher levels of education in a *taluk* during 1998-2003 was not correlated with the level of education in that *taluk* in 1998.

Household Level Analysis

Dependent variable was the same in all the regressions, namely, the unemployment rate (UNER)

1 UNER = (number of unemployed persons in a HH)/(number of persons in the labour force in the HH).

UNER is calculated for each household.

Several independent variables were tried

2 EDUC	=	1	if there is any highly educated (secondary or higher) person in the HH
	=	0	if otherwise
3 EMI	=	1	if there is any emigrant in the HH
	=	0	if otherwise
4 LPG	=	1	if the HH uses LPG for cooking
	=	0	if otherwise
5 HOUS	=	1	if the house occupied by the HH is luxurious or very good
	=	0	if otherwise
6 PHON	=	1	if the HH has a phone
	=	0	if otherwise
7 FRID	=	1	if the HH has a refrigerator
	=	0	if otherwise

All the bivariate correlation coefficients were statistically significant (See Annex A-7.1). But partial correlation coefficients were significant only in three cases:

- Unemployment rate and education (controlled for all other variables).
- Unemployment rate and emigration (controlled for all other variables).
- Unemployment rate and use of LPG for cooking (controlled for all other variables).

Multivariate Regression

Multivariate regression (See Annex A-7.1 for details) using all the variables indicated very strong positive association of the unemployment rate with:

1. Presence of a person with secondary or a degree in the household,
2. Presence of an emigrant in the household, and
3. Use of LPG for cooking by the household.

The analysis did not show statistically significant independent association with possession of a luxurious or very good house or possession of phone or refrigerator by the household. Thus, the hypotheses about the relationship between unemployment on the one hand, and education and emigration on the other are supported strongly by the SMS survey data. An important conclusion from this analysis is that the impact of emigration on unemployment works not only through improvement in education, but also through other channels. According to the flow chart (Figure 7.5), the other channels are: (i) financial security accruing from remittances which enables the unemployed to remain unemployed for long periods of time and (ii) replacement migration which substitutes for local workers. Thus, the regression analysis gives firm empirical backing to most of the hypotheses about increase in unemployment in Kerala given in this chapter.

Concluding Remarks

This concluding section touches on three different points.

First, a word of caution about the relation between emigration and education. Although emigration and remittances are given as factors for the increase in the proportion of the population with higher levels of education, they should be taken by no means as the only (or the major) factor. Increase in the number of persons opting for higher levels of education should be viewed in the context of the larger macroeconomic transition taking place in the state. The economic value of education has been on the increase in the state even much before the era of Gulf emigration. The importance of agriculture and other primary sector activities in the economy has been on the decline in Kerala for quite some time. In the light of this persistent trend, there were not many alternatives for an aspiring youngster in Kerala, but to try to get a good education and get into non-agricultural sector activity. Thus, irrespective of Gulf migration, the demand for higher education would have increased. What this chapter suggests is that the shift to higher education was accelerated by the increased demand for higher education (triggered by the possibility of emigration) and through the supply of funds for education that became available through remittances made by emigration.

Second, is unemployment as much an economic catastrophe as it is often portrayed to be? Unemployment is, no doubt, a major problem in Kerala. About 4 million (about 15 per cent of the adult population of Kerala) were registered with Employment Exchange in the state seeking jobs. About 2.3 million or 19.2 per cent of the labour force, 41 per cent of the female labour force, 35 per cent of the labour force in Thiruvananthapuram district, and about 50 per cent of labour force in the 15-24 age groups were unemployed. These figures certainly indicate the seriousness of the unemployment problem in the state. At the same time, they should be read along with other statistics indicating that the unemployment problem in the state is not very much an acute economic problem. First of all, nearly 75 per cent of the unemployed get a job within five years of waiting; and hardcore unemployment is confined to about 5 per cent (25 per cent of 19.2) of the labour force. Second, there is no geographical area that remains a high employment area for long periods of time. Areas of high unemployment rate undergo rapid transitions to lower rates and vice versa. The unemployment rate of a *taluk* in 2003 was found to be not correlated with its unemployment rate in 1998; the correlation coefficient between the two was not statistically significant. Third, the unemployment rate among persons of 30 years of age or above was only 6 per cent. Fourth, many of the unemployed come from well-to-do households possessing good houses and expensive household gadgets and equipment. Fifth, the unemployed are rarely the heads of households (breadwinners). They are mostly unmarried sons or daughters, or married females whose husbands are the breadwinners of the family.

Third, about policies to reduce unemployment. Creation of new jobs is, of course the direct route to reduce unemployment. There is, undoubtedly, plenty of scope for this line of approach in the state as most of the goods consumed in the state are produced outside the state. But there is only a small chance that any effort in this direction would yield positive results in the near future. A prior condition for such efforts to succeed is that our educated youth are "employable". A policy for tackling the unemployment problem in the state has to do with educational reform to make education relevant for employment. Educational reforms must be the number one priority. This is not a finding of this study, but it merits reiteration, in the context of policy suggestions to reduce unemployment.

Another relatively minor result of this study is also worth referring to here.

In 1998, the unemployment rate in the state was higher among degree holders than among persons with secondary school certificates: 31.4 per cent among degree holders and 23.1 among secondary school certificate holders. In 2003, the relationship was reversed. The unemployment rate was higher among persons with secondary school education (38.5 per cent) than among degree holders (36.4 per cent). The increase in the number of unemployed persons during 1998-2003 was 100 per cent for persons with secondary school education, but only 60 per cent for degree holders. One possible reason for this shift could be that by 2003, degrees holders in Kerala became more "employable" than they had been in 1998. The proportion of persons with technical degrees among all degree holders has increased in recent years, from 4.0 per cent in 1998 to 11.8 per cent in 2003. Could this increase in the relative share of technical graduates be the reason for the increase in the unemployment rate among degree holders being lower than that among the secondary school educated persons? Does it suggest that a cure for the unemployment problem lies in making the secondary school educated persons more employable by establishing some sort of match between education and the job market?

Annex A-7.1

Regression of Unemployment Rate on Education, Emigration, etc.

The relationship between unemployment rate (as dependent variable) and education, emigration and a few economic indicators (as independent variables) is analysed here with the help of multivariate regressions. This was done with *taluk* level data as well as with household level data.

Taluk Level Analysis

The following data were used in the analysis:

UNR03	=	Unemployment rate in 2003
UNR98	=	Unemployment rate in 1998
UNRIN	=	Increase in unemployment rate in 1998-2003
EDR03	=	Proportion with high education, 2003
EDR98	=	Proportion with high education, 1998
EDRIN	=	Increase in proportion with high education in 1998-2003
EMIR03	=	Emigration rate (per person) 2003

The results of the correlation analysis are given below:

Product Moment Correlation Coefficients

UNR03	UNR98	UNRIN	EDR03	EDR98	EDRI
UNR03					
UNR98	0.061				
UNRIN	0.874**	0.431**			
EDR03	0.366**	0.257	0.198		
EDR98	0.176	0.272*	0.027	0.647**	
EDRIN	0.296*	0.025	0.255*	0.508**	0.218
EMIR03	0.128	-0.036	0.143	0.131	-0.016

** statistically significant at 1 per cent level.

* statistically significant at 5 per cent level.

The analysis indicates a positive and statistically significant association of unemployment rate with the proportion with high education in a *taluk* in 1998 as well as in 2003.

Some of the other results of the analysis are as follows:

- The unemployment rate in 2003 has no statistically significant correlation with the unemployment rate in 1998.
- The increase in the unemployment rate during 1998-2003 is positively associated with the level of unemployment rate in 1998 and 2003 (statistically significant at 1 per cent level).

- The unemployment rate in 2003 has a statistically significant correlation with the increase in the proportion of persons with high education.
- The improvement in higher education in a *taluk* during 1998-2003 was not correlated with its level of education in 1998.

Household Level Data (2003)

Dependent variable was the same in all the regressions, namely, unemployment rate (UNER).

1 UNER= (number of unemployed persons in a HH)/(number in the labour force in the HH).

UNER is calculated for each household.

Independent Variables

Several independent variables were tried, such as the following:

2	EDU	= 1	if there is any highly educated persons in the HH (b6 = 6 or 7)
		= 0	if otherwise
3	EMI	= 1	if there is any emigrant in the HH
		= 0	if otherwise
4	LPG	= 1	if the HH uses LPG for cooking (b36 = 5 in SMS)
		= 0	if otherwise
5	HOU	= 1	if the house occupied by the HH is luxurious or very good (b37= 1 or 2)
		= 0	if otherwise
6	PHO	= 1	if the HH has a phone (b384 = yes)
		= 0	if otherwise
7	FRI	= 1	if the HH has a refrigerator (b387 = yes)
		= 0	if otherwise

Bivariate Correlation Coefficients*

UNER	EDU	EMI	LPG	HOU	PHO	FRI
UNER						
EDU	0.267					
EMI	0.162	0.053				
LPG	0.146	0.298	0.183			
HOU	0.099	0.232	0.208	0.362		
PHO	0.147	0.350	0.271	0.474	0.447	
FRI	0.129	0.302	0.240	0.516	0.507	0.596

* All the correlation coefficients were statistically significant at 1 per cent level.

The bivariate correlation coefficients varied from 0.099 to 0.596. In spite of this large variation, all the correlations were statistically significant at 1 per cent level.

Partial Correlations

UNER and EDU = 0.2280*** controlled for the remaining 5 independent variables

UNER and EMI = 0.1347*** controlled for the remaining 5 independent variables

UNER and LPG = 0.0469*** controlled for the remaining 5 independent variables

*** indicates that the correlation is statistically significant at 1 per cent level.

The other partial correlations were not statistically significant even at 5 per cent level.

Thus, education has the maximum correlation with unemployment rate. Next in importance was emigration. Possession of an LPG connection was the third in importance.

Multivariate Regression

Dependent Variable, 1 = UNER

Independent Variables 2 to 7 (see the list above)

	Independent Variable	*Beta Coefficient*	*t-value*	*Significance Probability*
2	EDU	0.238	21.6	.000
3	EMI	0.132	12.7	.000
4	LPG	0.052	4.3	.000
5	HOU	0.000	0.024	0.981
6	PHO	0.006	0.425	0.671
7	FRI	-0.003	-0.184	0.854

Multivariate regression confirmed the results of the analysis by partial correlations.

The regression analysis also indicated very strong positive association between unemployment rate and: (i) presence of a person with secondary level of education or a degree in the household, (ii) presence of an emigrant in the household, and (iii) use of LPG for cooking by the household.

The analysis did not show statistically significant independent association with possession of a luxurious or very good house and possession of phone or refrigerator by the household. Thus, the hypothesis about the relationship between unemployment on the one hand, and education and emigration on the other, is supported by the SMS survey data. An important aspect of the result of this analysis is that the impact of emigration on unemployment works not only through education, but also through other variables. Even after controlling for education, emigration has a significant effect on the unemployment rate in the state. According to the flow chart (Figure 7.5), emigration is hypothesised to have independent effect on unemployment through increased financial security accruing from remittances, which enables the unemployed to remain unemployed for long periods and in consequence of the replacement migration taking place in the state. Thus, regression analysis gives firm empirical backing to most of the hypotheses about increase in unemployment in Kerala.

8

Determinants of Women's Employment

ALICE SEBASTIAN and K. NAVANEETHAM

Introduction

The process of transformation of underdeveloped economies characterised by a production structure that used to be for subsistence involves several key changes that includes, among other things, substantial changes in the participation of women in the economic activities. In this context, it is generally hypothesised that the rate of economic growth and level of education have a significant positive impact on female labour force participation rates (Durand, 1975; Psacharopoulos and Tzannatos, 1991). It has been suggested that over a longer period, the pattern of labour force participation among women shows a U-shaped curve, first decreasing with urbanisation (as women stop working on family farms and on other household production activities) and then rising again once the demographic transition is completed (Sadie, 1965; Schultz, 1991; Goldin, 1995; Horton, 1996).

Participation of women in the labour force has increased worldwide during the past few decades. In developed countries, it increased from around 38 per cent in 1970s to around 45 per cent in 1990s and in developing countries, it increased from around 20 per cent to around 30 per cent (World Employment Report 1998-99). Since the pioneering works of Mincer (1962) and Cain (1966), the analysis of female labour force participation has been the subject of intensive research in recent years. Since most women are actually employed in some kind of productive/reproductive work, whether or not this is recognised and quantified by statistics, the issues relating to female employment are qualitatively different from those of male employment. This makes the study of work participation by women a more complex matter than is often recognised.

Participation of women in economic activities outside home has an important bearing on gender relations within the household. The inter relationship among economic power, gender and household variables started to receive the attention of researchers from the early 1980s only and that too mainly from sociologists. Dwyer and Bruce (1988) and Blumberg (1991) points out that the main factor that affects intra-household gender relations is relative incomes of males and females. Women's economic power (defined as control of key economic resources such as income, property and other means of production) relative to that of men is posited as the most important dependent variable affecting gender relations at the household level. There exist at least three important gender-based distortions in resource allocation: (i) discrimination against women in access to resources and services, (ii) unpaid work that women are obliged to undertake in social reproduction and family maintenance, and (iii) unequal exchange within households in terms of patterns of work and income distribution, reflecting conflict as well as cooperation (Elson and McGee, 1995).

The social influences of women's work are also quite extensive. Work opportunities outside home reduce the economic dependence of women on men and in turn, increase her economic command within the family. Women's work outside the household would alter the concept of male breadwinner and would reduce considerably the societal biases regarding the roles of women that are primarily responsible for underestimation of women's work. Women's earning give them access to and control over an independent income, which would make their economic contribution to the household visible and high (Basu, 1996). This, in turn, improves their access to and control over household resources and would offer them a better bargaining power (Dixon, 1978). This bargaining power can strengthen their participation in and the ability to influence household decisionmaking, which are crucial to women's autonomy in the household.

Situating Kerala

The study situates women's education and employment in the specific case of Kerala. In the context of female labour force participation, it has been generally hypothesised that economic growth and education increases female labour force participation. Kerala, where economic growth is higher than all India and where women are relatively more educated, experience the lowest female work participation and highest unemployment among the major states in India, especially among the educated. This is contradictory for a state, which ranks first in Human Development Index and Gender Empowerment Index among all Indian states. In the light of this contradiction, the study attempts to identify the factors that cause unemployment among the educated women in the state. The study tries to investigate how unemployment is related to educational achievements of women, conditioning on individual, household and demographic characteristics.

Falling Female Work Participation in Kerala

Work participation among women in Kerala is 22.9 per cent (NSS 1999-2000), which is one of the lowest in India. This low labour force participation is accompanied by high rates of unemployment. The most tragic failure of development in the state is the acute unemployment of both men and women. Reckoned in terms of all the three measures of unemployment—usual status, current weekly status and current daily status—used by NSS, Kerala has the highest incidence of unemployment both for males and females and in rural as well as urban areas. The overall unemployment rate in Kerala is 11.4, with a wide gender gap of 21.5 per cent for women and 7.4 per cent for men.

According to NSSO data, the percentage of women in paid jobs in the state is slightly less than 23 per cent. This is much less than the work participation rate of women in other Indian states with far lower levels of literacy. For example, states like Madhya Pradesh, Gujarat, Karnataka and Maharashtra with around 50 per cent of female literacy rate, report double the female work participation rate of Kerala. Figures from NSSO survey (1999-2000) show that the proportion of jobless women in Kerala is 10 times the national average (Table 8.1).

Table 8.1

Work Participation Rates Kerala and All India (UPSS)

	1987-88	*1993-94*	*1999-2000*
Total	38.6 (41.1)	38.3 (41.8)	38.7 (39.5)
Male	51.2 (53.1)	54.3 (54.4)	55.4 (52.7)
Female	26.5 (28.1)	22.9 (28.3)	22.9 (25.4)

Note: Figures in brackets refer to all India.
Source: NSSO Rounds on Employment and Unemployment.

While the male work participation rates improved in the last two decades, female work participation rates declined during the same period. Comparing it with the all India pattern, while male work participation rate in Kerala is higher than India (1999-2000), the trend is reversed in the case of women. This is paradoxical given the fact that, women in Kerala are believed to enjoy a higher status in terms of educational and health achievements compared to their counterparts elsewhere in the country. But this is not reflected in their work participation rates. The study attempts to explain the reasons behind this phenomenon.

Changing Pattern of Female Employment in the State

The most significant aspect of female employment in Kerala is the low proportion of women employed in the primary sector. In 1999-2000, primary sector accounted for 46.3 per cent of female employment in rural areas in Kerala as against 84.5 per cent at the all India level. The proportion of women employed in the secondary sector in Kerala is much higher than the corresponding all India figures for women.

In 1999-2000, the tertiary sector accounted for almost 25 and 56 per cent of total women employment in rural and urban sectors in Kerala; while at all India level, it declined for rural women from 12 per cent to 6.7 per cent and increased for urban women to 56.2 per cent. Thus, all India figure shows wide spatial difference in the tertiary sector employment of women compared to Kerala.

Table 8.2

Sectoral Composition of Workforce in Kerala and India

	1993-94				*1999-2000*			
	RM	*RF*	*UM*	*UF*	*RM*	*RF*	*UM*	*UF*
Primary sector	54.3 (74.4)	51.4 (85.2)	21.4 (10.0)	21.6 (20.0)	43.4 (71.8)	46.3 (84.5)	7.4 (7.4)	7.9 (15.0)
Secondary sector	17.8 (10.6)	27.5 (8.6)	27.3 (31.8)	33.5 (28.8)	22.9 (12.0)	28.9 (8.9)	33.3 (32.1)	36.0 (28.9)
Tertiary sector	27.9 (14.8)	21.1 (12.1)	51.3 (58.1)	44.9 (51.0)	33.6 (16.1)	24.9 (6.7)	59.3 (60.6)	56.1 (56.2)

Note: Figures in parenthesis refers to all India figures.
Source: NSSO Employment and Unemployment Surveys.

Table 8.2 clearly shows that structural transformation of women's economic activity have indeed taken place in the state with primary sector losing its importance and tertiary sector taking up its place.

Unemployment a Continuing Problem

Industrial backwardness of the state, together with the limited scope for absorption of more workers in agriculture and the considerable dependence on salaried employment has led to large-scale and growing unemployment in Kerala (CDS, 1975). The incidence of overall unemployment in Kerala is well over four times the national average for the last 25 years or so. The single factor of high unemployment alone takes away much of the sheen that Kerala may legitimately claim in respect of a number of achievements in the area of human and social development.

Table 8.3

Incidence of Unemployment: Unemployed as a Percentage of Labour Force (UPS)

Year	Rural			Urban			Total		
	Male	*Female*	*Total*	*Male*	*Female*	*Total*	*Male*	*Female*	*Total*
1977-78	13.6 (2.2)	29.2 (5.5)	19.2 (3.8)	16.2 (6.5)	39.5 (17.8)	23.5 (11.9)	14.0 (3.1)	30.6 (8.0)	19.8 (5.5)
1983	10.6 (2.1)	17.0 (1.4)	12.6 (1.8)	11.9 (5.9)	25.6 (6.9)	15.6 (6.4)	10.8 (3.0)	18.4 (2.7)	13.1 (2.9)
1987-88	12.5 (2.8)	25.0 (3.5)	16.6 (3.1)	14.2 (6.1)	34.0 (8.5)	19.6 (7.2)	12.8 (3.6)	26.3 (4.7)	17.1 (4.2)
1993-94	7.2 (2.0)	15.8 (1.4)	9.4 (1.8)	7.6 (4.5)	24.4 (8.2)	12 (5.2)	7.3 (2.6)	18.2 (2.5)	10.1 (2.6)
1999-2000	7.6 (2.1)	19.7 (1.5)	10.9 (1.9)	6.9 (4.8)	26.4 (7.1)	12.5 (5.2)	7.4 (2.8)	21.5 (2.4)	11.4 (2.7)

Note: Figures in parenthesis gives the all India figures.
Source: NSSO Employment and Unemployment Surveys.

This overall incidence is, however not distributed equitably as between men and women. In fact, it shows a sharp unequal distribution with women experiencing three to four times higher incidence than men do. While gender bias is more pronounced in the case of Kerala, it is the spatial bias that is more pronounced at the all India level.

Kerala has the highest female unemployment rates in the country according to various rounds of NSSO surveys on employment and unemployment. In 1999-2000, female unemployment rate in Kerala was 22 per cent. In Kerala, 19.7 per cent of women in rural areas and 26.4 per cent of women in urban areas are unemployed, which is far higher than the all India rate of 1.5 per cent and 7.1 per cent respectively (Table 8.3).

Nagaraj (1999) has argued that high unemployment rates for women in states such as Kerala *vis-a-vis* relatively backward states—UP, MP and Rajasthan—are largely due to constraints in 'skill utilisation'; work seekers may not be willing to accept employment at the wages being offered. Over time, this can result in discouraging women from entering the labour force preferring to remain primarily as housewives.

Educated Unemployment

Kerala stands in marked contrast to the rest of India in respect of a number of features of the unemployed population. One such feature is the high rate of unemployment among the educated labour force. But the contrast itself is the result of the structure of education in Kerala being widely different from that in other parts of the country. Apart from the characteristic performance of the primary school system, Kerala is also distinguished from other states by the difference in the structure of education at the other end of the pyramid, namely, higher education. Enrolment in higher education for girls in Kerala (3.3 per thousand population) is higher than all India level (2.9 per thousand population) while for boys (1.9), it is less than all India average of 4.8 per thousand (Institute of Applied Manpower Research, 2000-2001). Also, percentage of women enrolment in higher education to total enrolment in higher education in Kerala (55.9 per cent) is far higher than the corresponding all India figure of 37.7 per cent (Annual Report 2000-01, UGC). The rapid expansion of higher education in the state and the consequent steady increase in the supply of graduates swell the reservoir of educated unemployed in the state. There are distinct job preferences as between educated and uneducated person. Preference for salaried employment and aversion to self-employment among educated job seekers in Kerala were documented in a few recent studies (Mathew, 1997; Devi, 1996).

A state-wise analysis of educated unemployment shows that Kerala ranks second after Assam in rural areas and first in urban areas. Almost half of educated women in rural areas of Kerala are unemployed whereas this is less than 10 per cent for majority of the states. Other states which face the same problem of Kerala, but in less intensity, are Orissa, West Bengal, Punjab and Andhra Pradesh, which have unemployment rate above 15 per cent.

Another feature of unemployment in Kerala is the very high incidence of unemployment among educated women. When educational level are factored, women found themselves at a great disadvantage in the early eighties irrespective of their level of education. The situation at the end of the 1990s changed somewhat wherein women with higher qualifications experienced lower unemployment compared to less educated men and women. But still, the unemployment rate among educated women in Kerala is almost four times than that of educated men.

Educated unemployment has a differential impact on women in rural and urban centres. Educated women in rural areas register substantially high rate of unemployment than their counterparts in urban areas. But the trend is opposite in the case of general unemployment where urban women register a higher unemployment rate than rural women. This shows the difference in the nature of jobs available to and preferred by educated and uneducated women. The fact that educated women have distinct job preferences has been well documented in a few recent studies (Mathew, 1997; Devi, 2002). This job preference partially explains the high incidence of educated unemployment of women among rural areas. The kind of jobs available in rural areas may not suit the job preference of educated women and they opt to remain unemployed.

Table 8.4

State-wise Educated Unemployment Rate (Per 1000) in India (UPS) in 1999-2000

States	*Rural*			*Urban*		
	Male	*Female*	*Total*	*Male*	*Female*	*Total*
Andhra Pradesh	72	150	84	61	145	72
Assam	185	583	234	121	316	156
Bihar	71	69	71	124	294	134
Gujarat	14	3	13	27	52	30
Karnataka	43	73	46	48	94	56
Kerala	150	491	253	99	419	212
Madhya Pradesh	42	92	46	58	73	59
Maharashtra	70	72	70	68	117	75
Orissa	162	419	183	140	286	156
Punjab	48	215	60	47	64	49
Rajasthan	21	32	22	36	79	40
Tamil Nadu	106	149	113	51	148	70
Uttar Pradesh	37	71	39	71	172	79
West Bengal	110	379	130	98	292	121
India	68	204	82	66	163	79

Source: NSS Report No. 458: Employment and Unemployment Situation in India, 1999-2000.

The above analysis shows that the problem of unemployment in Kerala is basically one of educated unemployment. As will be evident from Table 8.5, for those below the primary level of education, chronic unemployment is almost negligible, i.e., less than two per cent for the last two decades. While it is around five per cent among those with middle school education, the rate is not high enough to be characterised as very serious or alarming. In this category, urban women have the highest incidence of unemployment.

The incidence of unemployment tended to rise with educational attainment till it reached a peak for those who had completed just secondary level of education with rates well above 30 per cent throughout the last two decades, with women registering the highest incidence. This phenomenon is explained in part by the widened scope for vertical mobility and the resulting increase in the number of matriculates. Girls are 50 per cent of total students at the secondary level, 60 per cent of the total students at the degree level and around 70 per cent in the postgraduate level (Government of Kerala, 2003) leading to a higher supply of educated girls in the job market.

Table 8.5

Unemployment Rate in Kerala according to Educational Attainments

	1983				1993-94				1999-00			
	Rural		Urban		Rural		Urban		Rural		Urban	
	M	F	M	F	M	F	M	F	M	F	M	F
Below Primary	1.3	8.5	6.7	8.4	6.2	2.1	0.3	1.0	1.2	1.3	0.1	0.30
Middle School	16.9	38.6	19.8	52.4	20.7	17.3	35.5	26.0	37.0	20.9	44.0	20.3
Secondary School	26.6	50.5	15.1	40.5	36.2	45.0	29.9	34.1	31.0	37.5	33.2	36.9
Graduate & above	10.5	43.4	11.3	25.6	19.9	20.0	10.0	22.0	9.8	24.9	5.4	21.6

But what is equally relevant is that employment opportunities for the educated do not seem to have been expanding at a rate fast enough to catch up with the increase in the number of educated (CDS, 1975). As a consequence, the stock of the educated unemployed as a percentage of the annual flow of the category has increased over time. As educational attainments increase further, the unemployment rate comes down to well over 15 per cent until the late nineties. But unemployment was still highest for the educated as a whole. And women experience three times higher incidence of unemployment than this category of educated men.

Persistence of large scale chronic unemployment clearly demonstrate the limited role that education can play as a catalyst for promoting social and economic equality, in the absence of adequate growth of employment opportunities all around.

Nature and Pattern of Educated Unemployment

The analysis is mainly drawn from the Centre for Development Studies survey on employment/unemployment conducted in three districts (Thiruvananthapuram, Ernakulam and Kannur) of Kerala. The survey covered only those having educational qualification of SSLC or more, and belongs to the age group of 15-59 years.[1]

1. The details about the survey can be found in Navaneetham and Kannan, 2004.

The study attempts to identify the factors that influence female labour force participation in the three districts of Kerala.

In the sample data collected from three districts in Kerala, the work participation rate among the educated shows wide divergence between males and females. Educated work participation rate among females (25.6 per cent) is less than half of males (70.5 per cent).

Table 8.6

Employment Status by Sex

	Male	*Female*	*Total*
Employed for salary/wage	729 (49.5)	342 (22.7)	1071 (36.0)
Self-employed	308 (21.0)	43 (2.9)	351 (11.8)
Unemployed	433 (29.5)	1119 (74.4)	1552 (52.2)
Total	1470	1504	2974

It was observed in the CDS survey that more than half of the labour force is unemployed and a major chunk of them (74.4 per cent) are women. Such high rate of unemployment among educated women is a cause of concern not only from development point of view but also from gender equity point of view. It reduces their mobility, tends to enhance women's dependence, making them economically vulnerable and hence, weaken their bargaining position within the household and outside it.

Level of Education and Nature of Female Employment

The data clearly shows the close association between nature of the job and level of education of women in the three districts. Majority of the casual women workers is from the lowest education category, i.e., secondary level. Among the graduates and above, only 4 to 5 per cent belongs to casual workers.

Those who have education of graduation and above, are found more in permanent jobs. While self-employed jobs are dominated by secondary educated women, permanent jobs are dominated by professional degree holders and regular jobs by graduates.

More than half of employed women (50.4 per cent) are in permanent jobs and another one-third in regular jobs. Casual workers consist only 6.8 per cent of total women workers. Thus, it can be said that the process of casualisation, which is observed for less educated women, has not affected the educated women workforce in these three districts of Kerala.

Table 8.7

Type of Female Employment by Level of Education

Educational Qualification	*Type of Female Employment*				*Total*
	Casual	*Regular*	*Permanent*	*Self-employed*	
Secondary	15.4	28.2	30.8	25.6	20.3
Higher secondary	6.5	39.1	39.1	15.2	11.9
Diploma	3.6	34.5	58.2	3.6	14.3
Graduation	5.8	36.0	47.7	1.5	22.3
Postgraduation	-	29.6	59.3	11.1	7.0
Professional	4.3	25.8	67.7	2.2	24.2
Total	6.8	31.7	50.4	11.2	100

Source: CDS Employment & Unemployment Survey, 2003.

Thus, the overall picture that emerges from the data is that education is an important factor that determines the nature of job of women; any policy for improving the quality of life of women through economic capacity creation must, therefore, start with improvement in their educational attainments.

Gender Segregation of Jobs

Gender segregation of jobs and its perpetuation over time to the disadvantage of women workers has been a widely discussed issue in women's studies. Social, cultural, historical and economic factors all play a role in determining the pattern of occupational segregation.

In a recent study covering over 40 countries, sex dominated occupations have been defined as those where workers of one sex constitute more than 80 per cent of the workforce (Anker, 1998). It is also found that women workers are employed in a narrower range of occupations while men are differentiated into a wider range of occupations, which lowers the scope for upward mobility of women.

A similar pattern of sex segregation of occupations is found in the three districts of Kerala. Among the seven occupational groups identified for salaried/wage-employed women, more than half of women are found in professional, technical and related category. Another 31 per cent are in clerical and related jobs. Together they account for 82 per cent of salaried/ wage-employed women in these three districts. This shows that women are employed in a narrower range of occupations.

Table 8.8

Occupational Group of Salaried/Wage Employed by Sex

Occupational Group	*Male*	*Female*	*Total*
Professional, technical and related	46.6 (20.7)	53.4 (50.6)	100 (30.3)
Administrative, executive and managerial	80.7 (6.3)	19.3 (3.2)	100 (5.3)
Clerical and related	59.7 (21.5)	40.3 (31.0)	100 (24.6)
Sales	76.3 (8.0)	23.7 (5.3)	100 (7.1)
Service	88.0 (10.0)	12.0 (2.9)	100 (7.7)
Farmers, fishermen, hunters, loggers and related	88.6 (5.3)	11.4 (1.5)	100 (4.1)
Production and related, transport equipment operators & labourers	91.5 (28.1)	8.5 (5.6)	100 (20.9)
Total	68.1 (100)	31.9 (100)	100

Source: CDS Employment & Unemployment Survey, 2003.

On the other hand, men have diversified into a wide range of jobs; top three categories of male dominated occupations, namely, production and related, transport equipment operators, labourers and clerical and related, and professional, technical and related, consists of 28 per cent, 21.5 per cent and 20.7 per cent of men respectively. Thus, men are not found crowded in any category of occupation.

In terms of sex domination of occupations, men form more than 80 per cent of workforce in administrative, executive and managerial jobs, in service sector, and production related, transport equipment operators and labourers. Only in one occupation, females outnumber males in workforce i.e., professional, technical and related area.

Total workforce also tends to concentrate in three main occupations *viz.*, professional, technical and related (30.3 per cent), and clerical and related (24.6) and production and related, transport equipment operators and labourers (20.9). These three categories constitute 75 per cent of total workforce.

Job Preference of the Educated Unemployed

Job preference plays an important role in determining the extent of unemployment among the educated. Type of work and place of work influence the individual preferences for jobs and this preference can be different for men and women. On account of their commitment to domestic duties and responsibilities, women may prefer to work at convenient place.

The gender aspects of the relationship between preference and unemployment have been given in Table 8.9. It shows that 94.2 per cent of women prefer to work at a convenient place and the corresponding figure for males is 69 per cent. It suggests that men have grater mobility in terms of job search while women's choices are restricted to household premises. Frank and Chasin (1996) observed that preference for jobs near home (in other words, the lack of mobility of women in Kerala) is one of the major reasons for female unemployment in the state. This makes it difficult for women to find an appropriate job commensurate with their qualification and force them to remain unemployed. When women seek employment only in a limited geographical location, their chances of getting a job of their preference reduces. This acts as a disincentive for women to enter the labour market.

Table 8.9

Preference for Job Location by Sex

Preference	*Female*	*Male*	*Total*
At convenient place	94.2	69.0	86.1
Outside India	5.2	19.3	9.7
Others	0.6	11.8	4.2
Total	67.6	32.4	100

People of Kerala have an inclination to migrate to other countries in search of jobs. Kerala has the highest proportion of population working outside the country (Zachariah *et al.*, 2003). Survey data also reflects this pattern of job search among the educated unemployed in the three districts. Almost 10 per cent of the unemployed expressed their desire to work outside India. But there is considerable gender difference in this pattern of preference. While nearly 25 per cent of males expressed their willingness to migrate for jobs, only 5.2 per cent of females are ready to migrate outside India for jobs. Women's inability to migrate puts them in a disadvantageous position in the labour market. It denies them access to the increased number of jobs available abroad and hence, limits their employment opportunities.

Job preference of unemployed women shows that higher educational qualifications are associated with stronger job preference. Accordingly, 63 per cent of professional women expressed their preference for a job commensurate with their qualification, while the figure was only 20 per cent for women who are higher secondary and below. The pattern of job preference also reveals that those who have skill-oriented education have more preference for jobs. Thus, half of diploma holders report their preference for jobs as per their qualifications while 32 per cent of postgraduates have no preference at all.

Table 8.10

Pattern of Job Preference of Unemployed Women

Educational Level	*Job Preference*		
	No Preference	*Any Permanent/ Temporary Job*	*Job as per Qualification*
Secondary and higher secondary	35.9	43.9	20.2
Diploma	25.6	23.1	51.3
Graduate	25.5	35.9	38.5
Postgraduate	31.8	25.0	43.2
Professional	14.3	22.9	62.9
Total	31.9	39.2	28.9

Source: CDS Employment/Unemployment Survey, 2003.

Thus, it becomes clear that lack of enough suitable employment opportunities along with aspiration for job of specific characteristics, has been fuelling the problem of unemployment among educated women in Kerala.

Voluntary Unemployment among the Educated Women

Among the unemployed, 10.7 per cent are not actively seeking for job due to several reasons. Women form a considerable proportion of this voluntary unemployed people. They form 67.6 per cent of total people who reported as 'not actively seeking employment'.

Table 8.11

Reasons for Not Seeking Job by Sex

	Female	*Male*	*Total*
Sick	0.4	14.7	1.9
Difficulty to get a job	92.6	64.7	89.6
Not interested	3.2	5.9	3.5
Others	3.9	14.7	5.0
Total	89.3	10.7	100

Source: CDS Employment/Unemployment Survey, 2003.

'Difficulty to get a job' has been sited by 89 per cent of unemployed, as the most important reason for not seeking a job. Data shows that women find it more difficult to get a job than men. Out of total women who reported as 'not actively seeking job', 92.6 per cent of them sited 'difficulty to get a job' as the reason for not seeking employment while 64.7 per cent of men sited the same reason. It shows that acute unemployment situation in the state discourages people from looking for a job. Lack of employment opportunities thus, emerges as the main factor that causes voluntary unemployment among the educated labour force.

But it needs to be stressed here that strong job preference of the educated in terms of location and type of job might make it difficult for them to find a job. One-third of the educated unemployed look for jobs commensurate with their educational qualification and 86 per cent of them want a job at a convenient place. These conditions make it difficult to find a job. In the case of women, these job preferences become much more restrictive because of their commitment to domestic responsibilities. Thus, it emerges that what is difficult is not to find a job, but to find a job of one's preference. Several studies on educated unemployed have reported the existence of strong job preference among the educated as the main factor that causes educated unemployment (Mathew, 1997; Mukherjee and Issac, 1994). Findings of this study also lead us to the same conclusion.

In the next section, we will focus on the factors that influence the labour market entry of women. Both individual level and household level characteristics are taken into consideration for explaining the observed difference in work participation of women.

Determinants of Female Labour Force Participation

An attempt is made in this section to determine the factors that affect female labour force participation using a multivariate logistic regression analysis. Educational level, family background and economic status of the household provide the context within which decisions are made regarding female employment. Both individual characteristics and household characteristics influence women's participation in paid work. The extent of influence of these variables is examined here using multivariate logistic regression analysis.

Two models are estimated, first model excludes two independent variables, husband's education and employment and second model excludes marital status. First model includes all observations and second model includes 499 married women whose information about husband's education and employment are available.

The regression results show that, of the six variables included in the model, five turned out to be significant in determining women's work participation. They are education, age, marital status, place of residence and economic status.

A variable, which is found to have a strong influence on female labour force participation, is women's educational level. All the four categories of education turned out to be quite significant. The odds ratio shows that compared to women with higher secondary and below education, women with diploma and professional education have 6 and 18 times more probability respectively, to be employed. It is to be noted that graduates and postgraduates are less likely to be employed compared to diploma holders. This shows the importance of skill-oriented education in improving the employability of women.

Age turned out to be an important factor determining the employment status of educated women. As the age increases, women's work participation also increases. Women in the age group of 40–59 have 13 times more probability to work than women in the age group of 15–24. This is an interesting result, which shows the important role life cycle plays in the employment decision of women.

Another factor found significant in the regression analysis is marital status. It shows that, single women have two times more probability than married women to have employment while controlling other characteristics. Religion does not exert any influence on women's employment as the coefficient of religion turned out to be insignificant.

Place of residence seems to exert an influence on women's employment. Women in Ernakulam district are two times more likely to be in the workforce than women belonging to Kannur district. It shows that employment opportunity in the place matter for women's employment. Ernakulam is an industrially and commercially more developed district in Kerala. This is reflected in the overall work participation rate also. Ernakulam records the highest work participation for both males and females (76 per cent and 32.6 per cent respectively) among the three districts.

The coefficient of economic status shows the nature of relationship between economic status and women's employment. It is found to be significant for women belonging to low economic status households. It shows that women from poor family are more likely to work than women from rich family. This is because women are forced to take up employment to supplement family income. The positive relationship between women's work participation and low economic status was due to the influence of education.

Table 8.12

Results of Logistic Regression Model

Variables	*Model 1*		*Model 2*	
	Odd Ratios	*S.E.*	*Odd Ratios*	*S.E.*
Level of Education				
H.S. & below®	1.00	-	1.00	-
Diploma	6.15	0.25 **	4.54	0.43**
Graduate	2.54	0.18**	2.13	0.31*
Postgraduate	3.83	0.29**	4.67	0.47**
Professional	18.63	0.24**	19.53	0.42**
Age Group				
Age 15-24®	1.00	-	1.00	-
Age 25-39	3.54	0.22**	1.24	0.42
Age 40-59	12.97	0.25**	6.35	0.44**
Marital Status				
Married®	1.00	-	-	-
Single	2.79	0.20**	-	-
Religion				
Muslim®	1.00	-	1.00	-
Hindu	1.32	0.28	0.80	0.53
Christian	1.49	0.297	1.17	0.56
Place of Residence				
Kannur®	1.00	-	1.00	-
Ernakulam	1.91	0.21**	1.40	0.41
Thiruvananthapuram	0.96	0.21	1.13	0.40
Economic Status				
High®	1.00	-	1.00	-
Medium	0.98	0.16	0.81	0.26
Low	1.86	0.25*	5.96	0.53**
Husband's Education				
Low®	-	-	1.00	-
Medium	-	-	1.13	0.29
High	-	-	0.70	0.44
Husband's Employment				
High®	-	-	1.00	-
Medium	-	-	0.53	0.29*
Low	-	-	0.40	0.36**
Constant	0.02	0.40*	0.11	0.79**
Number of Observations	1494	499		
-2 Log Likelihood	1316.58	462.63		
Model Chi Square	379.95	155.73		

Note: ® - Reference category ** $p < 0.01$, * $p < 0.05$

The second logistic regression model was attempted to explain the work participation of married women as they form 73 per cent of the total women. This model incorporates husband's education and employment as independent variables for explaining married women's work participation.

Out of 1105 married women, information about husband's education and employment are available only for 499 women. A logistic regression is run using 7 independent variables for these 499 women. Results of the model changes with regard to some variables.

Husband's employment turned out to be a significant variable in determining women's work participation. Level of husband's employment seems to have an impact upon women's employment prospects. An odds ratio less than one shows that, women whose husbands are employed at medium or low nature of work are less likely to enter into workforce compared to the high employment status of the husband. Odds ratio decreases with corresponding fall in the level of husband's employment. Thus, it can be concluded that women's employment has a significant and positive association with nature of husband's work.

Unlike husband's work, husband's education level is not significant in influencing women's employment, while controlling other characteristics.

It is interesting to note that in the case of married women, economic status plays a crucial role in determining their employment status. Married women from poor family are six times more likely to work. It shows that family obligations forces married women to opt for market work.

Conclusion

The study is mainly concerned with the problems of educated unemployment among women in Kerala. Our analysis shows that individual and household characteristics can go a long way in explaining women's entry into the labour market. The results show that education, age, marital status, place of residence, economic status and husband's employment turned out to be significant in determining women's entry into the workforce.

The study opens up potential for further research in many aspects of women's employment. The study raises more questions than answers about the causes of educated unemployment among women in Kerala. The conventional factors that influence labour supply like wage rate, demand for labourers and education level seems to be inadequate in explaining women's labour supply. When 70.5 per cent of men are able to find employment, 74.4 per cent of women remain unemployed. This shows that lack of employment opportunities cannot explain such wide gender differences in employment level. This prompts us to look into other likely factors that affect women's decision to work.

Educational achievements also fail to give any satisfactory explanation for low female employment rate. It is quite surprising to find that women are more educated than men across all educational categories except diploma and secondary education. In higher education also, women are more represented than men. But unfortunately women's edge over men in educational achievements is not translated into gainful employment opportunities. Though women are more educated than men, they suffer from almost three times the unemployment rate of men. Thus, it can be said that women's education has not played the transformative role so generally expected of it. Low levels of female employment and persistence of a gendered work structure have limited women's claims to independent sources of income.

The type of education women receive also contribute to their unemployment. Women are found to be over represented in general education without any skill orientation and professional qualification (Government of Kerala, 2003). This was particularly evident in the case of diploma education where 16 per cent of men and 7 per cent of women opting for it. It suggests the role of socio-cultural institutions such as families, which mediates micro level decisions regarding education and employment of women with the perceived requirements of marriage. Emerging norms of feminity dictate that women use their education in the interests of marriage to be accomplished wives and better mothers (Osella and Osella, 2000).

The relationship that exists between marital status, age and employment strengthens this argument. Our study finds that single women and older women are more likely to be employed. It suggests that persistence of gender differentiated family roles, with primary responsibility of domestic chores falling on women, constrain their options in other areas like employment. Given the very low employment level of women, high educational achievements attained by them does not seem to change the gender role assumptions in the society.

It, therefore, arises from our study that rather than labour market conditions, the likely explanation for such high levels of unemployment among educated women, lies in people's deep-seated beliefs about women's gender role in society. Any policy measure to improve women's employment situation in Kerala has to look beyond creating additional employment opportunities to changing gender roles within the household.

References

Anker, R. (1998). *Gender and Jobs: Sex Segregation of Occupations in the World.* Geneva: ILO.

Basu, Alaka Malwade (1996). "Women's Economic Roles and Child Health: An Overview", in *Population and Women.* New York: Population Division, UN.

Blumberg, Rae Lesser (ed.) (1991). *Gender, Family and Economy: The Triple Overlap.* U.S.A.: Sage Publications.

Cain, Glen (1966). *Married Women in the Labour Force: An Economic Analysis.* Chicago: The University of Chicago Press.

Centre for Development Studies (1975). *Poverty, Unemployment and Development Policy: A Case Study of Selected Review with Reference to Kerala*. New York: UN Publication.

Devi, L. (2002). "Education, Employment and Job Preference of Women in Kerala: A Micro-level Case Study", *Discussion Paper No. 42*, KRPLLD.

———. (1996). "Determinants of Labour force Participation among Women in Kerala: Some Evidence from a Micro-level Case Study", *The Asian Economic Review* 38, April.

Dixon, Ruth (1978). "Counting Women in Agricultural Labour Force", *Population and Development Review* 8(3).

Durand, John D. (1970). "Population Growth and Changing Structure of Economic Activity", Paper presented on *Interrelation between Population and Manpower Problems*, A Joint ECAFE/ILO Regional Seminar, Economic Commission for Asia and Far East. Bangkok: *Asian Population Studies* 7.

———. (1975). "The Labour Force in Economic Development and Demographic Transition", in Tabah Leon (ed.), *Population Growth and Economic Development in the Third World*. Vol. 1. Belgium: Ordina.

Dwyer, Daisy and Judith Bruce (1988). *A Home Divided: Women and Income in the Third World*. Palo Alto: Stanford University Press.

Elson, D. and R. McGee (1995). "Gender Equality, Bilateral Program Assistance and Structural Adjustment: Policy and Procedures", *World Development* 23(11).

Franke, Richard W. and Barbara Chasin (1996). "Female Supported Households: A Continuing Agenda for the Kerala Model?", *Economic and Political Weekly* 31(10): 625-30.

Goldin, C. (1995). "The U-Shaped Female Labor Force Function in Economic Development and Economic History", in T.P. Schultz (ed.). *Investment in Women's Human Capital*. Chicago: The University of Chicago Press.

Government of Kerala (2003). "Economic Review". Thiruvananthapuram: State Planning Board.

Horton, Susan (ed.) (1996). *Women and Industrialisation in Asia*. London: Routledge.

Mathew, E.T. (1997). *Employment and Unemployment in Kerala, Some Neglected Aspects*. New Delhi: Sage Publications.

Mincer, Jacob (1962). *Labor Force Participation of Married Women: A Study of Labour Supply*. Princeton, NJ. Aspects of Labour Economic Research.

Mukherjee, C. and T.M. Thomas Issac (1994). *A Review of the self Employment Programmes for Educated Unemployment in Kerala- Some Neglected Aspects*. New Delhi: Sage Publications.

Nagaraj, K. (1999). "Labour Market Characteristics and Employment Generation Programmes in India" in Barbara Harriss-White and S. Subramanian (eds.), *Ill-fare in India*. New Delhi: Sage Publications.

Navaneetham, K. and K.P. Kannan (2004). Educated Labour Force in Kerala: Pattern, Structure and Issues, Background paper prepared for Kerala Human Development Report, Centre for Development Studies.

Osella, Filippo and Caroline Osella (2000). *Social Mobility in Kerala: Modernity and Identity in Conflict*. London: Pluto.

Psacharopoulos, G. and Z. Tzannatos (1991). "Female Labor Force Participation and Education", in G. Psacharopoulos (ed.) *Essays on Poverty, Equity and Growth*. Oxford: Pergamon Press for the World Bank.

Sadie, J.L. (1965). *Proceedings of the World Population Conference Belgrade*. Vol. 1. Moderator's Report. Summary Report. New York: Department of Economic and Social Affairs. pp.219-24.

Schultz, T. Paul (1991). "International Differences in Labour Force Participation in Families and Firms", Papers 634. Yale-Economic Growth Centre.

Zachariah, K.C., E.T. Mathew and S. Irudaya Rajan (2003). *Dynamics of Migration in Kerala. Dimensions, Determinants and Consequences*. London: Orient Longman Pvt. Limited.

Section IV

Ageing

9

Population Ageing

S. IRUDAYA RAJAN and SABU ALIYAR

The sharp increase in numbers of older people and their proportion in relation to the working age population is a worldwide phenomenon, with vast economic and social implications. In India, the process is occurring much faster in the south, as compared to the northern states (Rajan, 2005). Among the south Indian states, Kerala is unique. As it is demographically ahead of the rest of the country and is in the final stages of the demographic transition (to low fertility and mortality), the ageing scenario of Kerala is much more prominent than in any other state in India (Zachariah and Rajan, 1997). For instance, a child born today in Kerala is expected to live over 71 years of age. (The female child is expected to live 76 years, six more than her male counterparts.) The younger age group, on the other hand, is shrinking. Thus, on an average, a woman in Kerala ends up producing just 1.6 children, which is a below replacement level of fertility. The recently released 2001 census shows that Kerala has more than 10 per cent of its population comprising of elderly. We have to give more attention to ameliorating their conditions.

In Kerala, as in other parts of the country, families have customarily supported elderly persons. With Kerala having undergone the demographic transition, however, the number of caregivers in families has been on the decline. Reduction in family size, national and international job-seeking flows out-migration, and a high work participation rate of women, have contributed to an attenuation of resources for the care of the elderly. At the same time, the increasing presence of older persons in the state is making people of all ages more aware that we live in a diverse and multigenerational society. It is no longer possible to ignore ageing, regardless of whether one views it positively or negatively.

Even when families can support the older generation, they essentially have difficulty in doing so because people above 60 years today live much longer than those of former generations, and require care and medical treatment for many more years. Many older persons in Kerala who have worked in the formal sector and who have participated in pension or other income security schemes will be able to economically support themselves in varying degrees during their post-retirement years. However, most of them are not covered by any such schemes and earn their livelihood in the informal sector by working even at the age of 80 years. The majority of them are women. They have not been able, for one reason or another, to accumulate sufficient savings to ensure their well-being in old age. It is vital that the social safety nets should be extended to cover all elderly persons.

Population Ageing: Inter-state Analysis

As of 2001, India accommodates 77 million elderly people, a figure second only to the number of elderly in China. Twenty-nine million of India's elderly are above 70 years and 8 million are above 80. Uttar Pradesh led with the highest number of elderly (11 million), followed by Maharashtra (8.5 million), West Bengal (5.7 million) and Tamil Nadu (5.5 million). The smallest number of elderly is found in the union territory of Lakshadweep. In terms of the proportion of elderly in the population, the low fertility state of Kerala ranks number one, with 10.5 per cent of its population comprising of elderly in 2001. Punjab and Himachal Pradesh occupy the second largest position in terms of percentage of elderly, followed by states of Tamil Nadu (8.9) and Maharashtra (8.7). Dadra & Nagar Haveli registered the lowest proportion (4). The percentage of elderly in the 80 years and above category is highest in Himachal Pradesh (1.3 per cent), followed by Kerala (1.2 per cent).

India is one of the few countries in the world where males outnumber females. However, among the elderly, female life chances are higher. Thus, at any age, there are more widows than widowers. Moreover, according to the 2001 census, the sex ratio among Indian elderly of 60 years and above is 1028 females for 1000 males. The trend is in favour of males in the age group of 70+ years, but then, it becomes favourable to females in the population of 80 years and above. Kerala has recorded the highest sex ratio—1247 females per 1000 males. The situation improves further to 1319 among elderly of 70+ years, and 1472 among elderly of 80 years and above (Table 9.2).

Table 9.3 shows various indices of population ageing in India. Kerala has registered the highest median age (27.9 years), indicating its status as a forerunner of demographic transition, followed by Goa (27.6 years), Tamil Nadu (27 years) and Pondicherry (26.5 years).

The highest index of ageing in the country is also reported for Kerala (40.2), followed by Goa (33.9), Tamil Nadu (33) and Pondicherry (30.8). This is also true for median age and age dependency ratio.

Table 9.1

Elderly in India, 2001

Rank	*India/States*	*60+*		*70+*		*80+*	
		Population	*%*	*Population*	*%*	*Population*	*%*
	INDIA	76826245	7.5	29376651	2.9	8060098	0.8
01	Kerala	3338428	10.5	1402678	4.4	389332	1.2
02	Punjab	2200153	9.0	939859	3.9	299106	1.2
03	Himachal Pradesh	548890	9.0	245121	4.0	81152	1.3
04	Tamil Nadu	5545499	8.9	2097100	3.4	557029	0.9
05	Maharashtra	8464895	8.7	3094957	3.2	780039	0.8
06	Goa	112858	8.4	41928	3.1	10969	0.8
07	Pondicherry	81082	8.3	31939	3.3	8223	0.8
08	Orissa	3044221	8.3	1168791	3.2	293770	0.8
09	Uttaranchal	655726	7.7	258515	3.0	70331	0.8
10	Karnataka	4065985	7.7	1611495	3.0	457643	0.9
11	Andhra Pradesh	5798171	7.6	2082435	2.7	505185	0.7
12	Haryana	1590118	7.5	656182	3.1	184587	0.9
13	Tripura	232896	7.3	106606	3.3	35296	1.1
14	Chhattisgarh	1506393	7.2	534077	2.6	135486	0.7
15	West Bengal	5708014	7.1	2275599	2.8	670812	0.8
16	Madhya Pradesh	4292242	7.1	1609752	2.7	436919	0.7
17	Uttar Pradesh	11701369	7.0	4470314	2.7	1273057	0.8
18	Gujarat	3502295	6.9	1310502	2.6	374579	0.7
19	Rajasthan	3829791	6.8	1473636	2.6	394208	0.7
20	Manipur	145775	6.7	61569	2.8	17211	0.8
21	Jammu & Kashmir	678384	6.7	274603	2.7	82415	0.8
22	Bihar	5513117	6.6	2046843	2.5	566871	0.7
23	Lakshadweep	3732	6.2	1288	2.1	381	0.6
24	Jharkhand	1580601	5.9	553844	2.1	148144	0.5
25	Assam	1562062	5.9	601856	2.3	169824	0.6
26	Mizoram	49066	5.5	20108	2.3	5313	0.6
27	Sikkim	29144	5.4	11018	2.0	2716	0.5
28	Delhi	720743	5.2	269146	1.9	70929	0.5
29	Daman & Diu	8045	5.1	2930	1.9	811	0.5
30	Chandigarh	44977	5.0	18170	2.0	5216	0.6
31	Andaman & Nicobar Islands	17478	4.9	6222	1.7	1676	0.5
32	Meghalaya	105870	4.6	39790	1.7	11258	0.5
33	Arunachal Pradesh	49967	4.6	18063	1.6	5655	0.5
34	Nagaland	90540	4.5	37709	1.9	13644	0.7
35	Dadra & Nagar Haveli	8818	4.0	2618	1.2	611	0.3

Source: Based on the 2001 census.

Table 9.2

Sex Ratio among Elderly, 2001 Census

India/State	*Sex Ratio (Females per 1000 males)*		
	60+	*70+*	*80+*
INDIA	1028	991	1051
Andaman and Nicobar Islands	766	827	932
Sikkim	772	734	752
Nagaland	780	786	765
Jammu and Kashmir	846	820	837
Bihar	882	827	811
Uttar Pradesh	886	821	830
Arunachal Pradesh	889	892	900
Chandigarh	891	887	953
Assam	949	876	923
Meghalaya	957	991	1050
Delhi	963	925	996
Punjab	971	865	922
Mizoram	977	1019	1184
Lakshadweep	979	1024	1177
Manipur	986	988	1033
Haryana	991	863	884
Uttaranchal	1002	952	984
Jharkhand	1005	945	891
Tamil Nadu	1013	977	1040
Himachal Pradesh	1021	997	1027
Orissa	1022	958	892
West Bengal	1047	1032	1093
Tripura	1064	1105	1230
Rajasthan	1084	1108	1261
Madhya Pradesh	1084	1112	1240
Andhra Pradesh	1099	1051	1215
Karnataka	1111	1137	1258
Gujarat	1148	1239	1410
Maharastra	1150	1063	1218
Chhattisgarh	1181	1182	1175
Pondicherry	1222	1239	1249
Daman & Diu	1239	1370	1886
Kerala	1247	1319	1472
Goa	1260	1424	1553
Dadra & Nagar Haveli	1270	1381	1406

Table 9.3

Indices of Ageing, 2001 Census

State	*Median Age*	*Index of Ageing*	*Age Dependency Ratio*
Jammu and Kashmir	21.6	18.7	11.6
Himachal Pradesh	24.5	29.1	15.1
Punjab	24.2	28.8	15.2
Chandigarh	24.6	17.2	7.6
Uttaranchal	21.5	21.2	13.8
Haryana	21.8	20.9	13.3
Delhi	23.5	16.0	8.4
Rajasthan	20.1	16.9	12.8
Uttar Pradesh	19.6	17.2	13.6
Bihar	19.5	15.8	13.0
Sikkim	21.6	15.4	9.0
Arunachal Pradesh	19.8	11.3	8.3
Nagaland	20.0	12.4	7.7
Manipur	23.1	20.6	11.1
Mizoram	21.7	15.6	9.3
Tripura	23.3	21.6	12.3
Meghalaya	18.1	10.8	8.6
Assam	21.6	15.7	10.3
West Bengal	24.1	21.4	11.9
Jharkhand	20.6	14.7	10.8
Orissa	24.1	24.9	14.1
Chhattisgarh	22.3	19.6	13.0
Madhya Pradesh	21.1	18.4	13.1
Gujarat	23.6	21.0	11.5
Daman and Diu	23.7	18.6	7.5
Dadra and Nagar Haveli	22.3	11.3	6.6
Maharashtra	24.4	27.2	14.8
Andhra Pradesh	24.4	23.7	12.6
Karnataka	24.3	24.1	12.7
Goa	27.6	33.9	12.5
Lakshadweep	23.0	18.0	10.3
Kerala	27.9	40.2	16.5
Tamil Nadu	27.0	33.0	13.9
Pondicherry	26.5	30.8	12.6
Andaman and Nicobar Islands	24.5	16.7	7.5
All India	**22.7**	**21.1**	**13.1**

Ageing in Kerala

According to the first census (1961 census) of Kerala state (Kerala state was formed as an independent state in 1956), the number of elderly aged 60 and above was just 10 lakh. It increased to 26 lakh in 1991 (a 160 per cent increase). According to the latest 2001 census, Kerala had 33 lakh elderly persons representing around 10.5 per cent of the total population. Their numbers are expected to increase to 57 lakh in 2021 and 120 lakh in 2061 and the proportion is likely to reach 40 per cent in 2061. While the Kerala population is growing at less than one per cent, the growth of the elderly over the 1991-2001 decade was much faster, and the trend is likely to continue over the next few decades. Over 1961-1991, the growth rate among the old old hovered around 3 per cent. It is expected to register a growth rate of around 4 per cent in the coming decades.

Table 9.4

Demographic Profile of Elderly, 1961-2061

Year	*Number of Aged (millions)*			*Percentage Total*			*Growth Rate (per cent)*		
	60+	*70+*	*80+*	*60+*	*70+*	*80+*	*60+*	*70+*	*80+*
1961	0.99	0.36	0.09	5.1	1.9	0.4	-	-	-
1971	1.33	0.50	0.13	6.2	2.3	0.6	3.47	3.66	4.71
1981	1.91	0.71	0.19	7.5	2.8	0.7	4.38	4.35	4.88
1991	2.57	1.00	0.29	8.9	3.4	1.0	3.48	4.06	5.59
2001	3.33	1.40	0.39	10.5	4.4	1.2	2.94	3.99	3.45
2011	4.20	1.94	0.54	12.2	5.6	1.6	2.61	3.86	3.85
2021	5.75	2.46	0.76	16.0	6.8	2.1	3.69	2.68	4.07
2031	7.78	3.52	1.01	21.3	9.7	2.7	3.53	4.31	3.29
2041	9.88	4.86	1.48	27.8	13.7	4.2	2.70	3.81	4.65
2051	11.48	6.22	2.11	34.4	18.6	6.3	1.62	2.80	4.26
2061	11.95	7.18	2.76	39.6	23.8	9.1	0.41	1.54	3.08

Note: Compiled by the authors for the periods 1961-2001 using the Indian censuses. The figures for the years from 2001 to 2061 are extracted from the population projections done by the authors.

The number of the oldest old (aged 80 and above) in Kerala was just 2,90,000 in 1991. It is expected to increase to 8 lakh in 2021 and further to 27 lakh by 2061. The growth rates among the oldest old is higher than the young old and old old in Kerala over the last 40 years and it is expected to slow down in the coming decades. The age pyramids for Kerala are presented (2001 and 2061) to indicate the speed of ageing in Kerala. Though the number of elderly in Kerala is much lower as compared to the populous states of India, Kerala leads with the highest proportion of elderly among

Indian states and union territories, and has relatively more women as compared to male elderly than in any other state in India. Kerala has the highest female expectation of life at birth and the gender gap was around 6 years in 2000. At age 60, a Malayali woman is expected to live 21 years, as against 19 years in the case of their male counterparts.

Figure 9.1

Age Pyramids for Kerala, 2001 and 2061

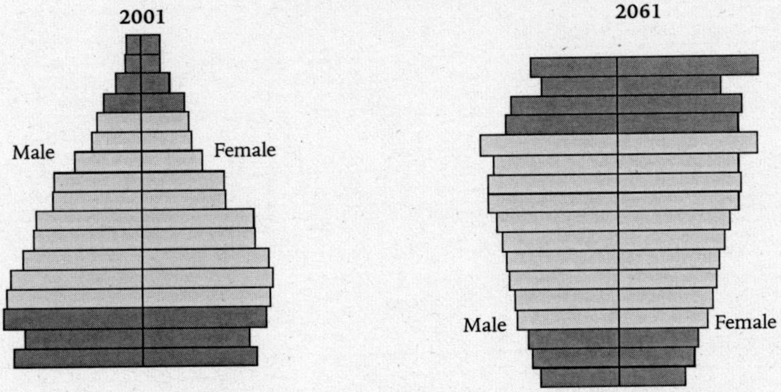

Figure 9.2

Sex Ratio among Elderly in Kerala 2001-2061

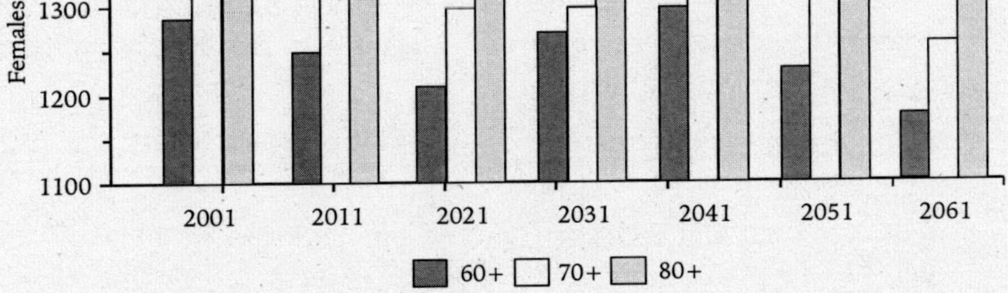

Figure 9.3

Expected Crossover Between the Young and the Aged in Kerala

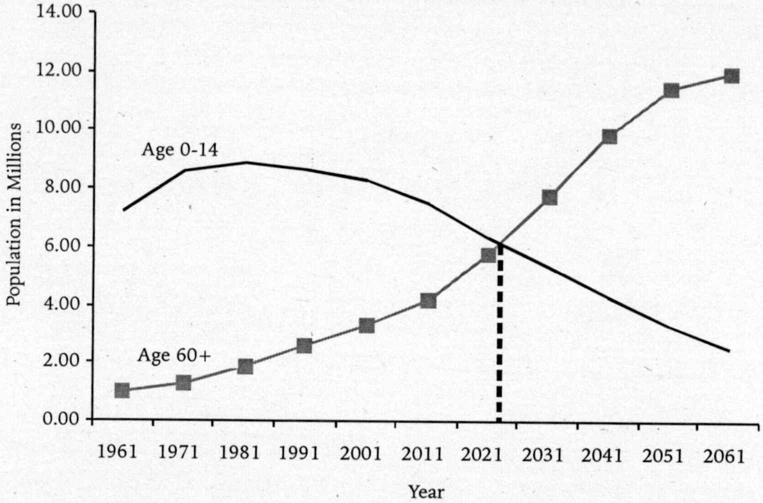

Dependency Ratios

The following ratios are presented for Kerala for the periods 1961 to 2061 (Table 9.5).

- *Young Dependency Ratio*: The number of persons aged 0-14 to per 100 persons of intermediate age (working age 15-59).
- *Aged Dependency Ratio*: The number of persons aged 60 years and above per 100 persons of working age (15-59).
- *Total Dependency Ratio*: The number of persons in the non-working age group (0-14 and 60+) to per 100 persons of working age (15-59).
- *Index of Ageing*: The proposition of the population aged 60 and above to the population aged 0-14. It is intended to measure the structure of dependency.
- *Index of Children*: The population of aged 0-14 per 100 to population aged 60 years and above.
- *Index of Parents to Children*: The population aged 60-74 per 100 to population aged 40-44.
- *Index of Oldest Old to Young Old*: The population aged 80 years above per 100 to population aged 60-64.

The young dependency ratio, 82.7 in 1961, declined to 75.2 in 1971, 61.5 in 1981 and 49.9 in 1991, whereas the aged dependency ratio increased from

11.3 in 1961 to 11.6 in 1971, further to 13.2 in 1981 and 14.4 in 1991 respectively. The increase of the aged dependency ratio was by 3 points whereas the decrease in the child dependency ratio was by 23 points. At the present juncture, households in Kerala have gained in terms of reduced burden of dependents, having to take care of fewer children without having too much strain of having to care for elderly persons. Currently, every 100 persons in the working age group take care of 17 old people.

The decline in fertility has reduced the overall dependency burden from 94.0 in 1961 to 64.3 in 1991. Though the aged dependency ratios are on the increase, the overall dependency ratio has shown a decline of 30 points during 1961-1991.

The projected age dependency ratios for the period 2001-2061 are also shown in the same table. During this period, the young dependency ratios are expected to decline from 41 in 2001 to 16 in 2061. On the other hand, the aged dependency ratios are expected to increase from 17 in 2001 to 76 in 2061. The implications of these ratios for the future is that, instead of every six working age persons there would be only two working persons in 2061 who will have to share the responsibility of taking care of at least one aged person. Moreover, the probability of this aged person being a woman, who is a widow, less skilled, less educated and not working, non-recipient of social security allowance, unhealthy without health insurance, is also much higher.

Table 9.5

Dependency Ratios, Ageing Index and Familiar Dependency Ratios for Kerala, 1961-2061

Year	*Dependency Ratio*			*Familial Dependency Ratio*			
	Young	*Old*	*Total*	*Index of Ageing*	*0-14/ 60+*	*60-74/ 40-44*	*80+/ 60-64*
1961	82.7	11.3	94.0	13.7	731	105	23
1971	75.2	11.6	86.9	15.5	647	107	26
1981	61.5	13.2	74.7	21.6	466	134	27
1991	49.9	14.4	64.3	28.9	370	136	33
2001	41.1	16.5	57.6	40.1	250	130	38
2011	32.8	18.4	51.2	56.1	178	123	42
2021	26.6	24.0	50.6	90.4	111	148	44
2031	22.8	33.3	56.1	146.2	68	194	45
2041	20.3	46.3	66.6	228.2	44	255	55
2051	18.1	61.9	80.0	342.7	29	332	78
2061	16.0	76.1	92.0	476.1	21	377	109

Note: All ratios refer to 100.

The index of ageing, nearly 14 in 1961, increased to 15 in 1971 and 29 in 1991. We can also see from the table that the increase between 1961 and 1971 was by only 2 points, whereas this increase was 6 points between 1971 and 1981 and another 7 points between 1981 and 1991 indicating the acceleration of the ageing process in Kerala. Our projections indicate that the ageing index for the year 2041 will be 228, 5 times higher than 2001's value of 40. This simply means that in Kerala, the rate of increase among elderly persons will be much higher. In 2061, there is likely to be 476 elderly persons for every 100 children in Kerala.

In other words, in the future, every household in Kerala has to take care of one child and an aged mother or father or both. The implications of this to the family would be quite substantial as the cost and care of an older person is different from that of a child.[1] For society, this shift in the dependency structure will mean a substantial change in the type of public sector expenditure. Furthermore, while the care of the child is the direct responsibility of the parents, the care of the extreme elderly has only a social obligation without any legal sanction.

Migration Surveys, 1999 and 2004

The Centre for Development Studies completed two migration surveys in Kerala in 1999 and 2004, covering 10,000 households throughout the state (Zachariah *et al.*, 2003; Zachariah and Rajan, 2004). We have extensively tabulated raw data from this source for this chapter so as to assess the various issues pertaining to the elderly.

In 1999, around 58 per cent of households in Kerala did not have any elderly persons. The number declined further to 52 per cent in 2004—a decline of six percentage points—indicating a changing household atmosphere, due to which the elderly do not stay with other members of the family. As almost half of the households in Kerala have no elderly persons to live with, they do not understand the advantages and disadvantages of elderly persons living with them. Another 33 per cent of households in Kerala accommodate just one elderly—either a widow or widower of either from the husband's or wife's side. Two elderly living in the same households have gone up from 11 per cent to 14 per cent, indicating an increase in the life expectancy among elderly males and females. Almost one in six couples in Kerala live beyond 60 as couples without losing their partners. Households with more than three elderly formed less than one per cent in 2004.

---

1. In a recent discussion with a group of elderly in an institutional setup, an elderly couple remarked to the senior author: "We want to stay with our children and grandchildren but they are not interested in us, hence we stay alone, and ourselves manage our day to day affairs."

Table 9.6

Distribution of Households by the Number of Elderly, 1999 and 2004

No. of Elderly	*2004*	*1999*
Nil	51.46	58.00
One	33.47	31.00
Two	14.19	10.50
Three	0.76	0.50
Four	0.12	0.00

Note: Special tabulations from the Kerala Migration Survey and South Asian Migration Surveys.

To understand the district profile, we have tabulated the proportion of elderly in all districts of Kerala for the years 1999 and 2004, from the migration surveys. The results are presented in Table 9.7. Between 1999 and 2004, the proportion of elderly to the total population in Kerala has increased from 11 to 14 in the last five years. Among the districts of Kerala, in 2004, the highest proportion of elderly is found in Pathanamthitta, followed by Kottayam. Ernakulam, Alappuzha and Thiruvananthapuram districts were above the state average. The lowest proportion was found in Wayanad. However, 12 out of 14 districts in Kerala have already crossed 10 per cent mark, with Pathanamthitta district showing the maximum of 21 per cent—double than the Malappuram figure. Districts which were the forerunners in the fertility and mortality transition, have reported higher proportion of elderly (Guilmoto and Rajan, 2001; 2002; 2005). In 2004, almost all the districts of Kerala have reported more proportion of female elderly in the population than males, except the three districts of Kollam, Idukki and Malappuram. Hence, any social policy measures to enhance the welfare of the elderly should take note of this phenomenon.

Among the elderly in Kerala, close to 56 per cent belong to young old (60-69 years). Another 31 per cent are old old (70-79 years) and only 13 per cent are oldest old (80 and above). Among the elderly, there are more females than males (Gulati and Rajan, 1999). The sex ratio (males per 1000 females) of all the elderly age groups indicates the preponderance of women among elderly. In the age group 85 and above, there are 647 males for 1000 females. Most of the women lose their husbands in old age due to sex differentials in mortality and age differentials at the time of marriage. This is reflected among the sex ratios of the widowed. All these dimensions of widowhood among the aged should be considered very seriously when formulating economic and social security measures.

Table 9.7

District-wise Proportion of Elderly Population in Kerala, 1999 and 2004

Districts	*1999*			*2004*		
	Male	*Female*	*Total*	*Male*	*Female*	*Total*
Thiruvananthapuram	10.60	11.10	10.90	13.62	13.92	13.77
Kollam	10.70	12.00	11.40	13.21	12.27	12.73
Pathanamthitta	17.50	13.60	15.50	20.48	21.21	20.86
Alappuzha	13.90	13.10	13.40	14.29	15.60	14.97
Kottayam	12.80	12.60	12.70	17.30	19.34	18.32
Idukki	8.90	6.10	7.60	11.43	9.47	10.47
Ernakulum	12.00	13.30	12.70	15.01	16.31	15.67
Thrissur	10.50	12.00	11.30	12.25	13.89	13.11
Palakkad	11.70	11.30	11.50	12.57	14.27	13.47
Malappuram	7.90	7.70	7.70	9.64	9.58	9.61
Kozhikode	10.00	11.00	10.50	13.15	13.07	13.11
Wayanad	7.40	7.60	7.50	8.57	10.14	9.38
Kannur	8.70	10.20	9.40	12.06	13.60	12.87
Kasaragod	8.00	8.60	8.30	10.51	10.53	10.52
Kerala	10.70	11.00	10.90	13.17	13.85	13.52

Note: Special tabulations from the Kerala Migration Survey and South Asian Migration Surveys.

Table 9.8

Age Structure of Elderly in Kerala, 2004

Age	*Male*	*Female*	*Total*	*Sex Ratio M/F*1000*
60-64	30.44	31.02	30.75	869
65-69	25.24	25.86	25.57	865
70-74	19.45	17.67	18.50	975
75-79	12.60	12.13	12.35	921
80-84	7.86	7.29	7.56	956
85+	4.17	5.61	4.94	647

Note: Special tabulations from the South Asian Migration Surveys.

The majority of the men (86 per cent) were married; but among women, the majority (56 per cent) came under the 'widowed' category. Similarly, close to 5 per cent of women were reported as either single or divorced or separated as against 2.5 per cent among men. Women require more social and economic attention in old age as most of them have no property or assets in their name. In an earlier study, around 60 per cent of rural and urban elderly females and 30 per cent of rural and urban males in India had no valuable assets in their name. Among the major states in India, Kerala ranks first in this regard, with 76 per cent of its elderly women reporting no financial assets in their name (Rajan, 2004)

Table 9.9

Marital Status of the Elderly in Kerala, 2004

Marital Status	*2004*		
	Male	*Female*	*Total*
Single	2.0	3.1	2.6
Married	85.9	39.4	61.2
Widowed	11.5	55.9	35.1
Divorced/separated	0.4	1.4	1.0

Note: Special tabulations from the Kerala Migration Surveys.

We have also analysed the status of current co-residence arrangements among the Kerala elderly by sex as of 2004. Interestingly, in both Kerala and India, 2.5 per cent of elderly live alone in their respective households (Rajan and Kumar, 2003). Four per cent of them are females and most likely, all of them are widows. Another 8 per cent of elderly live with their spouses. Three-fourth of elderly males live with their spouses, children and grandchildren compared to 50 per cent in the case of females. On the other hand, almost 40 per cent of females live in Kerala without spouses but with their children and grandchildren as against just 11 per cent in the case of males. Elderly living with strangers or non-relatives in a household is not common in Kerala. The number of old age homes in Kerala is 134, one-fifth of India's number. Currently, at least 5 old age homes are coming up every year. The number of inmates reported in the survey was 5076 persons, of which 60 per cent are females (Rajan, 2002).

Table 9.10

Living Arrangements among Elderly in Kerala, 2004

Living Arrangement	*Male*	*Female*	*Total*
Living alone	0.95	3.94	2.54
With spouse alone	10.56	5.07	7.65
With spouse, children and grandchildren	76.11	50.51	62.54
Without spouse but with children, grandchildren	11.42	38.47	25.76
Without spouse, but with relatives other than children and grandchildren	0.79	1.87	1.36
With non-relatives	0.17	0.15	0.16
Total	100	100	100

Note: Special tabulations from the Kerala Migration Surveys.

Social Security

Kerala has made remarkable progress in its demographic transition. The state has achieved below replacement level of fertility two decades ahead of the all-India target year of 2011. The TFR (total fertility rate denotes the average number of children that would be born to a woman during her life time, if she passes through her child bearing years confirming the current age specific fertility rates) declined from a high level of 5.6 in 1951-1961 to about 1.7 in 1993, a level which is very much below the replacement level of 2.05. The population growth rate has declined to about 1 per cent per annum in 1995 from 2.3 per cent per year during 1961-1971. Among all the states of India, longevity is highest in Kerala, for both men and women (Zachariah and Rajan, 1997; Rajan and Zachariah, 1998). While Kerala has the unique distinction of being the first state in India to complete the demographic transition, one of the immediate consequences has been population ageing. In this context, let us briefly assess the social security programmes in Kerala.

Successive governments in Kerala have introduced 35 social security and assistance schemes, which are currently being implemented. Among the southern states, Kerala spends close to 3 per cent of its budget for social security programmes and for the neighbouring states of Tamil Nadu and Karnataka, the expenditure ranges between 2.3 and 2.5. Brief details about each scheme such as eligibility criteria, year of introduction and annual expenditure incurred are given elsewhere (Rajan *et al.*, 1999). The schemes are classified into four categories and we shall list the programmes meant for elderly.

A. **Schemes which are fully financed by the state and Central governments:**

1 National Old Age Pension

B. **Schemes which are fully financed by the state:**

2 Kerala Destitute and Widow Pension Scheme

3 Kerala Agricultural Workers Pension Scheme

4 Special Pension Scheme for the Physically Handicapped and Mentally Retarded

5 Old Age Pension to Craftsmen

6 Pension to Sportsmen in Indigent Circumstances

7 Pension to Journalists in Indigent Circumstances

8 Pension to Cine Artists in Indigent Circumstances

9 Pension to Freedom Fighters

10 Pension to Second World War Veterans

C. **Major schemes which are financed with partial state support:**

11 Kerala Coir Workers' Welfare Fund

12 Kerala Construction Workers' Welfare Fund

13 Kerala Fishermen' Welfare Fund

D. **Schemes which are financed outside the budget and operated by respective boards:**

14 Kerala Headload Workers' Welfare Fund

15 Kerala Abkari Workers' Welfare Fund Scheme

16 Kerala Toddy Workers' Welfare Fund

17 Kerala Agricultural Workers' Welfare Fund

Among the programmes, the highest number of beneficiaries is reported for agricultural worker pension (5.3 lakh), followed by widow/destitute pension (2.1 lakh), pension for persons with disabilities (1.5 lakh) and national old age pensions (1.4 lakh) (for details see Table 9.11). In total, close to 12 lakh elderly persons are receiving some financial assistance from the Kerala government. Do they get the money regularly? Is it enough for sustaining the livelihood? We have to do more field level research on this subject. In this chapter, we would like to document the agricultural workers pension scheme in detail.

Table 9.11

Social Assistance and Security Programme Beneficiaries in Kerala, 2003

Schemes	*Beneficiaries*
National old age pension	134600
Agricultural workers	527647
Widow/destitute pension scheme	208445
Special pension for persons with disabilities	148553
Building and construction workers	37969
Second world war veterans	5690
Handloom workers	7407
Tailoring workers	5450
Pension to journalists	398
Pension to toddy workers	14929
Coir workers	67000
Fishermen	28190
Ration dealers	252
Abkari workers	97
Cine artists	146
Khadi workers	17
Freedom fighters	8888
Kerala	1195678

Source: Compiled from the latest *Economic Review* published from the State Planning Board, Government of Kerala, Thiruvananthapuram.

The district level profiles of beneficiaries for the three major pension schemes are presented in Table 9.12. The highest number of agricultural pension beneficiaries is reported for Thiruvananthapuram, followed by Alappuzha and Kozhikode. On the other hand, Malappuram leads with the highest number of widow/destitute pension beneficiaries, followed by Kollam and Kozhikode. In terms of national old age pension schemes, Palakkad leads with the highest, followed by Kollam and Malappuram. Is there any link between the number of elderly persons and the number of beneficiaries? It calls for further investigation.

Table 9.12

Major Pension Scheme Beneficiaries in Kerala by Districts, 2003

District	*Agricultural Workers*	*Widow/Destitute Pension*	*National Old Age Pension*
Thiruvananthapuram	91024	26484	9292
Kollam	33077	28133	15971
Pathanamthitta	17933	6636	3641
Alappuzha	68500	13969	7569
Kottayam	33560	10770	8890
Idukki	7979	2792	3930
Ernakulum	33870	16426	13994
Thrissur	50650	19143	11708
Palakkad	57154	19593	18748
Malappuram	52846	29345	15175
Kozhikode	62085	27290	9454
Wayanad	11843	4475	1448
Kannur	42908	15195	9171
Kasaragod	15635	10131	5609
Kerala	527647	208445	134600

Agricultural Workers Pension Scheme

One of the major social assistance schemes implemented in Kerala is the Kerala Agricultural Workers Pension Scheme which came into existence in 1980 (for more details, see Gulati, 1990; Rajan *et al.*, 1999). The pension amount was originally fixed at Rs. 45; it was raised to Rs. 60 in 1987, to Rs. 70 in 1991 and again to Rs. 100 in 1996. According to the provisions of the scheme, the beneficiaries should be agricultural workers above the age of 60 and whose annual income does not exceed Rs. 11000 (State Planning Board, 2005). An agricultural worker is defined as workers, other than those covered by Plantation Labour Act, depending principally on agricultural wages for livelihood and residing within the state for a continuous period of at least 10 years, immediately preceding the date of application. Agricultural workers with physical infirmity are also eligible for pension. The State Labour Commissioner is the administrator of the scheme. The amount is payable once in three months, in January, April, July and October by money order.

In 1999, 3.1 lakh persons had benefited by the scheme, of which, 58 per cent were women. Kerala had 19.47 lakh agricultural labourers and the scheme covered 16 per cent of them. The expenditure on this pension scheme increased sharply from Rs. 1615 lakh in 1986-87 to Rs. 2690 lakh in 1991 and to Rs. 3720 lakh in 1999 (Table 9.13). The increase was due to increases in the coverage of workers and the upward revision of the rates effected in 1988 and 1991.

Table 9.13

Agricultural Workers Pension Scheme Beneficiaries and Its Expenditure, 1980-81 to 1999-2000

Year	*Beneficiaries*	*Expenditure (in lakhs)*
1980-81	293778	1092.3
1981-82	172376	744.2
1982-83	139817	446.0
1983-84	217659	1188.0
1984-85	250116	1132.0
1985-86	277821	1801.0
1986-87	261584	1615.0
1987-88	286733	1469.5
1988-89	299758	1925.7
1989-90	308346	2197.1
1990-91	316509	3062.3
1991-92	344301	2515.8
1992-93	340776	2690.3
1993-94	345650	3551.0
1994-95	344946	2000.0
1995-96	312944	3457.3
1996-97	312944	3457.3
1997-98	300784	4301.0
1998-99	304638	3720.0
1999-2000	436452	NA

Source: Various (annual) issues of *Economic Review*, the State Planning Board, Government of Kerala, Thiruvananthapuram.

Concluding Observations

Can Kerala afford to provide social security or assistance or financial security for the growing number of elderly? Let us assess it with facts and figures. According to the 2001 census, the number of elderly in Kerala in 2001 was 33 lakh. Kerala has approximately 4 lakh pensioners (retired from the Kerala government services plus retired from other state governments outside Kerala and returned to Kerala after retirement plus the military, railways, post and telegraph pensioners). In other words, close to 15 per cent of the elderly in Kerala are the creamy layers of the senior citizens. They are not looking for any assistance from the Kerala government.

The work participation rates among elderly based on the NSS 1999-2000 round was around 50 per cent for elderly in Kerala. One has to view these trends in work participation rates in the context of widespread poverty and inadequate social security system. In Kerala, even at the age of 80, 10 per cent of elderly continue to work. As long as they work, theoretically, they do not look for free money from the government.

Two other important observations also can be made in this context. The absolute number of children has come down in Kerala and it has already led the Kerala government to close uneconomic schools. It simply means that the government can divert some money from primary education to social security.

Similarly, the fertility levels in Kerala are too low and according to our own predications, it will hover around 1.5 children per woman. Recent studies indicated that more than 70 per cent of women in Kerala are protected by various family planning methods and 80 per cent of them are sterilised. What is the role of the family planning programme in Kerala in the future? If this is the ground situation in Kerala, the government can also divert some money from family planning to social security.

According to the latest economic review, around 12 lakh elderly are beneficiaries of various social security and assistance schemes in Kerala. They account for 40 per cent of the elderly population. Not even a single systematic study exists in Kerala to assess the real beneficiaries.

If the government can implement all the schemes very seriously and provide assistance to the real needy among elderly (the senior author filed observations which indicate starvation among Kerala elderly), Kerala can continue to run the social assistance schemes without much financial constraints. The budget for social welfare can be increased by diverting money from family planning and primary education. We hope that the government, through *panchayat* level institutions, will be able not only to identify the needy (real) beneficiaries but also enhance the financial assistance from the current level of Rs. 110 to Rs. 300 per month. (Incidentally, West Bengal pays Rs. 300 as old age pension.) For this, a bold step in the right direction is needed.

References

Christophe, Z. Guilmoto and S. Irudaya Rajan (2001). "Spatial Patterns of Fertility Transition in Indian Districts", *Population and Development Review* 27(4): 713-138.

———. (2005). *Fertility Transition in South India*. New Delhi: Sage Publications.

Gulati, Leela (1990). "Agricultural Worker's Pension in Kerala: An Experiment in Social Assistance", *Economic and Political Weekly* XXV(6): 339-344.

Gulati, Leela and S. Irudaya Rajan (1999). "The Added Years: Elderly in India and Kerala", *Economic and Political Weekly* XXXIV(44): WS-46-51.

Guilmoto, C.Z. and S. Irudaya Rajan (2002). "District Level Estimates of Fertility from India's 2001 Census", *Economic and Political Weekly* XXXVII(7): 665-672, February 16.

Irudaya, Rajan S. (1989). "Aging in Kerala: One More Population Problem?" *Asia-Pacific Population Journal* 4(2): 19-48. June.

———. (2001). "Social Assistance for Poor Elderly: How Effective?", *Economic and Political Weekly* XXXVI(8): 613-617. February 24.

———. (2002). "Home away from Home: A Survey of Oldage Homes and Inmates from Kerala, India", *Journal of Housing for the Elderly* 16(1 and 2): 125-150.

———. (2002). "Social Security for the Unorganized Sector in South Asia", *International Social Security Review* 55(4): 143-156.

———. (2004). "Chronic Poverty among Indian Elderly", Chronic Poverty Research Centre and Indian Institute of Public Administration *Working Paper* 17, Indian Institute of Public Administration, New Delhi.

———. (2005). "Introduction: Emerging Demographic Change in South India", in Christophe Z. Guilmoto and S. Irudaya Rajan, *Fertility Transition in South India*. New Delhi: Sage Publications. pp.23-52.

Irudaya, Rajan S. and K.C. Zachariah (1998). "Long Term Implications of Low Fertility in Kerala", *Asia-Pacific Population Journal* 13(4): 41-66.

Irudaya, Rajan S. and Sabu Aliyar (2004). "Demographic Change in Kerala in the 1990s and Beyond", in B.A. Prakash (ed.). *Kerala's Economic Development: Performance and Problems in the Post-Liberalization Period*. New Delhi: Sage Publications.

———. (2004). "Gender, Ageing and Social Security". *SAMYUKTA, Journal of Women's Studies* IV(2), July.

———. (2005). "Fertility Change in Kerala", in Christophe Z. Guilmoto and S. Irudaya Rajan (eds.). *Fertility Transition in South India*. New Delhi: Sage Publications. (forthcoming).

Irudaya, Rajan S. and Sanjay Kumar (2003). "Living Arrangements among the Indian Elderly: New Evidence from the National Family Health Survey", *Economic and Political Weekly* XXXVIII(1): 75-80. January 4.

Irudaya, Rajan S., U.S. Mishra and P.S. Sarma (1995). "An Agenda for National Policies on Aging in India", *Research and Development Journal, Journal of Helpage India* 1(2): 38-53.

———. (1999). *India's Elderly: Burden or Challenge?* New Delhi/Thousand Oaks/London: Sage Publications.

Jhabvala, Renana and R.K.A. Subrahmanya (eds.) (2000). *The Unorganized Sector: Work Security and Social Protection*. New Delhi: Sage Publications.

Phoebe, S. Liebig and S. Irudaya Rajan (eds.) (2003). *An Aging India: Perspectives, Prospects, and Policies*. New York, United States of America: The Haworth Press Inc.

Robert, J. Palacios and S. Irudaya Rajan (2004). "Safety Nets for the Elderly in Poor Countries: The Case of Nepal", World Bank Pension Primer *Working Paper* No. 44.

State Planning Board (1996). *Social Security Initiatives in Kerala—Report of the Expert Committee*. Thiruvananthapuram: Government of Kerala.

———. (2005). *Economic Review 2004*. Thiruvananthapuram: Government of Kerala.

Zachariah, K.C. and S. Irudaya Rajan (eds.) (1997). *Kerala's Demographic Transition: Determinants and Consequences*. New Delhi/Thousand Oaks/London: Sage Publications.

———. (2004a). *Gulf Revisited. Economic Consequences of Emigration from Kerala – Emigration and Unemployment*. Thiruvananthapuram: Centre for Development Studies.

———. (2004b). "Malayali Emigration Moving in to a Higher Orbit", *Passline* 8(7).

Zachariah, K.C., E.T. Mathew and S. Irudaya Rajan (2003). *Dynamics of Migration in Kerala: Determinants, Differentials and Consequences*. Orient Longman Private Limited.

10

Fiscal Pressure on Pension System

SYAM PRASAD

Introduction

In India as well as other countries, there used to be several mechanisms to provide economic and social safety nets to the economically and socially vulnerable groups. In broad terms, it is achieved through the formal or informal social security system that ensures equitable justice in the society (Heller, 2003). This notion of the safety net enabled in all societies led to the social security system.

It received widespread attention with the spread of the ideology of the paternalist state and its welfare norms originated in the human mind as a part of its social, ethical and political consciousness. Social security as a system evolved first in the Western countries during the industrial revolution. The two models under which social security systems can be classified are the German model (Bismarckian model or social security/social market economy model) and the British model (Beveridgean model or the basic-income model). The Bismarckian model focused on maintenance of living standards and the benefits were earnings-related; on the other hand, the Beveridgean model guaranteed only a subsistence income to all elderly people at a flat, universal rate (Armingeon *et al.*, 1999).

The civil pension is considered to be an important component of the broader concept of social security provision to the elderly to enable them to maintain a better life after their retirement. Broadly, pensions as a concept can be defined widely as retirement income contracts between the employee and employer and represent the benefit payable, either as a lump sum amount or in the form of annuities, by an employer to an employee, for the services rendered. Pensions are also viewed as means of transferring purchasing power from the working phase to the retirement phase of the life cycle (Algoed and Spinnewyn, 2000).

The Supreme Court of India (1982) defined pension as 'a term applied to periodic money payments to a person who retires at a certain age considered age of disability; payments usually continue for the rest of the natural life of the recipient'. The pension provision should target at poverty relief, consumption smoothing and insurance in respect of longevity (Barr, 2000). According to the Asian Development Bank (ADB), old age pensions are designed to meet the requirements of an individual when, due to ageing, his/her capacity for work declines to the point where he/she is unable to be self sufficient (ADB, 2001). The World Bank (1994) argues that pension should have an objective of consumption smoothening and the acceleration of social insurance in the context of extended longevity of life. In short, pension can be considered as a means of livelihood to the elderly.

In general, government through public pillar of government leads the provisioning of the pensions and social security to the elderly. This chapter mainly looks into the state supported pension system in India and its fiscal pressure on the eve of living long as a process of ageing with special focus on the most ageing state of Kerala.

The Pension System in India

In the traditional Indian society, the family relationships and moral ethics had maintained an informal way of caring for the elderly. The complexity of the modern society and a paradigm shift in the demographic scenario had resulted in an inadequacy of the informal elder caring system (Goswami, 2001). Available evidence suggests that the origin of social security in India dates back to third century B.C. Different social assistance institutions and welfare centres were established in the ancient Indian society, which were concerned with the relief and alleviation of sickness, poverty and distress (Srivastava, 1966).

In modern India, we do not have a universal social security system to protect the elderly against economic deprivation. Perhaps, higher levels of poverty and unemployment act as deterrents to institute a pay-roll tax financed state pension arrangement for each and every citizen attaining old age. Instead, India has adopted a social insurance and pension policy that largely hinges on financing through employer and employee participation and restricting the coverage to the organised sector workers. In India, the most important state sponsored and also unfunded pay-as-you-go (PAYG) pension system is that which consist of the civil service pensions. It is mainly restricted to the formal employees in the organised government sector.

The Civil Service Pensions in India

The history of a formal civil service pension system in India can be traced back to the colonial period. The first award regarding pension benefits for government employees were given by the Royal Commission on Civil Establishments in 1881 (Goswami, 2001). This was essentially contributory in character; members of the Indian Civil Service were to contribute four per cent of their basic salary. Apart from a pension, the civil servants were also entitled to a family pension under the Indian Civil Service Family Pension rules. These pensions and other benefits payable under these rules were divided into two portions *viz.*, those met from contributions of subscribers and those met from the exchequer.

On the recommendations of the Royal Commission presided by Lord Islington, four per cent contribution that the employee had to make to earn the pension was abolished in 1920 and the Government undertook to meet the full expenditure on the pension. However, in order to earn a full pension, a worker should have completed the full term of 25 years. In the Government of India Act, 1919, provisions were made for retiring those who joined government service before 1920 as temporary employee were eligible to get pension at proportion to his service in the job at the time of retirement.

In 1924, the Lee Commission apart from recommending an increase in pension, also recommended that if and when the work for which a civilian had been recruited was transferred, it should be optional for that employee to retire on a proportionate pension. Further, provident fund was suggested as an alternative to pension system for all future recruits. Also, the Indian civil servant could, under certain conditions, commute for a lump sum payment not more than half of any pension that was statutorily granted.

The Government of India Act, 1935 also protected the rights and privileges of the members of the civil services (Srivastava, 1966). These schemes were later consolidated and then enlarged to provide retirement benefits to all who retired from government employment, later to entire public sector workers. It acted as a guideline to the sanctioning of civil service pensions in independent India.

The civil service pension system (CSPS) covers the entire gamut of the salaried workers in Central and state governments and union territory administrations in independent India. Within the Central government, pension schemes are organised for different departments and ministries with separate rules—which have somewhat different rules of eligibility—for railways, telecommunications, defence and other Central government employees. These benefit programmes are typically run on a PAYG, defined-benefit basis. The schemes are non-contributory; and the entire pension expenditure is charged to the annual revenue expenditure account of the Government. Table 10.1 gives an overview various of pension provisions in India.

In general, the basic pension amount is calculated with reference to average basic pay drawn by the state government employee during the last 10 months of service. The basic pension is computed on the basis of the last pay drawn by the employee. The full pension amount is 50 per cent of the average pay, payable to employees who have completed 33 years of qualifying service.

Table 10.1

Types of Civil Service Pensions in India

(i)	**Superannuation Pension:** A Government servant who retires on attaining the age of superannuation is granted this pension (Rule 35).
(ii)	**Retiring Pension:** A Government servant who retires or is retired prior to the stipulated age of superannuation or under FR 56 or Article 459 of civil service rules (CSR) and also one who opts for voluntary retirement on being declared surplus, are granted this pension (Rule 36).
(iii)	**Invalid Pension:** A Government servant who is retired from service on account of any bodily or mental infirmity, which permanently incapacitates him/her for the service, is eligible for Invalid Pension, which is granted only on the recommendation of a Medical Board constituted for the purpose (Rule 38).
(iv)	**Compensation Pension:** A Government servant who is discharged from service owing to the abolition of his/her permanent post is granted this pension (Rule 39).
(v)	**Compulsory Retirement Pension:** A Government servant who is retired compulsorily from service as a measure of penalty is granted this pension. An authority can sanction him/her either pension or gratuity or both at a rate not less than 2/3rd and not more than full compensation pension or gratuity or both (Rule 40).
(vi)	**Compassionate Allowance:** A Government servant who is dismissed or removed from service by the Competent Authority, and if the case deserves special consideration, is granted this allowance. Such allowance shall not exceed 2/3rd of pension or gratuity or both which would have been admissible to him/her had he/she retired on compensation pension (Rule 41).
(vii)	**Pension on absorption in or under a Corporation/Company/Body:** A Government servant who has been permitted to be absorbed in or under a corporation, company or body substantially owned or controlled by the Central government/state government in or under a body controlled or financed by Central government/state government is allowed this benefit.

Source: Report of High Level Expert Group on New Pension System, Govt. of India, 2002.

There are three types of gratuity available to Central and state government employees as retirement benefits from the government, which are financed by state's revenue:

Retirement Gratuity: A minimum of five years qualifying service is essential to make an employee eligible to get this one time lump sum benefit. Retirement gratuity is calculated at the rate of one-fourth of the last basic pay for each completed six monthly period of qualifying service.

Death Gratuity: This is one time lump sum benefit payable to the nominee of the deceased employee.

Service Gratuity: An employee is entitled to receive gratuity (and not pension), if total-qualifying services is less than 10 years. Admissible amount is half-month basic pay for each completed six monthly period of qualifying service. There is no maximum or minimum monetary limit on the quantum. This one time lump sum payment is paid over and above the retirement gratuity.

The provision of the commutation of pension as integral part of the pension provision in India is followed in almost every state. A pensioner has the option to commute a portion of his/her pension, not exceeding 40 per cent of basic pension, as a lump sum payment from exchequer. Some state governments, however, limit the commutation amount to one-third of the basic pension. The lump sum amount payable is calculated with reference to the commutation table constructed on an actuarial basis. The commuted pension is deducted from monthly pension, full time pensions is being restored on the expiry of 15 years from the date of receipt of the commuted value of pension. Dearness relief on pension, however, continues to be calculated on the basis of the original pension, i.e., without reduction of commuted portion.

The civil servants in India are acknowledged to get the benefit from other pension benefits such as provident funds. The pension coverage under the banner of state sponsored pension system becomes more extensive if we include the pension schemes under Employees Provident Fund Organisation (EPFO), which are partially funded by either state or Central government. In all the states, pension schemes cover all state government employees. With regard to the employees of grant-in-aid institutions (GIA), the pension schemes differ across the states. With regard to GIA institutions, which are mostly educational institutions, in some states are fully covered by the government pensions. For example, in West Bengal, the number of pensioners belonging to direct state government service is more or less the same as that belonging to GIA institutions and local bodies. As a result of increased coverage and with rise in longevity, there has been a phenomenal growth in the number of the pensioners occurred in India.

Table 10.2 provides the coverage of the government pension system in India under civil pensions both at Centre and state including partially funded EPFO. In the year 2004, there were 85 lakh government pensioners with both Centre and state governments with almost identical share while it was around 52 lakh in the year 1991 and around 60 lakh in the year 1996. There was witnessed a sharp increase in the number of pensioners in India both under state and Central government. They account for about 11.5 per cent of the elderly in India.

Table 10.2

Civil Service Pensioners in India, 1991-2004 (31st March)

Years	*Central Government Pensioners*	*State Government Pensioners*	*Government Pensioners*
1990-91	2594237	2568737	5162974
1991-92	2638184	2611933	5250117
1992-93	2716390	2689361	5405751
1993-94	2797200	2769367	5566566
1994-95	2880821	2852156	5732977
1995-96	2967202	2937677	5904879
1996-97	3105234	3074336	6179570
1997-98	3376717	3343118	6719835
1998-99	3430868	3396730	6827597
1999-2000	3829218	3250000	7079218
2000-01	3938806	3365400	7304206
2001-02	4046396	3525000	7571396
2002-03	4152682	3855456	8008138
2003-04	4256062	4214228	8470290

Source: Calculated from CSO abstracts.

The Civil Service Pensions in Kerala

The pension system in Kerala is mandatory to the civil servants, government employees and other employees of aided private college and school staff and governed by the Kerala Service Rules (KSR, 2000). According to existing service rules, the pension and other retirement benefits can be extended to other autonomous institutions and local bodies at the discretion of the state government (KSR, 2002). In Kerala at present, civil service pension covers almost the entire workforce in the government, public sector undertakings under Kerala government such as Kerala State Electricity Board, teachers and non-teaching staff of aided schools and colleges, and employees in local bodies.

The civil pension system in Kerala has a long history. In the time of the Cheras and later during the time of Zamorins, there existed a crude system of retirement benefits provided by the king to the members of the court and this expenditure had been met from the state's treasury. The provision of such kind was extended only to the servants of the royal court. This provision of that time was considered as one of the paternalist activities of the king to its servants for the lifelong service provided to the kingdom. The existing pension system of current nature is only a legacy of the last century. The government of Travancore introduced a comprehensive pension system for its employees in 1902 A.D (1077 Malayalam Era), which provided post-retirement benefits to the retirees from the administrative service of Travancore. In 1932 (1107 ME), the government introduced both superannuation pension and commutation benefits at the time of retirement. The provision of the retirement benefits was extended to other branches of government service other than administrative departments (Pillai, 1940).

Government had also introduced a system of state provident fund in 1932 for the government employees. The government servants had to contribute a part of their pay to get the retirement benefits either at the termination of the service or after the death of the employee. The contribution to this employee-funded scheme was compulsory to those appointed in the government service after 17th August 1932. In addition to it, government extended insurance coverage to the employees other than retirement benefits (Pillai, 1940). In 1957, with the formation of the Kerala state, there occurred a major policy shift on the part of the then government in order to enhance the welfare of the government servants. In 1958, government extended the pension and other retirement benefit to all government servants who are employed in Kerala government service with effect from 1st January 1955, either as a part of Madras provincial government or Travancore-Cochin government (Government order dated 8-11-1958).

With effect from 1968, the pension and other retirement benefits were extended to other institutions such as aided education institutions and other autonomous institutions, which fell directly under government jurisdiction and control. Since then, the pensions and other retirement benefits of the government servants became a right of the employees and an obligation from the part of the government. The pension benefits in Kerala have different components, multi-structural in character. The main components of the pension benefits to the government employees are as follows:

Superannuation Pension: A government servant who retires on attaining the age of retirement is granted this pension. By rule 1 of 151 of simplified pension rule and pension commutation rule, any retiree from Kerala government service has eligibility to get pension in the post-retirement period. Full pension at 50 per cent of the average pay is payable for those employees who have 33 years of qualifying service. For those employees who have not completed 33 years of service, the basic pension is calculated on a proportionate basis. A pensioner is eligible to get half if service is for 10 years.

The superannuation pension has two components, the basic pension and dearness allowance, which are frequently revised by the government. The basic pension is usually equated to 50 per cent of the basic pay drawn by the retiree in the last month of the service. The full pension accrued to the retiree is calculated on the basis of the basic pension indexed by using dearness allowances.

Retiring Pension: A government servant who retires or is retired prior to the age of superannuation or under FR 56 of Kerala service rules (KSR) and who opts for voluntary retirement on being declared surplus, are granted this pension. The pension benefits are mostly the same as in the case of normal pensions. Here, as per the rule if the retirement is after 20 years of service, there is eligibility for full pensions.

Invalid Pension: As per rule 32 of liberalised pension rule of 1966, a government servant who has retired from service on account of any bodily or mental infirmity, which permanently incapacitates him/her for the service, is eligible for Invalid Pension, which is granted only on the recommendation of a medical board constituted for the purpose. By the 1974 amendment, the minimum service requirement has been relaxed to 15 years to get full pensions.

Pension Commutation: A pensioner has the option to commute a portion of his/her pension, not exceeding 40 per cent of basic pension, into a lump sum payment, which is calculated with reference to a commutation table constructed on an actuarial basis that is reviewed by the government (Pension rule, 1966). The monthly pension will stand reduced by the portion commuted and the commuted portion will be restored on the expiry of 15 years from the date of receipt of the commuted value of pension.

Gratuity: Gratuity is another major component of the retirement benefit met by the government as a part of civil service pensions. Depending on the period of service, three types of gratuity are available to state employees: (i) retirement gratuity, (ii) death gratuity, and (iii) service gratuity. All types of gratuity are calculated on the basis of basic pay and service period. An employee with minimum of five years qualifying service is eligible to receive retirement gratuity/pension as a lump sum benefit. Retirement gratuity is calculated at the rate of one-fourth of the last basic pay for each completed six monthly period of qualifying service. The death gratuity is a lump sum benefit payable to the nominee of the deceased employee. Retirement gratuity and death gratuity are subject to a ceiling that varies across various levels of government employment in the state from Rs. 2.5 lakh to 3.5 lakh. An employee with less than 10 years of service is eligible to get a lump sum payment at the time of retirement not as pension. This is calculated on the basis of qualifying service in the government. In Kerala, it is half-month basic pay for each completed six monthly period of qualifying service (LPR Amendment, 1996) with minimum and maximum limit.

Family Pension: According to Kerala service rules as amended in 1972 and liberalised pension rule (Amendment, 1974), a family pension is provided to the dependent of a pensioner after his death. The pension is paid either to wife of the deceased pensioner, or to the children if they are minors, or to the daughter if she is unmarried (LPR, Amendment 1982). The family pension is granted on the basis of a calculation formula as in the case of other individual pensions and is indexed with variation of DA. The beneficiaries are eligible to receive the pensions as long as the dependent is alive. The benefits mentioned above are granted to those who retires from government employment in Kerala along with other non-pensionary benefits at the time of retirement such as leave encashment, government employees insurance schemes, etc. Besides, the individual's accumulation to the provident fund is that on which an interest is accrued to the employees on the decision of the government.

In general, the pensions and other retirement benefits have become an integral part of government service. The system provides an extensive coverage of the employees in various departments and other public sector and government aided institutions. There is an increase in the civil service pensioners in Kerala in the last two decades as the pensioners are living longer and change in the age structure of the employees. Moreover, there prevails a relatively low retirement age (55 years), resulting in an increase in the pensioners as more and more years are added to life.

Fiscal Pressure of Pension Burden in India

Throughout the developed world, the demographic transition and phenomenon of living longer have created fiscal imbalances. The low birth rates and increased longevity of life had pushed the population across the world into a vicious phenomenon of ageing, which has both short-run and long-run fiscal impact and it has serious implication on fiscal planning and forecasting (Auerbach and Lee, 2001).

In an ageing society, the government has to bear more expenditure on its welfare activities in the form of health and social security provisioning. The state administered pension system has been maturing alongside with the maturing of the population. The system's stability is to be disturbed as the PAYG system is being affected by the long span of life of the pensioners and less period of contribution by the workforce to the existing PAYG system as intergenerational liability. The demographic phenomenon had thus, put most of the pension system under severe economic pressure. The pension systems all over the world have been affected by the rapidly changing demographic regimes as a result of fast ageing population and the phenomenon of living longer (World Bank, 1994). The crisis of the pension system, which has traditionally state run, is largely due to the fact that the pensions contribute a sizeable part of government expenditure. As the population ageing gets accelerated, the system gets affected by the high incidence of the pension expenditure which is mostly paid out of payroll tax as the change in the age structure affects the intergenerational distribution across the old (pensioners) and young (workers) (Atkinson, 2001). The balance is also disturbed by the change in the life longevity of the period of pension to become lengthier than the period of the pay rolltax contribution by the same employee. As the ageing process advances, the state sponsored pension system has to bear large economic liability to be paid out of the fiscal expenditure. Thus, the pension system came on the verge of a crisis (World Bank, 1994). Various pension systems across the globe showed an element of the pension crisis, as there is an increased life expectancy. Thus, the widespread notion of the unsustainabilty of the government-run defined benefits and non-contributory pension system became a matter of concern (Swain and Sen, 2004).

At present, the salary and pension bill of both the Centre and the state governments accounts for a large share of the public expenditure from the fiscal front. They together constituted 9 per cent of GDP in 2003-04 while it was only 7.9 per cent in 1990-91. The increase in this expenditure was very sharp in the late nineties as a result of huge liability created in the context of Fifth Pay Commission recommendations.

The disaggregation of the government liability for salary and pensions shows that the share of pension expenditure as government liability is about 2.5 per cent of total GDP in 2003-04 as against 1.3 per cent in 1990-91. The pension expenditure of the government is even more than most of the other social sector expenditure of the government meant for the welfare and rehabilitation to the poor and socially disadvantaged groups.

The pension expenditure disaggregated by state and Centre shows an unprecedented increase in the pension expenditure in the nineties and in this decade. Table 10.3 indicates that the total pension liability went up from Rs. 6870 crore in 1990-91 to Rs. 49260 crore in 2001-02. During the same period, the pension expenditure of the country registered a growth of 16 per cent.

Table 10.3

Pension Liability of both Centre and States (Rs. in crores)

Year	*Centre*	*State*	*Total*
1990-91	3278.4	3592.0	6870.4
1991-92	3748.2	3715.0	7463.2
1992-93	4585.8	4379.0	8964.8
1993-94	5206.0	5107.0	10313.0
1994-95	5733.4	6123.0	11856.4
1995-96	6928.1	7813.0	14741.1
1996-97	8252.6	9826.0	18078.6
1997-98	11375.2	11667.0	23042.2
1998-99	15345.7	16166.3	31512.1
1999-2000	19444.9	22679.0	42123.9
2000-01	20617.7	25452.5	46070.2
2001-02	21411.3	27849.4	49260.7

Source: The pension expenditure calculated by the researcher based on budget and economic survey estimates.

The significance of this trend of the pension expenditure is that both the expenditure of the Centre and state governments witnessed almost same acceleration. The overall burden of Centre went up from Rs. 3278 crore in 1990-91 to Rs. 21411 crore in 2001-02 at an acceleration of 17 per cent per annum. While in the case of states, the same degree of acceleration was from Rs. 3592 crore to Rs. 27849 crore in the same period which resembles to an average growth of 16 per cent per annum. The emerging burden of the pension liability of the both governments reveals the fiscal stringency as a part of the "pension crisis" in India.

The "pension stringency" in India occurred in different states as the impact of demographic achievements and coverage of the pension system looks distinctly different in different states of India. The fiscal stress is very high in the states such as Tamil Nadu, Kerala, West Bengal, Andhra Pradesh, where the life expectancy and the coverage of pension system are considerably high. The extent of the fiscal stringency in the Indian states on the account of the rapidly rising pension expenditure can be measured in terms of two fiscal indicators: the pension expenditure as a share of revenue receipts and pension expenditure as a percentage of states own revenue. The share of the pension expenditure as a portion of the revenue receipt is one of the most visible sign of fiscal stringency arising from that of the pension system. At national level, the pension expenditure as a percentage of revenue expenditure accounts 12 per cent of the revenue expenditure of the government in 2001-02 as it was as low as 2 per cent in 1980-81 and 5 per cent in 1990-91. It may be noted that pension expenditure as a per cent of revenue expenditure went up sharply in the nineties and thus resulted in fiscal constraint. The desegregated figures of this expenditure (Table 10.4) reveal that there is a considerable difference in different states. The states like Kerala, Tamil Nadu, West Bengal, Bihar and Maharashtra are much above the national average. Kerala ranks highest among the states with more than 23 per cent of the revenue earmarked for the pension payment as a part of the revenue expenditure in 2001-02. The general trend of this indicator shows a faster growth of pension liability in almost every state in the late 1990s as a result of rising longevity and the implementation of the Fifth Pay Commission.

Table 10.4

Pension Payments of States as Per cent of Revenue Receipts

States	*1980-81*	*1990-91*	*2001-02*
Andhra Pradesh	3.2	6.2	10.6
Assam	1.3	2.8	12.3
Bihar	1.0	4.3	17.4
Gujarat	2.2	6.0	9.4
Haryana	1.2	3.7	8.6
Karnataka	4.6	6.9	10.7
Kerala	5.1	12.2	23.0
Madhya Pradesh	1.4	3.7	9.0
Maharashtra	1.7	3.3	8.6
Orissa	1.4	3.4	14.6
Punjab	1.6	6.4	11.2
Rajasthan	3.3	4.3	13.9
Tamil Nadu	2.3	6.8	16.2
Uttar Pradesh	1.2	2.8	9.3
West Bengal	1.6	4.5	15.5
India	2.1	4.7	11.0

Source: Pension expenditure calculated by the researcher based on budget and economic survey estimates.

The pension payment as a percentage of "States Own Revenue (SOR)" further highlights that how much internal resources of the states are allocated for the pension payment that covers less than 15 per cent of the workforce and elderly. Table 10.5 presents the allocation of the states own revenue for the pension payment in India by 15 major states. The drain of the states resources own account for the pension payment has been proceeding in an alarming pace in the last two decades. In the year 1980-81, the average spending was 3.4 per cent of the SOR at national average, increased sharply in the eighties and doubled to 7.9 per cent in 1990-91 in almost all the states. The latter part of the nineties witnessed a sharp increase and ended up in an average pension liability in terms of SOR at national level to 18 per cent. In Bihar, proportion went up to an unprecedented high of 63.5 percentage drain of SOR for the pension payment. The states like Orissa and West Bengal had reported figures around 30 per cent and Kerala allocates 28.5 per cent for the pension payment during the same period.

Table 10.5

Pension Payments of States as Per cent of Own Revenue Receipts

States	*1980-81*	*1990-91*	*2001-02*
Andhra Pradesh	5.0	9.6	14.1
Assam	2.0	7.0	34.8
Bihar	2.8	9.8	63.5
Gujarat	3.1	7.3	11.5
Haryana	1.6	4.5	9.9
Karnataka	6.5	9.4	15.0
Kerala	7.5	19.0	28.4
Madhya Pradesh	2.5	6.5	16.0
Maharashtra	2.2	4.1	10.0
Orissa	3.4	8.6	31.8
Punjab	2.0	8.2	13.3
Rajasthan	5.7	7.7	23.5
Tamil Nadu	3.4	9.9	20.9
Uttar Pradesh	2.7	6.0	16.4
West Bengal	2.6	7.8	31.0
India	3.4	7.9	17.2

Source: Calculated by researcher based on budget documents.

Thus, in the changing situation of both demographic and macroeconomic front, the fiscal stress of the pension payment thus act as an indicator of "Pension Crisis" in the India.

Pension "Crisis" in Kerala

Kerala state has reached what demographers call the final stage of demographic transition. This is the stage at which there are fewer births and deaths in a population. From the demographic point of view, Kerala is about 25 years ahead of the rest of the country. A male child born today can expect to live 70 years. A girl child will have even better—she can hope to live to 76. More importantly, the growth rate for the "oldest old" (eighty plus) is the highest in Kerala among different Indian states. It is interesting that Keralites spend one-fifth of their life span in old age. One of the consequences of the demographic transition is that of the financial insecurity of the aged.

Moreover with a higher proportion of government employees and organised workforce in Kerala, the coverage of the workforce under various pension schemes is higher. With the retirement age for the state government service fixed at 55 years coupled with higher average life expectancy at old age, it creates lot of imbalances in the society. With a continuous increase in the life expectancy, the pensioners spend longer time in post-retirement and receive enhanced pension benefits from time to time. The phenomenon of living longer as a consequence of demographic phenomenon had put aside an increase in the pension burden of the state and which in turn leads to a serious fiscal stringency on the state treasury with an immense drain of the resources for the pension payment.

Table 10.6 shows that the pension payments paid out by the government of Kerala witnessed an alarming growth in the past two decades. The actual expenditure went up from Rs. 33 crore in 1980-81 to Rs. 1990 crore in the year 2003-04. The growth of pension expenditure in Kerala was at 22 per cent per annum, which was above the national average. In the nineties, the expenditure registered a higher rate growth of 24 per cent.

Table 10.6

Pension Expenditure of Kerala

Year	*Pension Expenditure (Rs. crores)*	*Pension Expenditure as Percentage of NSDP*
1980-81	33	0.75
1990-91	284	1.2
1993-94	465	1.8
1994-95	565	2.0
1995-96	717	2.4
1996-97	754	2.4
1997-98	923	2.9
1998-99	1154	3.4
1999-2000	1808	5.0
2000-01	1930	5.1
2001-02	1938	5.1
2002-03	1968	4.8
2003-04	1990	4.6

Source: Calculated by the researcher based on budget documents.

The state witnessed an alarming increase in the pension burden. It shot up both in absolute and relative terms as a proportion of NSDP. The pension expenditure as a proportion of NSDP went up from 1.2 per cent in 1990-91 to 3.8 per cent in 1998-99, 5.0 per cent in 1999-2000 and 4.6 per cent in 2003-04. This crucial economic indicator is relatively higher than the national average of 2.5 per cent of GDP to pension expenditure.

It will also be interesting to note that the government as a part of fiscal allocation finances the large share of the expenditure on the pension. The extent of fiscal allocation can be noted as a percentage of revenue receipts of the government to total pension expenditure. Figure 10.1 gives the per cent of pension expenditure (pension liability) in terms of revenue receipts in Kerala over a period of time.

Figure 10.1

Pension Expenditure as Percentage of Revenue Receipts in Kerala

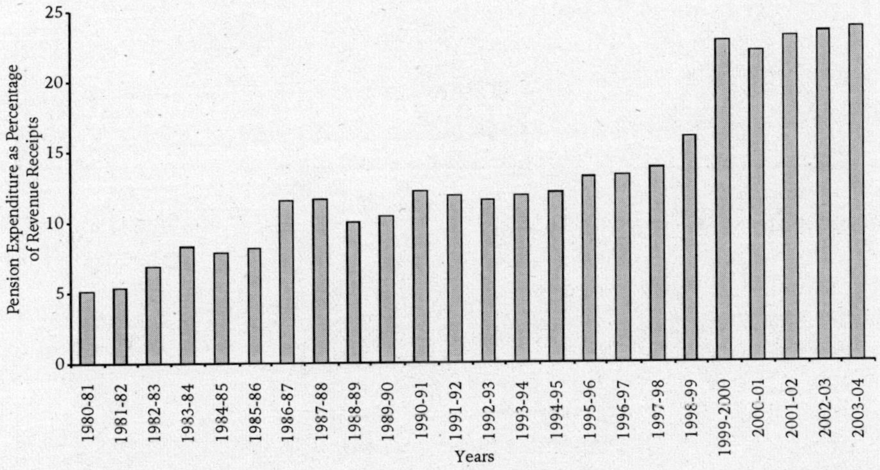

The drain of the state's resources caused by the pension payments has shown tremendous increase in the last two decades. The allocation which was just 5 per cent of the revenue receipts in 1980-81 shoot up to a level of 10 to 15 per cent in the nineties. In the beginning of the last decade on the eve of the Fifth Pay Commission recommendation and phenomenon of living longer, the pension payment registered its all time high in terms of revenue receipts. In this period, it ended up to a peak level of more than 22 per cent of the revenue receipts allocated for the pension payments. Also, the pension payments drains a large chunk of the states own resources. The pension payment in 2003-04 accounted for 30.5 per cent of the internally mobilised resources (state's own resources) of the government in Kerala as it was only 3 per cent in 1980-81 and 19 per cent in 1990-91. This really takes into account the fiscal imbalance in Kerala caused by the pension liability of the government.

The pension system in Kerala thus diverts a large chunk of the revenue of the state resources for the payment of the pensions to the retired civil servants of the government. The notion of a structural crisis with overwhelming financial liability in Kerala can be addressed on the basis on the coverage of the system and its dependency ratio to address the sustainability of the system. The coverage of the state pension system by the government, which targets the state civilian employees, is having a limited coverage among the total elderly of the state. It covers all the government employees and other employees of aided and grant-in-aid institution and also their family members, if one of them dies (family pensioners). Table 10.7 provides detailed data on different types of pensioners in Kerala. Over the years, the number of family pensioners has shown an increase and it is about 22 per cent in recent years.

Table 10.7

The Classification of the Pension Beneficiaries in Kerala

Year	*Service Pensioners*	*Family Pensioners*	*Total*
1970-71	112365	NA	112365
1980-81	146985	NA	146985
1990-91	209546	NA	209546
1999-2000	248920	58200	307120
2000-01	252768	58500	311268
2001-02	253125	59200	312325
2002-03	259040	62500	321540
2003-04	263895	64000	327895

Source: Government Treasury and Pension Bhavan.

With relatively large pension expenditure, the Government of Kerala spends Rs. 61,000 per individual pensioners per annum as on 31-3-2004. This per capita pension spending raises the question about the long run stability of the state-run unfunded pension system in the context of fiscal pressure.

In brief, the pension system in India and Kerala are suffering from the challenges caused by the demographic phenomenon of ageing and increased longevity as it causes unsustainable pension burden as the pensioners live longer. The existing pension system targets a minority of the aged population but accounts for higher government expenditure that result in fiscal stringency. It is high time to restructure the pension system to provide the basic security to the elderly with minimum cost on the part of the government.

In the state, the system dependency of the pension system (ratio of pensioners to employees in the payroll) is on an increase as the financing of the pensions is unsustainable for long run. Table 10.8 shows the system dependency ratio of the government pension system is higher than the demographic dependency ratio (of the population above 55 years to that of population 18-55 who are in a period eligible to get the government employment) which was just 15.0, 16.5, 19.8 and 23.0 in 1971, 1981, 1991 and 2001 censuses respectively.

Table 10.8

System Dependency Ratio in Kerala

Years	*System Dependency Ratio*
1970-71	34.47
1980-81	34.75
1990-91	45.95
1993-94	48.43
1994-95	48.47
1995-96	48.09
1996-97	47.03
1997-98	46.84
1998-99	46.42
1999-2000	45.93
2000-01	45.65
2001-02	45.42
2002-03	46.09
2003-04	46.67

Note: Estimated by the researcher based on estimated pensioners and employees, Finance Dept, GoK.

The system dependency was hovering around 35 during seventies and eighties and then shot up to 45 in the beginning of the nineties and it was estimated at 46.67 in 2003-04. With an increased life expectancy, the public pension system met out of the government is unsustainable in Kerala. The financial burden of the system makes serious fiscal stress on the government, which is affecting the macroeconomic stability. With an ageing population, the pension system is likely to allocate large financial resources to a system with limited coverage among the elderly.

Projection of the Pension Burden in Kerala

There is a common belief that the pension bill has the potential to reach an unsustainable level, or perhaps even exceed the wage bill, does not appear to be borne out by the recent trend or based on any realistic assessment of such liabilities in the future. In this context, the chapter is making an attempt to assess the pension liability for the state of Kerala using the existing data on elderly persons (population projections), life expectancy at older ages, current pensioners and employees. Projections for Kerala's pension burden involve two steps: estimation of pensioners for future from the available trends by ages of employees and pensioners. The estimation pension burden is on the basis of the estimated pensioners.

Estimation of the Number of Pensioners

The projections of the number of pensioners are done up to 2019 with a five-year interval based on the age profile of the existing employees and pensioners as per 31-3-2004. The simple demographic projection using component method is done on the basis of adjusted surviving rates. After projecting the number of individual pensioners by using the demographic methods, the number of total pensioners is estimated with help of a restricted assumption that number of the family pensioners will remain as 25 per cent (based on long run trend from 1990) of the service pensioners.

Table 10.9

The Number of Pensioners in Kerala (Projections)

Year	*Number of Pensioners*
2003-04	327895
2008-09	397100
2013-14	452647
2018-19	489287

Source: Projections by the researcher in consultation with demographers at Centre for Development Studies.

The projection shows that there will be an alarming increase in the number of pensioners from 3.3 lakh in 2004 to 4.0 lakh in 2009 and then to 4.5 lakh in 2014 and 4.9 lakh in 2019. The increase in the number of pensioners is due to new pensioners as well long life span of the existing pensioners.

Estimation of the Pension Burden

We have projected pension liabilities based on two broad assumptions.

Projections based on the assumption that there is no pension revision. The projection uses two cases to estimate future pension burden. In the first assumption, there will be no revision of pensions and per capita pension expenditure remains constant at Rs. 61000 per annum. Based on these assumptions, the projected pension expenditure is likely to be in and around Rs. 2422 crore in 2009, Rs. 2761 crore in 2014 and Rs. 2985 crore in 2019.

Table 10.10

Projected Pension Expenditure without Revision

Year	*Pension Expenditure*
2003-04	1990
2008-09	2422
2013-14	2761
2018-19	2985

The following projections assumed 20 per cent pay increase in every five years.

Table 10.11

Projected Pension Expenditure with Revision

Year	*Pension Expenditure*
2003-04	1990
2008-09	2907
2013-14	3976
2018-19	5157

Assuming a 20 per cent increase in pensions as a result of pay revisions once in every five years is considered to be more realistic and thus, the pension expenditure is likely to increase to Rs. 2907 crore in 2009, Rs. 3976 crore in 2014 and Rs. 5157 crore on 2019.

Our two projections are based on two different assumptions that are expected in the future and it is evident that the pension expenditure is likely to result in an alarming proportion in near future, resulting in a financial crisis. The enormous increase in the pension expenditure can also act as a deterrent to steady economic and social development. Added to this, the changing intergenerational balance in an ageing society like Kerala will make this expenditure unsustainable.

Conclusion

The chapter has made an attempt to understand the existing fiscal dilemma that exists in the Indian pension system. The study mainly examines how demographic phenomenon of "living longer" result in a grave fiscal dilemma. Long term stability and the fiscal constraints of the state-run pensions in an ageing society are the major focus of the chapter. Here the study looks into the overwhelming fiscal stress of the state sponsored pension system in India with special reference to Kerala.

The chapter highlights the ever-growing fiscal constraints on account of the pension liability, which in the recent past has proved to be a serious threat to the fiscal stability of the governments. The pension liability on the part of the government through civil service pensions went drastically upward in India both at Centre and states in the last two decades. The total pension liability of both Centre and states went up from Rs. 6870 crore in 1990-91 to Rs. 55711.6 crore in 2001-02. The emerging burden of the pension liability of the both governments reveals the fiscal stress due to pension liability. The fiscal strain is very high in states such as Tamil Nadu, Kerala, West Bengal, Andhra Pradesh etc., where the life expectancy and coverage is high. The study also reveals that at national level, the expenditure on pension as a per cent of revenue expenditure accounts for 12 per cent of the revenue expenditure and 17.6 per cent of the states own revenue of the governments in Indian states.

In the last two decades, the pension expenditure of the government of Kerala went up from Rs. 33 crore in 1980-81 to Rs. 1990 crore in the year 2003-04. The pension liability was revolving around 4.5 to 5 per cent of NSDP in the recent years. The pension expenditure is accounted to almost one-fourth of the revenue expenditure and nearly 30 per cent of the own revenue of the state, which added to the financial burden of the state. The pension system in Kerala that drains huge fiscal resources covers only 10 per cent of the aged in the state. The study has also examined the sustainability question of the pension system in the long run as the system dependency ratio is much higher than the demographic dependency ratio. This shows a structural crisis in the pension system with huge fiscal stress on the government treasury. The chapter also projects unsustainable increase in the pension payment in future.

In brief, the pension system in India and Kerala are suffering from the challenges caused by the demographic phenomenon of ageing and increased longevity. The pension system of the present kind targets a minority of the aged population and accounts for higher government expenditure that result in fiscal stringency. So it is high time to restructure the pension system to provide the basic security to the elderly with minimum cost on the part of the government.

References

Algoed, Koen, Frans Spinnewyn (2000). "Pensions", in Boudewijn Bouckaert and Gerrit De Geest (eds.), *Encyclopedia of Law and Economics*. Volumen IV—The Economics of Public and Tax Law. Cheltenham: Edward Elgar. Páginas 311-327.

Amedick, Sigrid (2000). "Old Age Security in a Community Service Administration: The Example of the Bavarian State Railway, 1844-1914—Pension Systems for Public Servants in Western Europe", *Yearbook of European Administrative History* (JEV) 12: 55-75.

Armingeon, K., F. Bertozzi and G. Bonoli (1999). "Convergence Towards a Unique Continental Model of the Welfare State in Europe? The Importance of Regional Integration for Swiss Welfare State Reform". *(mimeo). http://www.swisss cience.org_sppzch/posterpdf/Poster_Armingeon48.pdf 4*

Asian Development Bank (2001). *Social Protection for Asia and Pacific*. Manila

Atkinson, P. (2001). "The Fiscal Impact of Population Change", *Federal Reserve Bank Boston Conference Series*.

Auerbach, A. and R. Lee (ed.) (2001). *Demographic Change and Fiscal Policy*. London: Cambridge University Press.

Barr, Nicholas (2000). "Reforming Pensions: Myths, Truths, and Policy Choices", *IMF Working Paper* No.WP/00/139 August. New York.

Boldrin, M., S. Jimenez-Martin and F. Peracchi (1999). "Social Security and Retirement in France", in J. Gruber and D.A. Wise (eds.), *International Social Security Comparisons*. Chicago: The University of Chicago Press.

Fox, L. and E. Palmer (2001). "New Approaches to Multipillar Pension Systems: What in the World is Going On?" in Robert Holzmann and J.E. Stiglitz (eds.) *New Ideas about Old Age Security: Towards Sustainable Pension Systems in the 21st Century*. New York: World Bank.

Goswami, Ranadev (2001). "Indian Pension System: Problems and Prognosis", Paper presented in the *IAA Pensions Seminar*. June.

Government of India (2000). *The Project Oasis Report*. Submitted by the Expert Committee for Devising a Pension System for India, January.

———. (2002). *Report of High Level Expert Group on New Pension System*. Volume One: Main Report, February.

Government of Kerala (various dates). *The Liberalized Pension Rules (1966, 1974 & 1982) and its Amendments*.

———. (various dates). *Kerala Service Rules Amendments* (various reviews). Thiruvananthapuram.

Heller, S. Peter (2003). *Who Will Pay? Coping with Ageing Society, Climate Change and Other Long Term Fiscal Challenges*. New York: International Monetary Fund.

Pensions Internationals. *www.pensioninternational.co.uk*

Pillai, T.K. Velu (1940). *Travancore State Manual*. Vol. III. State Government Press.

Srivastava, G.P. (1966). *The Indian Civil Service*. New Delhi: S. Chand and Co.

Swain, Sibani and Pronab Sen (2004). "Pension Liabilities of the Central Government: Projections and Implications", Planning Commission, Government of India.

The World Bank (1994). *Averting the Old Age Crisis: Policies to Protect the Old and Promote Growth*. Washington D.C.: Oxford University Press.

11

Welfare Fund Boards and Social Security

S. IRUDAYA RAJAN

In India, well-organised social security and pension system exist only for formal sector employees in government, semi-government, local and private sectors and accounting for about 10 per cent of the workforce. The unorganised sector employees have no formal security and welfare benefits either during their working lives or old age. Generally, workers in the unorganised sector receive low wages and no permanency of employment. In order to provide social assistance to workers, the concept of labour fund has been evolved. Figure 11.1 illustrates this point vividly. The advantage of the welfare fund model is that the workers join the fund and contributes to the growth of the fund and receive various types of social security benefits in areas such as health, education, housing, recreation, water supply, death allowance, gratuity and old age pension.

Figure 11.1

Social Security and Welfare Schemes in Kerala

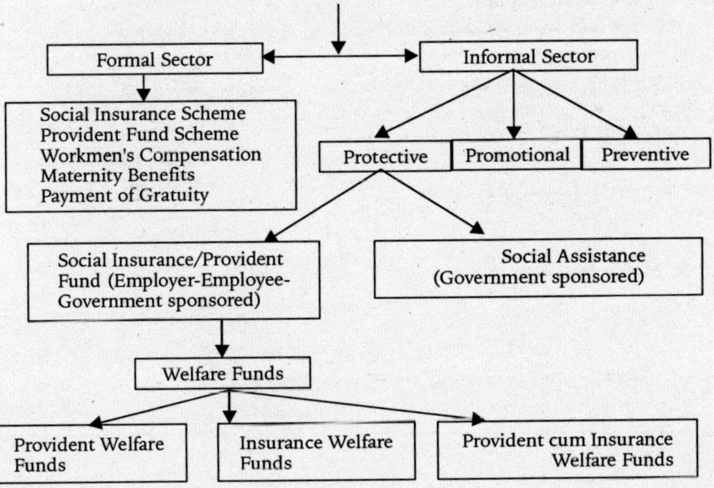

Welfare Fund Boards in Kerala

Kerala occupies a unique role in creating and maintaining several welfare fund boards for the benefit of unorganised sector workers. As of 2005, Kerala maintains 24 welfare fund boards; the first was introduced for toddy workers as early as 1969 and the latest addition was for ration dealers in 2000. Table 11.1 lists the welfare fund boards, its year of introduction, estimated and registered workers in each board and the proportion of workers covered as of 2002. We were not in a position to collect the latest information from 7 out of 24 welfare funds; however, wherever possible, we have used the existing information from various published sources and publications.

Table 11.1

Established Year and Workers Covered in Welfare Funds in Kerala, 2004

Name of the Welfare Fund	*Year of Initiation*	*Estimated Workers*	*Workers Covered*	*Per cent Covered*
Kerala Toddy Workers Welfare Fund	1969	44351	41428	93.41
Kerala Staff Welfare Fund	1972	n.a	25022	n.a
Kerala Nurses Welfare Fund	1974	n.a	n.a	n.a
Kerala Labour Welfare Fund	1977	482000	477024	98.96
Kerala Head Load Workers Welfare Fund	1983	n.a	63865	n.a
Kerala Motor Transport Workers Welfare Fund	1985	191000	45496	23.81
Kerala Advocate Clerks Welfare Fund	1985	n.a	2569	n.a
Kerala Artisans and Skilled Workers Welfare Fund	1986	n.a	202930	n.a
Kerala Cashew Workers Relief and Welfare Fund	1988	180000	137343	76.30
Kerala Khadi Workers Welfare Fund	1989	n.a	12293	n.a
Kerala Coir Workers Welfare Fund	1989	n.a	72908	n.a
Kerala Fishermen Welfare Fund	1989	189200	172000	90.91
Kerala Handloom Workers Welfare Fund	1989	125000	46869	37.49
Kerala Abkari Workers Welfare Fund	1990	n.a	13800	n.a
Kerala Building and Construction Workers Welfare Fund	1990	1500000	950000	63.33
Kerala Agricultural Workers Welfare Fund	1990	1800000	1745773	96.97
Kerala State Lottery Agents Welfare Fund	1991	10000	3919	39.19
Kerala Document Writers and Stamp Vendors Welfare Fund	1991	6000	4126	68.77
Kerala Auto Rickshaw Workers Welfare Fund	1991	155931	16704	10.71
Kerala Anganwadi Workers Welfare Fund	1991	50000	34851	69.70
Kerala Tailoring Workers Welfare Fund	1994	500000	237000	47.4
Kerala Beedi and Cigar Workers Welfare Fund	1996	160000	30521	15.26
Kerala Etta, Kattuvalli Workers Welfare Fund	2000	200000	6978	3.48
Kerala Ration Dealers Workers Welfare Fund	2000	n.a	11330	n.a
Total			4354749	

Source: Compiled by the author from the Welfare Fund Board records.

The first welfare fund came into existence in 1969 for toddy workers, followed by staffs, nurses, labourers, head load workers, motor transport workers, advocate clerks, artisans and skilled workers, cashew workers, *khadi* workers, coir workers, fishery workers, handloom workers, *abkari* workers, construction workers, agricultural workers, lottery agents, document writers and stamp vendors, *rickshaw* workers, *anganwadi* workers, tailoring workers, *beedi* and cigar workers, *kattuvalli* workers and ration dealers. Interestingly, the growth of the welfare funds was during certain periods as reflected in the political history of the state. The successive left and right governments had played a major role in creating more welfare fund boards to satisfy different section of labourers. The highest number of welfare fund boards (8) was initiated during 1985-1989 and 1990-1995; 4 in 1989, 3 in 1990 and again 4 in 1991.

As of 2003, 44 lakh unorganised labourers in the state of Kerala are registered with one or other types of welfare fund boards and receive various welfare benefits including old age pensions. The highest number of workers is registered with agricultural workers welfare fund (17 lakh), followed by construction workers (9 lakh) and 5 lakh in the labour welfare funds. Around 1 to 2 lakh workers are registered in the following welfare funds (artisans and skilled workers welfare fund, cashew workers, fishermen welfare fund and tailoring workers). More than 90 per cent of workers in the following sectors (agriculture, fishery, labour and toddy workers) have already enrolled as members in the respective funds. According to the 2001 census, Kerala has enumerated 102 lakh main and marginal workers. The planning board of Government of Kerala reports that 12 lakh persons are employed in organised sectors. Thus, around 50 per cent of the unorganised workers are registered with the 24 welfare funds (44 lakh out of 90 lakh) existing in Kerala.

Each welfare fund board has its own definition of workers for enrolment. For instance, Kerala fishermen welfare fund board membership is extended to all the fishermen who are employed for wages on a fishing boat or self employed persons who are registered as members of fishermen's welfare society. The eligible criteria of different welfare funds in Kerala are presented in Table 11.2.

Most of the welfare funds receive income from government, employer and employees. However, six welfare fund boards receive no grants from government and another five receive no income from employers (for details, see Table 11.3). Kerala handloom workers pay just rupee 1 per month to become member and acquire all welfare benefits including old age pension. This is also true for agricultural workers (Rs. 2 per month). Few welfare fund board employees pay 8 to 10 per cent of wages. They are: toddy workers, head load workers, *khadi* workers and *abkari* workers. For some welfare funds, employers and employees contribute the same amount of money (for instance, auto *rickshaw* workers welfare fund) to the welfare funds and some they differ in their contribution (for instance, tailoring workers). In some cases, government contribute sum equal to the contribution by the employees (for instance, Kerala *beedi* and cigar workers welfare fund) but in most of the cases, government contributes 10 per cent of the member's contribution (for instance, *anganwadi* worker welfare fund). Kerala government contributes Rs. 30 million for pension payments and another 17 million for insurance premiums per year to the Kerala fishermen welfare fund. However, government grants are irregular in many cases and the state of Kerala is in severe financial crisis.

Table 11.2

Eligibility Criteria among Welfare Fund Boards in Kerala, 2004

Name of the Welfare Fund	*Eligibility Criteria*
Kerala Toddy Workers Welfare Fund	Any person who works directly or indirectly in the production (tapping), collection and distribution of toddy for his/her livelihood.
Kerala Labour Welfare Fund	Workers in factories or plantations employing 10 employees and above, shops and commercial establishments employing two and above and cooperative institutions employing 20 workers and above are covered by the Fund.
Kerala Head Load Workers Welfare Fund Board	Person engaged directly or through a contractor in or for an establishment whether for wages or not for loading or unloading or carrying on head or person or a trolley any article or articles into or from a vehicle or any place in such establishment and includes any person not employed by any employer or contractor but engaged in the loading or unloading or carrying on head or person or in a trolley any article or articles for wages. For administrative purposes, they are divided into three broad groups: Attached group (permanently employed by the employer in an establishment: employee-employer relationship is clear), Unattached group (workers working for more than one identified employer in towns and urban areas: no definite employer-employee relationship) and Scattered group (no identified permanent employers—those engaged in work at forest, bus stands, boat jetties, railway stations and so on).

contd...

...contd...

Name of the Welfare Fund	*Eligibility Criteria*
Kerala Motor Transport Workers Welfare Fund	A person who is employed for wages in a motor transport undertaking directly or through an agency to work in a professional capacity on a transport vehicle, like driver, conductor, cleaner, station staff, cash clerk, time keeper, watchman or attender. An employee becomes eligible for membership on completion of three months of service within the age limit of 60 years.
Kerala Advocate Clerks Welfare Fund	A person who functions as an advocate clerk, registered under the Kerala Advocate Clerk Welfare Act who is with in the age limit of 20 and 70 are eligible for membership.
Kerala Artisans and Skilled Workers Welfare Fund	Workers in the informal sector such as tree climbers, gold smiths, *pappad* makers, carpenters, shoe makers, potters, *chakku* oil extractors, cycle *rickshaw* workers, gunny bag collectors, cycle repairers, milk and news paper distributors, watch repairers, ice makers, barbers and *dhobies* and other workers who do not come under any of the welfare schemes in the state, within the age limit of 18 and 55 are eligible for membership in this scheme.
Kerala Cashew Workers Relief and Welfare Fund	A cashew worker is a person, who is engaged in any form of employment in the processing of cashew. The scheme applies to cashew workers and their dependents (husband/wife, unmarried daughters and minor sons and parents, minor brothers and unmarried sisters, fully dependent on the beneficiary).
Kerala Khadi Workers Welfare Fund	The workers who are employed for wages under employers, contractors, in cooperative or self-employed for subsistence in *khadi* industries are eligible to be a member of the scheme.
Kerala Coir Workers Welfare Fund	Membership is extended to any person, employed by any other person or a self employed person in the coir industry and his dependents.
Kerala Fishermen Welfare Fund	Membership is extended to all the fishermen who are employed for wages on a fishing boat or self-employed fishermen who are registered as members of Fishermen's Welfare Society.
Kerala Handloom Workers Welfare Fund	All the handloom workers who have completed 3 months of service and all self employed persons in the handloom industry are eligible to register their names in the Board. The handloom workers and self employed persons so registered are the members and the beneficiaries of the Fund.

contd...

...contd...

Name of the Welfare Fund	*Eligibility Criteria*
Kerala Abkari Workers Welfare Fund	A worker shall be entitled to become a member under the scheme from the date on which he has completed 3 months continuous service in the *abkari* trade (excluding toddy shops i.e., arrack shops, foreign liquor shops and bar etc.).
Kerala Building and Other Construction Workers Welfare Fund	Every building worker who has completed 18 years of age but is not above 60 years of age and who is not a member in any other welfare fund, established under any law in force and who has completed 90 days of service as a building worker in the immediately preceding year shall be eligible for membership.
Kerala Agricultural Workers Welfare Fund	All workers who are engaged in the operation of agricultural work within the age group of 18 and 60 are eligible to become member.
Kerala State Lottery Agents Welfare Fund	Membership in the scheme is open to all who possess a valid registration in the form of an identity folder as a regular agent issued under the Rules and to those of who purchase tickets with face value of Rs. 200 or above as monthly commission from the purchase of tickets from the registering authorities of various lotteries conducted by the Government of India.
Kerala Document Writers Scribes and Stamp Vendors Welfare Fund	Person who function as a document writer or vendor and scribe and is licenced under the Kerala Document Writers or the Kerala Manufacture and Sale Stamp Rule (1960). Membership is opened to any person holding a valid licence and age below 65 years.
Kerala Auto Rickshaw Workers Welfare Fund	Membership of workers in this scheme is optional. Any person between the age of 20 and 48 years employed in an auto rickshaw used for the purpose of transporting passengers and goods are eligible to become the members of the Fund.
Kerala Anganwadi Workers Welfare Fund Board	Membership in this scheme is open to all persons who are working as a permanent staff in *anganwadi*, like health worker, teacher and helper.
Kerala Tailoring Workers Welfare Fund	A person who is employed for wages to do any work in connection with the various processes in tailoring work or embroidery work with or without the assistance of the machine, and who gets his wages directly or indirectly from the employer includes any person employed by or through a contractor depends mainly on tailoring work for his livelihood are covered under the scheme.

contd...

...contd...

Name of the Welfare Fund	*Eligibility Criteria*
Kerala Beedi and Cigar Workers Welfare Fund	All the *beedi* and cigar workers who have completed three months' continuous service, and who have completed 18 years of age, but not completed 55 years of age are entitled to and are required to be members of the Fund and shall register their names in the Board. The workers and the self employed persons so registered are the members and the beneficiaries of the Fund.
Kerala Etta, Kattuvalli Workers Welfare Fund	According to the Act, 'Bamboo, Kattuvalli and Pandanus Leaf Worker' means any person who is employed for wages to do any work in connection with or incidental to the bamboo industry or Kattuvalli industry or Pandanus leaf industry, as the case may be, and who gets his wages, directly or indirectly from the employer, dealer or producer of bamboo products or *kattuvalli* products or, as the case may be, pandanus leaf products and includes any person employed by or through a contractor or through an agent and depends mainly on bamboo industry, *kattuvalli* industry or pandanus leaf industry for his livelihood. Every bamboo, *kattuvalli* and pandanus leaf worker and self-employed persons in the above industry who has attained the age of 18 years and not completed 60 years is eligible to become the member of the Fund, but it does not include a person engaged in collecting bamboo, reed or cane for the purpose of making pulp, paper and artificial threads with mechanical aid.
All Other Welfare Fund Boards	n.a.

Source: Compiled by the author from the Welfare Fund Board records.

Kerala welfare fund boards offer various benefits to its members such as old age pension, provident fund, gratuity, retirement benefits, ex-gratia payments, disability allowance, funeral expenses, educational allowances (scholarships and cash awards), medical allowances, marriage grant, maternity benefits, unemployment benefits, housing loans and other special schemes. Let us examine each one separately to assess the welfare fund boards in Kerala.

Table 11.3

Resource Mobilisation of Welfare Fund Boards in Kerala, 2004

Name of the Welfare Fund	*Government*	*Employer*	*Employee*
Kerala Toddy Workers Welfare Fund	Nil	8% as provident fund contribution and 5% as gratuity as the wages of the employee	8% of the wage
Kerala Labour Welfare Fund	No fixed grant. Until today, Rs.63 lakh have been paid	Rs. 16 per year per employee	Rs. 8 per year
Kerala Head Load Workers Welfare Fund	Nil	25% of wages	10% of the wages
Kerala Motor Transport Workers Welfare Fund	Nil	8% of the workers wage plus another 5% of wages as gratuity	8% of the wages
Kerala Advocate Clerks Welfare Fund	Rs. 90 per year per member	Nil	Rs. 60 per annum. It can be paid by two instalments
Kerala Artisans and Skilled Workers Welfare Fund	Rs. 2 per every Rs. 10 contributed by the worker	Nil	Rs. 10 per month
Kerala Cashew Workers Relief and Welfare Fund	Re. 1 per worker	Re. 1 per worker for every working day	50 paise per worker for each working day
Kerala Khadi Workers Welfare Fund	10% of workers wage	10% workers wage	10% of the wage
Kerala Fishermen's Welfare Fund	Rs. 30 million for pension and Rs. 17 million for insurance per year	Dealers (1% of sales turn over). Exporters (1% of sales turn over). Prawn/fish farmer (2% of sales turn over) Boat owners: < 15 GRT (Gross Registered Tonnage): Rs. 100 per month for nine months; 15-25 GRT: Rs. 200 per month for nine months; 24-35 GRT: Rs. 400 per month for nine months; > 35 GRT: Rs. 1000 per month for nine months; Catamaram owners (non-motorised: Re. 1 per month for 9 months; Motorised: Rs. 2 per month for 9 months; Other Craft owners < 9 mts, non-motorised: Rs. 3 per month for nine months; < 9 mts, motorised:	Rs. 50 per year

contd...

...contd...

Name of the Welfare Fund	*Government*	*Employer*	*Employee*
		Rs. 5 per month for nine months; > 9 mts, non-motorised: Rs. 5 per month for nine months; > 9 mts, motorised: Rs. 7 per month for nine months; Chinese- and stake-net owners: Re. 1 per month for nine months.	
Kerala Handloom Workers Welfare Fund	Rs. 2 per month for workers and Rs. 4 per month for the self-employed	1% of the annual turn over and an amount equal to workers contribution	Rs. 1 per month for workers and Rs. 2 per month for the self-employed persons
Kerala Abkari Workers Welfare Fund	Nil	15% of workers wage (including 5% gratuity)	10% of the wage
Kerala Building and Other Construction Workers Welfare Fund	Nil	Employers contribution at the rate of 1% of the estimated cost of all construction works and for residential building only those whose estimate is beyond Rs. 10 lakh need to pay the cess	Rs. 20 per month
Kerala Agricultural Workers Welfare Fund	Nil	Rs. 10 per annum by the landowners of less than one hectare and Rs. 15 per annum for those who have more than one hectare	Rs. 2 per month
Kerala State Lottery Agents Welfare Fund	20% of the total respectively amount contributed by the member per annum	Nil	Category A and B contributes Rs. 15 and Rs. 10 per month
Kerala Document Writers Scribes and Stamp Vendors Welfare Fund	10% of the members contribution	Nil	Rs. 25 per month
Kerala Auto Rickshaw Workers Welfare Fund	10% of the members contribution	Rs. 25 per month	Rs. 25 per month
Kerala Anganwadi Workers Welfare Fund	10% of the members contribution	Nil	Worker Rs. 20 per month and helper Rs. 10 per month
Kerala Tailoring Workers Welfare Fund	10% of the contribution made by the worker every year	Rs. 5 per month for each worker	Rs. 10 per month for both workers and self-employed

contd...

...contd...

Name of the Welfare Fund	*Government*	*Employer*	*Employee*
Kerala Beedi and Cigar Workers Welfare Fund	Grant equal to the contribution paid by the employees	Rs. 6 per month per worker	Rs. 3 per month for worker and Rs. 5 per month for self-employed
Kerala Etta, Kattuvalli Workers Welfare Fund	Grant equal to the contribution paid by the employees and self employed	Rs. 7 per month for each worker	Rs. 7 per month for each worker and the self-employed
All Other Welfare Fund Boards	n.a.	n.a.	n.a.

Source: Compiled by the author from the Welfare Fund Board records.

Old Age Pension

Out of 24 welfare fund boards, 14 funds (58 per cent) offer old age pensions to its members (see Table 11.4). The first such old pension was implemented for Kerala agricultural workers in 1980 and currently they are paid Rs. 120 per month and the total number of beneficiaries is around 5 lakh. Among them, half of them are women. The eligible agricultural labour can avail the old age pension without being member of the Kerala agricultural workers welfare fund; however, this programme is being managed by the same board in recent years. It is one of the most popular cash transfers in Kerala. During 1987, fishermen welfare fund board offered pension to its members and another three (handloom, cashew and *khadi* workers welfare fund) joined the club in 1989. Though the toddy worker welfare fund came into existence as a pioneer welfare fund model in Kerala, it offered old age pension to its members only in 1997, after 28 years of its existence. The monthly pension varies from the minimum of Rs. 100 person to maximum Rs. 200 per person. The national old age pension initiated by the Government of India offers only Rs. 75 per month. Few welfare funds do not maintain proper data on the pension payments. As of 2002, around 7 lakh senior citizen received old age pension through different welfare fund boards and the coverage is likely to be around 25 per cent of old population in Kerala (7 lakh against 31 lakh).

Table 11.4

Pension Schemes Offered by the Welfare Fund Boards in Kerala, 2004

Name of the Welfare Fund	*Remarks*
Kerala Toddy Workers Welfare Fund	Eligibility: Minimum 10 years of continuous membership at the time of superannuation. Rate: Rupees 100 per month and additional Rupees 10 for each additional year completed than the required 10 years membership. Year of introduction: 1997 Number of recipients: 13116 (2002) Total amount disbursed: 759.99 lakh
Kerala Head Load Workers Welfare Fund	Eligibility: 6 years of qualifying service at the age of 60. Rate: Rupees 200 per month (minimum) and the maximum Rupees 2400 based on the length of service and the wages earned; in case of pensioner dies, Rupees 100 to the family as family pension. Year of Introduction: 1999 Number of recipients: n.a
Kerala Motor Transport Workers Welfare Fund	Eligibility: Pension scheme for workers who retire from service after completion of 10 years of service. Rate: n.a. Year of introduction: 2001. Number of recipients: n.a
Kerala Artisans and Skilled Workers Welfare Fund	Pension is proposed in 2002
Kerala Cashew Workers Relief and Welfare Fund	Eligibility: The members on termination of their service on attaining the age of superannuation or who suffer from permanent disablement will be granted monthly pension from the fund. No minimum qualifying service is prescribed for eligibility to pension. Rate: Rupees 125 per month in the case of the daily rated worker and rupees 200 per month in respect of monthly paid staff. Year of Introduction: 1989. Number of recipients: 40467 (2002)
Kerala Khadi Workers Welfare Fund	Eligibility: Minimum 10 years as a member at 60 years. If his service is less than 10 years, he is eligible to get only his contribution. Family pension is given in the event of death of the pensioner at the same rate. Date of introduction: 1990. Rate: Rupees 100 to 300 per month depending on the year of membership. Number of Recipients: 134 (2002)
Kerala Coir Workers Welfare Fund	Eligibility: Pension after completing 60 years and family pension in the event of death of the member. Date of introduction: 1989. Rate: Rupees 100 per month. Number of Recipients: 59923 (2002)
Kerala Fishermen's Welfare Fund	Eligibility: Completion of 60 years. Date of introduction: 1987. Rate: Rupees 120 per month. Number of Recipients: 27000 (1998)

contd...

...contd...

Name of the Welfare Fund	*Remarks*
Kerala Handloom Workers Welfare Fund	Eligibility: The members on termination of their service on attaining the age of superannuation, i.e., retirement on completion of the age of 60 years. Date of introduction: 1989. Rate: Rs.100 per month. Number of Recipients: 7146 (2002) Total amount disbursed: 67.44 lakhs
Kerala Abkari Workers Welfare Fund	Eligibility: Workers who retire from the service on superannuation. Minimum pension is applicable to members who prematurely retired from service due to permanent disability. Year of Introduction: 1993. Rate: Minimum is Rs. 200 and the Maximum is Rs. 300 depending upon their length of service. Number of Recipients: 115
Kerala Building and Other Construction Workers Welfare Fund	Eligibility: Workers who retire from the service on superannuation. Date of Introduction: 1991. Rate: Minimum pension is Rs. 200 and an additional Rs. 20 per year of service beyond five years. Number of Recipients: 36223 (2002) Family Pension: When a pensioner dies, the spouse become eligible for family pension. This is limited to half of pension received by the pensioner or Rs. 100 which ever is higher. Date of introduction: 1996. Number of Recipients: 672
Kerala Agricultural Workers Welfare Fund	Eligibility: Agricultural workers who have completed 60 years of age and whose annual income does not exceed Rs. 11000 are eligible. Year of introduction: 1980. Rate: Rs.120 per month. Number of Recipients: 527647 (2002)
Kerala Tailoring Workers Welfare Fund	Eligibility: Pension to members after 60 years and minimum of 9 years of service required. Date of introduction: 2000 Rate: Rs. 100 to Rs. 430. Number of recipients: 850 (2002)
Kerala Beedi and Cigar Workers Welfare Fund	Eligibility: Completion of 60 years with minimum 3 years of service. Date of introduction: 1997. Rate: Rs. 100 per month. Number of Recipients: 524 (2002)
Kerala Ration Dealers Welfare Fund Board	Eligibility: Completion of 65 years with minimum 10 years of service. Date of introduction: 2000 Rate: Rs. 150 per month. Number of Recipients: 57 (2002)
All Other Welfare Fund Boards	Nil

Source: Compiled by the author from the Welfare Fund Board records.

Retirement Benefits

Half of the welfare fund boards in Kerala offer either provident fund or gratuity or other terminal retirement benefits to its members. Provident fund provision exists only in toddy welfare fund and motor transport workers welfare fund. In addition to the above two welfare funds, gratuity also exists in *abkari* workers welfare fund. Terminal retirement benefits are based on the member's contribution and the length of membership. For instance, Kerala tailoring worker welfare fund offers retirement benefits to its members with a minimum of Rs. 100 to maximum of Rs. 60000 depending upon the length of the membership at age 60. On the other hand, Kerala agricultural workers fixed its minimum payment as Rs. 5000 as against Rs. 15000 by the Kerala head load workers welfare fund. Detailed information of various aspects of retirement benefits of different welfare fund boards are presented in Table 11.5.

Table 11.5

Provident Fund, Gratuity and Retirement Benefits Offered by the Welfare Fund Boards in Kerala, 2004

Name of the Welfare Fund	*Remarks*
Kerala Toddy Workers Welfare Fund	Provident Fund: All contribution along with interest thereon when the employee retires from service either on superannuation, invalidation or retirement or death. Gratuity: Gratuity to the employees is payable at the rate of 15 days wages for each completed year of service subject to a maximum of 20 months.
Kerala Head Load Workers Welfare Fund	Terminal Benefit: 10% of total wages earned during the entire period of service on superannuation, retirement, death, disability as terminal benefit or gratuity. Special Super-annuation Assistance: If the worker does not have minimum of Rs. 15,000 due to short service, he will be paid Rs. 15,000, if he worked at least 180 days in each year.
Kerala Motor Transport Workers Welfare Fund	Provident Fund: Total accumulated contribution along with 9% interest per annum will be paid at the time of the superannuation, retirement, dismissal and death. Gratuity: 15 days of wage for each completed years of service upto maximum of 6 months.
Kerala Advocate Clerks Welfare Fund	Terminal Benefit: Rs. 10000 paid as retirement if he completed 30 years of service.
Kerala Artisans and Skilled Workers Welfare Fund	Terminal Benefit: A member who completes the full term of 42 years in service will get an amount of Rs. 62720 as retirement benefit. Members who retire before 42 years will get retirement benefit proportionate to their duration of membership. Minimum retirement benefit admissible is Rs. 600 for which has to complete two years in the scheme.

contd...

...contd...

Name of the Welfare Fund	*Remarks*
Kerala Abkari Workers Welfare Fund	Gratuity Benefit: It is fixed at the rate of 50% of the average monthly wage for each completed year of service subject to a maximum of 20 months wage.
Kerala Agricultural Workers Welfare Fund	Superannuation: Members with the fund for 40 years of continuos contribution is entitled for Rs. 25000. However, member is entitled to the minimum amount of Rs. 5000 if the member is with the und not less than 36 months.
Kerala State Lottery Agents Welfare Fund	Retirement Benefit: Member completes the full term of 40 years service at age 60, is entitled for Rs. 62700.
Kerala Document Writers Scribes and Stamp Vendors Welfare Fund	Terminal Benefit: Members receive their contribution depend on the year of services.
Kerala Auto Rickshaw Workers Welfare Fund	Retirement Benefit: If a member completed 30 years of service at superannuation, he will receive a consolidated amount of Rs. 145264. Others will get depend on their year of contribution made to the fund.
Kerala Anganwadi Workers Welfare Fund	Terminal Benefit: Member completes five years of continuous service and contributed monthly is entitled to get an amount contributed with 11 per cent interest plus 10 per cent Government contribution. In the case of a member who failed to make the contribution for five years are not eligible for the government contribution and interest.
Kerala Tailoring Workers Welfare Fund	Retirement Benefit: Minimum of Rs. 100 to maximum Rs. 60000 is paid depends upon the years of service at age 60.
All Other Welfare Fund Boards	Nil

Source: Compiled by the author from the Welfare Fund Board records.

Ex-gratia Payment, Disability Allowance and Funeral Expenses

Out of the 24 welfare fund boards, six welfare funds neither offer any ex-gratia payment nor disability allowances and funeral expenses (Table 11.6). Of the 18 welfare funds, which offer above benefits, toddy workers welfare fund and *abkari* workers welfare fund provide no ex-gratia payments. Almost half of the welfare fund boards (9 out of 18) provide no funeral expenses; however, only six of them execute any disability allowance. The lowest amount of ex-gratia payment of Rs. 2500 exists in two welfare fund boards (labour welfare fund and cashew workers relief welfare fund), and the highest amount of Rs. 100000 (1 lakh) offered by two welfare fund boards (head load workers welfare fund and building and other construction workers). Vast difference exists among different welfare fund boards in its policy towards ex-gratia payments. Funeral expenses offered by the board also varied considerably (for instance, toddy workers welfare fund gives 5000 as funeral expenses whereas artisans and skilled workers welfare fund fixed the amount as Rs. 500). Most of the welfare fund provides one time grant as disability allowances (ranging from Rs. 5000 to 25000), however, five welfare fund boards (toddy workers welfare fund, head load workers welfare fund, artisan and skilled workers welfare fund, building and construction workers welfare fund and tailoring workers welfare fund) offer disability allowance per month until death (ranging from Rs. 100 to 150).

Table 11.6

Ex-gratia, Disability Allowance and Funeral Expenses Offered by the Welfare Fund Boards in Kerala, 2004

Name of the Welfare Fund	*Remarks*
Kerala Toddy Workers Welfare Fund	Ex-gratia payment: Nil Disability allowance: Totally and permanently, disabled workers, due to fall from the tree, while engaging in toddy tapping work are eligible for this benefit. Rate: Rupees 150 per month until death of the member. Number of beneficiaries: 289 Funeral expenses: Rupees 5000 is given to the legal heir, if the member dies while in service.
Kerala Labour Welfare Fund	Ex-gratia payment: Rs.2500 is paid as death benefit for the immediate relief to the dependants of the deceased employee. Disability allowance: Nil Funeral expenses: Nil
Kerala Head Load Workers Welfare Fund	Ex-gratia payment: In the event of death of a worker while in the rolls, his heir/nominee will be eligible for special death ex-gratia to the tune of Rs.15000 for normal death, Rs. 30000 for accidental death and Rs. 100000 for death in an accident in the course of his employment. Disability allowance: Monthly pension of Rs. 150 will be paid till death. Funeral expenses: On the death of a worker an amount of Rs. 3000 is paid.
Kerala Motor Transport Workers Welfare Fund	Ex-gratia payment: Rs. 25000 is paid to the dependants of a deceased worker. Disability allowance: Member worker in the event of becoming permanently or totally disabled as a result of an accident is being paid an amount of Rs. 25000 as disability allowances.
Kerala Artisans and Skilled Workers Welfare Fund	Ex-gratia payment: Nominee of the deceased member is entitled to receive death benefit of Rs. 10000.

contd...

...contd...

Name of the Welfare Fund	*Remarks*
	Funeral expenses: On the death of a worker an amount of Rs. 500 is paid towards funeral expenses. Disability allowance: Any member sustains fatal injury during the course of his work will get financial assistance of Rs. 1000. If the injury prohibits the member permanently to continue in work, a monthly assistance of Rs. 100 will be given until death.
Kerala Cashew Workers Relief and Welfare Fund	Ex-gratia payment: Rs. 2500 is paid under circumstances such as accidental death, prolonged illness and permanently disabled; in the case of accident death, the payment is made to the dependants. Disability allowance: Nil Funeral expenses: Rupees 1000 and Rupees 500 respectively to the nominee of the dependents, if the member is in service or the member who receives pension.
Kerala Handloom Workers Welfare Fund	Ex-gratia payment: Dependent of the deceased member who dies while in employment will be paid Rs. 5000. Disability allowance: Disability allowance is paid up to a maximum of Rs. 5000 to a member under special circumstances like prolonged illness or permanent disablement of the member incapacitating him to continue as a handloom worker. Funeral expenses: Nil
Kerala Abkari Workers Welfare Fund	Ex-gratia payment: Nil Disability allowance: A member of the fund incapacitating to continue in work due to permanent disablement, the member shall be eligible for disability allowance of Rs.5000 to Rs. 10000 respectively. Funeral expenses: The dependent of the deceased person shall be eligible for payment of Rs.1000 for funeral expenses.
Kerala Building and Other Construction Workers Welfare Fund	Ex-gratia payment: When a member dies, his dependent is eligible to get Rs. 15000. If the death is due to an accident at the work spot during employment, his dependent is eligible to get Rs. 100000. Disability allowance: If permanent disability is resulted, worker gets Rs. 50000. When a worker becomes invalid due to disease or accident, he/she becomes eligible for invalid pension to the tune of Rs. 150 per month. Number of Recipients: 404 (2002) Funeral expenses: Dependent of a deceased worker gets Rs. 1000.

contd...

...contd...

Name of the Welfare Fund	*Remarks*
Kerala Agricultural Workers Welfare Fund	Ex-gratia payment: In the event of a death of a member before superannuation and after the contribution for 12 months, an amount of Rs. 1000 shall be paid to the dependent of the member. Disability allowance: Nil Funeral expenses: Nil
Kerala Document Writers Scribes and Stamp Vendors Welfare Fund	Ex-gratia Payment: Rs. 50000 is paid in the case of a member dies before the retirement. Disability allowance: Nil Funeral expenses: Nil
Kerala Auto Rickshaw Workers Welfare Fund	Ex-gratia payment: In case of the death of a member his nominee will get Rs. 25000 as death benefit. Disability allowance: Nil Funeral expenses: Nil
Kerala Anganwadi Workers Welfare Fund	Ex-gratia payment: In the event of accidental death of a member, dependent of the deceased person will be eligible for Rs. 10000, if the member completed two years of continuos contribution to the fund. Disability allowance: Nil Funeral expenses: Nil
Kerala Tailoring Workers Welfare Fund	Ex-gratia payment: Rs. 10000 is paid to family members in the case of death. Disability Allowance: Disability pension to disabled workers/self-employed tailors who obtained the age of 60 years. Rate: Rs. 100 per month. Number of Recipients: 3045 (2002) Funeral expenses: Nil
Kerala Beedi and Cigar Workers Welfare Fund	Ex-gratia payment: The nominee or the dependent of a member is eligible for a lumpsum payment of Rs. 10000 in the event of death. Disability allowance: Financial assistance is made to a member up to a maximum of Rs. 10000 under special circumstances like prolonged illness or permanent disablement of the worker or member incapacitating him to continue his work or to do any manual labour. Funeral expenses: Nil
Kerala Bamboo, Kattuvalli and Pandanus Leaf Workers Welfare Fund	Ex-gratia payment: Dependent of a member will be paid Rs. 10000 if the member dies in an accident. Disability allowance: Member suffers from permanent disablement is entitled to get Rs. 10000. Funeral expenses: Nil
All Other Welfare Fund Boards	Nil

Source: Compiled by the author from the Welfare Fund Board records.

Educational Allowances

Half of the welfare fund boards in Kerala offer scholarships and cash awards to children of enrolled members to improve the educational situation among unorganised workers. Education grants to school students from 8th to 10th standards are provided with Rs. 250 per annum among 3000 children belonging to Kerala labour welfare fund members. Recently, Kerala agricultural workers welfare fund introduced an incentive scheme of Rs. 200 for admission into 1st standard to promote primary education. Few (*anganwadi* workers welfare fund, motor transport workers welfare fund and bamboo, *kattuvalli* and pandanus leaf workers welfare fund) funds provide loans to members for their children's education. More details can be seen from Table 11.7.

Table 11.7

Educational Allowances (Scholarships and Cash Awards) for Children Offered by the Welfare Fund Boards in Kerala, 2004

Name of the Welfare Fund	*Remarks*
Kerala Toddy Workers Welfare Fund	Scholarships: Available for the children and dependants of toddy workers studying in the Govt. school and colleges or Govt. approved institutions from 8th standard to professional courses. Minimum 40% marks in the exams is a pre-requisite. Cash Awards: Cash awards are given to the students appeared in the Secondary School Leaving Certificate Examination and who secured the highest mark in the district level and state level. Candidate with the highest mark in state is given Rs. 1500. In the districts, the first rank holder will get Rs. 1000, the second rank holder will get Rs. 500 and the third rank holder will get Rs. 250 respectively.
Kerala Labour Welfare Fund	Scholarships: Educational grant to school students (8th, 9th and 10th) at Rs. 250 per annum to 3000 students. Educational grants for higher education to the children of members ranging from Rs. 400 to Rs. 1800 per annum depend upon the nature of the professional course. Craftsman training: Board imparts training to 230 students in 12 Government industrial training institutes on 13 different trades and provide a stipend of Rs. 150 per month. Computer training: The Board in association with the Lal Bahadur Shastri Centre, Trivandrum and DITS at Kannur, conducts training programme to the children of the members at concessional rate for four courses with 50 students each.

contd...

...contd...

Name of the Welfare Fund	*Remarks*
Kerala Head Load Workers Welfare Fund	Scholarships: Grants to workers whose children study in school/colleges will be paid Rs. 200 at the reopening time. Annual scholarships ranging from Rs. 100 to 3000 are paid to children studying in technical and professional courses.
Kerala Motor Transport Workers Welfare Fund	Scholarships: Annual scholarships ranging from Rs. 1000 to 3000 are paid to children studying in technical and professional courses. Loans: The member can avail of educational loans not exceeding Rs. 1200 at a time.
Kerala Artisans and Skilled Workers Welfare Fund	Scholarships: Educational grants for higher education to the children of members ranging from Rs. 500 to Rs. 2500 per annum depending upon the nature of the professional course.
Kerala Cashew Workers Relief and Welfare Fund	Scholarships: Educational grants for higher education to the children of members ranging from Rs. 500 to Rs. 2500 per annum depending upon the nature of the professional course.
Kerala Handloom Workers Welfare Fund	Scholarships: Grants to the children of the members are being paid between Rs. 250 to 5000 per year depending upon the professional course. Cash Awards: Rs. 500 is being paid to the member's son/daughter who scores highest mark in the Secondary School Leaving Certificate examination in each district every year.
Kerala Building and Other Construction Workers Welfare Fund	Scholarships: Children of members are eligible to get scholarship for pursuing post-matric studies. Cash Awards: Those who score higher marks in the Secondary School Leaving Certificate in the state are eligible to get cash award. Entrance Coaching Fees: Board has decided to pay a maximum amount of Rs. 5000 to the children of the workers to undergo entrance coaching classes for the professional courses.
Kerala Agricultural Workers Welfare Fund	Scholarships: Nil Cash Awards: Children of the members who have scored higher marks in the Secondary School Leaving Certificate examination. Primary Education: To promote primary education among the workers, children admitted to 1st standard are given Rs. 200 as incentive.
Kerala Anganwadi Workers Welfare Fund	Loans: Members can avail the loan upto Rs. 1000 for higher education of their children.
Kerala Tailoring Workers Welfare Fund	Scholarships: Grants are offered between Rs. 600 to Rs. 3000 to children undergoing various professional courses. Cash Awards: Awards for students who secured highest marks in the Secondary School Leaving Certificate examination.

contd...

...contd...

Name of the Welfare Fund	Remarks
Kerala Bamboo, Kattuvalli and Pandanus Leaf Workers Welfare Fund	Loans: Non-refundable advance up to 80% amount can be available for children education. Scholarships: Scholarship is given to 15 students (Rupees 1000 per annum for two years) who secured 65% marks in the Secondary School Leaving Certificate Examination, to pursue plus two course.
All Other Welfare Fund Boards	Nil

Source: Compiled by the author from the Welfare Fund Board records.

Medical Allowances

Currently, 10 welfare funds in Kerala offer some allowances for medical treatment and other expenses. Workers who suffer from any serious diseases or undergo surgery are given payment up to Rs. 10000 by Kerala labour welfare fund. Medical expenses are reimbursed upto Rs. 5000 for any serious diseases or operations among *anganwadi* workers welfare fund. Besides, they also reimburse between Rs. 200 to Rs. 500 for out-patient treatment for every year and Rs. 1000 for in-patients (see Table 11.8).

Table 11.8

Medical Allowances Offered by the Welfare Fund Boards in Kerala, 2004

Name of the Welfare Fund	Remarks
Kerala Toddy Workers Welfare Fund	Aid for cancer treatment: A member of this fund who is suffering from cancer is eligible for Rs. 7000.
Kerala Labour Welfare Fund	Workers suffer from serious diseases and operations are given payment up to Rs.10000.
Kerala Head Load Workers Welfare Fund	The worker is hospitalised for treatment beyond two days in any registered/recognised hospitals, the expenses incurred for the treatment is reimbursed on claims subject to a maximum of Rs. 5000 per annum. In the case of his spouse, children below 18 years and aged parents, the amount is limited to Rs. 2000 per year.
Kerala Motor Transport Workers Welfare Fund	Member can avail loan for medical treatment subject to a maximum amount equal to 3 months of his basic wages. Member is entitled for medical benefits subject to a maximum amount of Rs. 25000 or 50% of the actual expenses which ever is less for certain chronic diseases.
Kerala Khadi Workers Welfare Fund	Loan up to 50% of his contribution for his or his

contd...

...contd...

Name of the Welfare Fund	*Remarks*
	dependent medical treatment; provision for medical grant of Rs. 500.
Kerala Building and Other Construction Workers Welfare Fund	When a worker is hospitalised due to accident/ disease, he gets medical benefits. If the patient is hospitalised for five days, he is eligible for Rs. 300. An additional amount of Rs. 50 is given for every additional day of hospitalisation.
Kerala Agricultural Workers Welfare Fund	A member is entitled for reimbursement of Rs. 1000 in connection with medical expenses.
Kerala Anganwadi Workers Welfare Fund	Medical expenses are reimbursed up to Rs. 5000 for workers who suffer from serious diseases and conduct major surgeries. Medical reimbursement between Rs. 200 to Rs. 500 for out-patient treatment is allowed for one year; Rs. 1000 for in-patients.
Kerala Tailoring Workers Welfare Fund	Medical expenses up to Rs.10000 are given one time for workers suffering from serious diseases and operations; Rs. 5000 for physically handicapped members for purchase of artificial limbs and crutches.
Kerala Bamboo, Kattuvalli and Pandanus Leaf Workers Welfare Fund	Member is given non-refundable advance up to 80% of amount in the account.
All Other Welfare Fund Boards	Nil

Source: Compiled by the author from the Welfare Fund Board records.

Marriage and Maternity Benefits

Out of 24 welfare funds, 10 welfare funds give marriage grants ranging from Rs. 1000 to Rs. 3000 (Kerala Bamboo, Kattuvalli and Pandanus Leaf Workers Welfare Fund) to the members towards marriage of their daughter (for more details, see Table 11.9). However, Kerala head load workers welfare fund offer an interest free loan of Rs. 5000 to the daughter's marriage. On the other hand, only 8 welfare funds provide maternity allowances to members or spouses of the members ranging from Rs. 500 to Rs. 2000 only for two deliveries. The exception is cashew workers relief and welfare fund in which the maternity benefit is provided upto three children.

Table 11.9

Marriage and Maternity Benefits Offered by the Welfare Fund Boards in Kerala, 2004

Name of the Welfare Fund	*Remarks*
Kerala Head Load Workers Welfare Fund	Marriage loan: Workers will be paid an interest free loan of Rs. 5000 in connection with daughter's marriage. After marriage celebration, an amount of Rs. 1500 will be paid to the worker as grant. Maternity Benefit: Nil
Kerala Artisans and Skilled Workers Welfare Fund	Marriage Assistance: Member is eligible to get Rs. 2000 for the marriage of their daughter. Maternity Benefit: Women members are entitled to get an amount of Rs. 750 as maternity benefit upto 2 children.
Kerala Cashew Workers Relief and Welfare Fund	Marriage Assistance: Widowed members are provided with a financial assistance of Rs. 1000 for marriage of their daughters subject to a maximum of two times. Maternity Benefit: Rs. 1000 granted to women employees who are deprived of the benefit of any other schemes, upto three children.
Kerala Handloom Workers Welfare Fund	Marriage Assistance: All members are eligible to get Rs. 2000 for their daughter's marriage. Maternity Benefit: Woman member is eligible to get Rs. 500 as maternity benefit.
Kerala Building and Other Construction Workers Welfare Fund	Marriage Assistance: Women workers and daughters of members are eligible to get Rs. 3000 as marriage assistance. Male members and son of members will be paid Rs. 2000 for their marriage. Maternity Benefit: Women workers are eligible to get maternity benefit of Rs. 2000 for two times.
Kerala Agricultural Workers Welfare Fund	Marriage Assistance: Financial assistance is given to the marriage of female member or the marriages of daughters of the all members are entitled to get Rs. 2000. Maternity Benefit: A women member is eligible to get a benefit of Rs. 1000 for two deliveries.
Kerala Anganwadi Workers Welfare Fund	Marriage Assistance: Loan for the marriage of the member or their daughters to the extent of Rs. 2000. Maternity Benefit: Nil
Kerala Tailoring Workers Welfare Fund	Marriage Assistance: Rs. 1000 each is given for the marriage of the female member and for two daughters of each member. Maternity Benefit: Rs. 600 towards maternity benefit is given to the women workers for two deliveries.

contd...

...contd...

Name of the Welfare Fund	*Remarks*
Kerala Beedi and Cigar Workers Welfare Fund	Marriage Assistance: Female member is eligible to get Rs. 2000 for her marriage. Maternity Benefit: Female member is also eligible for maternity benefit of Rs. 500.
Kerala Bamboo, Kattuvalli and Pandanus Leaf Workers Welfare Fund	Marriage Assistance: Rs. 3000 as grant for marriage of female member or daughter of the members. Maternity Benefit: Rs. 1000 to female members as maternity benefit for two deliveries.
All Other Welfare Fund Boards	Nil

Source: Compiled by the author from the Welfare Fund Board records.

Housing Loans

Only six welfare funds offer housing loan facilities to its members. According to the head load workers welfare fund, if the worker owns three cents of land, he is eligible to avail the loan of Rs. 100000 for new house construction and Rs. 50000 for repair/extension. However, bamboo, *kattuvalli* and pandanus leaf workers welfare fund provides 50 per cent loan and 50 per cent grant subject to the availability of fund, if the member has completed five years of membership in the fund (for more details, see Table 11.10).

Table 11.10

Housing Loans Offered by the Welfare Fund Boards in Kerala, 2004

Name of the Welfare Fund	*Remarks*
Kerala Head Load Workers Welfare Fund	If the worker owns 3 cents of land, he is eligible to avail the loan of 100,000 for new house construction and 50000 for repair/extension.
Kerala Motor Transport Workers Welfare Fund	Non-refundable advances paid for construction or purchase of a house.
Kerala Handloom Workers Welfare Fund	Assistance is paid to a member for purchase or construction of a house.
Kerala Building and Other Construction Workers Welfare Fund	Members are eligible to get advance at the rate of Rs. 50000 for the construction of residential house.
Kerala Anganwadi Workers Welfare Fund	Housing advance of Rs. 10000 is payable to members for construction of a house. An advance of Rs. 5000 is paid for renovation, extension or alteration.
Kerala Bamboo, Kattuvalli and Pandanus Leaf Workers Welfare Fund	If the member completed five years of service, they can get 50% loan and 50% grant subject to the availability of funds.
All Other Welfare Fund Boards	Nil

Source: Compiled by the author from the Welfare Fund Board records.

Other Programmes

Toddy workers welfare fund and motor transport workers welfare fund provide unemployment benefits to its members (Table 11.11). Similarly, labour welfare fund gives grant to libraries, tour subsidies and financial assistance to physically handicapped for purchasing artificial limbs upto Rs. 5000. Head load workers welfare fund offers bonus to every worker at 11.5 per cent of the total wages earned by him during each financial year in connection with festivals plus holiday allowances for 9 days at the rate of average daily wages annually (Table 11.11).

Table 11.11

Unemployment Benefits Offered by the Welfare Fund Boards in Kerala, 2004

Name of the Welfare Fund	*Remarks*
Kerala Toddy Workers Welfare Fund	Provide unemployment loan to its members.
Kerala Motor Transport Workers Welfare Fund	Give financial assistance to its members for the period of unemployment not exceeding an amount of the provident fund contribution in his credit.
All Other Welfare Fund Boards	Nil

Source: Compiled by the author from the Welfare Fund Board records.

Table 11.12

Special Schemes Offered by the Welfare Funds in Kerala, 2004

Name of the Welfare Fund	*Remarks*
Kerala Labour Welfare Fund	Grant to Libraries: Grant to libraries mainly used for workers for purchase of books up to Rs. 5000.
	Tour Subsidy: Workers and their family members can avail tour subsidy at holiday home at Thekkady/Kumily with Rs.125 per day with concession price for food and accommodation.
	Financial assistance to physically handicapped for purchasing artificial limbs, crutches up to Rs. 5000.
Kerala Head Load Workers Welfare Fund	Bonus: Every worker is paid bonus at 11.5% of the total wages earned by him during each financial year in connection with festivals.
	Holiday Allowance: Workers are paid holiday allowance for 9 days at the rate of average daily wages annually.
All Other Welfare Fund Boards	Nil

Source: Compiled by the author from the Welfare Fund Board records.

Conclusion

The labour welfare fund is voluntary in nature. The number of workers and establishments registered fluctuates widely so the income and the resources base of the fund is loosely targeted and the administrative expenses are extremely high. They can enhance the contribution and introduce old age pension so that it can benefit the large number of workers.

References

Das, S.K. (2001). *A Better Deal for Beedi Workers*. Report submitted to the International Labour Organisation, New Delhi.

Government of Kerala (1996). *Social Security Initiatives in Kerala*. Thiruvananthapuram: State Planning Board.

———. (1997). *Report of the Task Force on Social Security and Welfare*. Thiruvananthapuram: State Planning Board.

Irudaya, Rajan S. and S. Harichandran (1994). "Social Security and Assistance Schemes in Kerala". *International Conference on the Elderly Proceedings*. International Federation on Ageing. Chapter 55: 331-347.

Irudaya, Rajan S. and U.S. Mishra (1997). "Population Ageing: Causes and Consequences. Chapter 12, pp. 222-237" in K.C. Zachariah and S. Irudaya Rajan (eds.) (1997). *Kerala's Demographic Transition: Determinants and Consequences*. New Delhi: Sage Publications.

Irudaya, Rajan S. (1999). "Aging and Social Security". Chapter 3, pp. 49-71 in B.A. Praksh (ed). *Kerala's Economic Development: Issues and Problems*. New Delhi: Sage Publications India Private Limited.

Irudaya, Rajan S., U.S. Mishra and P.S. Sarma (1999). *India's Elderly: Burden or Challenge?* New Delhi: Sage Publications.

Irudaya, Rajan S. (2000). "Social Security and Safety Nets for Unorganized Sector in India", Paper Presented at the *Workshop on Reforming Pension System in South Asia* organised by the Asian Development Bank Institute, held at the Oberoi Hotel, New Delhi, 23 November-2 December.

———. (2001). "Social Assistance for Poor Elderly: How Effective?", *Economic and Political Weekly* XXXVI(8): 613-617. February 24.

Jhabvala, Renana, Neelam Gupta and Nita Mishra (2000). *Losing Work: A Study of Beedi Workers in India*. New Delhi: International Labour Organization.

Jhabvala, Renana and R.K.A. Subramanya (2000). *The Unorganized Sector: Worker Security and Social Protection*. New Delhi: Sage Publications.

Kannan, K.P. (2002). "The Welfare Fund Model of Social Security for Informal Sector Workers: The Kerala Experience", *Working Paper No 332*. Thiruvananthapuram: Centre for Development Studie.

Kurien, John and Antonyto Paul (n.d.). "Social Security Nets for Marine Fisheries: The Growth and Changing Composition of Social Security Programmes in the Fisheries Sector of Kerala State", *Working Paper No. 318*. Thiruvananthapuram: Centre for Development Studies.

Ministry of Labour. Various annual reports.

Nata, Duvvury and Sabu George (1997). *Social Security in the Informal Sector: A Study of Labour Welfare Funds in Kerala*. UNDP sponsored project. Trivandrum: Centre for Development of Imaging Technology.

Pillai, S. Mohanan (1992). *Social Security Schemes for Workers in Unorganised Sector: A Case Study of Head Load Workers Welfare Fund Schemes in Kerala*. M.Phil Thesis Submitted to Jawaharlal Nehru University, Thiruvananthapuram: Centre for Development Studies.

———. (1996). "Social Security for Workers in Unorganized Sector: Experience of Kerala", *Economic and Political Weekly* 31(31): 2098-2107.

State Planning Board (2003). *Economic Review 2002*. Government of Kerala, Thiruvananthapuram.

Vijayasankar, P.S. (1986). *The Urban Casual Labour Market in Kerala: A Study of the Head Load Workers in Kerala*. M.Phil Thesis Submitted to Jawaharlal Nehru University. Thiruvananthapuram: Centre for Development Studies.

12

Ageing, Widowhood and Health Vulnerability

SREERUPA

Introduction

An improvement in the life expectancy of population has been experienced by most of the countries around the globe as a result of the process of economic development and public health achievements. The expectation of life at birth among females and males in India has risen from 49 and 50.5 years during 1970-1975 to 63 and 61.3 during 2001 (i.e., by 14 and 10.8 years respectively). The expectation of life at 60 has also risen by 3.8 year from 14.3 to 18.1 years among females and by 2.6 years from 13.4 to 16 years among males. Undoubtedly, years have been added to the life of the elderly but the question remains that whether life has been added to these years. Decline in health, though, just one of the possible risks associated with old age apart from a prospective fall in income, dependency and loneliness, remains one of the dominant concerns among the aged (Jai Prakash, 1999). This is not surprising as studies have shown that health is one of the crucial factors that determine the quality of life among the elderly (Wiggins *et al.*, 2004). Moreover, poor health would be a cause of worry among the elderly since illness episodes in general have the potential to cause economic shock (Crystal *et al.*, 2000), leading to financial dependency (Pal, 2004), loss of autonomy, reduced social contact and loneliness.

Literature on health clearly shows that a positive relation exists between age and morbidity among the adults, i.e., at old age there is higher prevalence of morbidity implying that the risk of illness and morbidity is higher among the aged (Duraisamy, 2001). However, even among the aged there could be individuals or group of individuals, experiencing a greater risk to health deficits in comparison to the other aged. A systemic concentration of poor health among a certain group of the elderly population is a marker of their health vulnerability. These vulnerabilities are socially constructed and are rooted in structural inequalities associated with certain debilitating characteristics or social conditions. Among the aged, female gender and widowhood may be two such characteristics associated with poor health.

Ageing, Widowhood and Health: A Review

There is a wealth of literature in the western societies which has examined the health status of the aged and the differences therein on the basis of age, gender and marital status. The relation between marital status and mortality has been widely studied especially in the western societies. These studies have documented that mortality rates are higher for non-married[1] people than married people, and are especially high for the formerly married (Gove, 1973; Trovato and Lauris, 1989). In general, these studies have shown that widowed individuals have poorer health than do the currently married, with differences being greater for men than for women. On the whole, studies have found marital differences in health and mortality to be similar. The divorced and separated people appear least healthy, followed by widowed, then single people, while the married people appear most healthy (Hu and Goldman, 1990; Umberson *et al.*, 1992; Verbrugge, 1979; Wyke and Ford, 1992).

However, the effect of marital status on health varies substantially by gender. The mortality studies show that non-married men have much higher mortality rates than married ones, while the difference for women is smaller (Zick and Smith, 1991). Hence, it was argued that men are more affected by the non-marriage and behave in ways that increase their health risks as marriage appears to provide a greater protective affect for men than for women (Gove, 1973; Zick and Smith, 1991). While mortality studies have found men to be more sensitive to marital status, surprisingly, women appeared to be more sensitive than men to their marital status in morbidity and disability studies (Verbrugge, 1979). The experience of the dissolution of marriage has been found to have a longer lasting effect on women's health than on men's health (Murphy *et al.*, 1997).

Further, the pathways of health benefits from marital status have been widely noted to vary with gender. While women benefit via an increase in socio-economic status, men benefit via an increase in social support (Hu and Goldman, 1990; Zick and Smith, 1991). Based on data on Dutch persons in the age group of 25-74 years, Joung *et al.* (1997) studied the relative contributions of psychosocial conditions, material circumstances[2] and health behaviours to differences in physical and mental health by marital status. While the study found that non-married have higher morbidity rates than married one, it also revealed that psychosocial conditions contributed most to the explanation of morbidity differences among men, but material circumstances contributed most among women. The indicators of psychosocial

1. Non-married persons include unmarried persons as well as 'have-been married' persons.
2. The material circumstance was captured using household income, financial problems, crowding and housing condition.

condition used in this study were emotional support, instrumental support, partner loss in the previous year and other life events which also capture an element of quality of the social support. There has been a long standing stream of research in the Western societies which has engaged with issues like marital status and health (even among aged), impact of bereavement or the shock of widowhood on health and investigations into the gender differences in these interrelations. But there is dearth of comparable research studies in diverse cultural settings. The association between marital status and health is a highly under-researched area in South Asia, particularly India. Here, marriages are near-universal, the dominant patriarchal ideology creates sharp gender differences in the access to resources and much of such claim on resources for women comes through marriage. Further, the society is predominantly community-oriented rather than being individualistic; all these unique characteristics provide a very different cultural setting from that of the western societies. Hence, there is scope for significant contribution to the existing body of knowledge by studying the association of marital status and health of aged in India. Hence, the aim of this study is to extend previous research done in this area in western societies, by undertaking a gender analysis of the association between health and marital status among the aged in a contrasting cultural setup of India. The study examines whether aged widows experience relatively poor health status when compared to all aged women or men of comparable age and marital status groups; further possible explanations for health vulnerability of aged widows is explored in their differential access to material and care resources.

Demographic Profile of Ageing in India

It is a combination of high fertility and falling mortality during the 20th century which has brought about rapid increases in the elderly population in the country, as successively larger cohorts enter the spin of old age (Rajan *et al.*, 2003). According to the Census 2001, India had an elderly population of 77 million. The proportion of elderly persons in India has been rising from 5.63 per cent in 1961 to 6.08 per cent in 1991 (Rajan *et al.*, 1999) to 7.5 per cent in 2001.

A look at the break-up of the population age structure on the basis of sex immediately reveals the trend of feminisation of ageing i.e., an increase in the share of the female in the older population. India is one of the few countries in the world where males outnumber females in the general population. But a look at the sex ratio of the females, in the age group of 60 and above, shows an improvement from 94 aged females per 100 males in 1991 to 103 in 2001. This phenomenon is a result of faster reduction in female than male mortality in the recent past and also due to a slightly higher female life expectance at ages 60 and above than that of males.

An emphatic feature of the demographic profile of the female aged is the higher proportion of widowhood. More than half of all aged women in India are widowed compared with less than 10 per cent of men in India. The higher female life expectancy at ages 60 and 70, universal tendency for women to marry men older than themselves and the social restrictions on widows to remarry have led to a high incidence of widowhood among the female aged (Gulati, 1993). The incidence of female widowhood is slightly more than three times that of male widowhood at the national level. Seventy-one per cent of women are widowed as against 29 per cent of men among the oldest old age group i.e., those 80 years and above of age. It can be seen that at any given age, there are more widows than widowers and as age advances, the prevalence of widowhood also increases.

Given the backdrop of a significant proportion of the aged women spending their extended life as widows, our study takes a critical look at the condition of the elderly women especially the widows from a gender perspective, giving due recognition to the structural disadvantages faced by them under the patriarchal system. Under patriarchy, the death of a husband brings tremendous changes in a woman's life in terms of her social identity and relationships, her living arrangements and her access to property (Chen, 2000; Dreze, 1990). Thus, widowhood could make the situation of a woman vulnerable in both economic and social terms.

A Conceptual Framework for Understanding Health Vulnerability

Literature on widows and aged persons has presented both groups as vulnerable, referring to their general powerless state. Despite a growing literature, there is no consensus on defining vulnerability (Ruof, 2004). Vulnerability is widely associated with 'fragility, defenselessness and lack of means to cope without damaging loss, on being exposed to a risk or a shock' (Chambers, 1989). The emphasis is on the inherent defenselessness or lack of ability to cope rather than concentrating only on risks.[3] Thus, vulnerability of a person or a group of persons is associated with certain characteristics or social condition. In general, the aged population has a higher risk of morbidity, but neither do all aged suffer equally during an illness episode nor

3. The focus on the 'lack of ability to cope' rather than risk is based on the line of argument put forward by the structuralist school of thought which asserted the need to place greater emphasis upon the vulnerability of a population as a determinant of disaster rather than the severity of the hazard. The logic being that the interaction with a vulnerable population is critical in deciding whether, the hazard remains a hazard or turns into a disaster.

do they encounter the same handicaps during the period of recovery. Among the aged, female gender and widowhood are two such debilitating characteristics associated with poor health status. Thus, during old age when the risk of morbidity is high, gender and marital status become two of the critical characteristics which shape the vulnerability of a person or group of persons, thereby determining whether the experience of old age becomes a personal 'catastrophe' or not.

Figure 12.1

Interlinkages between Health and its Socio-economic Correlates

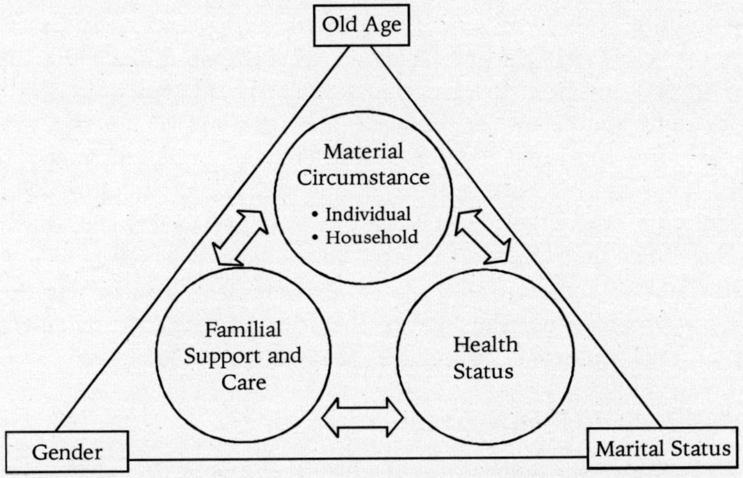

Based on theoretical considerations and the review of previous research largely in developed countries, two set of important factors have been identified which are critical for the well-being of the aged in terms of health, and they are material circumstances and familial support (as shown in Figure 12.1). When considering access to material resources for the aged, both individual as well as household characteristics have been considered. At the individual level, the economic independence, education and ownership of property and finance could indicate the aged person's access to economic resources; while per capita monthly expenditure quartiles and social groups capture the household socio-economic condition. In the South Asian cultural context, caring resources for the aged mainly comes from the family and close kin, as there is no systematic provision of extra-familial care from either the state or the market. So we limit our analysis to the support and care available from the family. And given the limitation of the data in terms of availability of a direct measure of health care provided by the family members, we take 'relation with the head of the household' and 'living arrangement' as a proxy for the same. However, it is important to placc our understanding of these capacities of the aged within the structure of old age, gender and marital status, since they have a critical role in determining the distribution, access and control of these assets and capabilities among the aged. Gender also plays a major role in the kin availability, support in old age and resource availability, particularly through the status of parenthood and widowhood. This is important more so for women whose access to extra-familial sources of livelihood and support are limited and grow more so with age. Among the familial ties, the role of marital status is important given its potential to confer health related benefits mainly through the pathway of improved socioeconomic status for women and care and social support for men (Goldman *et al.*, 1995; Hu and Goldman, 1990; Ross *et al.*, 1990; Zick and Smith, 1991) apart from the emotional support and companionship which would be quite significant for the aged. However, the gendered pathway for health benefits accruing from marriage charted out by scholars is only indicative, may not be universally applicable and would be culturally specific. Gender plays a crucial role in a largely patriarchal society like ours where losing the spouse not only means a fall in the economic status of a woman, given her lack of access to extra-familial resources but also puts her in a socially unfavourable position due to the stigma attached to widowhood in certain cultural contexts (Chakravarti, 1998; Chen, 2000).

Markers of Health Vulnerability

According to our framework, poor health status is the adverse outcome against which vulnerability among the aged is assessed. For the purpose of this study, the indicators of health status used are: perceived current health status, prevalence of chronic ailment and prevalence of disability. The latter two morbidity measures are generally of two types, namely, self-perceived and observed (Murray and Chen, 1992). Self-perceived morbidity measure is based on morbidity information provided by the respondent during the survey. Observed morbidity measure, on the other hand is based on the illness pattern as assessed by an independent trained observer using specific methods that lend themselves for repetition with some degree of consistency (Duraisamy, 2001). For the purpose of this study, we are using the former measure of morbidity due to the unavailability of the observed measure in a large scale sample survey data like NSS and acknowledge the limitations of the same. Nevertheless, it would be worth mentioning that studies have found self-perceived health to be a reliable predictor of future functional status and even mortality (Idler and Benyamini, 1997; Idler and Kasl, 1995), thereby providing empirical support for the use of the same as a measure of overall health.

The analyses in this study has been extensively based on the unit level data of the 52nd Round (July 1995–June 1996) survey, conducted by the National Sample Survey Organisation, on Morbidity, Health Care and the Conditions of the Aged. Though the NSS 60th Round Survey (January-June 2004) Report has been published in March 2006, the unit level data had not been released, thereby limiting the scope for any in-depth analysis of the same. Given this scenario, the unit level data of NSS 52nd round is one of the most suitable recent source of information for ascertaining the health status and general condition of the aged all over India. The survey had a nationwide coverage with 33,982 elderly sample. The unit level data in the 52nd round of the NSS provides data on the morbidity patterns, use of medical facility, hospitalisation and related details for the general population for 1995-96. We have used this part of the survey to cull out the relevant information for the aged. Further, we have referred to the module on the aged, which provides additional information pertaining to their social and economic position. It also gives additional information on specific health condition of the aged like information on physical mobility, disability, current state of health, relative state of health etc.

Measuring Health Status of the Aged across Marital Status Groups

In this chapter, we try to identify the 'vulnerable groups' by exploring the systematic disparities in the health status of the aged across gender and marital status. So to examine the identify the 'vulnerable group(s)', we have divided the aged population into four exhaustive groups[4]—married male, widowed male, married female and widowed female. Here we use two different approaches to measure the poor health status of the aged population. Firstly, we have calculated the prevalence rates for each of the above mentioned health attributes. A prevalence rate tells us the total number of persons who have an attribute or illness at a given moment in time divided by the population at risk of having the attribute or illness.

Finally, we calculate the relative risks, which is a ratio measuring the strength of an association that compares two populations, a population exposed to a particular risk factor (e.g. old age) to a population who is not (e.g. not old). A relative risk of 1 means there is no association (e.g. risk of

4. Both the category of married and widowed elderly refers to the currently married and currently widowed elderly.

having an illness is the same for persons exposed to poor work environment and otherwise). A relative risk greater than 1 suggests that persons exposed to the factor increases the likelihood of having an illness. The stronger the association, the higher will be the relative risk. Generally relative risks below 2 are considered weak, since a large proportion of relative risks in the profile are less than 2. We include levels of significance obtained from chi-square test to strengthen our confidence in associations. Relative risks have been used for assessing socio-economic inequalities in health by comparing the disadvantaged group(s) to the most advantaged group. But here we use this measure to assess the inequalities in the health status by comparing the group which emerges as the most disadvantaged during the analysis with the rest of the groups, to underscore the relatively greater risk experienced by the former.

Assessing Self-reported Health Status

Prevalence of Poor Health Status, Disability and Chronic Illness

Self-assessed current health status is a subjective measure closely associated with the feelings of well-being and quality of life. In the survey when asked to rate their health status (as 'excellent', 'very good', 'good/fair' or 'poor'), more than 79 per cent of aged reported their health status to be ranging from 'excellent' to 'good/fair', with nearly 70 per cent reporting 'good/fair' health status. This is despite a large number of the elderly, nearly 66 per cent, reporting to be suffering from at least one disability or chronic ailment. The reason could be that many of them perceive illness and health problems as a part of old age and may be responding to the question accordingly.

In the survey, the respondents were asked whether or not they were suffering from any of the following disabilities related to old age: visual, hearing, speech, locomotion and senility. We constructed a binary variable which took the value of 1 if the response is "yes" to any of the above set of questions. We found that 39.1 per cent elderly had at least one disability. Nearly a quarter of the elderly reported visual disability, making it the disability showing the highest prevalence. Another indicator of health status is the prevalence of chronic illness.[5] In the survey, the respondents were asked whether they suffered from each of the eight listed chronic ailments and the responses were coded as 'yes', 'no' and 'not known'. Here again we constructed a binary variable which took the value of 1 if the response is "yes" to any of

5. Generally, chronic ailment refers to a long duration illness for a period of six months or more. But as per the definition used for the compilation of NSS data, an illness lasting for more than 30 days has been termed as chronic illness.

the above mentioned ailments. It was observed that 52.6 per cent of the elderly had at least one of the eight listed chronic ailment.

Table 12.1

Current State of Health, Prevalence of at least One Disability and Chronic Illness by Sex and Marital Status (in %)

Sex	*Marital Status*	*Poor*	*At Least One Disability*	*At Least One Chronic Ailment*
Male	Currently married	15.42	35.46	51.88
	Widowed	21.41	42.40	55.87
	Total	16.67	36.90	52.71
Female	Currently married	15.51	30.74	47.57
	Widowed	24.82	48.24	55.75
	Total	21.09	41.22	52.46
Total	Currently married	15.45	33.84	50.40
	Widowed	23.97	46.77	55.78
	Total	18.91	39.10	52.58

Note: 1. At least one disability includes disability of vision, hearing, speech, locomotor and mind (amnesia/senility).

2. At least one chronic ailment includes ailments like cough, piles, problems of joints, BP, heart disease, urinary problem, diabetes and cancer.

Source: Estimated by the author using the unit level NSS data (52nd round).

From the above table, we can see that there is gender difference in the reporting of health status with more elderly women reporting their health status to be poor (21.1 per cent) as compared to their male counterparts (16.7 per cent). But a closer look reveals that not all aged women have a greater likelihood of suffering poor health, only 15.5 per cent of married women report poor health status as against 24.8 per cent widows. Widowhood seems to be associated with similar adverse health outcome even among the elderly men. However among the four groups, higher percentage of aged widows report their current health status to be poor.

Table 12.1 shows that more aged women (41.2 per cent) have at least one of the five disabilities as compared to the aged men (36.9 per cent). Similarly, higher percentage of the elderly widowed report at least one disability as compared to the married ones, irrespective of their gender. However, the effect size seems to be larger/stronger among the women than men. These results are in line with the evidence provided by the literature (Sengupta and Agree, 2003).

As far as the prevalence of chronic ailment is concerned, there doesn't seem to be a gender difference. Once again we find a significant difference on account of the marital status, with the influence being strongest among the females. Nearly 37 per cent of the elderly have reported having problems with the joints making it the most common health problem reported. Slightly higher number of women report this problem than men, the reason could be the higher prevalence of musculoskeletal condition and osteoporosis among the elderly women as compared to the men (WHO, 2003). Similarly, the gender difference in chronic cough may be rooted in the higher consumption of tobacco and subsequent higher incidence of lung disease among men (Sengupta and Agree, 2003).

While ailments like chronic cough, piles, problems of the joints and urinary problems could be diagnosed without formal medical diagnosis, others like hypertension, diabetes and heart disease would require formal diagnosis. Studies in South Asia have found a female disadvantage in the use of health services and doctor visits (Sengupta and Agree, 2003), so when it comes to the reporting of such ailments requiring formal diagnosis, it is quite possible that the female respondents may underreport.

There may be an argument that a part of the gender and marital status difference in reported health results from age differences, particularly if women tend to be older because their adult mortality rates are lower as also widows since are concentrated in the older age groups (as seen in the previous sections). To check for this possibility we stratified by age group and found that both gender and marital differences within age groups persist (results not shown).

Relative Risks by Marital Status Groups in Health Outcomes

Finally, we calculate the relative risks, which is a ratio measuring the strength of an association that compares two populations.

Table 12.2 indicates that compared to all other groups, the aged widows report the worst health status. In other words, the relative risks suggest that being an elderly widow is associated with relatively greater risk for poor health outcomes. Associations are particularly pronounced for poor perceived health and disability.

The relative risk for poor health is greater for widows when the reference group is married female rather than widowed male. So it gives the impression that marital status is more significant than gender (when we control for gender and marital status respectively) as a risk factor for poor health among the widows. However, the last two columns show that widows have a greater risk to poor health outcome than widowers when the reference group is married men, implying that the gender of the widows makes them more at risk and possibly vulnerable than the widowers. Finally, the relative risks for the widowed with respect to their married counterparts shows that widowhood is a greater risk factor for the aged women as compared to the men. The relative risks calculated for widows of different age groups indicates that for the most part, widowhood as a risk factor for poor health status appears to become less important with the advance of age i.e., the association between widowhood and poor health weakens with age.

Table 12.2

Comparison of Selected Health Status Indicators, Prevalence and Relative Risk by Sex and Marital Status

Indicators (%)	*Female*			*Male*				
	Widowed (1)	*Currently Married* (2)	*RR* (1)/(2)	*Widowed* (3)	*RR* (1)/(3)	*Currently Married* (4)	*RR* (1)/(4)	*RR* (3)/(4)
Poor status of health	24.82	15.51	1.60**	21.41	1.16**	15.42	1.61**	1.39**
At least one disability	48.24	30.74	1.57**	42.40	1.14**	35.46	1.36**	1.20**
At least one chronic ailment	55.75	47.57	1.17**	55.87	1.00	51.88	1.07**	1.08**

Note: Statistical significance of these risks were estimated through chi-square test; *$p<.05$, **$p<.01$.

Source: Estimated by the author using the unit level NSS data (52nd round).

The analysis of the health status of the elderly reveals that widowed of both sexes are a disadvantaged group, with the magnitude of the disadvantage being more severe for the widows. Analysis of the relative risks revealed that being an elderly widow was a risk factor for poor health outcomes. Finally, a comparison of the relative risks for the widowed with their married counterparts revealed that widowhood is a greater risk factor for the aged women as compared to the men.

A possible explanation of the greater health vulnerability of widowed elderly lies in their adverse socio-economic condition. A perusal of the health literature reveals strong association between socio-economic condition and health status. Hence, exploring the differences in the material circumstances and care resources among the elderly could be informative in disentangling inequalities in health status among the elderly groups. In the next section, we would be exploring the socio-economic factors that are associated with vulnerability to poor health among the widows. Firstly, we would start by giving a brief overview of the socio-economic condition of the aged widows.

Differential Economic Capacity and Social Support across Marital Status Groups

Our framework identifies material circumstances and familial support and care as important elements of the capacity of an aged which would have a positive association with the health outcomes. Further, in old age the socio-economic circumstances like the availability of economic resources, support and care provided by the kin, are associated with the gender and marital status of a person. Thus, we keep gender and marital status throughout our analysis of socio-economic capacity of the aged. In our study we try to capture the material circumstances of the elderly by examining their level of economic dependence, education, ownership and management of property and financial assets.[6] Their relation with the head of the household and living arrangement could be good proxy for indicators which capture the access to familial support.

Table 12.3

Pattern of Differential Economic Capacity by Sex and Marital Status

Sex	*Marital Status*	*Illiterate*	*Fully Economically Dependent*	*No Property*	*No Financial Assets*
Male	Currently married	51.98	27.35	16.86	26.85
	Widowed	67.98	43.29	26.90	34.49
Female	Currently married	82.37	66.52	47.10	51.16
	Widowed	87.17	75.46	57.95	65.29

For the above table, we have considered the worst economic condition with respect to each of the indicators, and we find that widows top all of them. The highest number of illiterates are also concentrated among the widows. The pattern of disadvantage is the same as before with clear disadvantages on account of gender and marital status. Majority of the aged widows (75.5 per cent) are fully dependent on others. Similarly, 63 per cent and 56 per cent of elderly widows neither own nor manage any financial assets or property respectively. This is in stark contrast to the elderly married male who seems to fare much better. The glaring material disadvantage faced by women in general and widows in particular, has its basis in

> ...the social expectation of their financial dependence on men within marriage. Women's generally lower pay, together with the constraints on participation in

6. Ownership and management of property and financial assets are highly correlated, hence, only the former would be used in the further analysis.

the paid work placed on those who perform a reproductive role, has profound implications for women in later life, especially following widowhood or divorce (Arber and Ginn, 1991: 69).

Married women gain their power and access to resources via their spouse but with the breakdown of marriage, the women are forced to seek new channels of support. But as the proximity in the relationship with the patron increases, the claim on the economic as well as care resources diminish. Similarly, examining the aged person's relation with the head of the household and their living arrangement helps us to assess their position in the power equation of the household. This should give us a fair insight into their claim on familial support available within the household.

Table 12.4

Pattern of Familial Support Available to the Aged by Sex and Marital Status

Sex	*Marital Status*	*Living Arrangement*				*Relation to Head*			
		Living Alone	*Living with Spouse Only or with Other Members*	*Living with Children*	*Living with Other Relations*	*Self*	*Spouse of Head*	*Father/ Mother/ -in-laws*	*Other Relatives*
Male	Currently married	0.92	94.62	3.17	0.44	89.11	0.19	9.47	1.03
	Widowed	8.26		73.86	8.82	60.01		32.84	5.81
Female	Currently married	1.00	92.32	5.19	0.55	1.17	82.44	14.79	1.45
	Widowed	9.38		78.10	8.20	23.55		67.76	7.30

Source: Estimated by the author using the unit level NSS data (52nd round).

The highest proportion of aged widows (68 per cent) are living in households headed by either their children or the spouse of their children.[7] The majority of the other aged either are head (especially among men) or spouse of the head of the household (among married women) which would be a position of advantage due to the proximity in relation with the head of the household. Headship represents status, power and authority in the family; hence, Sivamurthy and Wadakannavar (2001) underscores the importance of looking into the household headship information regarding aged households since for an aged person to be considered as the head of the household means to a large extent guarantee of availability of better care and support from the

7. The NSS data gives a common designation 'father/mother/in-law' for any relation ranging from the head of the household being own son or daughter to spouse of son or daughter, in the process losing out valuable information about the sex of the head of the household and nature of relation with the elderly.

family members. Empirical support is available in Rahman's (1999) study of the impact of relationship to head of the household on aged mortality in rural Bangladesh, which revealed that being the head of the household had a significant impact on reducing aged mortality for both men and women.

Another point to note is that only the older widowed persons are living alone in significant numbers and even among them, more than 63 per cent are widows. This is quite an ironical situation for the aged women, since throughout their life, they provide care for their husband and other older relatives and finally in their old age when they need help, they are left alone with no one to care for them. Meanwhile, most of the married older persons co-reside with their spouse and children, thereby having access to the care and support of both spouse and children. On the other hand, the widowed are completely dependent on their children for the same.

Association between Health Status and Socio-economic Capacity of Aged

Health economics literature is replete with evidence showing strong association between health and socio-economic conditions. Studies have shown that even at older ages the health of a person is related to his or her socio-economic condition. In the previous section, we have shown that in the old age the socio-economic circumstances like the availability of economic resources, support and care provided by the kin, are associated with the gender and marital status of a person, with the aged widows being in the most powerless position. Thus in this section, we investigate the association between health outcomes[8] and socio-economic indicators for all aged in general and widows in particular.

Comparisons of prevalence and relative risks of health problems across the various socio-economic indicators[9] are presented in Appendix Table A-12.1.

Table A-12.1 as well as Figure 12.2 shows that economic dependency[10] is a risk factor for poor health outcomes (i.e., self-reported health status, prevalence of at least on disability and prevalence of at least one chronic illness) for both all aged and widows, more so for the aged. 'Neither owning nor managing of property', and 'owning but not managing' of the same, both

8. The health outcome variables considered are the same as those used in the previous chapter i.e., self-reported health status, prevalence of at least one disability and prevalence of at least one chronic illness.

9. Ownership and management of financial assets and property are highly correlated variables hence, the former has been dropped in all further analysis.

10. Even partial economic dependency turns up as a risk factor for poor health outcome (results not shown).

turn out to be risk factors for poor health outcomes. These results compliment the literature on health which has shown that even at old ages, the health of a person is related to her or his socio-economic condition (Fenwick and Baressi, 1981; Mutchler and Burr, 1991).

Figure 12.2

Association between Health Outcomes and Economic Indicators among Aged Widows

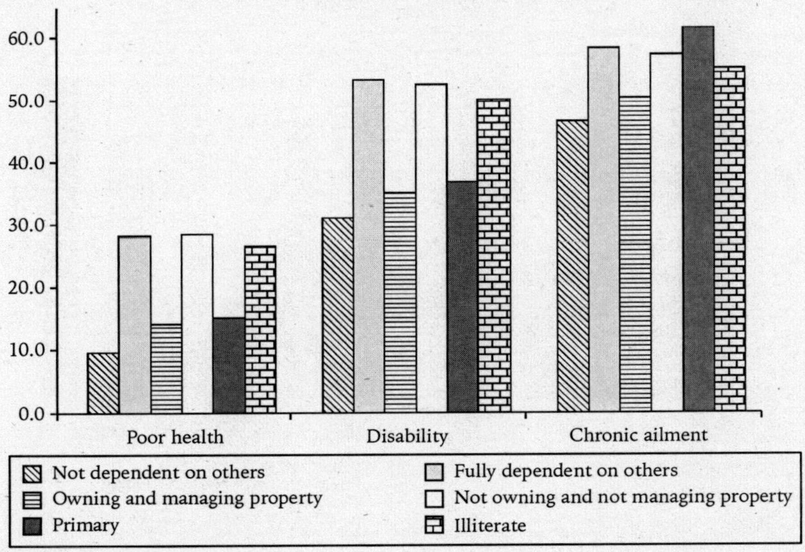

Source: Estimated by the author using the unit level NSS data (52nd round).

However, the association of economic capacity and chronic illness is relatively weaker, may be because there are certain chronic lifestyle ailments which tend to be concentrated among the economically better off and thereby, negating the higher prevalence of general chronic illness among the economically worse off. The higher relative risk of poor health outcomes among the all aged compared to the widows with respect to the economic variables is mainly because the health outcomes of the aged men are more sensitive than women to their level of economic dependence (results not shown). This is understandable given the norms of our society which does not encourage women to be economically independent at any stage in their life; rather they are expected to be financially dependent on their male kin. At the same time, men are expected to be economically independent throughout their working life and as long as possible, hence, a change in status towards economic dependency may be more risky for them.

In the case of relation with the head of the household, living in a household headed by one's children or some other relative is a risk factor for poor health among the widows. In other words, being the head of the household (whether living alone or not) seems to be associated with relatively better health status for the widows.

Figure 12.3

Association between Health Outcomes and Familial Support Available to the Aged Women

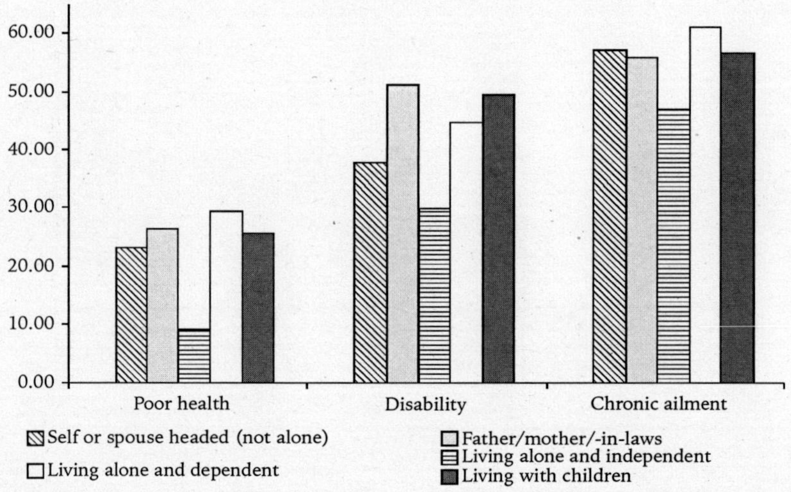

Source: Estimated by the author using the unit level NSS data (52nd round).

In the case of all aged, being spouse of the head appears as the most advantageous position in terms of health outcome (followed by those who head the household with other members), which is almost exclusively representative of the aged married women, a majority of whom live in households headed by their spouse. Meanwhile, losing the headship of the household is a risk factor for the aged men. On investigating further, we found that more than half of the widows (and most of the other aged except married women) heading the household were living with their children. Undoubtedly, heading the household while co-residing with the children, is probably the most advantageous position for an aged.

Older adults who have supportive social networks tend to enjoy better physical and mental health than those without. In a study addressed to examine the question of whether social support from different sources (i.e., spouse, children, and other relatives and friends) have differential impact on mental health, Okabayashi *et al.* (2004) found that among the older persons without a spouse, only greater support from children was significantly correlated with higher positive well-being, less distress and less cognitive impairment.

Except when an aged is economically independent and living alone, for all other cases our analysis also reveals that co-residence with spouse/children is the best living arrangement for the aged with respect to their reported health status and chronic illness. Only in the case of disability, living with children is associated with a higher prevalence of disability among the widows. This is indicative of the possibility that the living arrangement of the aged is determined by their health status (Pal, 2004), hence it calls for caution while interpreting the association between health outcomes and living arrangement. Even if the aged are choosing co-residence with children as a strategy to ensure care and support, it is important to note that some among them do not even have this option like childless widows/widowers who constitute the highest proportion of aged living alone, especially widows. It has been found that for cultures that value family interdependence, older people who live alone or those who do not get emotional and instrumental support from their children (especially those who have lost their spouse) face negative health effects (Zunzunegui *et al.*, 2001).

Summary and Conclusion

Our analysis of the unit level data revealed the presence of disparities in the health status of the aged by gender and marital status. Being an aged widow/widower was a risk factor for poor health status. Widows were particularly vulnerable to poor general health status and disability. The results provide strong support to our hypothesis that the experience of widowhood will be very different for men and women due to the structural disadvantages associated with gender and marital status. A comparison revealed that widowhood is a much greater risk factor for the aged women as compared to the men.

Further, we had explored possible explanations for health vulnerability of aged widows in their differential access to material and care resources. It was found that economic dependency[11] was a risk factor for poor health outcomes (i.e., self-reported health status, prevalence of at least one disability and prevalence of at least one chronic illness) for both all aged and widows. However, contrary to our expectations it was a greater risk factor for the other groups than the widows. 'Neither owning nor managing of property',

---

11. Even partial economic dependency turns up as a risk factor for poor health outcome (results not shown).

and 'owning but not managing' of the same, both turn out to be risk factors for poor health outcomes. These results compliment the literature on health which has shown that even at old ages the health of a person is related to her or his socio-economic condition (Fenwick and Baressi, 1981; Link and Phelan, 2000; Mutchler and Burr, 1991).

In brief, our study highlights the need for modifying our understanding of the association of health and marital status among the aged men and women based on research from diverse cultural settings. The findings of studies from the western societies need not hold true in other societies where the cultural significance and value attached to marriage and widowhood for men and women may be very different.

Similar research needs to be carried out across different cultures to better understand the significance of marital status for the health and well-being of the aged persons in diverse settings. Moreover, the interaction of gender with these aspects of an aged person's life may also vary across cultures. Similarly, there is a strong case for interstate analysis within India. Chen's work on widows in India gives a rich description of the vast diversity in the experience of widowhood in the northern and southern parts of the country emerging from the largely lower status of women in the northern and north-western states. Further, our analysis has revealed how gender and marital status structures the access to resources even among the aged. Hence, there is a need to study the intra-household allocation of resources and how it affects the more vulnerable among the aged. One such vulnerable category of aged persons is the severely disabled or chronically ill aged persons who may be completely dependent on family members for economic support and physical care.

References

Arber, S. and J. Ginn (1991). *Gender and Later Life: A Sociological Analysis of Resources and Constraints.* London: Sage Publication.

Chakravarti, U. (1998). "Gender, Caste and Labor: The Ideological and Material Structure of Widowhood", in *Widows in India: Social Neglect and Public Action,* edited by Martha Alter Chen. New Delhi, India: Sage Publications.

Chambers, R. (1989). "Vulnerability, Coping and Policy", *IDS Bulletin* (Institute of Development Studies, University of Sussex) 20(2): 1–7.

Chen, M. (2000). *Perpetual Mourning: Widowhood in Rural India.* Philadelphia: University of Pennsylvania Press.

Crystal, S., R.W. Johnson, J. Harman *et al.* (2000). "Out-of-pocket Health Care Costs among Older Americans", *Journal of Gerontology B Psychology Sci Soc Sci* 55(1): S51-62.

Dreze, J. (1990). *Widows in Rural India.* STICERD DEP No. 26. London School of Economics, London.

Duraisamy, P. (2001). "Health Status and Curative Health Care in Rural India", *Working Paper* Series No. 78, National Council of Applied Economic Research.

Fenwick, R. and C.M. Baressi (1981). "Health Consequences of Marital Status Change among the Elderly: A Comparison of Cross-sectional and Longitudinal Analyses", *Journal of health and Social Behaviour* 22(2): 106-116. June.

Goldman, N., S. Korenman and R. Weinstein (1995). "Marital Status and Health among the Elderly", *Social Science and Medicine* 40(12): 1717-1730.

Gove, W.R. (1973). "Sex, Marital Status and Mortality", *American Journal of Sociology* 79: 45-67. July.

Gulati, L. (1993). "Population Ageing and Women in Kerala State, India", *Asia-Pacific Population Journal* 8(1): 53-63.

Hu, Y. and N. Goldman (1990). "Mortality Differentials by Marital Status: An International Comparison", *Demography* 27: 233-250.

Idler, E.L. and Y. Benyamini (1997). "Self rated Health and Mortality: A Review of Twenty-seven Community Studies", *Journal of Health and Social Behavior* 38(1): 21-37.

Idler, E.L. and S.V. Kasl (1995). "Self-Ratings of Health: Do They Also Predict Change in Functional Ability?", *Journals of Gerontology: Social Sciences* 50B: S344-S353.

Jai Prakash, I. (1999). *Ageing in India.* Draft. Geneva: World Health Organization.

Joung, I.M.A., K. Stronks, H. van de Mheen, F.W.A. van Poppel, J.B.W. van der Meer, J.P. Mackenbach (1997). "The Contribution of Intermediary Factors to Marital Status Differences in Self Reported Health", *Journal of Marriage and the Family* 59: 476-90.

Link, B.G. and J. Phelan (2000). "Social Conditions as Fundamental Causes of Disease", *Journal of Health and Social Behaviour* (Extra Issue): 80-94.

Murphy, M., K. Glaser and E. Grundy (1997). "Marital Status and Long Term Illness in Great Britain", *Journal of Marriage and the Family* 59(1): 156-164.

Murray, C.J.L. and L.C. Chen (1992). "Understanding Morbidity Change", *Population and Development Review* 18(3): 481-503.

Mutchler, J.E. and J.A. Burr (1991). "Racial Differences in Heath and Health Care Services Utilization in Later Life: The Effect of Socio-economic Status", *Journal of Health and Social Behaviour* 32(4): 342-356. December.

Okabayashia, H., J. Liangb, N. Krausec, H. Akiyamad, H. Sugisawae (2004). "Mental Health among Older Adults in Japan: Do Sources of Social Support and Negative Interaction make a Difference?", *Social Science & Medicine* 59: 2259–2270.

Pal, S. (2004). "Do Children Act as Old Age Security in Rural India? Evidences from an Analysis of Elderly Living Arrangements", *http://129.3.20.41/eps/lab/papers/0495/0405002.pdf*

Rahman, M.O. (1999). "Age and Gender Variation in the Impact of Household Structure on Elderly Mortality", *International Journal of Epidemiology* 28: 485-491.

Rajan, S.I., P.S. Sarma and U.S. Mishra (2003). "Demography of Indian Aging, 2001-2051", in *An Ageing India: Perspectives, Prospects, and Policies,* edited by P.S. Liebig and S.I. Rajan. New York: The Haworth Press. pp.11-30.

———. (1999). *Indian Elderly: Burden or Challenge*. New Delhi: Sage Publication.

Ross, C., J. Mirowsky and K. Goldsteen (1990). "The Impact of the Family on Health: The Decade in Review", *Journal of Marriage and the Family* 52: 1059-1078.

Ruof, M.C. (2004). *Vulnerability, vulnerable populations, and policy*. National Reference Center for Bioethics Literature. Georgetown University, Washington DC, USA. *http://www.ncbi.nlm.nih.gov/entrez/query.fcgi?cmd=Retrieve&db=PubMed&list_uids=15812988&dopt=Abstract*

Sengupta, M. and E.M. Agree (2003). "Gender, Health, Marriage and Mobility Difficulty among Older Adults in India", *Asia-Pacific Population Journal* 18(4): 53-65. December.

Sivamurthy, M. and A.R. Wadakannavar (2001). "Care and Support for the Elderly Population in India: Results from a Survey of the Aged in Rural North Karnataka, India", Paper submitted to the IUSSP General Population Conference held in Salvador (Brazil), during 18th-24th August. 2001.

Trovato, F. and G. Lauris (1989). "Marital Status and Mortality in Canada: 1951-1981", *Journal of Marriage and the Family* 51: 907-922.

Umberson, D. (1992). "Gender, Marital Status and the Social Control of Health Behaviour", *Social Science and Medicine* 34: 907-917.

Verbrugge, M. (1979). "Marital Status and Health", *Journal of Marriage and the Family* 41(2): 267-285.

Wiggins, R., P. Higgs, M. Hyde and D. Blane (2004). "Lifecourse and Contextual Factors that Influence Quality of Life in Early Old Age", *Ageing and Society* 24: 693-708

World Health Organization (2003). "Gender, Health and Ageing", *http://www.who.int/gender/documents/en/Gender_Ageing.pdf*

Wyke, S. and G. Ford (1992). "Competing Explanations for Associations between Marital Status and Health", *Social Science and Medicine* 34: 523-532.

Zick, C.D. and K.R. Smith (1991). "Marital Transitions, Poverty, and Gender Differences in Mortality", *Journal of Marriage and the Family* 53(2): 327-336. May.

Zunzunegui, M.V., F. Beland and A. Otero (2001). "Support from Children, Living Arrangements, Self-rated Health and Depressive Symptoms of Older People in Spain", *International Journal of Epidemiology* 30: 1090-1099.

Annex Table A-12.1

Association between Health Outcomes and Socio-economic Indicators

Socio-economic Indicator	*Group of Aged*		*Poor Health Status*		*At Least One Disability*		*At Least One Chronic Ailment*	
			%	*RR*	*%*	*RR*	*%*	*RR*
State of economic dependence	Widow	Not dependent	9.79		31.25		46.62	
		Fully dependent	28.30	2.89**	53.24	1.70**	58.34	1.25**
	All aged	Not dependent	7.78		26.49		44.77	
		Fully dependent	26.84	3.45**	48.42	1.83**	58.30	1.30**
Ownership and management of property	Widow	Owning and managing	14.22		35.17		50.24	
		Owning but not managing	26.47	1.86**	51.12	1.45**	60.11	1.20**
		Not owning and not managing	28.71	2.02**	52.53	1.49**	57.21	1.14**
	All aged	Owning and managing	10.56		29.19		47.84	
		Owning but not managing	27.66	2.62**	49.33	1.69**	59.40	1.24**
		Not owning and not managing	25.80	2.44**	47.26	1.62**	56.40	1.18**
Relation with the head of the household	Widow	Self (not alone)	23.10		37.88		57.04	
		Mother/-in-laws	26.40	1.14**	51.21	1.35**	55.89	0.98
		Other relatives	26.17	1.13**	57.11	1.51**	55.11	0.97
	All aged	Self or spouse (not alone)	15.81		33.61		51.26	
		Father/mother/-in-laws	25.71	1.63**	48.85	1.45**	55.58	1.08**
		Other relatives	22.02	1.39**	54.68	1.63**	51.45	1.00**
Living arrangement	Widowed	Living alone and independent	8.98		29.85		47.02	
		Living alone and dependent	29.39	3.27	44.75	1.50**	61.14	1.30**
		Living with children	25.74	2.87	49.54	1.66**	56.62	1.20**
		Living with other relative	25.27	2.81	46.90	1.57**	49.04	1.04**
	All aged	Living alone and independent	7.64		31.13		49.42	
		Living alone and dependent	29.73	3.89**	46.33	1.49**	60.34	1.22**
		Living with spouse/children	19.11	2.50**	38.92	1.25**	52.80	1.07**
		Living with other relative	20.96	2.74**	42.45	1.36**	46.44	0.94**

Note: Statistical significance of these risks were estimated through chi-square test; *p<.05, **p<.01.

Source: Estimated by the author using the unit level NSS data (52nd round).

13

Health Concerns among Elderly

S. IRUDAYA RAJAN, SHANTHI JOHNSON
and SABU ALIYAR

As Kerala stands ahead of at least 30 years of the rest of the country in its achievement in reaching the final stage of demographic transition (low fertility and mortality), the ageing scenario of Kerala calls for special research unlike that in any other states in India (Zachariah and Rajan, 1997; Rajan and Zachariah, 1998; Rajan and Aliyar, 2004; 2005; see Chapter 9 in this volume). In this context, Kerala Ageing Survey (2005) has been completed with funding support from the Indo-Dutch Programme on Alternatives in Development (IDPAD) of the Indian Council for Social Science Research, New Delhi, Shastri Applied Research Project (SHARP) of the Shastri Indo-Canadian Institute, New Delhi and the Global Health Initiative of the Canadian Institutes of Health Research, Canada. The survey is co-ordinated by the senior author of this chapter at the Centre for Development Studies. The survey consists of two parts: one household survey (elderly living with families) and other institutional survey (elderly living in old age homes). The household survey was conducted in 2004 and the institutional survey was completed in 2006. This major survey has targeted several social, economic and health issues pertaining to the elderly in Kerala.

Sampling Design: Kerala Ageing Survey

The sample for Kerala Ageing Survey is based on the second Kerala Migration Survey (2003) conducted by the Centre for Development Studies, Thiruvananthapuram (for details, see Zachariah and Rajan, 2004; 2005; Chapters 3 and 7 in this volume). Household was the ultimate sample unit for the Kerala Migration Survey. On the basis of our earlier experience in conducting large-scale sample survey, it was decided that 10000 households should be sufficient to provide relatively accurate estimates of migration at the state level. It was also decided that nearly half the number of households in the sample households should be the same as those canvassed in the first Kerala Migration Survey in 1999 (for details, see Zachariah *et al.*, 2003).

Out of the 200 sample *panchayat*/municipal wards (localities) in the 1999 migration survey, 125 localities were retained. From each of these 125 localities, 40 households were selected from among those 50 selected in the 1999 study. This gave 5000 of the 10000 sample households. Actually only 4795 households could be matched. The other 5000 households were selected from 100 *panchayats* which had not been covered in the earlier survey selected at random giving weight to the total number of households in each locality according to the 2001 census. The new localities gave a total of 5000 new households for the sample (Table 13.1).

Table 13.1

The Second Kerala Migration Survey 2003: Sample Size by Districts

Districts	*Sample Localities*			*Sample Households*			*Sample Population*
	Total	*New*	*Old*	*Total*	*New*	*Old*	
Thiruvananthapuram	25	11	14	1110	550	560	4726
Kollam	20	9	11	890	450	440	3662
Pathanamthitta	11	5	6	490	250	240	2018
Alappuzha	16	7	9	710	350	360	3206
Kottayam	15	7	8	670	350	320	3111
Idukki	9	4	5	400	200	200	1700
Ernakulam	23	10	13	1020	500	520	4493
Thrissur	21	9	12	930	450	480	4311
Palakkad	18	8	10	800	400	400	4009
Malappuram	20	9	11	890	450	440	5445
Kozhikode	19	9	10	850	450	400	4432
Wayanad	5	2	3	220	100	120	970
Kannur	16	7	9	710	350	360	4008
Kasaragod	7	3	4	310	150	160	1739
KERALA	225	100	125	10000	5000	5000	47830

Source: Zachariah, K.C. and S. Irudaya Rajan (2006). "Gulf Revisited", Thiruvananthapuram: Centre for Development Studies.

Kerala Ageing Survey 2004

Kerala Ageing Survey (KAS) was conducted in 2004 in all migration survey households which reported at least one elderly in the household. The purpose of the KAS was to examine the determinants of healthy ageing, social security, property rights and institutional provisions in the context of care for elderly. Other than the socio-economic characteristics of elderly, the survey also canvassed issues such as children and grandchildren, attitudes and beliefs, old-age support systems, subjective well-being inventory (SUBI), general health enquiry (GHQ), property rights, labour force participation, pensions and social security, lifestyle and life satisfaction, health problems and health utlisation, disability, activities of daily living scale (ADL), instrumental activities of daily living scale (IADL), falls, behavioural factors, food frequency, eating behaviour and nutritional assessment. In order to accomplish the main objectives, a representative sample of 5013 elderly from throughout Kerala covering both gender groups and rural and urban areas was studied. As we can see from Figure 13.1, the sample elderly declines with the increasing age indicating the sampling is appropriate for providing major conclusions. However, we shall limit our presentation to health concerns and health care utilisation among elderly in Kerala in this chapter.

Table 13.2

Kerala Ageing Survey 2004

District	*Sex*		
	Male	*Female*	*Total*
Thiruvananthapuram	218	266	484
Kollam	178	175	353
Pathanamthitta	142	185	327
Alappuzha	149	168	317
Kottayam	221	263	484
Idukki	52	46	98
Ernakulam	257	317	574
Thrissur	155	203	358
Palakkad	184	205	389
Malappuram	225	253	478
Kozhikode	237	271	508
Wayanadu	31	48	79
Kannur	180	250	430
Kasaragod	62	72	134
Total	2291	2722	5013

Institutional Survey

As stated earlier, to study the similarities and dissimilarities of the elderly living in households as well as institutions (old age homes), we have expanded the survey to cover all old age homes and its inmates in Kerala in 2006. However, some of the elderly could not be interviewed due to their unwillingness to participate, extreme old, bedridden, elderly with mental and hearing disabilities. In total, we have visited 157 old age homes throughout Kerala and interviewed 4865 inmates of which 60 per cent are women. The break-up data is presented in the Table 13.3. Among the total old age homes, two-thirds of them are found in just four districts of Thiruvananthapuram, Kottayam, Ernakulum and Thrissur. Only one old age home is located in the tribal district of Kasaragod. About 25 per cent of inmates surveyed are from Ernakulam.

Figure 13.1

Percentage of Elderly by Age Groups, KAS 2004

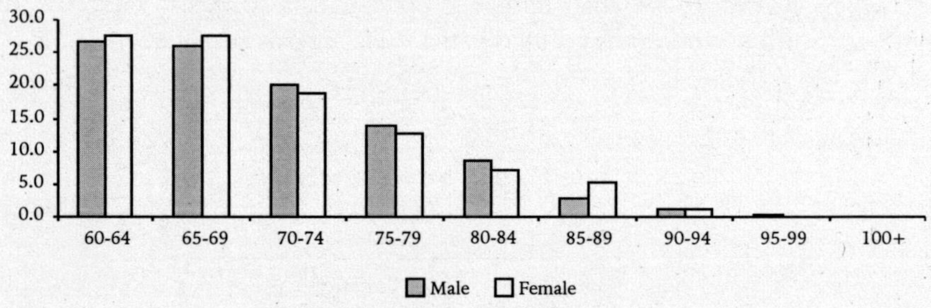

Table 13.3

Kerala Institutional Ageing Survey 2006

	No. of Old Age Homes	*Sex*		
		Male	*Female*	*Total*
Thiruvananthapuram	22	185	230	415
Kollam	10	62	128	190
Pathanamthitta	5	37	48	85
Alappuzha	8	62	103	165
Kottayam	25	446	516	962
Idukki	4	111	138	249
Ernakulam	27	401	829	1230
Thrissur	26	183	397	580
Palakkad	3	52	30	82
Malappuram	2	10	16	26
Kozhikode	7	92	126	218
Wayanad	8	98	90	188
Kannur	9	161	276	437
Kasaragod	1	14	24	38
Total	157	1914	2951	4865

Morbidity and Chronic Illness

Our results have shown that the age of participants ranged from 60 to over 100 years of age with 54 per cent of participants being women. The study showed that joint pains were the most often reported morbidity among elderly, with women reporting higher percentage (53 per cent) compared to men (41 per cent). The next highest morbidity seems to be forgetfulness or loss of memory with again females (33 per cent) outnumbering male elderly (27 per cent). Other common health problems which more than 10 percentage elderly reported include: having no energy (27 per cent), sleep problems (21 per cent), chest pain (20 per cent), stomach problems (14 per cent), chewing or dental problems (13 per cent) (for more details see Table 13.4). Two more important observations can be made: firstly, all the morbidly enquired in the Kerala Ageing Survey, women reported higher prevalence rates compared to men and similarly, as the age increases, morbidity levels also increase with the highest prevalence among the oldest old.

Table 13.4

Morbidity among Elderly in Kerala, KAS 2004

	60+			60-69		70-79		80+	
	Male	*Female*	*Total*	*Male*	*Female*	*Male*	*Female*	*Male*	*Female*
Having no energy	23.6	29.8	26.9	16.3	23.1	28.4	34.9	39.8	44.4
Forgetfulness/Loss of memory	27.0	32.6	30.1	19.8	26.3	30.2	35.3	47.4	51.9
Sleep problems	19.4	22.4	21.0	15.3	19.5	21.2	23.8	30.6	31.3
Chewing/Dental problems	12.2	13.9	13.1	8.7	10.9	14.6	16.4	19.7	20.3
Chest pain	18.2	21.1	19.7	16.7	20.5	21.5	21.1	15.5	23.0
Joint pains	41.0	53.2	47.6	37.6	51.0	43.4	57.2	48.4	52.4
Immobility	5.4	8.1	6.9	3.2	6.4	6.9	7.7	10.2	15.8
Incontinence (no bladder control)	2.7	3.9	3.3	1.3	2.5	2.8	4.1	7.9	8.6
Stomach problems	13.1	14.1	13.6	12.2	12.7	12.6	16.2	17.8	15.2

Note: Special tabulations from the Kerala Ageing Survey.

Along with common morbidity, the Kerala Ageing Survey also canvassed the prevalence of some common chronic illnesses among the elderly. They are: arthritis, asthma, emphysema or bronchitis, Alzheimer's, cancer, diabetes, heart problems, hypertension, blood pressure and osteoporosis (Table 13.5). Out of the eight chronic diseases which needs continuous treatment, the prevalence rate is much higher among women compared to men in four diseases. High blood pressure/hypertension emerges as the single largest chronic disease among the elderly in Kerala, followed by arthritis, asthma, emphysema or bronchitis and diabetes. Osteoporosis, which is an emerging chronic disease, was reported less often. This was perhaps related to the silent nature of this disease.

Table 13.5

Chronic Illness among Elderly in Kerala, KAS 2004

	60+			60-69		70-79		80+	
	Male	*Female*	*Total*	*Male*	*Female*	*Male*	*Female*	*Male*	*Female*
Arthritis	18.9	24.5	22.0	16.4	23.5	21.8	27.8	21.7	21.1
Asthma, emphysema or bronchitis	14.2	10.4	12.2	12.1	10.0	16.0	11.1	17.8	10.4
Alzheimer's/Dementia	1.4	1.5	1.5	3.2	4.4	4.6	5.7	7.2	5.4
Cancer	1.5	1.3	1.4	1.5	0.9	1.8	2.0	1.0	1.3
Diabetes	18.2	15.8	16.9	17.7	17.6	19.6	15.4	16.1	9.6
Heart problems	10.6	8.4	9.4	8.9	7.6	13.1	9.5	10.5	9.4
Hypertension/High blood pressure	26.2	36.0	31.5	23.6	34.9	30.0	39.3	26.6	33.4
Osteoporosis	2.4	4.2	3.4	2.3	4.5	2.9	4.8	2.0	1.6

Note: Special tabulations from the Kerala Ageing Survey.

Health Care Utilisation and Physical Activities

For medical needs, close to 40 per cent accessed public hospitals and 56 per cent used private hospitals. The reasons for access to private *versus* public varied. Most of them accessed public hospital for the free service provided whereas those who accessed private hospitals did so for the availability of better services, good care and attention.

Table 13.6

Health Care Utilisation among Elderly in Kerala, KAS 2004

	60+			60-69		70-79		80+	
	Male	*Female*	*Total*	*Male*	*Female*	*Male*	*Female*	*Male*	*Female*
Government hospital	38.93	40.85	39.98	39.30	41.74	38.42	40.09	38.82	39.04
Private hospital	57.66	55.62	56.55	56.62	54.78	59.41	56.15	57.24	57.75

Note: Special tabulations from the Kerala Ageing Survey.

In our study, only about 36 per cent had routine medical check-up—slightly higher among elderly men compared to women. Among them, monthly check-up is about 27 per cent indicating that one-fourth of elderly only received proper medical attention and care in the later years of age. This may be due to the fact that the elderly are not covered by any health insurance to undertake medical check-up except for the hospitalisation charges. Among the elderly, one in two elderly were taking medications on a regular basis. The cost of managing any chronic disease in old age is extremely high. It is high time that we develop policies and programmes for each disease management so that we can help the poor elderly for maintaining good health in old age.

Table 13.7

Medical Check-up and Medication among Elderly in Kerala, KAS 2004

		60+			*60–69*		*70–79*		*80+*	
		Male	*Female*	*Total*	*Male*	*Female*	*Male*	*Female*	*Male*	*Female*
Routine medical check-up		36.14	35.01	35.53	34.4	34.6	39.8	37.0	33.6	32.1
Frequently go for medical check-up	Weekly	2.40	2.68	2.55	1.5	2.5	3.6	3.2	3.0	2.4
	Monthly	27.59	26.78	27.15	26.3	26.2	30.4	28.8	25.3	24.3
	Yearly	3.32	2.31	2.77	3.7	2.1	3.1	2.6	2.3	2.7
Now taking medications		49.37	51.73	50.65	45.4	50.7	55.6	55.1	49.0	48.1

Note: Special tabulations from the Kerala Ageing Survey.

Approximately, 60 per cent of the elderly participated in physical activities mostly in the form of household activities and this reduced from 66 per cent among young old to 36 per cent among the oldest old of 80+ age group. Physical activity decline among females as age advances and it may be due to the high prevalence of joint pains among them. Self-reported participation in physical activity decreased with age.

Table 13.8

Elderly Undertake Physical Activities, KAS 2004

Age Group	*Sex*	*Per cent*
60+	Male	59.4
	Female	58.2
	Total	**58.7**
60–69	Male	65.5
	Female	66.4
	Total	**65.9**
70–79	Male	57.1
	Female	55.8
	Total	**56.6**
80+	Male	41.1
	Female	31.0
	Total	**35.8**

Note: Special tabulations from the Kerala Ageing Survey.

Disability Profile

In the Kerala Ageing Survey, we enquired about prevalence of disability and it plays a crucial role in the quality of life of an elderly. Among the three disabilities enquired, the problem of vision is reported with very high prevalence with over 70 per cent. This visual disability increases with age with close to 80 per cent reported among the oldest old and it is slightly higher among males in all elderly age groups (Table 13.9). The second disability faced by the elderly in Kerala is the problem of walking with one out of five elderly reporting this handicap. As against vision handicap, walking disability is highly prevalent among women compared to men with 46 per cent females reported as handicap among the oldest old. In hearing and walking disability at later ages, women overtake men.

Table 13.9

Disability Profile among the Elderly in Kerala, KAS 2004

	60+			60–69		70–79		80+	
	Male	*Female*	*Total*	*Male*	*Female*	*Male*	*Female*	*Male*	*Female*
Vision problem	71.89	69.76	70.74	67.6	64.8	74.9	74.8	80.9	78.1
Hearing problem	13.57	14.36	14.00	7.1	6.7	16.3	17.2	32.2	38.5
Walking problem	18.64	22.15	20.55	11.7	13.8	21.6	26.1	38.2	46.3

Note: Special tabulations from the Kerala Ageing Survey.

As disability in seeing and walking can lead to falls among elderly, we have enquired about falls and the injuries sustained. One out of four elderly had fallen down during the last few years and it is slightly higher among women compared to men among all the elderly groups. Among them, 4 per cent had no injuries sustained, 10 per cent had continuous pain, 5 per cent minor cuts and another 6 per cent with fractures (Table 13.10). Falls lead to dependency and bedridden among elderly and reduce the quality of life in old age. It is time, India develop fall prevention strategies to help the elderly. The study also showed that prevalence of falls and the fracture rates were high resulting in further disability.

Behavioural Factors and Dietary Patterns

As some of the behaviours during adult ages and continuous usage of certain substance have serious implications on the health at later ages of life, the Kerala Ageing Survey canvassed three behavioural patterns among the elderly: smoking, drinking and chewing. Gender differences were clearly observed for behavioural factors with men smoking cigarettes and drinking alcohol whereas women chew betel leaf more often. One out of four elderly men was addicted to smoking and it declines from 32 per cent among 60-69 years to 15.79 among aged 80 and above (Table 13.11). Similarly, one out of five elderly men was addicted to alcohol and it declined from 22 per cent among young old to 13 per cent among the oldest old.

Table 13.10

Falls among Elderly in Kerala, KAS 2004

	60+			*60–69*		*70–79*		*80+*	
	Male	*Female*	*Total*	*Male*	*Female*	*Male*	*Female*	*Male*	*Female*
Fallen down	20.82	27.88	24.66	20.9	25.3	20.0	31.4	22.7	30.2
Injuries sustained									
None	3.32	3.93	3.65	3.4	3.5	3.4	4.7	2.6	4.0
Pain	8.86	11.61	10.35	8.7	11.4	8.3	13.0	10.9	9.4
Minor (cuts, bruises)	4.19	4.78	4.51	4.2	3.8	3.9	5.6	4.9	6.7
Fracture	4.45	7.57	6.14	4.6	6.6	4.3	8.1	4.3	10.2

Note: Special tabulations from the Kerala Ageing Survey.

Table 13.11

Behavioural Factors among Elderly in Kerala, KAS 2004

Behavioural Factors	*60+*			*60–69*		*70–79*		*80+*	
	Male	*Female*	*Total*	*Male*	*Female*	*Male*	*Female*	*Male*	*Female*
Smoke cigarettes/*Beedi*	27.54	0.92	13.09	31.6	0.9	25.8	0.9	15.8	0.8
Drink alcohol	19.82	1.10	9.65	22.3	0.7	18.6	1.5	13.2	1.9
Chew betel leaf	13.44	18.99	16.46	12.9	18.1	13.1	19.3	16.4	21.9

Note: Special tabulations from the Kerala Ageing Survey.

Dietary patterns showed that 90 per cent of both elderly men and women consume three meals a day with a greater tendency for the young old and the oldest old age groups to skip or miss meals. Our survey indicates that about 14 per cent miss meals among 60-69 years and increased to 21 per cent among aged 80 and above. Among the oldest old, 21 per cent of them miss meals and it needs serious investigation (Table 13.12). This may be due to stomach problems or the non-availability of special meals suggested by doctors or problems of dental health. Interestingly, 80 per cent of elderly in Kerala reported to be non-vegetarians. Also, the type of food changed from non-vegetarian to vegetarian as people aged with the onset of the problems of digestion and teeth. Approximately, 30 per cent were on special diet such as diabetic diet or low salt diet.

Table 13.12

Eating Behaviour among Elderly in Kerala, KAS 2004

		60+			60-69		70–79		80+	
		Male	Female	Total	Male	Female	Male	Female	Male	Female
Meals per day	One meal (B/L/D)	2.05	2.28	2.17	1.8	1.9	2.4	2.6	2.0	2.9
	Two meals (B/L/D)	7.90	9.40	8.72	7.7	7.7	7.4	10.6	10.2	13.6
	Three meals	90.05	88.32	89.11	90.5	90.4	90.2	86.9	87.8	83.4
Missing meals		14.01	17.23	15.76	13.7	13.6	13.1	20.8	17.4	23.8
Type of food eating	Vegetarian	17.77	20.17	19.07	16.9	18.5	17.9	21.9	20.7	23.0
	Non-vegetarian	81.80	79.24	80.41	82.6	81.1	81.7	77.4	78.9	76.2
	Eggetarian	0.35	0.33	0.34	0.4	0.3	0.3	0.4	0.3	0.3
	Others	0.09	0.26	0.18	0.1	0.1	0.1	0.4	0.0	0.5

Note: Special tabulations from the Kerala Ageing Survey.

Mental Health

Mental health is often not discussed when we discuss about the general health. As Kerala leads in the country with the highest suicide rates (32 per 1 lakh population as against 8 for India as a whole), the Kerala Ageing Survey made an attempt to assess the mental health using two sets of modules: Subject Well-Being Inventory (SUBI) and General Health Questionnaire (GHQ).

SUBI was developed by Sell and Nagpal (1992). The original version consists of a 40-item questionnaire. For each item, there are three response options. It yields a total score as well as subscores for the positive (well being) and negative aspects (ill-being). This is validated through factor analysis. Eleven factors are identified from which a short version consisting of three very sensitive factors are taken for the purpose of the study. This short version is an 8-item questionnaire and the factors are general well being—positive effect, expectation achievement congruence and confidence in coping. Human well-being is measured on the basis of 8 questions with 3 multiple choices and the scores are based on the chosen answer (see Appendix A-13.1 for details). The lower the score the better is the well-being of individuals and vice versa. In our earlier Kerala Mental Health Survey, Keralite men report comparatively higher levels of well-being than women. The mean score for men (17.35) is significantly lower than that for women (17.9). The difference is statistically significant. Well-being diminishes as age advances in both men and women (Mohamed *et al.*, 2002).

SUBI is influenced by a host of socio-economic and demographic variables which explains individual differences. It contains three primary components:

people's emotional responses, depressive symptoms and life satisfaction, and it was able to tap into the components of SUBI and found some pair-wise differences between age groups that emerged as significant. The maximum scores are 24 and minimum 8. Elderly men have comparatively higher levels of well-being compared to women, except the oldest age group of 90 and above. The mean score for men of 15.88 is significantly lower than that of women (16.91). The difference is statistically significant (Table 13.13).

Table 13.13

Index of Subjective Well-being Inventory by Age and Sex: KAS 2004

Age	*Number of Elderly*		*Mean*			
	Male	*Female*	*Male*	*Female*	*t value**	*Significance*
60-69	1194	1487	15.41	16.57	-1.934	0.036
70-79	790	839	16.08	17.09	-1.186	0.127
80-89	274	341	16.94	17.70	-1.658	0.059
90+	33	40	19.12	18.93	-0.940	0.181
Total	2291	2707	15.88	16.91	-2.1489*	0.0242

Note: Special tabulations from the Kerala Ageing Survey.
* t values are highly significant.

Well-being diminishes as age advances in both men and women. However, among men a sudden decline is observed in well-being between the ages of 80 and 90 indicating the widowhood and loss of care by their spouses at extreme old age. The woman's well-being declines marginally after 60 years and continues further to reach 18.93 among 90 and above.

Table 13.14

Negative and Positive Symptoms among the Elderly in Kerala, KAS 2004

	At least one Negative Symptoms (Per cent)		
	Male	*Female*	*Total*
60–69	27.9	33.7	31.1
70–79	31.6	42.0	37.0
80–89	40.5	46.0	43.6
90+	57.6	57.5	57.5
	At least one Positive Symptoms (Per cent)		
	Male	*Female*	*Total*
60–69	38.0	28.7	32.9
70–79	32.2	27.1	29.5
80–89	29.6	23.2	26.0
90+	21.2	22.5	21.9

Note: Special tabulations from the Kerala Ageing Survey.

Analysis of one positive and negative symptoms based on eight questions indicates that about 31 per cent of elderly reported at least one symptom of emotional or depressive or life dissatisfaction and it increases to 58 per cent among elderly above 90 years. There is a clear gender difference among men and women. Similarly, 33 per cent of elderly in the age group 60-69 reported one positive symptom and it declined to 22 per cent among the oldest old. Though there is clear differentials reported among men and women in the young old, the gender differences become negligible once they reach 90 years (Table 13.14).

Developed by Goldberg (1972), GHQ has found application in a variety of psychiatric and non-psychiatric contexts and has been translated, revalidated and used in many countries including India. It has been used in many studies related to the economic situation, occupation and unemployment (Strandh, 2000; Warr *et al.*, 1988; Banks *et al.*, 1983). The GHQ is available in several versions of varying length. The 12-item GHQ has the advantage of brevity and hence, convenience of administration and scoring. It is also as sensitive and valid as are the longer versions. It consists of the 12 "best items" of the original 60-item questionnaire, that is, those items that were most discriminating in determining clinical status and were not endorsed by a physically ill control group. In India, the 12-item GHQ has been validated against the Indian Psychiatric Survey Schedule and has been found to demonstrate excellent sensitivity and specificity, that is, it is able to accurately identify the presence of psychological disturbance with few false negatives and false positives (Shamsunder *et al.*, 1986). Each of the 12 items of the questionnaire has four possible response choices (see Appendix A-13.2). The scoring is simple, the total score being a summation of the score on each item. In surveys, the GHQ can be used as a dimensional measure of psychological disturbance and can also be used to identify a "case". In the former situation, the total score is used to indicate the degree of psychological distress. In the latter situation, a threshold score is used so that persons scoring above the threshold are identified as potential psychiatric cases. Thus, for the 12-item GHQ, the recommended threshold score is 2 and above. The higher the score, the lower is the mental health. Keralites show significant gender disparity in mental health. In general, females are lower in scale compared to men in mental health (Mohamed *et al.*, 2002). This is true based on the results from Kerala Ageing Survey. As age advances, the mental health deteriorates both among men and women with the score of 2.6 and it is highly significant (Table 13.15).

Table 13.15

Index of General Health Questionnaire, KAS 2004

Age	Mean			t value*	Pearsons R	Significance
	Male	Female	Total			
60-69	2.0	2.1	2.1	-1.000	0.8049	0.16
70-79	2.1	2.3	2.2	-1.430*	0.6124	0.08
80-89	2.2	2.5	2.4	-1.360*	0.4524	0.09
90+	2.6	2.6	2.6	-0.752	0.0628	0.23

Note: Special tabulations from the Kerala Ageing Survey.
* t values are highly significant.

Several epidemiological studies have reported that the physical, mental and social well-being of elderly individuals are very closely interrelated. With the rapid increase in the elderly population, the health of the elderly individuals and those with mental depression has become a major public health problem in Kerala. In this situation, an extension of life span is no longer the goal of the elderly, an improvement in functional independence and the achievement of a better quality of life is more important. It is necessary to improve not only physical function but also mental health condition to achieve a better quality of life. In Kerala, no previous studies have been conducted on the mutual relationship between physical function and mental health status. In this study, we estimate the correlation between these functions in the elderly population. The study clearly observed various mental health problems among the elderly in Kerala. Females have lower mental health irrespective of their age; this disparity is particularly significant in two broad age groups 70-79 and 80-89. In the case of other age groups, the differences exist but they are not statistically significant. As age advances, mental health declines for both men and women. Even when we break the GHQ into three components, males fare better compared to females in terms of mental health (Table 13.16).

Although this study focuses on the health of elderly in the state of Kerala, the information gained from the surveys has striking similarities to those in other nations in the Asian and non-Asian world alike. Understanding the determinants of healthy ageing might be similar if not identical to those in other areas that are of similar social and environmental make-up. As such, the findings and evidence-based recommendations have international applicability.

Table 13.16

Anxiety, Social Dysfunction and Severe Depression among Elderly, KAS 2004

Age	Anxiety		Social Dysfunction		Severe Depression		No. of Observations	
Male	Female	Male	Female	Male	Female	Male	Female	Male
60-69	2.04	2.20	2.04	2.18	1.88	2.03	1194	1487
70-79	2.20	2.35	2.17	2.32	2.04	2.15	790	839
80-89	2.31	2.51	2.28	2.50	2.13	2.33	274	341
90+	2.67	2.64	2.62	2.70	2.47	2.54	33	40
Total	2.14	2.29	2.12	2.27	1.97	2.11	2291	2707
	Minimum Value=1				*Maximum Value= 4*			
			Mean Age		*Standard Deviation*			
Total			69.97		7.45			
Male			70.14		7.75			
Female			69.97		7.62			

Note: Special tabulations from the Kerala Ageing Survey.

References

Banks, Michael H., Paul R. Jackson, Elizabeth M. Stafford and Peter B. Warr (1983). "Unemployment and Psychological Distress in Young People: The Moderating Role of Employment Commitment", *Journal of Applied Psychology* 68(3): 525-535.

Goldberg, D.P. (1972). *The Detecting of Psychiatric Illness by Questionnaire: A Technique for the Identification and Assessment of Non-Psychotic Psychiatric Disease*. Oxford: Oxford University Press.

Gulati, L. and S. Irudaya Rajan (1999). "The Added Years: Elderly in India and Kerala", *Economic and Political Weekly* XXXIV(44): WS-46-51.

Irudaya, Rajan S. (1989). "Aging in Kerala: One More Population Problem?", *Asia-Pacific Population Journal* 4(2): 19-48. June.

———. (2001). "Social Assistance for Poor Elderly: How Effective?", *Economic and Political Weekly* XXXVI(8): 613-617. February 24.

———. (2002a). "Home Away from Home: A Survey of Oldage Homes and Inmates from Kerala, India", *Journal of Housing for the Elderly* 16(1 and 2): 125-150.

———. (2002b). "Social Security for the Unorganized Sector in South Asia", *International Social Security Review* 55(4): 143-156.

———. (2005). "Chronic Poverty Among the Indian Elderly", Chapter 5, pp.168-197 in Aasha Kapur Mehta and Andrew Shepherd (eds). *Chronic Poverty and Development Policy in India*. New Delhi: Sage Publications.

———. (2006). "Social Safety Nets for the Vulnerable Poor and Elderly in India", Chapter 11, pp.233-260 in Nisha Srivastava and Pravesh Sharma (eds). *Protecting the Vulnerable Poor in India: The Role of Social Safety Nets*. New Delhi: World Food Programme.

Irudaya, Rajan S. and K.C. Zachariah (1998). "Long Term Implications of Low Fertility in Kerala", *Asia Pacific Population Journal* 13(3): 41-66. September.

Irudaya, Rajan S. and Sabu Aliyar (2004). "Demographic Change in Kerala in the 1990s and Beyond", in Chapter 3, pp.61-61 in Baroda A. Prakash (ed). *Kerala's Economic Development: Performance and Problems in the Post-Liberation Period*. New Delhi: Sage Publications.

———. (2005). "Fertility Change in Kerala", Chapter 5, pp.167-190 in Christophe Z. Guilmoto and S. Irudaya Rajan. *Fertility Transition in South India*. New Delhi: Sage Publications.

Irudaya, Rajan S. and Sanjay Kumar (2003). "Living Arrangements among the Indian Elderly: New Evidence from the National Family Health Survey", *Economic and Political Weekly* XXXVIII(1): 75-80. January 4.

Irudaya, Rajan S. and U.S. Mishra (1997). "Population Aging: Causes and Consequences", Chapter 12, pp.222-236 in K.C. Zachariah and S. Irudaya Rajan (eds) (1997). *Kerala's Demographic Transition: Determinants and Consequences*. New Delhi: Sage Publications.

Irudaya, Rajan S., U.S. Mishra and P.S. Sarma (1999). *India's Elderly: Burden or Challenge?*. New Delhi/ Thousand Oaks/London: Sage Publications.

Mohamed, E., S. Irudaya Rajan, K. Anil and Mohammed, P.M. Saidu (2002). *Gender and Mental Health in Kerala*. Report of the Kerala Mental Health Survey (KMHS) submitted to the Gender Network, Institute of Social Studies Trust, New Delhi.

Phoebe, S. Liebig and S. Irudaya Rajan (eds) (2003). *An Aging India: Perspectives, Prospects, and Policies*. New York, United States of America: The Haworth Press Inc.

Sell H. and R. Nagpal (1992). "Assessment of Subjective Well-Being", *SEARO Regional Health Paper* No. 24.

Shamsunder, C., T.G. Sriram, S.G. Muraliraj and V. Shanmughan (1986). "Validity of a Short 5-Items Version of the General Health Questionnaire", *Indian Journal of Psychiatry* 28: 217-19.

Strandh, M. (2000). "Different Exit Routes from Unemployment and their Impact on Mental Well-Being", *Work, Employment & Society* 14(3): 459-479.

Warr, P., P. Jackson and M. Banks (1988). "Unemployment and Mental Health: Some British Studies", *Journal of Social Issues* 44(4): 47-68.

Zachariah, K.C. and S. Irudaya Rajan (2004). "Gulf Revisited". Centre for Development Studies *Working Paper* No. 363, September. Thiruvananthapuram (*www.cds.edu*)

———. (2005). "Unemployment in Kerala at the Turn of the Century: Insight form CDS Gulf Migration Studies", *Working Paper No 374*, CDS, Thiruvananthapuram (*www.cds.edu*)

Zachariah, K.C. and S. Irudaya Rajan (eds.) (1997). *Kerala's Demographic Transition: Determinants and Consequences*. New Delhi/Thousand Oaks/London: Sage Publications.

Zachariah, K.C., E.T. Mathew and S. Irudaya Rajan (2003). *Dynamics of Migration in Kerala. Dimensions, Determinants and Consequences*. Hyderabad: Orient Longman Pvt. Limited.

Appendix A-13.1

Subjective Well-being Inventory (SUBI)

1. Do you feel your life is interesting?

   1. Very much 2. To some extent 3. Not so much

2. Compared with the past, do you feel your present life is?

   1. Very happy 2. Quite happy 3. Not so happy

3. On the whole, how happy are you with the kind of things you have been doing in recent years?

   1. Very happy 2. Quite happy 3. Not so happy

4. Do you think you have achieved the standard of living and the social status that you had expected?

   1. Very much 2. To some extent 3. Not so much

5. Do you normally accomplish what you want to?

   1. Most of the time 2. Sometimes 3. Hardly ever

6. Do you feel you can manage situations even when they do not turn out as expected?

   1. Most of the time 2. Sometimes 3. Hardly ever

7. Do you feel confident that in case of a crisis (anything that substantially upsets your life situation) you will be able to cope with it/face it boldly?

   1. Very much 2. To some extent 3. Not so much

8. The way things are going now, do you feel confident in coping with the future?

   1. Very much 2. To some extent 3. Not so much

Appendix A-13.2

General Health Questionnaire (GHQ)

We would like to know if you have had any medical complaints and how your health has been over the past few weeks. Please indicate the answer, most closely applies to you. We want to know about your recent complaints.

Have you recently:

1. Been able to concentrate on whatever you're doing?
   1. Better than usual 2. Same as usual
   3. Less than usual 4. much less than usual
2. Lost much sleep over worry?
   1. Not at all 2. No more than usual
   3. Rather more than usual 4. Much more than usual
3. Felt that you are playing a useful part in things?
   1. More so than usual 2. Same as usual
   3. Less useful than usual 4. Much less useful
4. Felt capable about making decisions about things?
   1. More so than usual 2. Same as usual
   3. Less capable than usual 4. Much less capable
5. Felt constantly under strain?
   1. Not at all 2. No more than usual
   3. Rather more than usual 4. Much more than usual
6. Felt that you couldn't overcome your difficulties?
   1. Not at all 2. No more than usual
   3. Rather more than usual 4. Much more than usual
7. Been able to enjoy your normal day-to-day activities?
   1. More so than usual 2. Same as usual
   3. Less so than usual 4. Much less than usual
8. Been able to face up to your problems?
   1. More so than usual 2. Same as usual
   3. Less able than usual 4. Much less useful
9. Been feeling unhappy and depressed?
   1. Not at all 2. No more than usual
   3. Rather more than usual 4. Much more than usual

10. Been losing confidence in yourself?

1. Not at all	2. No more than usual
3. Rather more than usual	4. Much more than usual

11. Been thinking of yourself as a worthless person?

1. Not at all	2. No more than usual
3. Rather more than usual	4. Much more than usual

12. Been feeling reasonably happy, all things considered?

1. More so than usual	2. Same as usual
3. Less so than usual	4. Much less than usual

14

Seniors' Social Lives

MANJA BOMHOFF

It is my knee that makes me old (Annie)

If ageing is a biological process, old age is a construct of culture

—Tilak, 1989:xi

Introduction

In this chapter, some of the most important, yet preliminary findings of my study of elderly men and women in Kerala will be discussed. This study was undertaken during five months period of research in Thiruvananthapuram in 2005. Thiruvananthapuram is the capital of the Indian state of Kerala and has a population of about 745 thousand. This research functioned as a sequel to an earlier performed study in 2003 and was part of the IDPAD/IIAS study titled *Care of the Aged: Gender, Institutional Provisions and Social Security in India, Netherlands and Sri Lanka*. The research population consisted of urban living, well-educated and financially privileged seniors. Purpose of the study was to research the discourse on ageing and the social lives of elderly. The research methods used were primarily intensive semi-structured individual interviews, but also group interviews, (participant) observation, and literature and media analysis. The individual interviews lasted from 20 minutes to 4 hours, depending on many factors and most importantly on the respondent's physical condition.

There are three main sections to this chapter: one on ageing in general and the different aspects to this process; one on the various discourses that exist on ageing and one on the living arrangements of seniors.

In examining the concept of ageing, it is important to give attention to the distinction between 'ageing' and 'getting old'. Whereas 'ageing', according to Desai (1999), encompasses all the biological changes that occur over a lifetime, 'getting old' is a social concept, only slightly related to those biological processes of ageing. Ageing is a lifelong process: a progressive and irreversible changing of the structures and functions of a living organism and an integral part of living (Tilak, 1989: 1). Nevertheless, in the popular sense of the word, 'ageing' refers to the elderly only and this is also the sense in which the word is used in most academic writing.[1]

Tilak explains how "[e] ach distinct culture tends to introduce a unique set of stresses in the ageing individual and his/her family and community with respect to age-specific roles, norms, statuses and social worth" (1989: 4). One of the more prominent issues being investigated by anthropologists interested in ageing has, therefore, been that of cross-cultural variation in response to this pan-human experience of growing old. Gerontology then is the organisation of concepts, theories and normative practices concerning both ageing as a process and the aged themselves. It is seen as a cultural system linking ageing and the human response to it (Tilak, 1989: 3).

However subjective and unclear the term 'old' might be, it is still used as a "generalised way of marking and signifying someone whose body, demeanor, behavior, social position, or history is suggestive of the later decades of the life course in a given place or time" (Cohen, 1998: 33). Statistical and comparative purposes often make the use of numerical age categories indispensable. Those that have been used to signify the 'old' vary from 45 and older to 60 and more (Rajan and Mishra, 1997; Rajan, 1989; Vatuk, 1980). Yet, because of the obvious arbitrariness of a numerical definition of this sort, some researchers have chosen to use emic definitions instead: categorising those people as 'old' who are described as such by themselves and others in their surroundings (see Lamb, 2000; Vatuk, 1980).[2]

Since my research was not to contain any large-scale quantitative comparisons, I felt at liberty to concentrate as much as I could on the emic definition(s) of the 'old'. Let me start by mentioning those who were not happy about one or more of the definitions used. First, there was my

---

1. There is a difference between population ageing and individual ageing. The first is not only determined by the number of persons within the society who have reached a certain age, it is also influenced by the number of children and middle-aged persons in that society. This is because the ageing of a society is a relative concept that indicates its composition (Rajan and Mishra, 1997: 222). Throughout this study I will, as a rule, always refer to the process of individual ageing, unless explicitly noted otherwise.

2. 'Emic' and 'etic' (derived respectively from 'phonemic' and 'phonetic') designate two contrasting levels of data or methods of analysis. An emic model is one which explains the ideology or behaviour of members of a culture according to indigenous definitions. An etic model is one which is based on criteria from outside a particular culture (Barnard, 1996: 180). Problematic about these concepts is that anthropologists often present emic models "as though they are 'discovered' rather than 'invented'. However, emic models, [...] are ultimately exogenous constructions, formalised by the analyst on the basis of distinct features present in indigenous usage." (181). Still, notwithstanding possible criticism of the concepts, I am using the distinction here to show the crucial differences between a definition of 'aged' fixed by the researcher beforehand and consequently applied to respondents in the field and a definition of 'aged' based on reactions of respondents to stimuli given by the researcher.

informant Dr. Elizabeth who did not reveal but was explicit about her rejection of the term:

> 'Elderly' is not such a good classification. I may be over sixty, but I'm not helpless and manage very well. It is better to use the word 'senior' if you want to use a word. Upper class Indians don't see themselves as old because they don't need any help. You should use the word 'senior citizen'. You see, I'm very busy and always occupied so I'm not 'old' as such."

Dr. Elizabeth was definitely not the only one who discarded the term and those who did all made the same link to their high levels of activity. 'I'm not old because I'm active' seemed to be their adagio, a way of defining 'old'. Apart from those who rejected the term 'old' altogether, there were those who made a distinction between several different aspects of growing old. Like the 68-year-old man who told me: "[...] I am not senior either. By age and by mental stature I am old, but physically I am fit to do any normal work, including housework and driving the car [...]". For this category of respondents, becoming 'old' is defined as a full package of ageing mentally, physically and in years. Since these processes of ageing do not always carry on at the same speed, these respondents conclusively only consider 'old', those people who have aged in all areas mentioned.

When turning to those who did accept the definition of 'old' and applied it to themselves, it is interesting to see how they did so for different reasons. One of the reasons mentioned during my interviews corresponds closely to a point first established by Lamb and Vatuk. These researchers both pointed out that the marriage of one's son or daughter and the birth of grandchildren may mark the start of old age much more clearly than the passing of another calendar year (Lamb, 2000: 43-45; Vatuk, 1980: 138-140). In my respondent's words, this would simply mean that: "When grandchildren come, you feel you've become old", as a 62-year old grandmother of two said.

Apart from the birth of grandchildren or the marriage of children, retirement was also indicated as an important event indicating seniority. One retired male government officer was negative about the existence of an obligatory retirement and felt he had been "declared aged" on the day he stopped working. Lata, a female retired auditor had also experienced her retirement as a defining moment but saw it in a much more positive light. She simply stated that she had felt 'senior' ever since that day. Apart from her retirement, she also saw 'experience' in general as something that made people 'aged' and 'senior'. With a sense of pride, she told me how she likes saying she is 'senior'. "It is because of all the experience. I brought up my children very well and 69 is a good age. At this age there are so many things that we have seen and difficulties that we have had." Another respondent, Christina, put it as follows:

> Senior, elderly, old lady. All are good terms. They are dignified titles showing that you have more experience and should have more knowledge. Not necessarily do, but should. It also means that you have interacted with so many people. We have learned that life is not all roses. There are good things and bad things. If you are young, you have no problems, the worries come with age.

Finally there were those, whose physical situation had made them 'old', whether or not they were happy with the term. In *India's Elderly: Burden or Challenge?*, the authors find that: "[m] ost of the elderly who participated in the discussion are still working and are against the chronological definition of 60 years as the cut-off point for defining the elderly. [...] They seem to believe that declining health status as well as restrictive activity pattern should be the criterion for defining elderly"[3] (Rajan *et al.*, 1999: 268-270). It was my very first respondent, Annie who used this definition the most literally when she said:

> It is not so much age that is a problem. It is my knee that makes me old. That really is a problem; the rheumatics in my knee make it very difficult to walk. It makes me slow. I have to ask for help for many things I would like to do by my self.

The quote tells us that Annie doesn't think much has changed for her with getting older. Still, the only thing that really interferes with the way she wants to lead her life is that knee she refers to. Her rheumatic knee not only makes walking difficult but also causes her a lot of pain and makes her much more dependent on her co-habiting offspring than she would ideally want to be.

Thus, a definition of 'old' based on the number of years lived was definitely not the most often heard emic description forwarded by my respondents. On the contrary, definitions based on matters such as experience, retirement, the birth of grandchildren and health seemed a great deal more defining, and matched much better to these people's own feelings and thoughts on the subject. It is interesting to see that while the relation between health and feeling 'old' could be seen as correlating negatively, all the other definitions seem to entail a positive relationship.[4]

We can therefore, conclude that speaking of 'old age' is really not all that straightforward. There are different ideas about what is considered 'old' and

---

3. This opinion was recorded amongst agricultural workers in Kerala's neighbouring state Tamil Nadu. Still, however different these respondents' situations, there are apparently some commonalities in how they think about the definition of 'old' (Rajan *et al.*, 1999).

4. A negative relationship meaning: the worse the overall health situation, the more respondents define themselves as 'old'. A positive relationship meaning: the more experience (privately and professionally), married children and born grandchildren, the more respondents define themselves as 'old'.

all respondents experience their ageing differently. Also, there are characteristics that can greatly influence one's ageing experience, such as gender, religion or one's financial situation, making it a unique and individual experience for everyone. Still, through a close look at the interviews and observations, several patterns and common issues that are of importance to all respondents did come forward, such as for instance a fear of losing health and becoming dependent.

Be graciously old but keep yourself busy.

I will now focus more specifically on the actual discourses on elderly in Thiruvananthapuram. Even though human responses to ageing differ across cultures and are influenced by differences in cultural discourse, gerontologists have proposed general theories to explain attitudes and reactions. Two of these theories, 'activity theory' and 'disengagement theory' have long divided gerontological thinking in two camps (Vatuk, 1980: 126). 'Activity theory' suggests that the ageing individual aspires actively to extend the norms of middle age as long as it is physically and mentally possible to do so. Successful ageing to activity theorists is related to maintaining reasonable levels of activity and substituting new roles for those lost with retirement. To the contrary, 'disengagement theory' posits that with age every individual comes under increasing pressure to cede control and power to the younger members of the family or the community.[5] Withdrawal, according to this theory, is a normal aspect of ageing since both the individual and its surroundings are preparing for the ultimate disengagement: death (Vatuk, 1980; Tilak, 1989).

During my own research period in Thiruvananthapuram, I found the discourse on ageing amongst elderly themselves, to contain characteristics of both the 'activity' as well as the 'disengagement' theory. Supporting the 'disengagement theory' for instance would be that people often told me the importance of growing old 'graciously'. However, after all the preparatory reading, I was surprised to simultaneously find a social situation that was in many ways almost opposite to the one described by Tilak (1989) and Lamb (2000). Rotary clubs, Lion clubs, Inner Wheel factions, the YWCA, religious book reading groups, all had a large share of active elderly members who came to meetings, organised functions and enjoyed their social life. In an article titled "Old and the beautiful" in the Kerala edition of *The Hindu*, the author paints a similar picture for the senior women of the city.[6] According

5. Although the 'disengagement theory' was originally put forward as a universal development for all ageing men and women, modifications have been made to allow for more variation, depending on the social or cultural milieu (Vatuk, 1980; Tilak, 1989).

6. Although the financial situation of these ladies remains undiscussed, it is clear, both from the text and from the accompanying pictures, that the author is referring to the well-off senior women of the city.

to Nagarajan, it is a *joie de vivre* that characterises this population group, pointing to an attitudinal change in society. "Old age is not a disadvantage. On the other hand, it is a time to embark on a voyage of self-discovery. Many of these women in the 50-plus age group attempt to revive talents that were put on the backburner while they were busy with their children and homes", the author writes (Nagarajan, 2003). Activities mentioned are theatre, writing, catering, teaching and singing. When I told Lata about this article, she wholeheartedly agreed:

> It is true what they say in that article. Women have gotten very aware. There are some that will go to flower making classes to learn and teach others how to do flowers. Even at the age of 70 or even 80 they are realising that they can do anything. So they want to give others what they have, their talents. Me too. I'm teaching children on Sundays. I teach the children of poor families. I teach them Hindi for 1½ hours. When I am teaching I come closer to the children, which makes me feel good. I also prepare the classes myself before I teach.

Another respondent explained: "We try to keep ourselves busy and that is a good way of growing old." Several added that it was not only a good way to grow old but even the only way to remain happy and avoid depression.

To me, this shows how even though there might be an orthodoxy with close resemblance to the disengagement theory, stating that the last years in life need to be in preparation for death and in separation of the social world, a different practice has started a different discourse (heterodoxy), stating that the only way to grow old in happiness is by engaging in social activities. This latter discourse is much more in line with the activity theory.

Although not all senior respondents said that things had been better in the past, all told me about the enormous changes their society had gone through during only a couple of decennia.

> It is true that the youngsters look upon the old as remnants of a bygone age, and as obstacles to progress. And, there are difficulties in bridging the gap between the old and the young. One factor in this is consumerism, the attendant selfishness and the feeling of each for himself.
>
> Fr. Anthony, Professor of Sociology (All India Radio, 21/11/2003)[7]

Most saw those changes as a *fait accompli* and felt there was not much to do about them; several told me that change was simply a part of progress, whether it was good or bad. All the same, 'the generation gap' became a recurring theme during my interviews with both senior and young people and it enlightened me on the perceived changes in society and the individual's role in them.

7. Original radio discussion was in Malayalam. The text was transcribed for me in English by one of its participants, Mr. Menon.

Because of the particular focus of this research, I was most interested in changes as perceived by my respondents. First, because it is hard to find correct and reliable matching longitudinal data that would clearly indicate such structural changes in society. Second, when one studies the experience of seniors it is much more interesting to find out about the perception of these changes and the impact they are thought to have on individual lives, than to learn about these changes themselves. Eighty-four year old Leela for instance, felt she had experienced a great many changes throughout her life, some of which she found quite extreme:

> Our generation was brought up in an entirely different way. Respect, courtesy and politeness were the most important values that we were taught. There is very much a generation gap. I don't think anybody who is 50 years of age at this moment, will experience that much of a gap, as my generation does. Modern girls are all educated, working and rather selfish... In the joint family everybody would be sharing. Sometimes even 2 couples would be sharing one bedroom, now you wouldn't even be able to make a child share his or her room with another child... There used to be this unselfishness and a division of labour. In every attitude, everything has changed. Even the dress has changed into jeans instead of a skirt. ...Sometimes my children tell me: 'you are living in another world'. Then I sometimes answer that I prefer that old world. It doesn't make me sad as such, even my own children and grandchildren are like that and live like that. But the [...] patience and unselfish habits that we were brought up with are not there that much anymore. If my father came into the room we would all automatically stand up and wait with sitting down until he sat down. Nowadays they'll just stay seated with their legs crossed and tell you 'hi'. There is such a difference... But me too, I'm getting used to it. The old world is not coming back anyways.

Do you have feelings of melancholy or not?—"No, I don't have those."

The two greater processes that Leela describes in the quote above can be categorised as materialism and individualism. Materially, these seniors' children's generation of affluent Malayalis has seen a large increase in luxury and comfort. According to the seniors then, it is in particular because of the importance the younger generations attach to these new commodities and their behaviour related to them, that they feel a change has occurred. On the one hand, it has given 'the young' knowledge and interests about things, 'the old' know and care much less about.[8] On the other hand, it has made 'the young' greedy and more demanding than 'the old' would like them to be.

The other process that Leela describes, and with her many others I spoke to, is of a rise in individualism. According to this view, people have become more interested in their own personal gain and have lost the interest and the will to sacrifice for the common good. Evidence hereof would be children's

8. In an interview with All India Radio (21/11/2003), Mr. K.R. Menon says: "Another factor contributing to the gap between the old and the young is the progress in information technology! Letter writing has ceased. Now, it is only a few lines by e-mail once in a way". Original interview in Malayalam, transcribed by Mr. Menon himself.

desire to find their own future partner in marriage, rising rates of divorce, leaving the extended family and moving abroad whilst leaving one's elderly parents alone or in an old age home. In general, these changes would all come down to one thing: young people have gotten a will of their own and have stopped listening to their seniors. Most respondents saw these changes as negative, but irreversible. When I asked Annie whether she thought there was anything she could personally do to resist the changes she had just described, she replied:

> No, it is the society that changes, you can't do much about it. Family ties were greater [in the past]. We are beginning to follow the lifestyle of a foreign country.

However, not all respondents were negative about changes or saw them as singularly attributable to the younger generation. One male respondent of 67 years told me he thought it was mostly the seniors themselves who created a gap between the generations.

> Seniors in general like to impose though, which should be avoided. You shouldn't expect anything from others as a senior because they will never live up to your expectations. You can't ask your children for too much and should allow them to be on their own. It is not good to control them; you'll only be disappointed. All the failures and the non-fulfilment of desires will only be to blame on the seniors who expect too much. [...] Also, seniors will often think they are supreme. But children too may know a lot. When I was young, we didn't have anything like a television, cars, computers and such. There is a very fast technical advancement and this generation knows a lot about those things. You should therefore try to learn from your children.

Also, children's changed attitudes towards marriage were not described as negative by all. Even though the orthodoxy amongst seniors seems to hold that a formally arranged marriage is the best option for parents and child, several of my respondents were quite vocal in proclaiming their opposing views on the matter. Nevertheless, these remained exceptional and the reactions against them were strong.

Reactions on old age homes were just as strong and almost always extremely negative:

> Sending aged people to old-age homes is not right for a civilised society like ours. Dependence on such institutions arises only when sons and daughters are away or are neglecting the parents. [...] I think it is the duty of all sons and daughters to look after their parents in their old age. If the present generation deviates from this path, the next generation is sure to repeat this mistake [...] S.K.Vijayan, Alappuzha (A reader's view in the newspaper *The Hindu*, 17/04/2004).

Among the major states in India, Kerala has the highest number of aged persons (21.89 per cent) in homes (Rajan *et al.*, 1999: 239). Tamil Nadu follows with 20.28 per cent and the next is Karnataka (13.93 per cent) (*ibid.*). For a state that has a rising number of old age homes, discourse on the institutions is in general quite negative:

> Ninety per cent of the seniors are against that development. Many will talk negatively about it. For instance, a lot of the children go abroad. Many parents will then complain: our children are putting us in old age homes (67 year old male respondent).

Talking to respondents and reading several reader's views in *The Hindu* newspaper, I found there to be a strong orthodoxy regarding 'old age homes'. According to this orthodoxy, it is the negative changes as described in the previous paragraphs that force some desperate elderly into these homes.

> In several cases, it is nothing short of filial ingratitude that sends the aged and ailing to old-age homes. But, in some other cases, it is sheer compulsion of the situation that necessitates the lodging of them in an old-age shelter. As the nuclear family takes root, we have to accommodate the 'necessary evil' that the old-age homes have come to be [...] N.K. Vijayan, Kizhakkambalam (A reader's view in the newspaper *The Hindu*, 17/04/2004).

What is interesting about these views is that the homes are seen as symbolic for the neglect of elderly in society. They are seen as negative, 'necessary evil' for that which they represent: the abandonment of needy old people; more than for what they are. Only rarely did people write on the actual condition of one or more homes that they had personally visited. The vibrant debate on 'old age homes' amongst the English speaking population of Kerala remains therefore an ideological discussion, much more than a practical one.

Under One Roof

> Give generously to your children while you live, but keep to yourself a house and the wherewithal for living in your old age. Some parents give away their house(s) and other assets to their children on their marriage or otherwise and opt to live with one child or another. But, they come to grief soon. Speech on "What old age has taught me" by the president of the SCA during a one-day seminar organised by HelpAge India, Kerala on the 28th of October 2003.

Since one major objective of this fieldwork was to carefully explore the social lives of seniors, it is important at this point to address how, where and with whom these seniors live.[9] The average household[10] size in Kerala is, with 5.3 persons in 1991, just a little bit smaller than the national average of 5.5.

---

9. The general concept used to describe these phenomena, is the 'household'. Within anthropological literature, it is proven difficult to find one agreed to definition of the household. This is because people within different contexts seem to attribute different meanings to the concept. According to the *Encyclopedia of Social and Cultural Anthropology*: "Many keystrokes have been registered, and much ink spilt, in attempts to produce a universal, etic, one-size-fits-all definition of household. None exists" (Sanjek, 1996). In the light of my 'grounded theory' approach, I have used a flexible definition of household that respondents themselves could give shape to. During interviews I would first ask respondents directly how many people were living in their household. Next, I would ask more detailed questions about these persons and possible other visiting guests, tenants or servants, in order to get an understanding of what the 'household' really meant to the elderly. The interesting conclusions that this led to, will receive due attention in this chapter.

10. Here, a demographic definition of the 'household' is used, which the authors have not elaborated upon.

The same holds for the percentage of extended households in Kerala at 17.7 compared to 21.2 in India as a whole (Gulati and Rajan, 1999). More recent statistics from the district level for Thiruvananthapuram corporation in 2001 show us a total population of 524,006 with 107,892 households, making the average household size for this urban part of the district lower still at 4.86 (Government of Kerala, 2001). The percentage of female-headed households however, was in 1991 with 19.4 per cent in Kerala much higher than the 10 per cent for India.[11] Gulati and Irudaya Rajan mention four possible reasons for this remarkable difference: a) there is a persistence of matrilineal traditions, b) women have greater access to property and regular work, c) the state has large-scale male migration and d) a higher incidence of ageing and widowhood (1999). Data on living arrangements for the elderly in Kerala show us that an overwhelming majority of the elderly live with their offspring. Nevertheless, since most families in Kerala opt for a small well-endowed family over an ill-endowed large one, the average family size is shrinking (Rajan and Zachariah, 1997: 21).

On average in India, 60+ elderly reside in households with at least seven members, often consisting of three generations. Only 6 per cent of the Indian elderly are living with their spouses alone, another 6 per cent live in a household "where their immediate kinship is not present" (Rajan and Kumar, 2003: 79). Nevertheless, when looking at these statistics one needs to realise that these elderly are of course not equally 'scattered' over the households. Whereas 60 per cent of the Indian households have no elderly persons amongst them, 31 per cent have one and 11 per cent have two elderly members (Rajan, 2001: 614).

Whereas statistics like those above on household size and composition are on the respected demographer's terrain, it is the equally important but less easily quantifiable data on opinions, feelings, discourse and practice that should be the anthropologist's territory. A 90 year old lady living with her daughter, son-in-law and three grandchildren might feel terribly deserted if she thinks she is being neglected or misunderstood. A 60 year old widow who lives alone on the other hand, may finally experience intellectual fulfilment after her bedridden husband has passed away and she has taken up theatre as a newfound hobby. It is these hidden realities behind the data on household composition that I have tried to unravel. What is to be expected from this exercise is not an account of how 'the average Keralite elderly' lives and with whom, but an investigation of how elderly honestly feel about their

11. Census definition of 'head of household': "the person who has chief responsibility for the economic maintenance of the family"(In Gulati and Rajan, 1999).

living arrangements, how they see the role of their children and the actual practicalities of living 'independently' or with family.

When talking with respondents about their children, I was pointed to a very important distinction. Not once but several times, was I told about the significance of the difference between living with your children and having your children live with you.[12] The disparity in power that is implied in these terms was explained to me and quite a few times was I told explicitly that it was the children who were living with the respondent and not the other way around. Whilst obviously being a major issue for the elderly I spoke to, I came to see that there is really only a thin line that separates these two possibilities. To illuminate the not easily visible power relations within a household, census questionnaires talk of 'a head of household' to indicate that member of the household who holds chief responsibility for the economic maintenance of the household. However, this does not seem to be the (only) issue in seniors' perceptions of their living arrangement with children.

Sen is right in describing the household as a remarkable and complex institution (1993). He explains how economists have often ignored the household in their analysis or have used over-simplifications that lack all resemblance with reality.[13] For a correct understanding, it is important to recognise the inequalities that exist within it and to see household economics as a bargaining problem with co-operative conflicts (Sen, 1993). The most empowering issue in my analysis turned out to be house ownership, to which we will come back later in this chapter. A great part of the respondents lived in a house that they had themselves inherited from their parents. This naturally gives the houses a lot of personal history and emotional value, and makes their ownership more than only a financial matter. Apart from house ownership, it also seemed to matter to the respondents, who had been first to live in the house. Respondents would often tell me about the construction process of their house and about all the adjustments they had made after coming to live there. Often these adjustments would have had something to do with other family members coming to stay or leaving them. Like building an extra floor on top of the existing building, or shutting off floors and sub

12. The first respondent to make me aware of this difference said: "The children have always lived with me. That is very different from me living with my children. This was my house and the children were free to stay with me. But staying with the children is very different, definitely."

13. Sen distincts three models used by economists to analyse the family: in the glued-together family, the family is taken as a unit in terms of which decisions are taken and economic processes function; within the super-trader family, the individuals are assumed to be relentlessly pursuing their individual utilities and in the despotic family, a despotic head of the family takes all decisions while the others obey (1993). In reality however, the workings of the family turn out to be far too complex and specific to fit neatly into these three categories.

renting them to students or other families. All this personal history makes of course, that the oldest resident will naturally have most affinity with the house.

House ownership and personal history in the house are however, not the only aspects that give authority. Even in old family mansions, where seniors may have lived throughout their lives, roles can be reversed and elderly respondents can suddenly find themselves 'living with their children'.[14] When focusing on women in particular, I would say that the defining moment that effectuates this transfer of authority for senior women would be the moment in which the household duties are slowly or abruptly taken over by the younger generation.

One 87 year old respondent, Premila, put some of the frustrations and pain into words that accompany this process when she told me: "I don't have any work to do. They are not making me do anything. They want me to sit still and be quiet. I want to be with God. I can't do anything here." Premila's 53 year-old daughter explained to me how this can also be a sad and stressful change for the one who takes over. At one moment, when Premila had drifted off for a while, she told me a little defensively: "See, that's why I don't let her do any work. She is forgetful and falls asleep. If I would let her work in the kitchen that would be dangerous, she would leave the gas on or something."

Those senior women who were on the other hand 'still' responsible for their household duties would tell me so, proudly and explicitly. Like the 78 year old former professor who lived with her daughter and son-in-law and who told me about her daily routine: "At 5.45 I wake up and help in the kitchen, I prepare the coffee for the entire family. Tell the cook what to prepare. The house is still managed by me, not by my daughter. I am the one who decides what to purchase and what to cook." Or the 78 year old widow, Pankajam, who lived with her daughter, son-in-law and granddaughter and said without any probing: "I wake up at 5.30 and make tea for everyone. [...] It is me who runs the household and gives the instructions. Only when I'm not here, does my daughter take over."

These stories show us how important physical and psychological well being is for these elderly women's sense of authority. Keeping a close watch on what goes on in the household and protection of the established authority is necessary to maintain control. This is, of course, only possible if the senior lady herself is fit in body and mind. However, it is clear that having servants

---

14. The process is sadly but beautifully portrayed in Rohinton Mistry's novel *Family Matters*, which describes the relationships 79 year old Nariman, living in an apartment building in Mumbai, has with his co-residing (step) children (2002).

will allow her to continue with her tasks a lot longer than the poorer elderly woman who has to depend more on her own physical abilities.

I would argue that to the elderly women I met, above-mentioned factors are all very important for their feelings about authority and power. Next to, of course, the personalities of all those living in the house and other emotional issues that might interfere. Concluding, one could say that the earlier mentioned 'head of household' is an over-simplified definition that takes no account of these complex subtleties. In a next study, it would be interesting to ask respondents who they would consider 'head of household'; see whether they would be able to make a choice and in what ways they would motivate their choice.

Although census figures on household numbers and arrangements might suggest otherwise, the elderly women and men I spoke to had a serious tendency to move. One daughter told me about her mother: "She sometimes stays with her brother. She doesn't like to stay in one place continuously, she gets bored. Last July I went to pick her up. She had stayed with her brother for 8 months." A change of home is not such a big deal for any of those involved and can be quickly realised. Risseeuw made a similar point about seniors in Sri Lanka, when she explained how to them, relations seem more important than localities (2005). She reported the same phenomenon as I did in Thiruvananathapuram and appropriately called those senior women who frequently change locations: 'travelling grannies' (Risseeuw, 2005)

As briefly mentioned, this flexibility not only restricted itself to 'hopping' from one child to another. During the four months I stayed in Thiruvananthapuram, I came across several even more different living arrangements that taught me about the enormous range of possibilities in space and duration. There was, for instance, this one professor who was herself specialised in care and very conscious about the needs of elderly. Since she had taken an interest in several senior people she knew, she had started to feel so responsible for them that she had ended up having her old *guru* and four distantly related aunts and uncles share her house. Then there was this other expert interview during which I learnt that the senior expert himself was living with his 14 year old granddaughter during the week. According to him, this was a mutually beneficial situation. For the granddaughter, his house was closer to her school and so she had less travelling to do. For him, this arrangement meant that he wasn't by himself all week and had some enjoyable company for most of the time.

In conclusion, one could say that this study was not about how 'the average Keralite' lives and with whom, but much more about proper ways to research the household situation of elderly and about some of the complexities that may come along. As Sen explains, the household is a remarkable and complex institution, which researchers have too often ignored, or described with over-simplifications that lack all resemblance with reality (Sen, 1993).

References

All India Radio: *Senior Citizens: A Source of Power in Society*. Discussion with Mr. K. Menon, Prof. Indukumari & Fr. Anthony (21/11/03). Translated from Malayalam to English by Mr. K. Menon.

Barnard, A. (1996). "Emic and Etic", in A. Barnard & J. Spencer (eds.) *Encyclopedia of Social and Cultural Anthropology*. London: Routledge.

Cohen, L. (1998). *No Aging in India: Alzheimer's, the Bad Family, and Other Modern Things*. California: University of California Press.

Desai, M. (1999). "Ageing of Women in Post-Menopausal Stage: Need for Intervention", in *Economic and Political Weekly* 34(44).

Government of Kerala (2001). *Panchayat Level Statistics*.

Gulati, L. and S. Irudaya Rajan (1999). "The Added Years: Elderly in India and Kerala", in *Economic and Political Weekly* 34(44).

Irudaya Rajan, S. (1989). "Aging in Kerala: One More Population Problem?", in *Asia-Pacific Population Journal* 4(2): 19-48.

———. (2001). "Social Assistance for Poor Elderly: How Effective?", in *Economic and Political Weekly* 36(8): 613-617.

Irudaya Rajan, S. and U. Mishra (1997). "Population Ageing: Causes and Consequences", in S. Irudaya Rajan & K. Zachariah (eds.) *Kerala's Demographic Transition: Determinants and Consequences*. New Delhi: Sage Publications.

Irudaya Rajan, S. and K. Zachariah (eds.) (1997). *Kerala's Demographic Transition: Determinants and Consequences*. New Delhi: Sage Publications.

Irudaya Rajan, S., U. Mishra and P. Sankara Sarma (1999). *India's Elderly: Burden or Challenge?* New Delhi: Sage Publications.

Irudaya Rajan, S. and S. Kumar (2003). "Living Arrangements among Indian Elderly: New Evidence from National Family Health Survey", in *Economic and Political Weekly* 38(1): 75-80.

Lamb, S. (2000). *White Saris and Sweet Mangoes: Aging, Gender, and Body in North India*. California: University of California Press.

Mistry, R. (2002). *Family Matters*. New York: Alfred A. Knopf.

Nagarajan, S. (2003). "Old and the Beautiful", in *The Hindu*, 20/10/2003.

Risseeuw, C. (2001). "Policy Issues of Inclusion and Exclusion in Relation to Gender and Ageing in the South", in *The European Journal of Development Research* 2: 26-48.

———. (2005). *Ageing, Vulnerability and Gender Compared within Urban, Mid-income Levels in Sri Lanka and the Netherlands*. [Unpublished].

Sanjek, R. (1996). "The Enduring Inequalities of Race", in S. Gregory and R. Sanjek (eds.), *Race*. New Brunswick: Rutgers University Press. pp.1-17.

Sen, A. (1993). "Economics and the Family", in P. Uberoi (ed.) *Family, Kinship and Marriage in India*. Oxford: Oxford University Press.

Tilak, S. (1989). *Religion and Aging in the Indian Tradition*. Albany: State University of New York Press.

Vatuk, S. (1980). "Withdrawal and Disengagement as a Cultural Response to Aging in India", in C. Fry (ed.) *Aging in Culture and Society*. New York: Praeger.

———. (1995). "The Indian Woman in Later Life: Some Social and Cultural Considerations", in M. Das Gupta (ed.) *Women's Health in India: Risks and Vulnerability*. Bombay: Oxford University Press.

Vijayan, S. (2004). "Bad Trend", in *The Hindu*, 17/04/2004.

Vijayan, N. (2004). "Necessary Evil", in *The Hindu*, 17/04/2004.

Section V

Other Emerging Issues

15

Child Crafting in Kerala

J. DEVIKA

I

Post-demographic issues of childhood will certainly figure as a major item on the emergent agenda of demographic research on Kerala. Even though the individual causal trajectories may indeed be varied in different societies, the links between increased costs of child bearing and rearing, changes in the value ascribed to children and the demographic transition, have been acknowledged as more or less universal (Goody, 2003). Both structural and ideological reasons have been noted (Bumpass, 1990; Main, 2006). It has been noted that modernisation and industrialisation pushes up the costs of bringing up children, and these result in falling birth rates; besides there are ideological reasons, which Arland Thornton has termed 'developmental idealism' (Thornton, 2001). Historically, these observations apply to Kerala's demographic transition as well. The early-mid twentieth century in Malayali society was characterised by both declining death rates and rising costs of rearing and bearing children, as a result of economic crisis and modernisation of the family and notions and practices of childcare (Devika, 2002).

Thus, during the period of the demographic transition, fundamental changes occur in the way parents and children are perceived, which has consequences for the shape taken by family life, parenting, schooling and children's health care, and the state's responsibility towards families. Research into post-demographic issues elsewhere have inquired into issues ranging from changes in the volume of parenting time and parental supervision (Sandberg and Hofferth, 2001; Bianchi, 2000; Casper, 2004), to access to resources of children of different types of families (McLanahan, 2004). More generally, much interest in the intersections of demographic and institutional changes, particularly in the family, has been evident (Bumpass, 1990; Morgan, 2003; Cherlin, 1999).

In Kerala, the mid-twentieth century developmentalist welfare state responded to the demands entailed by these changes through increased investment in public education and health care (Jeffrey, 2003). But we need to train attention to some other specific shifts in twentieth century Kerala, not merely related to state policy, in order to identify some of the emergent issues related to children, family and schooling that may call for the urgent attention of demographers. Indeed, in the contemporary context, many of the massive social changes afoot in the Malayali society in the twentieth century seem to have attained a climax. One crucial change has been the general loosening of community ties and the decline of the joint family, which began in the twentieth century, actually pursued actively by community reformisms here (Jeffrey, 2003). An important consequence of this shift has been that the care of children is now very clearly a responsibility of the nuclear family, and especially, of the mother (Devika, 2007). Also important is the fact that increasingly since the twentieth century, marriage and family in Kerala, across all communities, are being stabilised through transfers of wealth from the bride's family to the bridegroom's. This is coupled with an all-pervading ideological stress upon the necessity of marriage for respectable and secure female existence, which has prompted one scholar to term the present form of patriarchy in Kerala 'conjugal patriarchy' (Kodoth, 2006). This implies that those who have less wealth to transfer during marriage and are less subject to the ideology of marriage may face marital instability and family insecurity. Elsewhere, such situations of striking difference in stability and material endowments of families have been observed to have grim implications, pointing to the widening of the gap between children of better endowed/ stable marriages and those of less endowed/less stable marriages in the access to resources and opportunities available (McLanahan, 2004). A third development since the twentieth century is of the labour migration from Kerala since the early 1970s, and continuing, with interesting changes, at present (Zachariah *et al.*, 2003). The unremitting dependence of Malayalis on the global job market, as well as the strengthening of a host of values associated with globalised consumption, is now translating into significant changes in childcare practices both at home and at school. The fourth key shift continuing from the late twentieth century is, of course, the context of gradual withdrawal of the welfare state, which creates tensions in a post demographic transition, post-globalisation society in which the value of children and expectations about them are equally high.

For the rest of this chapter, I try to reflect briefly upon some of the concrete issues for research that emerge out of the four contexts of change outlined above. This is of course not to claim that some of the children's issues already acknowledged to be of concern have become inconsequential—such as for instance, child labour (Niuewenhuys, 1994). Indeed, we may find that many such issues have become all the more critical, given the above contexts. In the last section, I try to think of the methodological implications of identifying these areas as crucial for demographic research.

II

Recent anthropological work among the marginalised sections of people in Kerala have brought significant insights into the degree to which the institution of the family has been changing in the late twentieth century across class strata in Kerala. Marion den Uyl, for instance, remarks about the Dalit colony she studied that in this settlement, where traditional kinship structures were strong, in the recent years, "individualism and personal profit motive are seen to be eroding into the task of raising children, which is becoming an even-more tedious task, an individual one, with extended family ties waning." (Uyl, 1995: 175-9). These changes may be considered to be fairly complete among many other groups in Kerala (Puthenkalam, 1977; Osella and Osella, 2000; Devika, 2002). Indeed, Uyl's conclusion is that her study demonstrates that new values inherent in the adoption of the monogamous nuclear family are seeping into groups that were "outlier" in the sociological sense (Uyl, 1995: 265). Recent historical work into the transformation of working class life in Kerala also corroborates these findings (for example, Lindberg, 2001).

However, these scholars have also often pointed out that the changes in family size that have accompanied this need not necessarily be read as having positive effects for women, even though it may appear women now have greater freedom to pursue other kinds of activities and gainful work. Indeed, it may be possible to hypothesise that given the post-demographic transition scenario in which the value and costs of fewer children has risen dramatically, the burdens of mothering may indeed have increased instead. This, viewed alongside the decline of female work participation in Kerala and rising female unemployment, provides an interesting emergent scenario for demographers to investigate. The question of the extent to which the domestic agency opened up for women in the nuclear family has indeed affected women's entry into public life as workers and citizens is now well-discussed by now in the social scientific literature on Kerala, but the effects of such shifts on notions and practices of childcare, schooling and on expectations about children remain quite unexplored at the moment. These may, indeed, also have significant implications for the health, both physical and mental, of both mothers and children, all of which remain largely unexplored.

This applies not just to female-headed or female-supported households alone. There is reason to think, from the anthropological and historical studies cited above, that women's responsibilities as providers for the family are on the rise in Kerala. In fact, the extent to which the highly lauded anti poverty initiatives of the 1990s in Kerala, such as the Kudumbashree (characterised as a 'women-oriented poverty alleviation mission'), both draw upon these tendencies and intensify them is in itself an interesting research problem. Recent demographic work on women's work and childcare arrangements among the poor in Kerala has revealed the changing composition of women's work, their continuing and rising responsibilities as caregivers for children, and the increasing share of expenditure for children from the incomes of mothers (Thampi, 2007). Indeed, the present context has been identified as one in which female-headed or supported families are on the rise all over the world, and that very often they are endowed with much less resources than other families (Buvinvic and Gupta, 1997). Buvinic and Gupta point to two factors that may accelerate this phenomenon. Of these, the first is the disruption of traditional patriarchal governance in families which "weakens implicit and explicit contracts that enforce income transfers from fathers to mothers and their children." (Buvinic and Gupta, 1997: 262-3). They quote Nancy Folbre who remarks that this is a converging issue for women in the developing societies as and in the industrialising world, and that it is indexical not so much of women's choice not to depend on men, as of a forced independence (ibid.: 263). The second trend they identify relates to declining real incomes in the wake of economic crises which prompts men to give up supporting families (ibid.: 263).

Both seem to be applicable to Kerala judging from work done on the poor from other disciplinary perspectives. Also, preliminary fieldwork recently conducted on women supporting or heading their families in Kerala seems to confirm other observations made by Buvinic and Gupta, like for instance, the strong priority for children's education in female-headed households, compared to male-headed ones.[1] These observations may throw up fruitful hypotheses regarding childcare arrangements, child welfare and performance, for demographers to explore. Demographic work in the industrialised world seems to indicate that children of unstable and underprovided families are more disadvantaged than their counterparts in stable and materially well-off families (McLanahan, 2004). While one may not simply transfer such conclusions to other contexts, rising work loads for women in Kerala and their low earnings definitely allow one to explore the usefulness of such findings in Malayali society. Given the fact that some recent anthropological work seems to indicate that dowry transfers are a way in which Malayalis try to ensure stability in marriage (Kodoth, 2006; Gallo,

1. Interviews being conducted by researchers from the Centre for Development Studies with informal sector women workers (all them either heading their households or supporting them heavily) politicised by SEWA, Kerala for an ongoing project on the politicisation of women in Kerala have revealed the intense desire on the part of mothers to educate their children at all costs. However, age and levels of exposure to the public seem to be important variables determining the intensity of this desire.

2005), this may also make important contributions to the study of emergent socio-economic inequalities in post-globalisation Kerala.

However, in a context like Kerala in which much of the female headship arises from the 'left-behind' status of many women, the poverty-female headship correlation, and its implication for child welfare cannot exhaust the range of research questions that may be possibly posed.[2] Though the 'left-behind' female heads have received some attention recently, again, the implications of this change for parenting—and for the changing alignments of power within families along both the husband-wife and the parent-child axes—remains quite in the shadow. Here again, changes induced by the 'left-behind' status, combined with other aspects like the increased seeking of upward social mobility through the preparation of children for high-income and technically skilled jobs abroad, and the rising levels of education of mothers, have generated a situation that may be of interest to demographers.

As a historian, I would call this situation a direct effect of a long-term social process, which I call the 'domestication' of Malayalis, and a more recent one, the intensification of 'child-crafting' (as distinguished from 'childcare') in this society. By 'domestication' of Malayalis, I point to a process in and through which people have been directed towards investing most of their time, energies and desires in the home. At the same time, this also implies a certain 'taming', a making useful, a political docility, of individuals. Ever since the aspirations towards modernity became evident in Malayali society since the late nineteenth century, there has been an increasing thrust towards transforming domestic space into an individualising space (Devika, 2007). The home has increasingly been conceived as the space within which children were to be moulded into perfect, productive individuals capable of living within a liberal political order and thriving within a capitalist economic order. Nancy Folbre's notion of 'child-crafting' seems relevant here (Folbre, 1998). The more the domestic domain became a space for the shaping of perfect individuals, the more child-rearing has resembled a craft-like activity in which children are treated as a sort of 'raw material' upon which parents work. This offers the parents a tantalising mix of emotional intensities, pleasure and pain. Parenting is then persistent, even agonising labour,

2. Journalistic accounts of the rise in divorce rates in Kerala have also fuelled fears about the rise of the single-parent family in contemporary Malayali society. However, recent research into the solidification of conjugal marriage in Kerala has pointed out that these fears may be indeed exaggerated: the rising divorce figures may actually reflect the extent to which marriages have been legalised in Kerala, a phenomenon probably intensifying in the latter half of the twentieth century. Looser norms of marriage in matrilineal communities, and stronger joint- and extended family structures in earlier times seems to have assured that women did separate more frequently, easily and with less stress, from their husbands then. See Kodoth, 2006.

combined with the pleasure of near-total absorption and insulation from any larger worries stemming beyond the home, and the pleasurable, if precarious, expectation of a perfect end-product. The strains and tensions of domestic responsibilities and its pleasures and consolations all stem from a common source: the direction of a major share of the energies of men and women into their supposedly natural calling, parenting. This has had two important implications for participation in the public: one, parenting, as in handicraft, requires such constant attention to the 'work at hand', that it turns the person engaged in parenting completely away from the public; two, it shapes participation in the public in such a way that the interests of the household and family life acquire an inordinately high centrality within it. Thus, the householder seems to acquire a weight decidedly above the citizen in public life as well.

I do think that in the light of the above historical account, several issues regarding child welfare that have been discussed actively in the Malayali public recently may be real enough to be regarded as important issues for demographic research. For instance, there has been much concern expressed about the excessive regulation of time and activities of children and the general withdrawal of time and spaces for unsupervised play and interaction, especially for teenagers. Given the historical trajectory of the modern Malayali family, and given the present-day context of migration-dependence and aspirations of ever-greater sections towards upward mobility, the heightening pressure to mould children into the saleable professions is something that would follow. Or, take for instance, reports of increasing physical and mental violence against children from their parents and from school. This, again, may be hypothesised to be a predictable consequence of the tendency mentioned above, to treat children more as 'raw material' and less as human beings. This also brings up questions about human rights for children in Kerala, which is yet another poorly explored area. Indeed, this would also help us understand the extent to which the sexuality of children and teenagers are ignored in Kerala—for sexuality may be understood only as an attribute of active and living beings, and not of inert 'raw material'. Indeed, some recent research has brought to light the extent of ignorance that prevails among the general child population in Kerala, and worse, the dangerous misconceptions that seem to be abounding among them (Mathew, 2005). Another area of concern that is now ever-frequently a topic of public discussion is the rising burden of the instruction and supervision of children upon mothers and thus, the shifting of the responsibility of pedagogic supervision on to families, rather than schools. This, again, appears to make sense when hypothesised as the culmination of the tendency, gestured at above, to treat children as future contributors to the family, especially to family upward mobility, rather than as future citizens with moorings in the public. Exploring this as a hypothesis also appears to offer rich rewards when we consider the fact that in the social groups that have gained access to modern education in Malayali society in the twentieth century, the levels of education attained by mothers have been also steadily rising through the century. The impact of this shift in pedagogic and supervisory authority on the mental and physical well-being of children (which would mean moving beyond concerns about nutrition, literacy or basic health care), on domestic time-management regimes, resources spent on children across social groups etc., may indeed be considerable. These are undeniably important issues for research, and light into the wider implications of these, such as for inequalities of class, caste and gender in Malayali society, may be crucial inputs for both policy-making and civil social activism.

Simultaneously, such research into the newer forms of mothering could be of immense significance to those interested in the dynamics of gender in contemporary Kerala. The highly educated mother occupies a different position within the nuclear family in comparison with that of the less educated mother, especially in the tasks she is expected to perform at home. Indeed, it may even be possible to hypothesise that while the levelling of educational achievements between husband and wife in the nuclear family (as also the superior achievement of the wife, as is the case, in many Malayali families, especially those of migrants) may indeed soften the patriarchal undergirding of the husband-wife axis of power, it may actually enhance the parent-child axis of power. That is, children may indeed be now subject to greater degrees of control within the family when both parents are equally educated and upwardly mobile. It must be mentioned, though, that this does not unravel into an argument against higher education for women and mothers. It, however, may expose the consequences of the specific kind of agency of modern motherhood opened up within modernity for Malayali women. We may indeed see that this sort of agency for women has turned them into agents of patriarchal power located within the family, into vehicles of power exercised upon children, into the agents of 'delegated patriarchy'. At the same time, it simultaneously sanctions their exclusion from public forms of power. This, again, may result in research into the consequences the new mothering has for the mental health of mothers, their time management, the human capabilities they possess, and the success they achieve in translating them into desired and desirable functionings. Needless to say, these are matters of considerable relevance, again, for both policy makers and civil social organisations.

Besides the above, the contemporary context of globalisation has had important cultural effects on childhood and teenage, many of which have been explored elsewhere (for instance, Stearns, 2005). It may be interesting to investigate into the local manifestations of such global changes, especially for their implications for demographic change.

III

It may be evident by now that including the above concerns in the new agenda for demographic research indicates interdisciplinary methodological horizons. The issues mentioned certainly have aspects of interest to historical, sociological, psychological and anthropological researchers and the themes of interest shade into research in fields like gender, sexuality and family studies, cultural studies. The interdisciplinary turn in the social sciences has certainly not left demography untouched. In the last two decades, creative exchanges between demographers, cultural anthropologists and historians have highlighted the importance of the changing meanings of procreation, family life and the good life, for understanding changes in fertility (Caldwell *et al.*, 1987; Carter, 1988; Greenhalgh and Li, 1995). The editors of a recent special issue of the *Journal of Interdisciplinary History* call for an approach that "joins the quantitative strengths of demographic history with the interpretive power of cultural and oral history. The former can pinpoint when, where, and among whom significant changes in family formation occurred, but texts and testimonies are indispensable for a more complete understanding of why those changes occurred and what they meant to the groups and communities involved..." (Szretzer *et al.*, 2003: 154). Feminist interventions in demography too have attempted to shift emphasis from the 'big picture' of broad demographic changes to the local and the micro contexts of change, to generate non-linear accounts of change which take conflict, resistance and culture seriously (Greenhalgh and Li, 1995; McDaniels, 1996; Bledsoe *et al.*, 1999; Kaler, 2000).

These methodological innovations may indeed be of crucial significance to demographers dealing with the 'second-generation' or post-demographic transition issues in Malayali society precisely because unlike the 'first-generation' issues in child welfare, they may not be explored through quantitative methodologies alone. That is, while literacy, health, nutrition etc., were studied mainly through the analysis of quantitative data, the issues outlined above may require a more ingenious combination of quantitative and qualitative and even archival methods and textual interpretation, derived from sociology, anthropology, history, cultural studies and psychology.

Contrary to the common view, this may not diminish the status of demography as a 'policy science' (Ittman, 2003). With the attention it pays to power and inequality and its problematisation of governmental power, it may, however, completely change our notion of what 'policy' ought to be. If so, it may be evident that no longer can any 'policy knowledge' limit itself to the generation of manageable categories and quantifiable data. Indeed, many of the 'second generation' issues that have emerged are not ones that warrant simple, universal and familiar governmental solutions. The processes that shape them are not so readily discernible or easily enumerated. They arise at the conjunctures of distinct historical and social forces, and call for solutions that are complex but specific to this moment in Malayali society. In fact, the call for interdisciplinarity in demographic research has also been explicitly linked with the need to produce more balanced analysis for sound policy, and to prevent it from veering towards extreme positions (Cherlin, 1999). Thus, effective policy-making will itself require knowledge generated with a more varied set of tools. No doubt, as elsewhere in the world, demography here will rise to meet this new challenge.

References

Bianchi, Suzanne M. (2000). "Maternal Employment and Time with Children: Dramatic Change or Surprising Continuity?", *Demography* 37(4): 401-14.

Bledsoe, Caroline H., Allan H. Hill, Umberto D'Alessandro, Patricia Langerock (1994). "Constructing Natural Fertility: The Use of Western Contraceptive Technologies in Rural Gambia", *Population and Development Review* 20(1): 81-113.

Bledsoe, Caroline H., John B. Casterline, Jennifer A. Johnson-Kuhn, and John G. Haaga (eds.) (1999). *Critical Perspectives on Schooling and Fertility in the Developing World*. Committee on Population. National Research Council.

Bumpass, L.M. (1990). "What's Happening to the Family?: Interactions Between Demographic and Institutional Change", *Demography* 27(4): 483-98.

Buvinic Sym, Mayra and Geeta Rao Gupta. (1997). "Female-Headed Households or Female-Maintained Families: Are They Worth Targeting to Reduce Poverty in Developing Countries?", *Economic Development and Cultural Change* 45(2): 259-80.

Caldwell, John and Pat Caldwell (1987). "The Cultural Context of High Fertility in Sub-Saharan Africa", *Population and Development Review* 13(3): 409-437.

Caldwell, J.C., Bruce Caldwell and Pat Caldwell (1978). "Anthropology and Demography: The Mutual Reinforcement of Speculation and Research", *Current Anthropology* XXVIII: 25-34.

Carter, Anthony T. (1988). "Does Culture Matter? The Case of the Demographic Transition", *Historical Methods* XXI: 164-169.

Casper, Lynne M. (2004). "Self-Care: Why do Parents Leave their Children Unsupervised?", *Demography* 41(2): 285-301.

Cherlin, A.J. (1999). "Going to the Extremes: Family Structure, Children's Well-being, and Social Science", *Demography* 36(4): 421-28.

Devika, J. (2002). "Domesticating Malayalees: Family Planning, The Nation, and Home-Centred Anxieties, in Mid-Twentieth Century Kerala", CDS *Working Paper* No. 340. Thiruvananthapuram: Centre for Development Studies.

———. (2007). *En-Gendering Individuals: The Language of Re-forming in Early Twentieth Century Kerala..* Hyderabad: Orient Longman.

Folbre, N. (1998). "Patriarchy and Fertility Decisions", in P. Demeny and G. Mc Nicoll (eds), *The Earthscan Reader on Population and Development*. London: Earthscan. pp.121-42.

Gallo, E. (2005). "Unorthodox Sisters: Gender Relations and Generational Changes in Transnational Malayali Marriages". Paper presented at KCHR Colloquium, Feb. 5, Thiruvananthapuram.

Goody, Jack (2003). "Globalisation, Population and Ecology", Paper presented at the International Conference on Theoretical Topics in Ecological Economics, Trieste, Italy, February 10-12.

Greenhalgh, Susan (1990). "Towards a Political Economy of Fertility: Anthropological Contributions", *Population and Development Review* 16(1): 85-101.

Greenhalgh, Susan and Jiali Li (1995). "Engendering Reproductive Policy and Practice in Peasant China: For a Feminist Demography of Reproduction", *Signs: Journal of Women in Culture and Society* 20(3): 601-37.

Ittman, Karl (2003). "Demography as Policy Science in the British Empire, 1918-1969", *Journal of Policy History* 15(4): 417-48.

Jeffrey, Robin (2003). *Politics, Women and Well-Being: How Kerala Became a 'Model'*. New Delhi: OUP.

Kaler, Amy (2000). "Who Has Told You to Do This Thing? Towards a Feminist Interpretation of Contraceptive Diffusion in Rhodesia, 1970-1980", *Signs: Journal of Women in Culture and Society* 25(3): 677-704.

Kodoth, Praveena (2006). "Varante Vila Uyarunnu: Lingadhikaravum Vivahalochanayum Keralattil" (The Rising Price of Men: Gender in Marriage Match-making in Kerala), in (ed.) J. Devika, *Aanarashunattile Kazhcchakal: Keralam Streepakshagaveshanattil* (Sights in Male-dom: Kerala in Feminist Research). Thiruvananthapuram: Women's Imprint.

Lindberg, Anna (2001). *Experience and Identity: A Historical Account of Class, Caste and Gender among the Cashew Workers of Kerala, 1930-2000*. Lund: Department of History, University of Lund.

Main, Gloria L. (2006). "Rocking the Cradle: Downsizing the New England Family", *Journal of Interdisciplinary History* 37(1): 35-58.

Mathew, Phillip, K.M. (2005). "Attitudes of Adolescent Students in Thiruvananthapuram towards Gender, Sexuality, Sexual and Reproductive Health and Rights". Thiruvananthapuram: Achutha Menon Centre for Health Science Studies, Sree Chitra Tirunal Institute for Medical Sciences and Technology.

McDaniels, Susan (1996). "Towards a Synthesis of Feminist and Demographic Perspectives on Fertility", *Sociological Quarterly* 37(1): 83-104.

McLanahan, Sara (2004). "Diverging Destinies: How Children are Faring under the Second Demographic Transition", *Demography* 41(4): 607-27.

Morgan, S.P. (2003). "Is Low Fertility a Twenty-First-Century Demographic Crisis?", *Demography* 40(4): 589-603, November.

Nieuwenhuys, Olga (1994). *Children's Lifeworlds Gender, Welfare, and Labour in the Developing World*. London: Routledge.

———. (1999). *Children's Lifeworlds: Gender, Welfare and Labour in the Developing World*. New Delhi: Social Science Press.

Osella, Caroline and Filippo Osella (2000). *Social Mobility in Kerala: Modernity in Conflict*. London: Pluto Press.

Puthenkalam, J. (1977). "Marriage and Family in Kerala with Special References to the Matrilineal Castes", George Kurien (ed.), *Journal of Comparitive Family Studies Monograph Series*. Alberta: University of Calgary.

Sandberg, John F. and Sandra L. Hofferth (2001). "Changes in Children's Time with Parents: United States 1981-1997", *Demography* 38(3): 423-36.

Stearns, Peter. N. (2005). "Preface: Globalization and Childhood", *Journal of Social History* 38(4): 845-48.

Szrezer, C.S., R.A. Nye and F. van Poppel (2003). "Fertility and Contraception during the Demographic Transition: Quantitative and Qualitative Approaches", *Journal of Interdisciplinary History* 34(2): 141-54.

Thampi, Binitha V. (2007). "Economic Role of Women and Its Impact on Child Health and Care: A Study in Kerala", PhD Thesis submitted to ISEC, Bangalore.

Thornton, Arland (2001). "The Developmental Paradigm, Reading History Sideways, and Family Change", *Demography* 38(4): 449-65.

Uyl, Marion den (1995). *Invisible Barriers: Gender, Caste and Kinship in a Southern Indian Village*. Utrecht: International Books.

Zachariah, K.C., E.T. Mathew and S.I. Rajan (2003). *Dynamics of Migration in Kerala: Dimensions, Differentials and Consequences*. Hyderabad: Orient Longman.

16

Urbanisation in Kerala

REMYA PRABHA

Introduction

The state of Kerala presents a peculiar pattern of urbanisation among other Indian states. The continuous semi-urban appearance of regions within the state with little population density differences between towns and villages and the more rural to rural than rural to urban migration contributes to this unique pattern of urban growth. According to 2001 census, Kerala ranks seventeenth in the degree of urbanisation among the states and union territories in India.

At the beginning of 20th century, Kerala had a population of 63.9 lakh of which 59.4 lakh or 92.9 per cent resided in rural areas. The share of rural population to the total population of Kerala underwent significant decline in the succeeding decades and reached 74.0 per cent as per the 2001 census. It reveals that Kerala became slowly urbanised which is a clear sign of modernisation. In other words, Kerala economy is being transformed from a traditional agricultural society to a modern service sector economy—its urban proportion has shown an increase from 7.1 in 1901 to 25.9 in 2001, over the period of last 100 years. In Kerala, we are experiencing a tertiary pattern of development. Therefore, over-urbanisation (urbanisation without industrialisation) in the state is a serious concern. In this context, assessing the urban process of Kerala is extremely useful for policy makers to address the issues of low economic development and formulate policies to curb unemployment, poverty and other negative consequences of urbanisation.

In this chapter, we would like to examine the different factors contributing to the urban development of Kerala. The present study on Kerala's urbanisation is limited to the decades 1961 to 2001 for two reasons. Since 1961, the Census of India used uniform criteria for defining the urban areas. Secondly, the state of Kerala came into existence in 1956, comprising greater part of the old state of Travancore and Cochin, Malabar district and Kasaragod *taluk* of South Canara district in Madras Presidency (Sreekumar, 1993).

Growth of Urban Population

Kerala has had a relatively slow but consistent growth in the urban population till 1981—15.1 per cent in 1961 to 18.7 in 1981 (see Table 16.1). In 1991, the urban population had an unexpected rise to 26.4 per cent and could not keep its pace of urbanisation in 2001 resulting in a decline in its proportion to 25.9 per cent. A cursory glance at the data would reveal that Kerala has been invariably lagging behind the corresponding all-India figures except for the year 1991. In 1991, Kerala's urban population (26.4 per cent) was above the national average (25.7 per cent).

Table 16.1

Growth of Urban Population in Kerala and India, 1961-2001

Census Year	*Kerala*		*India*	
	Per cent Urban	*Urban Growth Rate*	*Per cent Urban*	*Urban Growth Rate*
1961	15.1	3.4	18.0	2.4
1971	16.2	3.1	19.9	3.3
1981	18.7	3.2	23.3	3.9
1991	26.4	4.9	25.7	3.1
2001	25.9	0.7	27.8	2.8

Source: Census of India, various issues.

A comparative analysis of the annual growth rate of urban population for India and Kerala reveals that Kerala has been falling below India except for the decade 1981-1991. The all-India urban growth rate had increased till 1981 and thereafter it declined. But for Kerala, the urban growth rate was highest during 1991 (4.9 per cent), much higher than the growth rate of India (3.1 per cent), then it had a steep fall to 0.7 per cent in 2001.

This slowing down of the pace of urbanisation in India became a matter of recent debate among the scholars (Mohan, 1996; Premi, 1991; Visaria, 1997). Initially, the reason for this decline was passed on to the data error, more particularly on the under-enumeration of urban population in 1991 census. More detailed studies, however, indicated that the recorded slowdown of the urbanisation was real and could not be attributed solely to under enumeration, and this phenomena of urban population growth rate was supported by the fact that a large number of states as well as urban centres at all levels experienced a decline in its pace of urbanisation (Mohan, 1996). Later on, few other studies attributed this slowdown due to identification of relatively fewer new towns, decline in the volume of rural to urban migration and increasing concentration of population in the rural areas adjacent to large urban centres. Nevertheless, most of the scholars considered this slowdown in urbanisation as only temporary-phenomena and commented that it "would be a mistake to presume that urbanisation will continue to be slow during 1990s and beyond" (Visaria, 1997). But the data available in the provisional 2001 census shows that the trend of this slowing down of urbanisation has continued even during the 1991-2001 decade.

The instability in Kerala's urban system and its lagging behind all-India figures are partly due to the peculiarity of Kerala's economic structure. The decay of traditional industries, rural to rural migration, absence of strong rural to urban migration, inability to absorb the growing population in non-agricultural activities and decline in natural rate of growth of population has resulted in the slow pace of urbanisation in Kerala (Sreekumar, 1990). Generally, increase in urban population growth rate is the result of over concentration in the existing cities especially metropolitan cities. This is true in the case of urbanisation in the other states of India. But in Kerala, the phenomenal increase in urban growth rate during the decade 1981-1991 was due to extensive reclassification of urban areas and inclusion of new towns (Census of India, 2001). The 2001 census indicates that Kerala's urban growth rate had a sudden fall to 0.7 per cent. The deceleration should be seen as a matter of serious concern in view of the fact that even in 2001, only little more than a quarter of the state's population lived in urban areas. In the next section, we would like to figure out some factors responsible for this slowdown in urban growth.

Slowing Down of the Pace of Urbanisation in Kerala: Plausible Explanations

First, an attempt has been made to analyse the components of urbanisation in Kerala. It is important to segregate the urban process in order to identify the various factors contributing to urbanisation. Based on the information obtained from this exercise we have explored other features, which could have contributed to the stagnant growth of urbanisation.

Components of Urbanisation

Urban population growth results from: 1) natural increase, 2) rural to urban migration, 3) reclassification and boundary changes of the existing urban centres (Mohan, 1996). However, it is difficult to calculate the precise contribution of the different components of urban population growth due to problems inherent in the required data availability. Data are available only on one or two components and the share of other components is often estimated as residual. The methodology adopted here is to estimate the migration component as the residual.

Table 16.2

Components of Urban Growth, Kerala and India, 1961-2001

Components	1961-1971		1971-1981		1981-1991		1991-2001
	Kerala	India	Kerala	India	Kerala	India	Kerala
Natural increase	42.6	61.6	44.5	41.2	26.9	54.8	14.4
Reclassification	70.1	19.7	81.7	19.2	59.1	17.3	-0.1
Migration	-12.6	18.7	-26.2	39.7	14.0	28.0	85.7

Note: For 1991-2001, estimates for Kerala made by the author using the same methodology. However, we could not obtain the estimates for India due to unavailability of the data.
Source: Bhasin (2001).

Of the three components of urbanisation, natural increase is the most important factor contributing to urban growth in India. Its share was 61.6 per cent in 1961-1971, it declined to 41.2 per cent in 1971-1981 but again it increased to 54.8 per cent in 1981-1991. The share of net immigration rose from 18.7 per cent in 1961-1971 to a high 39.7 per cent in 1971-1981 and then declined to 28.0 per cent in 1981-1991 and is considered as one of the main factors in the slowing down of urban process in India (Bhasin, 2001). The share of area reclassification declined over the decades from 19.7 per cent in 1961-1971 to 17.3 per cent in 1981-1991 and this is another most important factor in the slow growth of urban population during 1981-1991(Mohan, 1996). Thus, the process of urbanisation in India is less dependent on migration and reclassification and more on natural increase.

The case of Kerala is quite different from the all-India pattern. In Kerala, it is the reclassification component which is the most important factor contributing to urban growth. Its share rose from 70.1 per cent in 1961-1971 to a maximum of 81.7 per cent in the next decade (1971-1981). But it declined to 59.1 per cent in 1981-1991. From 1961-1981, the migration component is negative signifying the fact that the number of out-migrants is more than the number of in-migrants. Out-migration was the highest during 1971-1981 because of the "Gulf Boom" in the 70s (Prakash, 1999). The share of net migration during 1981-1991 was 14.0 per cent indicating considerable in-migration into urban Kerala. On the other side, the share of natural increase has declining trends implying that Kerala is in the final stage of demographic transition with low death and birth rates. Using the methodology adopted by Bhasin, we estimated the share of each component for the period 1991-2001 for Kerala and presented in Table 16.2.

An analysis of the components of urbanisation in Kerala for the period 1991-2001 shows a pattern quite different from that in the previous decades. The share of reclassification component has lost its dominating position since 1991. In fact, its share is negative which shows that the decrease in urban population due to declassifying erstwhile urban areas as rural is much greater than the increase in urban population due to the emergence of new towns. This could be a reason for the decline of degree of urbanisation from 26.4 per cent in 1991 to 25.9 per cent in 2001. The share of natural increase has further declined to 14.4 per cent indicating the continuous decline of fertility rates in Kerala (Guilmoto and Rajan, 2005). The major contributing factor to Kerala's urban growth during the last decade is migration with as high as 85.7 per cent. Thus, the components of the urbanisation in Kerala during the last decade reveals that the natural increase contributing to urban growth has declined; migration's contribution to urban growth has increased tremendously and the contribution of reclassification is negative, signifying the fact that decline in urban population growth is due to declassification. The stagnancy of the urban process in Kerala could be better explained by looking at the factors contributing to urban growth.

Natural Increase

To examine the contribution of natural increase, Table 16.3 gives us an idea about the birth and death rates for India and Kerala, according to the Sample Registration System. The rate of natural increase is declining for both India and Kerala. The death and birth rates in India tend to be lower in urban areas than in villages. Compared to the all-India level, the birth and death rates for Kerala are much lower and also there is not much difference between rural and urban rates. Kerala has, in fact, entered the final phase of demographic transition. The rural rate of natural increase at the all-India level is much higher than the urban rate. Thus, in the absence of any rural-urban migration or reclassification, the rise in the rate of natural increase in rural India had resulted in higher population growth in rural India and it has contributed to the slower urbanisation (Visaria, 1997). But in Kerala, the rural rate of natural increase is almost the same as urban rate and is very low. Thus, we cannot say that the slower urbanisation is due to natural increase as the rate of increase is of the same degree in both rural and urban Kerala.

Reclassification

The process of reclassification of localities from rural to urban also declined during the last decade. Table 16.4 analyses the growth of towns in Kerala over the decades. In Kerala, there were 92 towns in 1961 with majority of urban population concentrating in Class IV and Class III towns. In 1971, the number of towns declined to 88 with 40 towns in Class III and 25 towns in Class IV. In 1981, there were 106 towns in Kerala of which 64 belonged to Class III towns. In 1991, there was a boom of 197 towns in Kerala with an explosion of towns in Class I; from just 6 towns in 1981 to 102 towns which pointed out that there was heavy concentration of population in Class I towns. Thus, the phenomenal increase in urban population during the period 1981-1991 was mainly due to the creation of new towns in the state and the inclusion of peripheral areas with pronounced urban characteristics as urban outgrowths (Census of Kerala, 2001). In the latest 2001 census, the number of towns was reduced to 159 towns with a reduction in the number of towns in all classes except in Class II and Class V. However, a good number of the towns in Kerala were included in Class I towns during this period.

Table 16.3

Birth Rate, Death Rate and Natural Increase, Kerala and India, 1995-2001

Nation/ State	*Year*	*Birth Rate*			*Death Rate*			*Natural Increase*		
		Total	*Rural*	*Urban*	*Total*	*Rural*	*Urban*	*Total*	*Rural*	*Urban*
	1995	28.3	30.0	22.7	9.0	9.8	6.6	19.3	20.2	16.1
	1996	27.5	29.3	21.6	9.0	9.7	6.5	18.5	19.6	15.1
	1997	27.2	28.9	21.5	8.9	9.6	6.5	18.3	19.3	15.0
India	1998	26.5	28.0	21.1	9.0	9.7	6.6	17.5	18.3	14.5
	1999	26.1	27.6	20.8	8.7	9.4	6.3	17.4	18.2	14.5
	2000	25.8	27.6	20.7	8.5	9.3	6.3	17.3	18.3	14.4
	2001	25.4	27.1	20.2	8.4	9.0	6.3	17.0	18.1	13.9
	1995	18.0	18.1	17.7	6.0	6.0	6.0	12.0	12.1	11.7
	1996	18.0	18.0	17.9	6.2	6.3	6.0	11.8	11.7	11.9
	1997	17.9	17.9	17.9	6.2	6.3	6.1	11.7	11.6	11.8
Kerala	1998	18.3	18.3	18.2	6.4	6.5	6.2	11.8	11.8	12.0
	1999	18.0	18.1	17.7	6.4	6.5	6.3	11.5	11.6	11.4
	2000	17.9	18.0	17.5	6.4	6.5	6.2	11.5	11.6	11.4
	2001	17.2	17.4	16.6	6.6	6.8	6.1	10.6	10.6	10.5

Source: SRS Bulletin, October 1998 and October 2002.

One of the objectives of the present study is to assess the near stagnancy of Kerala's urban growth during of the last decade. To understand the stagnancy, we need to look at some detail of the share of urban population in each size classes for the decade 1991-2001. The total number of towns in Kerala reduced from 197 in 1991 to 159 in 2001. The number of towns in Class I reduced from 102 to 78, those in Class III was reduced from 46 to 35 and number of Class IV towns fell to 26 from 34 during this period. In other words, during 1991-2001, 42 towns were declassified, 16 towns were merged with three corporations of Thrissur, Kollam and Thiruvananthapuram and 18 towns were newly added. Also, 2 declassified towns were continued as census towns. The declassified towns in 2001 census resulted in the loss of 6 per cent of the total urban population of Kerala in 1991 whereas the newly added towns contributed to only 3.7 per cent of the total urban population in 2001. The end result indicates that there was an insignificant decline in the percentage of urban population during 1991-2001.

Table 16.4

Total Number of Towns across Size Class in Kerala, 1961-2001

Size Class	*1961*	*1971*	*1981*	*1991*	*2001*
Class I	4	5	6	102	78
Class II	5	7	8	9	11
Class III	31	40	64	46	35
Class IV	33	25	21	34	26
Class V	15	9	6	6	9
Class VI	7	2	1	—	—
All classes	92	88	106	197	159

Note: (1) Total number of towns include both statutory and census towns.
(2) "—"indicates data is not available.

Sources: Census of India (1961); (1971); (1981); (1991); (2001).

Migration

One of the important factors affecting urbanisation is migration. It is one of the significant factors affecting population growth. Kerala was a net in-migrating state till 1940s. Then the state transformed itself into a net out-migrating state with migration having a negative effect on population growth. Table 16.5 indicates the migration trends in Kerala for the last four decades. A negative net migration rate signifies that migration out of Kerala exceeds migration into Kerala, resulting in a decline in population. The absolute migration rate is showing a constant trend of 0.2 per cent over the years with the maximum rate of 0.3 during 1991, which continued with slight decline in 2001.

Table 16.5

Migration in Kerala, 1961-2001

Census Year	*Net Migration Rate*
1961	-0.20
1971	-0.16
1981	-0.22
1991	-0.31
2001	-0.27

Source: Zachariah *et al.* (2003).

One of the major shortcomings of this analysis is the non-availability of migration tables from the Census of India, 2001. It is a serious constraint in analysing the factors contributing to the slower growth of urbanisation process in Kerala. But the migration tables for the previous decades provide some valuable information regarding the pattern of migration in Kerala which is contributing to the peculiar pattern of urbanisation which Kerala is experiencing. The rural-urban distribution of in-migrants gives valuable information regarding the urban process of Kerala (see Table 16.6).

Table 16.6

Share of Migrants in Kerala and India, 1971-1991

Year	*Kerala*			*India*		
	Rural	*Urban*	*Total*	*Rural*	*Urban*	*Total*
1971	20.8	27.6	24.2	28.2	38.8	30.4
1981	27.1	24.9	26.7	28.2	62.7	30.6
1991	22.7	18.3	22.1	25.7	31.4	27.2

Note: This table is based on POB criterion.
Source: Calculated by the author based on various migration tables.

At the all-India level, the share of urban migrants shows a fluctuating pattern; it increased from 38.8 per cent in 1971 to a high of 62.7 per cent in 1981 and declined 31.4 per cent in 1991. But the trend in Kerala is declining over the decades. The share of urban migrants declined from 27.6 per cent in 1971 to 24.9 per cent in 1981 and to 18.3 per cent in 1991. At the all-India level, the share of urban migrants to total urban population is much higher than rural migrants. This is an evidence for greater rural to urban migration in India. But in Kerala, the number of urban migrants as a proportion of total urban population is lower than the number of rural migrants except for the year 1971. This indicates that there is not much preference for the people to migrate to urban areas in Kerala. This is confirmed by the data presented in Table 16.7 on streams of migration in Kerala over the decades.

The all-India and Kerala pattern of migration stream is similar in the case of rural to rural (R-R) stream. The majority of the migrants are concentrating on the rural to rural stream and this is explained in terms of marriage migration and movements from areas of low agricultural productivity to areas of high agricultural productivity (Premi, 1991). But its share is declining over the years. The pace of this decline is different in Kerala as it declined from 73.4 per cent in 1971 to less than 58 per cent in 1991. But at the all-India level, it had just four points decline from 69.1 per cent in 1971 to 64.5 per cent in 1991. The contribution of rural to urban (R-U) stream and the urban to urban (U-U) stream is almost similar in Kerala and at the all-India level. Both these streams are showing an increasing trend over the years, but the volume of migration is much lower in Kerala. The substantial increase in the proportion of R-U and U-U migration is partly due to the emergence of a large number of new towns and the movement of people from towns of low economic bases to towns having strong economic bases (Premi, 1998). Another important point to be noticed is that in Kerala, the share of urban to rural (U-R) migration is also increasing. It rose from a mere 9.4 per cent in 1971 to as high as 15.2 per cent in 1991 whereas for all-India its share is declining. Thus, the dominating migration stream is the rural to rural stream in Kerala and also the share of urban to rural migration stream is increasing over the decades. Thus, most of the in-migrants ended up in moving to rural areas of Kerala (Rajan, 1998).

Table 16.7

Migration Streams in Kerala and India, 1991

Year	*Kerala*					*India*				
	R-R	*U-R*	*R-U*	*U-U*	*Total*	*R-R*	*U-R*	*R-U*	*U-U*	*Total*
1971	73.4	9.4	12.4	4.8	100.0	69.1	5.9	14.6	10.4	100.0
1981	65.7	12.3	14.7	7.3	100.0	65.3	6.1	16.7	11.9	100.0
1991	57.7	15.2	18.2	8.9	100.0	64.5	6.0	17.7	11.8	100.0

Note: This table is based on POB criterion.
Source: Calculated by the author based on various migration tables.

Net migration rate given in Table 16.5 not only include internal migration i.e., migration to other parts of India but also external migration that is moving abroad. The increasing share of external migrants could also be a plausible explanation for the slowing down of urban process in Kerala as it results in a loss of urban population. Table 16.8 shows the break-up of total net migration into external and internal migration for the period 1961 to 1991.

Table 16.8

External and Internal Migration in Kerala (in '000s)

	1961-1971	*1971-1981*	*1981-1991*
Total net migration	-318	-473	-744
Net internal migration	-298	-249	-189
Net external migration	-20	-224	-555

Source: Zachariah *et al.* (2003).

During 1961-1971, Kerala's loss due to external migration was quite insignificant. The net loss was 224,000 persons during 1971-1981 and in the next decade, it increased to 555,000 persons. It is to be noted that the urban population has a greater propensity to move out of Kerala than the rural population. The estimated proportion of urban population in Kerala in 1998 is about the same as the estimated proportion of emigrants originating in urban areas, about one-third of the total (Zachariah *et al.*, 2003). Thus, the loss of urban population due to external migration results in a slowdown in the urban growth of Kerala. Also, most of the emigrants had been labourers in non-agricultural sector before emigration and the emigration rate among them was 2.3 times that of general population (Zachariah *et al.*, 2003). This causes a loss of working population in the non-agricultural sector in the area of origin, which may result in low urbanisation. Table 16.9 shows the occupational distribution of emigrants before and after migration. The data reveals that 34.1 per cent of the emigrants were non-agricultural labourers before migration and 26.5 per cent were job-seekers.

Table 16.9

Occupational Distribution of Emigrants Before and After Migration

Occupation	*Before Migration*	*After Migration*
State/govt. employee	2.2	2.5
Semi-govt. employee	0.6	0.9
Private sector employee	15.1	40.8
Self-employed	13.9	4.4
Unpaid worker	0.8	0.0
Agri. labourer	1.8	0.1
Non-agri. labourer	34.1	47.5
Job-seeker	26.5	0.6
Voluntarily unemployed	0.2	0.2
Student	1.5	0.4
Household work	3.2	2.6
Old-age pensioner	0.1	0.0
All	100.0	100.0

Source: Zachariah *et al.* (2003).

Table 16.10 reveals the reasons for internal migration in Kerala from the 1991 census. The majority of the migrants in Kerala moved due to marriage. The proportion of rural migrants moved as a result of marriage was higher than the urban migrants. The second important reason for migration was family movement. It is important to note that the proportion of migrants moving for education, employment and business is much lower in Kerala. Also, it is to be noted that their share is very low in rural areas. This may be due to the availability of infrastructural facilities in rural areas. The villages in Kerala do not differ much from the towns in terms of several basic modern amenities accessible to the people (Kannan, 1986; National Sample Survey Organisation, 2002).

Table 16.10

Reasons for Out-Migration, Kerala, 1991

Reasons	*Rural*	*Urban*	*Total*
Employment	5.9	11.9	7.4
Business	0. 6	0.9	0.7
Education	1.2	2.7	1.6
Family moved	26.2	27.5	26.5
Marriage	42.3	34.8	40.5
Natural calamities	0.1	0.1	0.1
Others	23.7	22.1	23.3

Source: Rajan, 1998.

Migration leading to urbanisation is in turn affected by both push and pull factors. Population pressure, agricultural stagnation, education expansion and institutional failure in promoting secondary and tertiary sectors are the push factors determining migration from Kerala (Zachariah *et al.*, 2003). Pull factors represent rural population migrating to urban areas in response to favourable socio-economic and political factors like employment, higher wages, higher education and better health facilities. In Kerala, it is to be noted that, in recent years the pull factors affecting migration is losing its importance. This may be due to the fact that the infrastructural facilities are better dispersed in both urban and rural areas in Kerala. In the following segment, we would like to look at the spatial distribution of these facilities and try to find out whether this will reduce rural to urban migration and urbanisation.

Accessibility to Basic Amenities in Villages

In this section, we are making a hypothesis that the number of people migrating to urban areas of Kerala is becoming lower and lower, partly based on our observation of migration streams of Kerala. However, there was a heavy concentration of rural to rural migrants and increasing concentration of urban to rural migrants. In order to test our hypothesis, we make use of the data on availability of basic amenities at villages collected from NSS reports.

Before we discuss further on this issue, we would like to document that Kerala had the special advantage of high human density over a period of last 100 years. Among the major states, Kerala has the third highest density of 819 persons per sq.km next to West Bengal and Bihar in 2001 census. However, the density of population in Kerala is more than twice the all-India average of 324 persons per sq.km. This high density is one of the major contributory factors in greater accessibility of basic amenities and indirectly resulted in the slowing down of the process of urbanisation in Kerala.

The high density of population contributes to the development of social infrastructure in Kerala. Villages in Kerala are better equipped with all basic infrastructural facilities compared to other states as well as India as a whole, which probably prevented the rural folk not to migrate largely to urban areas in search of such services. The development of infrastructural facilities has also helped in bringing the industries to rural areas and provide non-agricultural employment there itself (Premi, 1991).

Table 16.11 gives distribution of various general facilities per 1000 villages in major Indian states. Among the major states, Kerala occupies the lead position in terms of availability of basic amenities. As can be seen, almost all villages in Kerala have metalled road, bus stop; 94 per cent of villages have fair price shop, 88 per cent of villages have post office; 76 per cent of villages have bank and 6 per cent of the villages have railway station within a distance of less than 2 km. The availability of better transport facilities also enables the rural folk to commute to their urban work place, thereby reducing the need for rural population to settle down in urban areas for sake of employment. This shows that the villages of Kerala are better linked with other parts of Kerala and they have all the necessary facilities accessible within a specified distance, which make the rural population less migratory.

Accessibility to Educational Facilities

Kerala is renowned for its social developments and educational attainments. There is no rural-urban difference in the availability of educational facilities in Kerala. The villages of Kerala are well networked with schools and colleges. Table 16.12 provides data on number of villages having educational facilities available within a distance of less than 2 km for major Indian states. Kerala has the largest number of villages having a higher secondary school or college with degree course located within a distance of less than 2 km and has the second largest number of villages having a middle school and secondary school, next to Haryana. Almost 95 per cent of villages in Kerala have a primary school within a distance of 2 km. Thus, it is clear that Kerala villages have all necessary educational facilities in its proximity.

Table 16.11

No. of Villages (Per 1000) having General Facilities Located within a Distance of less than 2 Km from the Village

States	*Railway Station*	*Bus Stop*	*Metalled Road*	*Post Office*	*Bank*	*Fair Price Shop*
Andhra Pradesh	24	723	746	568	162	754
Assam	27	371	382	359	70	806
Bihar	42	278	401	428	183	597
Gujarat	31	815	877	410	98	662
Haryana	41	805	987	672	261	912
Karnataka	41	641	684	478	151	604
Kerala	67	993	1000	881	759	948
Madhya Pradesh	18	468	409	260	52	304
Maharashtra	23	704	790	442	191	779
Orissa	21	230	434	352	84	400
Punjab	67	662	962	557	316	722
Rajasthan	40	636	705	472	168	471
Tamil Nadu	55	832	906	683	288	881
Uttar Pradesh	48	330	718	607	225	852
West Bengal	52	383	501	807	555	274
All India	35	476	606	474	183	649

Source: NSS Report on Village Facilities, 58th Round, India, 2002.

Accessibility to Medical Facilities

Kerala occupies a prominent position in health attainments. Among major Indian states, Kerala has the maximum number of villages having a primary health centre, community health centre, private hospital and medical shop located within a distance of less than 2 km (see Table 16.13). It is important to note that 72 per cent of villages in Kerala have a sub-centre within the specified distance whereas the all-India average is just 32 per cent. Thus, the rural folk in Kerala need not have to come to cities for availing health related facilities. Villages in Kerala are better integrated with all the basic amenities, which are normally lacking in rural areas of other states in India. This is a possible reason for declining rural to urban migration in Kerala over the decades, which could have contributed to the slowdown of the process of urbanisation.

Table 16.12

No. of Villages (Per 1000) having Educational Facilities Located within a Distance of less than 2 Km from the Village

States	Primary School	Middle School	Secondary School	Higher Secondary School	College with Degree Course
Andhra Pradesh	827	537	332	62	24
Assam	848	594	310	116	23
Bihar	650	361	176	35	22
Gujarat	967	435	217	63	21
Haryana	990	811	606	269	3
Karnataka	774	586	246	74	37
Kerala	946	757	576	360	81
Madhya Pradesh	964	413	75	44	11
Maharashtra	1000	567	344	121	22
Orissa	744	475	304	48	23
Punjab	874	598	478	262	35
Rajasthan	976	538	246	66	2
Tamil Nadu	873	538	302	154	2
Uttar Pradesh	973	503	261	226	16
West Bengal	935	477	346	161	17
All India	885	505	264	124	22

Source: NSS Report on Village Facilities, 58th Round, India, 2002.

Table 16.13

No. of Villages (Per 1000) having Medical Facilities Located within a Distance of less than 2 Km from the Village

States	Sub-Centre	Primary Health Centre	Community Health Centre	Private Hospital	Medical Shop
Andhra Pradesh	317	99	75	54	228
Assam	288	156	66	23	143
Bihar	287	233	60	68	339
Gujarat	257	124	34	14	44
Haryana	583	234	82	39	394
Karnataka	258	205	73	72	165
Kerala	721	575	268	466	720
Madhya Pradesh	127	52	3	9	63
Maharashtra	335	122	47	84	165
Orissa	153	55	11	18	116
Punjab	515	267	44	170	444
Rajasthan	742	424	101	21	149
Tamil Nadu	442	267	109	137	252
Uttar Pradesh	352	206	47	81	388
West Bengal	524	205	74	23	218
All India	323	166	55	57	235

Source: NSS Report on Village Facilities, 58th Round, India, 2002.

Wage Rates

According to neo classical theories of migration, the movement of people from rural to urban areas takes place in response to the prevailing rural urban differences in employment opportunities and wages (Lewis, 1954; Todaro, 1976). Thus, a major economic pull factor for higher urban migration is the higher wage rates in urban areas compared to rural areas.

Table 16.14 analyses the average daily wages of casual workers in selected Indian states. The wage rates of informal sector (or casual) labourers in Kerala, for both rural and urban areas did not show much difference as compared to the significant rural urban wage differences at the all-India level. This could be a reason for the casual labourers in Kerala not migrating to urban areas looking for better wages. Even if rural workers find opportunities to work in urban areas, they retain their rural habitations and commute to urban centres for work. Such commutation is a low cost alternative to migration, which could be attributed to the better transport facilities in Kerala. Also, the wage rates of informal sector labourers in Kerala have come to be much higher than the national average and higher than the corresponding wage rates in states like Tamil Nadu and Maharashtra. Given such differences in wage rates of casual labourers between Kerala and the rest of India, it is likely that unskilled labourers of Kerala are losing their opportunities for work in the informal sector as they have been replaced by cheap labourers from other states.

Table 16.14

Average Daily Wages of Casual Workers: Rural and Urban Areas of Selected Indian States, 1999-2000 (in Rupees at Current Prices)

	Rural			*Urban*		
	Male	*Female*	*Persons*	*Male*	*Female*	*Persons*
Kerala	100.8	56.7	90.6	102.4	47.2	93.1
Maharashtra	41.3	25.3	34.0	61.7	29.2	54.1
Tamil Nadu	60.2	30.8	48.1	72.3	46.9	66.3
India	44.8	29.0	39.6	62.3	37.7	56.9

Note: The data corresponds to wages of casual workers of age 5 years and above, engaged in works (in farm or non-farm enterprises) other than public works.

Source: Thomas, 2003 and National Sample Survey, 2001.

The provision of modern amenities at the rural areas could be a possible explanation for peculiar pattern of migration i.e., high concentration of rural to rural migrants, increasing urban to rural migration and less number of people migrating due to reasons like education, employment and business.

Thus, the pull factors in urban areas contributing to migration are rather unwelcoming in Kerala as the favourable socio-economic and political factors like higher education, better health facilities and better wages are available in Kerala without any rural-urban distinction.

Kerala has a peculiar settlement pattern of rural-urban continuum in human habitations. This unique habitation emerged as a result of better infrastructural facilities. The improved accessibility to health services and education has in fact resulted in a decline in natural growth rate of population. The non-agrarian structure of Kerala economy together with the well developed transport and communication network resulted in a peculiar pattern of migration in Kerala with little preference for moving to urban areas. All these factors along with considerable reclassification have contributed to the stagnancy of urban growth in Kerala during 1991-2001.

Conclusion

The peculiar pattern in urban growth during the decades 1961-2001 is explained mainly in terms of reclassification of urban areas and migration. The emergence of large number of towns along with increased volume of urban migrants clarifies the high degree of urbanisation during 1981-1991. The factors like the peculiar settlement pattern in Kerala; a rural-urban continuum in human habitations emerged as a result of well developed transportation network; and improved accessibility to health services and education causing a decline in natural growth rate; a peculiar pattern of migration with little preference for moving to urban areas and considerable reclassification leading to a decline in the number of towns, all had contributed to the stagnancy of urban growth in Kerala for the period 1991-2001.

References

Bhasin, Reena (2001). *Urban Poverty and Urbanization*. New Delhi: Deep and Deep Publications.

Census of India (1961). *Cultural and Migration Tables*, Kerala, Volume VII, Part II-C, Directorate of Census Operations, Kerala.

———. (1961). *General Report*, Kerala, Volume VII, Part I-A (i), Directorate of Census Operations, Kerala.

———. (1971). *General Population Tables*, Series-9, Part II-A, Directorate of Census Operations, Kerala.

———. (1971). *Migration Tables*, Kerala, Volume VII, Part II-C, Directorate of Census Operations, Kerala.

———. (1981). *General Population Tables*, Series-10, Part II-A, Directorate of Census Operations, Kerala.

———. (1981). *Migration Tables*, Series-10, Part V-A&B, Directorate of Census Operations, Kerala.

———. (1991). *Final Population Totals*, Series-12, Paper 3, Directorate of Census Operations, Kerala.

———. (1991). *Migration Tables*, Series-12, Volume I, Part V-A&B, Directorate of Census Operations, Kerala.

———. (2001). *Provisional Population Totals: Rural-Urban Distribution*, Series- 33, Paper 2, Directorate of Census Operations, Kerala.

Guilmoto, C.Z and Irudaya Rajan, S. (2005). *Fertility Transition in South India*. London: Sage Publications Pvt. Ltd.

Kannan K.P. (1986). *Of Rural Proletarian Struggles: Mobilization and Organization of Rural Workers in Kerala India*, PhD Thesis, ISS, The Hague, The Netherlands.

Lewis, W.A. (1954). "Economic Development with Unlimited Supplies of Labour", *The Manchester School of Economic and Social Studies* 22: 139-191.

Mohan, Rakesh (1996). "Urbanization in India: Patterns and Emerging Policy Issues" in Gugler, J. (ed), *The Urban Transformation of the Developing World*. New York: Oxford University Press.

National Sample Survey (2001). *National Sample Survey*. New Delhi: National Sample Survey Organization, Government of India.

NSSO (2002). *NSS Report on Village Facilities*, Round 58th, Report No. 487, India.

Prakash, B.A. (ed) (1999). *Kerala's Economic Development- Issues and Problems*. New Delhi: Sage Publications.

Premi, M.K. (1991). "India's Urban Scene and Its Future Implications", *Demography India* 20(1): 41-52.

Rajan, S.I. (1998). *Internal Migration in Kerala, 1961-1991*. Centre for Development Studies, Trivandrum, Kerala.

Sreekumar, T.T. (1990). "Neither Rural nor Urban- Spatial Formation and Development Process", *Economic and Political Weekly* 25(35): 1981-1991. September 8.

———. (1993). *Urban Process in Kerala, 1900-1981*. Trivandrum: Centre for Development Studies.

Thomas, Jayan Jose (2003). "Labour and Industrialisation in Kerala", *Indian Journal of Labour Economics* 46(4): 575-92.

Todaro, M.P (1976). *Internal Migration in Developing Countries*. Geneva: ILO.

Visaria, Pravin (1997). "Urbanization in India: An Overview" in Jones, Gavin W. and Visaria Pravin (ed), *Urbanization in Large Developing Countries: China, Indonesia, Brazil and India*. New York: Oxford University Press.

Zachariah K.C., Mathew E.T. and Irudaya Rajan S. (2003). *Dynamics of Migration in Kerala*. Hyderabad: Orient Longman Private Limited.

17

Emerging Health Threats

C.R. SOMAN

In the last 50 years, Kerala's age structure has changed in favour of the aged. According to the census of the 1961, 41 per cent of children were below 15 years, while those aged 60 or above constituted 5.6 per cent. According to the census of India data for 2001, the proportion of children declined to 26 per cent while that of the aged rose to 10.5 per cent. It is also important to note that the age composition has shifted in favour of the healthy young adult population.

During this period, Kerala's health status has witnessed an amazing transformation for the better (Figure 17.1). These indices while being most welcomed do not give any indication of rapidly transforming picture of ill health that is characteristic of the adult population of Kerala. Health Action by People, an NGO, is involved in serious epidemiological studies of the rapidly changing pattern of morbidity in Kerala. Some of our salient observations concerning the prevalence of emerging chronic diseases are discussed below.

Principal Causes of Death in Kerala

We adopted a population residing in seven *panchayats* falling within the jurisdiction of Varkala ICDS Block. At the time of the first survey, the population comprised of 1,62,753 of which were 79,877 males and 82,876 were women. People aged 20 or more constituted 64 per cent of the population. During the first five years of observation, we lost 3,973 persons on account of death. The causes of death were ascertained carefully using the technique of verbal autopsy. They were grouped into major classes and analysed. The analysis reveals a disturbing picture (Figure 17.2).

Heart attack remains the single highest contributor to mortality in Kerala. 24.3 per cent of the deaths occurred on account of heart attack. Analysed separately for sexes, 32 per cent of deaths of males and 16.5 per cent of deaths of females were the contribution of heart attack. It should be remembered that two generations ago, all chronic diseases contributed to less than 25 per cent of mortality while the contribution of infectious diseases to death was over 60 per cent. The figure also demonstrates that the second contributor to death is stroke. Just over 11 per cent of the deaths were from stroke. Gender-specific analysis reveals that stroke deaths were more in women. Cancer deaths contributed just under 10 per cent to the overall mortality. Suicides contribute to over 6 per cent of all the deaths, a picture very disturbing. What is more striking is that all infectious diseases together are responsible for only 5 per cent of the deaths in Kerala.

Figure 17.1

Change in Health Indices in Kerala between 1956-2005

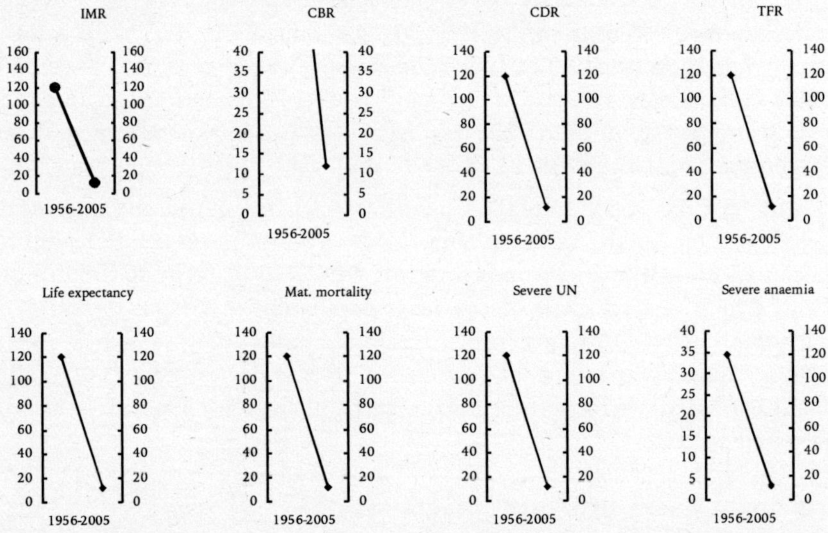

On the basis of these observations, it is projected that the number of persons who die of heart attack in Kerala are in the range of 45,000 to 50,000. It is estimated the survival rate after a heart attack is 75 per cent. On the basis of the above assumption, every year 180,000 to 200,000 people suffer heart attack in Kerala. The recent emergence of high-tech hospitals with specialised cardiac care facilities is a response to the growing epidemic of coronary heart disease. Our investigations also reveal that the proportion of adults aged 30 or more with cardiac abnormalities recorded in the ECG is just over 11 per cent. Extrapolated to the population, we can presume that at least 1.6 million people are living with clinically diagnosed cardiac diseases. At the same time, the number of HIV infected people in Kerala is put at anywhere between 50,000 to 70,000 only. The enormity of the problem of coronary heart disease in Kerala will be evident when we compare the death rates from CHD in Kerala with those of USA and UK (Figure 17.3).

Figure 17.2

*Principal Causes of Death in Kerala**

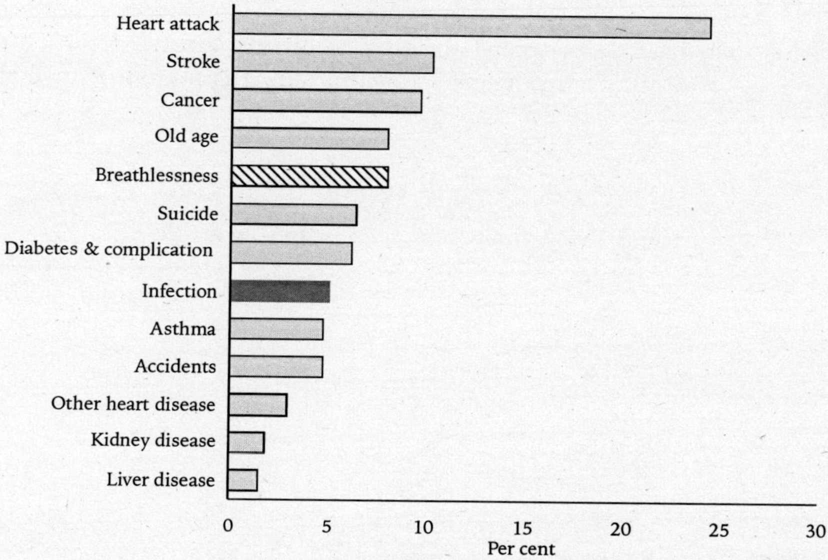

Note: *Population Registry of Lifestyle Diseases—ongoing study, Health Action by People.

Figure 17.3

Age-specific Death Rate from Heart Attacks: Varkala, Kerala, USA and UK

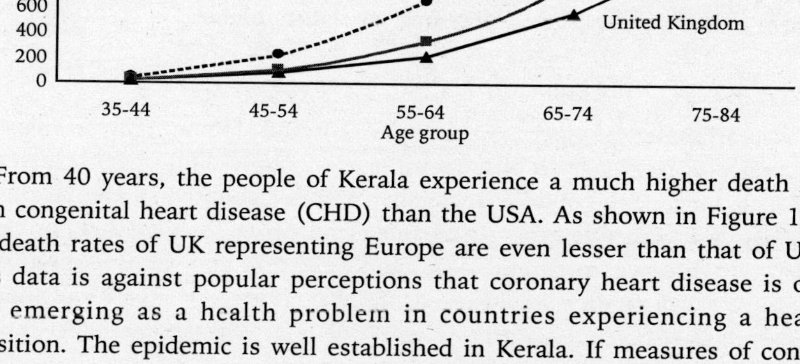

From 40 years, the people of Kerala experience a much higher death rate from congenital heart disease (CHD) than the USA. As shown in Figure 17.3, the death rates of UK representing Europe are even lesser than that of USA. This data is against popular perceptions that coronary heart disease is only just emerging as a health problem in countries experiencing a health transition. The epidemic is well established in Kerala. If measures of control are not imitated on a war-footing, we are in for catastrophic consequences, both in health and in our economy.

The problem in respect of the dominant disease contributing to death in Kerala is that these deaths occur much ahead of time for the victims. The median age of death from principal causes in Kerala is presented in Table 17.1.

Table 17.1

Age of Death from Principal Diseases in Kerala

Causes	*Mean*		*Median*	
	M	*F*	*M*	*F*
All	62.2	69.5	65.0	74.0
Heart attack	59.6	67.3	61.5	67.5
Cancer	56.7	59.5	61.5	63.5
Suicide	43.4	34.8	39.5	32.5
Accidents	39.7	58.0	34.5	70.0
Breathlessness	70.6	81.3	72.5	85.0
Diabetes	63.4	64.5	65.0	66.5
Stroke	69.8	65.7	71.5	70.0
Blood pressure	63.1	73.9	63.0	78.0

Source: Death Registry, Prolife—Health Action by People.

It may be noted that the median age of deaths from heart attack is much lower than the life expectancy of the people of Kerala. Both in men and women, the median age is lower than the respective life expectancy by over 10 years. The difference is still more in the case of diseases like cancer. The most dramatic difference is seen in accidents and suicides which take a very heavy toll of the young. The median age of deaths by suicides in women is only 32.5 as against 39.5 in men. The picture is similar in the case of accidents also, though the median age is slightly higher.

Prevalence of Non-communicable Diseases in Kerala

Populations that experience both health and demographic transitions experience an increase in the prevalence of non-communicable diseases (NCD). In view of the rapid changes that were experienced by the population of Kerala in the last two generations, one could expect an increased prevalence of lifestyle diseases attributable to modernisation and urbanisation. Only community level studies would reveal the magnitude and severity of lifestyle diseases in the population. Hitherto, we have only fragmentary statistics from hospitals in relation to these diseases. The dominant NCDs are diabetes mellitus, hypertension, coronary heart disease, stroke and various cancers. Overweight and obesity, not considered as major diseases, create favourable conditions for the onset of the other NCDs. Ongoing field studies in Kerala undertaken by Health Action by People reveal that the burden of illness from NCDs in our state is much higher than was feared. We discuss below the situation pertaining to some of the principal NCDs.

Diabetes Mellitus

Our investigations on the prevalence of diabetes were carried out in the population of Neyyattinkara *taluk* in the year 2000. Much to our surprise, the prevalence was higher than what was presumed on the basis of National Statistics. The age adjusted prevalence varied from 3.2 per cent in coastal fishermen to 21.4 per cent among urban males (Table 17.2).

Table 17.2

*Prevalence of Diabetes Mellitus in Neyyattinkara Taluk**

Region	*Sex*	*Diabetes*	*Overweight (BMI 25-29.99)*	*Obese (BMI >29)*
High land	Male	6.00	09.1	2.3
	Female	7.60	16.6	3.8
Midland	Male	12.1	15.2	0.4
	Female	8.30	22.5	6.6
Coastal	Male	3.20	20.6	2.0
	Female	4.10	25.3	9.2
Urban	Male	21.4	32.7	6.5
	Female	12.5	38.5	19.7

Note: * Study of prevalence of Type 2 diabetes in Neyyattinkara *Taluk*—Health Action by People 2003.

Much larger proportion of people had overweight/obesity, a favourable milieu for diabetes and other non-communicable diseases. Since the year 2003, we are carrying out more thorough investigations on the prevalence of diabetes mellitus, both in urban Trivandrum and rural Varkala. The figures are much more disturbing than what emerged from the Neyyattinkara study (Figure 17.4).

Figure 17.4

*Age-related Prevalence of Diabetes Mellitus in Kerala, 2004-2006**

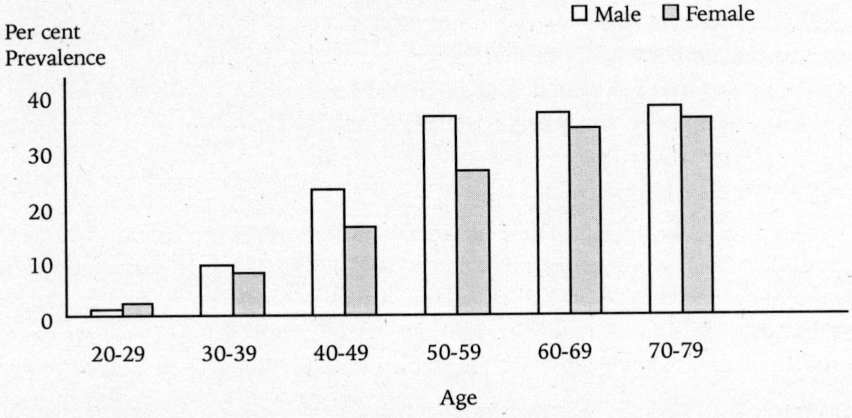

Note: *Prospective Rural–Urban Epidemiology study(PURE)-ongoing, Health Action by People.

The age standardised (>20 years) prevalence of diabetes was 14.9 per cent in males and 13.2 per cent in women. If these estimates were to be projected for the whole Kerala population, we have about 16 million males and 14 million women currently diabetic. Expressed in another way, nearly 9 per cent of the people of Kerala suffer from diabetes mellitus. The gravity of the situation is appreciated only when we realised that a diabetic individual is three times prone to suffer a heart attack or stroke. Diabetes also invites high blood pressure, retinal disease, kidney failure and neurological complications. Foot amputations consequent on diabetes complications is very rampant in Kerala. The prevalence of diabetes increases in relation to age and reaches levels of 37 per cent in males and 32 per cent in women aged 50 or above.

Hypertension

We estimated the prevalence of hypertension in our study of population. The prevalence is higher than that of diabetes in every age group in both sexes. A peak prevalence of 60 per cent or more is observed in those aged 60 years or more. For every age group, the prevalence of hypertension was higher among women. Nearly 60 per cent of the hypertension is newly discovered during the surveys. Hypertension is an important risk factor for heart disease and stroke. The high prevalence of hypertension and the need for life time medication make the burden of hypertension in our society, a major health challenge. The overall prevalence of risk factors for coronary heart disease is presented in Table 17.3.

Table 17.3

*Prevalence of Risk Factors in Rural and Urban Kerala**

Risk Factor/Disease	*Rural*		*Urban*	
	Men	*Women*	*Men*	*Women*
BMI ≥ 25	33.6	48.3	32.1	42.9
BMI ≥ 23	55.0	58.8	52.7	63.3
S. Cholesterol ≥ 200	68.9	73.8	68	73.7
S. Cholesterol ≥ 240	31.9	38.2	31	36.7
Blood pressure ≥ 140/90	44.4	42.4	37.7	36.7
Triglyceride ≥ 150	21.6	11.7	37.1	21.6

Note: *Prospective Rural–Urban Epidemiology study (PURE)-ongoing, Health Action by People.

Overweight and Obesity

As mentioned earlier, the prevalence of overweight and obesity in Kerala is alarmingly high. The irony is that the high prevalence co-exist with an energy intake still below the recommended dietary allowances. The paradox is understood in the context of massive unemployment and/or under employment in Kerala. The energy balance is shifted to a lower tire of low intake and still lower expenditure. The prevalence of overweight and obesity borders on 50 per cent among women and 40 per cent among men (Table 17.3). A peculiar feature of the problem of obesity in Kerala is the dominant deposition of fat in and around the abdomen. Abdominal obesity, marked by an increase in waist circumference poses considerably higher risk of diabetes and coronary disease. A body mass index (BMI) of 25 or above is considered the cut-off point for defining overweight. However, our studies suggests that when the BMI exceeds 23, the people of Kerala invite a three-fold risk of developing diabetes and hypertension.

Elevated Serum Cholesterol

Cholesterol is a vital lipid molecule, synthesised by every living mammalian tissue. However, if the cholesterol synthesis is in excess, its level increases in the plasma and poses a major risk of heart attack. Nearly 40 per cent of total risk of heart attacks is contributed by elevated serum cholesterol. The upper limit of desirable cholesterol is 200 mg/dl of plasma. For any subject with another risk factor for coronary disease, the desirable level is at a much lower value. Table 17.3 provides information on the proportion of people in Kerala with high and undesirably high serum cholesterol. Nearly 70 per cent of the people of Kerala have elevated serum cholesterol. The average level of cholesterol levels in Kerala is 13 mg higher than in USA and

50 mg higher than in other Indian states. The physicians' answer to elevated serum cholesterol is prescribing expensive cholesterol lowering statins. However, diet has an important bearing on the serum cholesterol. Populations consuming high amounts of saturated fats have elevated serum cholesterol. Irrespective of the source, fat people of Kerala consume disproportionately a large amount of saturated fats, mainly derived from fresh coconut. Among the free living population of the nations of the world, saturated fat consumption is highest in Kerala. Nearly 78 per cent of the fat/energy in the Kerala diet is derived from saturated fatty acids chiefly of the coconut origin. Our diet is much low in monounsaturated fat and precariously so in polyunsaturated fatty acids (Figure 17.5).

Figure 17.5

Relative Contribution of Fatty Acids in the Kerala Diet

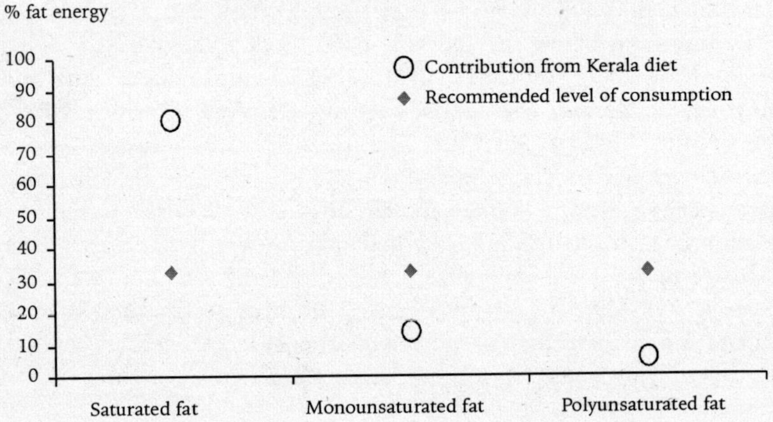

Source: Based on 2635 diet surveys.

Cancer

Cancer is yet another non-communicable disease showing a steady increase over the years. Every year, between 30,000–35,000 people develop cancer in Kerala. Nearly 10 per cent of the deaths are from cancers, while diabetes mellitus despite its high prevalence contributes to much less annual mortality. A great concern to Kerala is the rather alarming increase in the incidence of breast cancer in women. On an average, women of Kerala develop breast cancer 11 years earlier than the women of United States. Obesity, late marriage, early cessation of fertility and decrease in consumption of fruits and vegetables are implicated as risk factors.

Summary

The burden of non-communicable disease in Kerala threaten development in more than one way. When struck by these diseases, the quality of life suffers and the attendant's loss of productivity affects economic development. These lifelong diseases impose a heavy economic burden for primary treatment. Complications, when they occur inflict still higher expenditure. Premature mortality results in heavy economic losses to the family and to the nation. Preventive strategies with emphasis on exercise from childhood, eating grains, more of green leafy vegetables and fruits and avoiding tobacco and alcohol are among the principal successful interventions in the West. It is time that we wake up to the unpleasant realities and meet the challenges head-on.

18

Community-based Palliative Care Initiative

SAJAN THOMAS, AJU MATHEW and PRABHU DASS G.

An increasing ageing population and a greater than before incidence of chronic and lifestyle diseases has brought to fore the need of high quality end-of-life care across the developing world (Singer and Bowman, 2002; Rajagopal *et al.*, 2003, Casarett *et al.*, 2006). However, given the heterogeneous nature of the resource-poor societies in developing countries, institutionalisation of palliative care services has continued to be a challenging task. Besides region-specific issues, the adaptation and acceptability of such care in local cultures has also been identified as an important prerequisite (Pampallona and Bollini, 2004). In this context, the success of the palliative care experiment in northern Kerala demands both academic and policy-related inquiries. This chapter analyses the community-based palliative care initiative in the backdrop of a crisis of Kerala model of health, which is a vital component of the much acclaimed Kerala development experience.[1]

This chapter is organised into four sections. The first section deals with different dimensions of the health care crisis in Kerala, particularly in the

1. Ever since the publication of UN study *Poverty, Unemployment and Development Policy* (1975) by K.N. Raj and his colleagues at Centre for Development Studies, Thiruvananthapuram, Kerala's high achievements on the statistical indicators of development despite continuing low incomes (Franke, 1995) received much international attention. The paradoxical relationship between social and economic development in this south Indian state, often characterised as a model for developing societies, has been in the forefront of post-1970 development discourses. Discussions on Kerala's pathway of development are broadly clustered around four questions: Does a Kerala development model really exist? What are the factors that contributed to the evolution of this development experience? How much inclusionary is this development framework? Whether it can be sustained over generations or be replicated elsewhere? The questions on evolution is centred around endogenous explanations such as public action (Dreze and Sen, 1989), class mobilisation (Heller, 1999; Reynolds and Harilal, 2006) and radical reforms (Franke and Chasin, 1989), and the exogenous interpretations emphasise on the foreign links over centuries (Kawashima, 1998, Raman Kutty, 2000, Kannan, 2005; Harilal and Joseph, 2000). Meanwhile, the queries on sustainability and replicability focuses on concerns such as fiscal crisis (George, 1993), environmental sustainability (Chattopadhyay and Franke, 2006) and demographic transition (Zachariah and Rajan, 1997). However, there were also discussions with regard to the rationale of conceptualising development on the basis of certain quantifiable variables and the exclusionary tendencies inherent in Kerala's development experience. The latter debates are going on in relation to the multifaceted marginalisation of outliers i.e., *Dalits*, tribals, fisher folks and certain other socio-economic groups (Kurien, 1995; Kunjaman, 2002).

context of ageing and high morbidity scenario. The second section presents some relevant findings from *Morbidity, Health Care and the Condition of the Aged (2006)*, which is based on the 60th round of National Sample Survey (NSS) by the National Sample Survey Organisation (NSSO). The third section examines the community-based palliative care experiment by using the latest data of the palliative care clinics in northern Kerala (2005). This section also explores the emerging dimensions of community participation in the background of decentralisation, people's planning and the surfacing dynamism of neighbourhood networks in Kerala. The fourth section is the concluding observation on this palliative care experiment and its emerging potential as a facilitating institutional base for overcoming the health care crisis in the state.

Crisis of Kerala Model of Health

Various aspects of the health care outcome in Kerala have been subjected to detailed examinations in connection with the Kerala model discourses. Kerala's high health status in terms of standard health indicators like crude death rate, infant mortality rate and life expectancy with comparatively low governmental spending in health care services has prompted many analysts to talk about a unique Kerala Model of Health, worth emulating by other developing parts of the world (Ekbal, 2000). The sustained performance of Kerala in the health care sector—despite its disadvantageous geographical position in the tropics, high density of population and low per capita income—have been given different explanations. Prominent interpretations emphasise on factors like the unique socio-political environment in the state, a far above the ground health awareness due to high literacy level, an extensive and efficient public health care system, leading role by non-state actors like Christian missionaries, and higher accessibility to health care due to better infrastructure at the local level.[2] Instead of reducing the prevalent physical well-being to the health care sector, these explanations gave prominence to inter-sectoral factors such as the spread of education, political awareness, development of road networks and transportation and social movements with distributional biases.

However, there are concerns over the changing demographic pattern and high morbidity levels, the two constraining factors inherent in Kerala model

---

2. Heller mentioned about the highly educated, organised and activist populace which make strong demands on the government. Also, the poor populace considers health services as a right and there are instances of conflicts over the proper functioning of health care centres (MacDonald, 2005).

of health.[3] A structural shift in the age composition of population[4] is leading to an increased share of old age dependent population (*Kerala Human Development Report*, 2006). According to a projection of age composition of the population (1986-2026 A.D), Kerala's elderly populace is expected to increase from 2.2 million in 1986 to 4.6 million in 2011 and 8.3 million in 2026 (Rajan, 1989). This manifold increase in the elderly population, almost four times in the course of 40 years, needs to be analysed simultaneously with high morbidity levels in the state. The sustenance of high morbidity levels along with the highly acclaimed low mortality figures, the low mortality high morbidity syndrome (Panicker and Soman, 1984) has been the characteristic of Kerala for a long time. Nevertheless, Kerala's morbidity scenario worsened with the high incidence of chronic lifestyle and communicable diseases of recent times.[5] Contemporarily, Kerala is among the areas with the highest prevalence of chronic diseases in the country.

The ageing and morbidity figures is a cause of apprehension as the Kerala model of health care i.e., good health at low cost (Panicker, 1992), based on social justice and equity is in danger of being dismantled (Ekbal, 2005). The main reasons attributed to this crisis are catastrophic health care expenditure (George, 2006), switchover from process to a product patent regime (Ekbal, 2005) and a decline of public spending in health care due to the fiscal crisis (Vohra, 1999). This is regardless of the fact that Kerala is better positioned in connection with the efficient use of available resources[6] in the public health care sector. The state also gives a positive picture regarding the equality of access to health care notwithstanding class, caste, gender and regional considerations (Varatharajan, 2004). But the expansion of private sector, especially in rural areas, to fill the vacuum created by the government has a definite bearing on the cost of health care. The 52nd round of National Sample Survey ranks Kerala with the highest private health expenditure in

3. These concerns are outlined in the concept paper (draft version) on Kerala secondary health system project by the Department of Health & Family Welfare, Government of Kerala. This paper prioritised the areas to be focused between 2003 and 2008. It is accessible from *http://www.kerala.gov.in/dept_health/paper.pdf*

4. For a detailed discussion on the determinants and consequences of Kerala's demographic transition, see Zachariah and Rajan (1997).

5. The spread of AIDS and the sanctions imposed by the society on HIV carriers, despite high health awareness, add to this complexity. Moreover, Kerala has the highest suicide rate among Indian states, nearly three times the national average. In addition to the increase in lifestyle diseases such as obesity and diabetes, the state is also under the threat of communicable diseases and psychiatric disorders. Kerala is considered to be one of the largest markets for psychiatric drugs in south India. The recent spurt of insect-borne Chikungunya in the coastal districts expose the evolving environment-related health risks, which has already became a major concern for this densely populated state.

6. Although underutilisation of public health care system is a serious concern in India, Kerala has a notable track record when compared to other states.

India in terms of medical care (Arun and Varatharajan, 2005). The burgeoning health care expenditure in Kerala is detrimentally affecting the poor people's access to health care as the escalating costs of private services and reduced public investments could generate inequalities in access for the poor. A recent study on out-patient care utilisation in urban Kerala points to these inequalities in access despite the expansion of private health care (Levesque *et al.*, 2006). In the erstwhile period, the presence of an efficient and equitable public health system in Kerala served as a competitive threat to private facilities in determining the price of treatment (Krishnan, 1999).

The settling in of high morbidity levels and ageing figures has all-around implications for the policy makers. In the context of ageing, a considerable part of the resources which were earlier earmarked for other age groups would have to be diverted to take care of the elderly people's housing, food and health needs (Zachariah and Rajan, 1997).[7] Moreover, the policy framers have to identify the most vulnerable groups within the elderly population of Kerala. A survey on health and functional status of the elderly in Thiruvananthapuram city shows that the quality of life of the elderly is depended on gender and socio-economic class considerations (Kumar *et al.*, 1994). The plight of female elderly, especially the case of divorced and widowed, demand intervention considering their increasing economic dependence on others for livelihood.[8] Similar stories of deprivation were also reported among the elderly in backward socio-economic groups and rural areas. This points to the need for giving special consideration for the vulnerable groups within the state's elderly population. The implications of ageing on policy are mentioned in the draft approach paper for Kerala's Eleventh Five Year Plan (2007 to 2012):

> It is also disturbing for an additional specific reason, namely that the very success of Kerala in providing literacy and healthcare has not only brought down the birth rate and the infant mortality rate, but has also increased longevity. Consequently, the age composition of the population is changing significantly in favour of the older age groups. This fact is going to place an additional demand upon the health-care system of the state (even as the increased demand for pension payments further restricts the possibilities of raising plan outlays)

The Kerala government has already come with a policy for the elderly (December 19, 2006) that entrusts sons and daughters an equal responsibility to take care of their aged parents. It also stands for giving special privilege for elderly in buses and hospitals (*Kaumadi Online,* December 20, 2006).

---

7. The implication of an ageing population on the state sponsored pension system is analysed in Prasad (2005). The author situates the structural and fiscal crisis inherent in Kerala's pension system in the wake of an ageing population and poor fiscal management. The study finds that the fiscal burden of the pension system is in an unsustainable reach and suggests a restructuring to avoid the overriding fiscal stress of the pension system in Kerala.
8. The longevity of females in Kerala is more than the male population.

It is pertinent to note that the above mentioned concern has special importance as the prevalence of morbidity, hospitalisation, disabilities and other chronic conditions is comparatively high among the elderly in Kerala, particularly those in rural areas (Dilip, 2002). High incidence of degenerative diseases like cancer along with major reportable illnesses such as acute respiratory infection, asthma and tuberculosis among other age groups has also emerged as a major policy issue. This artificial difference in the morbidity and hospitalisation among different sub-groups of the population in Kerala (Dilip, 2002) has also become an inescapable challenge. This crisis of the Kerala model of health can be summarised as the decay of public health system, the uncontrolled/least regulated growth of private sector, escalation of health costs as well as marginalisation of the poor (Mishra, 2004). The very fact that this crisis is making a way into an ageing society with high morbidity figures is a cause of serious concern. As pointed out in several empirical studies, the 60th round of National Sample Survey (NSS) presents the severity of the Kerala case in comparison to other Indian states.

Findings of NSSO 60th Round

This section discusses the health care crisis in Kerala on the basis of 60th round of National Sample Survey (NSS) carried out from January to June 2004 by the National Sample Survey Organisation (NSSO).[9] The survey was spread over 4,755 villages and 2,668 urban blocks covering 73,868 households across the country. The report titled *Morbidity, Health Care and the Condition of the Aged* covers the curative aspects of the general health care system in India, utilisation of health care services provided by the public and private sector, and the expenditure incurred by the households for availing these services. In addition, information on the condition and problems of aged persons was also collected.[10] The following tables were based on the health care and ageing situation in Kerala.

Table 18.1 gives details regarding the number of people reporting ailment per thousand population (PAP), number of people reporting commencement of any ailment (PPC) and medical/non-medical expenditure in the state of Kerala. The NSSO data points to large discrepancies between Kerala and rest of the country with regard to the variables mentioned above. The morbidity level (PAP) in the rural parts of Kerala is 255 while the figure for the backward state of Jharkhand is only 33. Moreover, the PPC figures in Kerala are also high at 103 when compared to Jharkhand, Uttarakhand and Bihar.

9. National Sample Survey Organisation (NSSO) is under the Ministry of Statistics and Programme Implementation, Government of India.

10. Highlights of the report are accessible from *http://www.mospi.nic.in*

While higher health awareness in Kerala is responsible for more reporting of the ailments, the NSSO data points to the continuance of high morbidity levels in the state. One reason for this overall increase in morbidity level is the higher proportion of aged people (60 years and above) in Kerala as compared to other states.

Table 18.1

Morbidity and Medical Expenditure in Kerala

	Ailment (no.)		*Hospitalised (no.)*			*Expenditure (Rs.)*			
Rural	PAP	255	Rural	Govt.	356	Rural	Medical	Govt.	3
	PPC	103		Pvt.	644			Pvt.	179
Urban	PAP	240	Urban	Govt.	346	Urban	Medical	Govt.	5
	PPC	100		Pvt.	654			Pvt.	189

The table also throws light on the increasing dependence on private sector for health care and the expenses involved in medical treatments. Only 356 and 346 of the 1000 hospitalised cases are utilising the public health care facilities in rural and urban areas, respectively. It is relatable to note that these figures for Jammu and Kashmir are 913 and 865 respectively. This is pointing to the expansion of private health care in the state, both in urban and rural areas. The first implication of this development would be the escalation of medical expenses. The average medical expenditure of treatment per person during a period of 15 days for the rural and urban areas in Kerala is given in the table. The huge disparities on the public and private sector spending in rural and urban areas i.e., 3 and 179 in rural and 5 and 189 in urban, have a definite bearing on the Kerala model of good health at low cost.

Table 18.2

Ageing Situation in Kerala

Proportion of Aged in the Total Population Hospitalised (%)		*Population per Bed Hospitalised*	*Number of Aged per 1000 persons for Each Sex*				*Old Age Dependency Ratio*	
			Rural		*Urban*			
Rural	*Urban*		*Male*	*Female*	*Male*	*Female*	*Rural*	*Urban*
23	31	325	106	123	103	109	155	139

The second table is on Kerala's ageing population and their health related issues. According to 2001 census, Kerala's elderly population is 3.36 million, which is 10.5 per cent of the state population. The table shows a high old age dependency ratio in Kerala, which indicate a high dependence of aged to working age population. The estimated proportion of aged in the total hospitalised population is 23 per cent in rural areas and 31 per cent in urban areas. Only few states like Assam, Gujarat, Himachal Pradesh and Uttarakhand have relatively high proportion of aged persons who are in hospitals. In the case of persons hospitalised during a reference period of 365 days, Kerala has a relatively high figure of 325 per 1000 population. Given the context of high morbidity levels, more reported ailment cases, increasing percentage of aged people and disproportionate spending in the government sector, the findings of NSSO's 60th round is of immense importance at the policy level.

Community-based Palliative Care in Northern Kerala

The above mentioned crisis and concern on the future of Kerala model of health is almost instantaneous with wider discussions on the sustainability and replicability of Kerala's development experience. There is a general consensus among scholars that the fiscal crisis (George, 1993) unfolded out of the stagnation in productive sectors (Subramanian and Azeez, 2000, Kannan and Pushpangadan, 1988; 1990; Teearamangalam, 1998), and burgeoning social expenditure has severely constrained the capacity of state governments to respond to the redistributive social demands. This crisis has been interpreted as failure of the old Kerala model, which was characterised with socially sustained redistributive policies of the native and democratic state.[11] The continuance of low levels of income and productive capacity, which can also be seen to be inherent in the very pattern of Kerala's social, political and cultural development (Tharamangalam, 1998), has put Kerala's erstwhile way to development at a crossroads (Kannan, 2000). The subsequent shift in the developmental trajectory has been explained in various ways. One prominent explanation points a transition to new Kerala model that seeks reconciliation of social, productive and environmental objectives at the local level, and tries to develop synergies between civil society, local governmental bodies and the state government (Veron, 2001).

The ideological moorings of a new Kerala development model and the potential role of international development agencies in sustenance of the same has triggered political controversies and academic discussions at various

11. The benevolent policies of the native kingdoms, especially Travancore, have significantly contributed to the social development in the state. For instance, Amartya Sen (1990) has cited the instructions issued by Rani Gouri Parvathi Bai (the queen of Travancore), as early as 1817, in favour of government support for education.

levels. Most of these second generation debates on Kerala development experience focus on people's participation at the local level and the facilitational role of institutional transformations such as decentralisation and people's planning. Although Veron's (2001) depiction of this developmental transition—i.e., from the state-led development process to a community driven one—offers only a partial explanation, his characterisation provides a starting point for analysing many community-driven initiatives at the grassroots level. Given the background of a transition in the practice and conceptualisation of Kerala's development, this chapter discusses the community-based palliative care movement in the northern districts of Kerala as a response to the health care crisis in the state.

The community-based palliative care network in northern kerala is one of the largest of its kind in the developing world. It is estimated that 60 palliative care units in northern Kerala have a coverage of 70 per cent of the regional population, where the national average is mere one per cent. The worth mentioning part is that more than 80 per cent of the resources for this experiment is raised locally through small donations, often less than 10 rupees (20 cents). Approximately 5000-6000 patient contacts are happening in each week, and since 1993, more than 25,000 patients had undergone treatment. More than 8,000 patients with incurable diseases are currently under its care, which makes this one of the major networks of palliative care (Kumar, 2006). Given its wide acceptance in society and the social demand from other regions, the state government has made a special mention on palliative care services in its 2005 budget.

Several studies have discussed the different dimensions of the community participation in the northern Kerala experiment (Sallnow and Chenganakkattil, 2005; Paleri and Numpeli, 2005; Bollini *et al.*, 2004; Rajagopal and Palat, 2002). The palliative care movement in northern Kerala is an inimitable one because of its functioning through a neighbourhood network—Neighbourhood Networks in Palliative Care (NNPC). These neighbourhood groups are functioning in close cooperation with the decentralised state bodies, religious, social and political groups in the region. Unlike majority of its counterparts across the developing world, out-patient treatment with a supportive home care service was adopted as the main mode of operation of the clinics. Trained volunteers from the community assist in providing care and family members were empowered in order to ensure continuity of treatment (Bollini *et al.*, 2004). Besides empowering the local communities to identify the chronically/terminally ill (also paralysed and bedridden), the NNPC are also provide the patients with medical and non-medical rehabilitation services (Stjernsward, 2005). These services by the clinics, regardless of the disease or cause, are met with limited resources raised from the locality and without any outside economic support. There are occasions where the informed volunteers of palliative care clinics decide the health care priorities of the *panchayats* in *gramasabha* meetings. Accordingly, this community-based movement can strengthen not only government's capacity to deliver quality end-of-life care but also ensure a better utilisation of existing health care infrastructure of the state.

The northern Kerala experiment in community-based palliative care is of great importance in the backdrop of a transition in the practice and conceptualisation of Kerala development experience. The main components of the new Kerala model—participatory planning, decentralised decision-making, locally monitored implementation and fiscal devolution—are essential parts of this community-based initiative. The following analysis is based on the fieldwork data collected on the functioning of palliative care clinics in 2005.

Table 18.3

Patient Details

Type of Disease	*No. of Patients*
Cancer	4018
Backbone	459
Others	1521
Total	5998

Figure 18.1

Figure Showing the Patient Details

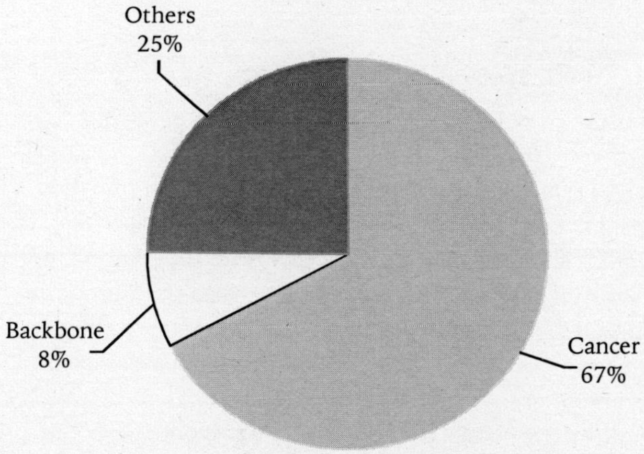

The relatively high correlation coefficient (.63) indicates a significant relationship between the total cost incurred and number of patients had undergone treatment. The total number of patients is 5998 and cost incurred is Rs.1,21,64,007. Figure 18.1 shows details of the patients at various palliative care units in the northern districts of Kerala. Although cancer patients constitute the majority, the chart also gives an idea about those with backbone-related and other diseases. While the cancer case is 67 per cent, patients with backbone and other diseases are 8 per cent and 25 per cent, respectively. There is a high volunteer to patient ratio of 1:2.56, which means 2339 volunteers for 5998 patients. From the above explanation, it is apparent that the palliative care units are capable enough to provide health care (not just palliative care) to a considerable number of patients. Before analysing the medical and non-medical services provided by the palliative care clinics, it is of great importance to have a discussion on the infrastructural base of palliative care units.

Figure 18.2

Infrastructure Facilities

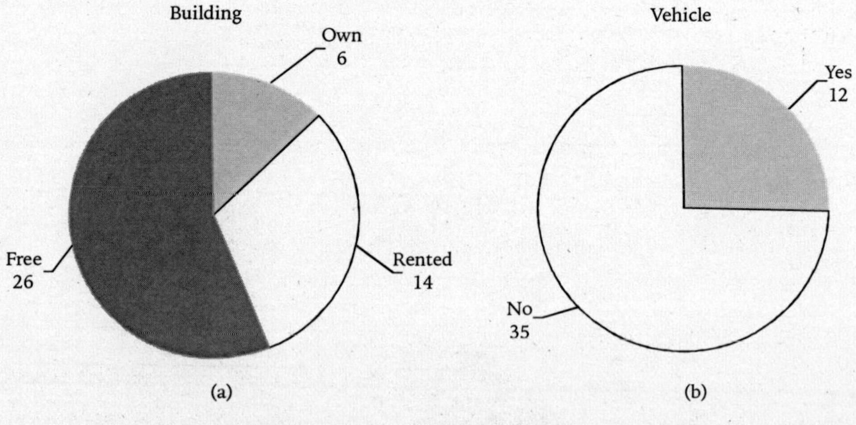

Figure 18.2(a) on infrastructural facilities shows that lion's share of the clinics have their own building either owned, rented or free. There are cases where the clinics function in buildings given by the elected representatives or in association with local self-government bodies and public health care centres. While 12 clinics have vehicles of their own (Figure 18.2(b)), the remaining depends on hired vehicles for bringing patients to clinics and for related needs. Moreover, clinics like Nilambur give travel expenses for patients to go to the medical college at Kozhikode.

Figure 18.3 throws light on the rehabilitation support provided by the 48 palliative care units in Kerala. The black bars indicate the medical services provided by the clinics and the grey bars show the non-medical facilities ensured in the year 2005. Few clinics provide all the above mentioned medical and non-medical services. Regarding medical facilities, 37 units provide wheelchair, 41 have water beds and 46 give painkillers to their patients. In the case of non-medical services, 16 units are endowed with employment opportunities, 24 provide educational facilities and 41 supply food. It is evident that while almost all of the clinics provide medical facilities, some of them also offer the non-medical services. The field work data on the palliative care clinics (2005) in regard to patient details, infrastructural facilities and rehabilitation services gives a brief picture of the northern Kerala experience. The increase in number of patients, considerable infrastructure facilities and rehabilitation services provided by the clinics along with the community participation makes this health care experiment a significant one for the ageing and highly morbid society in Kerala.

Figure 18.3

Rehabilitation Services

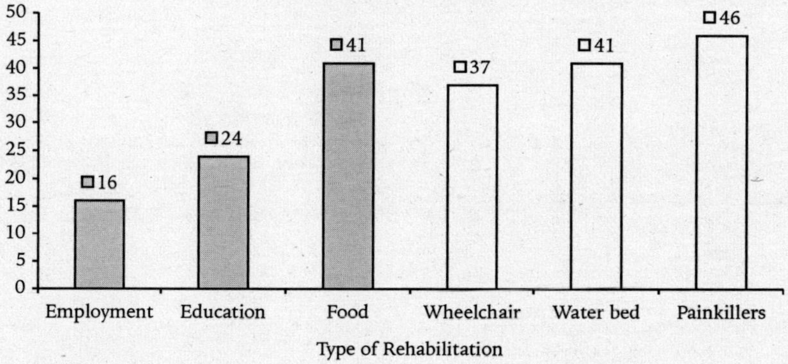

Conclusion

Experiences across the world shows that meaningful palliative care require a combination of socio-economic, cultural and medical solutions; the northern Kerala experiment has proved that community can take the responsibility of its chronically and terminally ill. It also demonstrates the ascendancy of a community-based initiative over the hospice approach or the institutionalised medical approach to palliative care. Given the concurrence of demographic and health transitions,[12] decline of publicly financed systems of health care and escalation of medical expenditure, this response from northern Kerala is a well-timed one.

This community-based experiment has special relevance in the context of the crisis to the Kerala model of health. Firstly, it showed that comprehensive and integrated palliative care programmes can be implemented at no additional cost to the existing health care system. The emerging partnerships with the local government institutions and its positive outcome with regard to the utilisation of funds and existing health care infrastructure; incorporation of more diseases/patients and the transition of NNPC to Neighbourhood Networks in Health Care (NNHC); the physical and financial self-sufficiency of palliative care units in the state; the promising role of religious and social actors, especially their role as volunteers; and the rehabilitation support provided to the patient and family points to the importance of this community-driven experiment. Given its sizeable infrastructure and firm enmeshment in local settings, the palliative care movement has immense potential as a facilitating institutional base for improving the health care system in the state. Its continuing success urges the need for framing policies for utilising human, physical and financial resources of this community-based movement for addressing the health care crisis in Kerala.

References

Arun, B. and D. Varatharajan (2005). "Appraising Government Healthcare Expenditure in Kerala using NHA Framework", Paper presented at Forum 9, Mumbai, India on 12-16 September.

Bollini, P., C. Venkateswaran and K. Sureshkumar (2004). "Palliative Care in Kerala, India: A Model for Resource-Poor Settings", *Onkologie* 27(2): 138-142.

Casarett, David J., Teno, Joan and Irene Higginson (2006). "How Should Nations Measure the Quality of End-of-Life Care for Older Adults? Recommendations for an International Minimum Data Set", *Journal of the American Geriatrics Society* 54(11): 1765–1771.

Chasin, Barbara H. and Richard W. Franke (1989). *Kerala: Radical Reform as Development in an Indian State.* San Francisco: Institute for Food and Development Policy.

Chattopadhyay, Srikumar and Richard W. Franke (2006). *Striving for Sustainability: Environmental Stress and Democratic Initiatives in Kerala.* New Delhi: Concept Publishing.

Chen, Lincoln C. (2001). *In Pursuit of Health Equity: The Kerala-Global Connections*, TN Krishnan memorial lecture at the Achutha Menon Centre for Health Sciences, Thiruvananthapuram, Kerala, India on January 28.

Department of Economic and Social Affairs (1975). *Poverty, Unemployment and Development Policy: A Case Study of Selected Issues with Reference to Kerala.* New York: United Nations.

12. According to Lincoln Chen (2001), the transition in health "is producing three epidemiological clusters simultaneously—a first generation of poverty-linked infectious diseases, a second generation of lifestyle-related chronic diseases, and the emergence of a "third wave" of fresh environmental, infectious and behavioral pathologies".

Dilip, T.R. (2002). "Understanding Levels of Morbidity and Hospitalization in Kerala, India", *Bulletin of World Health Organization* 80(9): 746-751.

Dreze, Jean and Amartya Sen (1989). *Hunger and Public Action*. Oxford: Clarendon Press.

Ekbal, B. (2000). "People's Campaign for Decentralized Planning and the Health Sector in Kerala", *Issue paper*, People's Health Assembly. Accessible from *http://phmovement.org/pdf/pubs/phm-pubs-ekbal.pdf*

———. (2005). "Kerala Model of Healthcare in Peril", *The Hindu*, Thiruvananthapuram edition, April 24.

Franke, Richard W. (1995). "Is there a Kerala Model?", Paper presented at World Malayalee Convention on July 1-3, 1995 at New Jersey, USA.

George, Asish Thomas (2006). *Catastrophic Health Care Expenditure and Impoverishment in Kerala: An Analysis Based on NSSO 55th Round, 1999-2000*, Thesis of M.phil 2003-2005. Centre for Development Studies, Thiruvananthapuram.

George, K.K. (1993). *Limits to Kerala Model of Development: An Analysis of Fiscal Crisis and its Implications*. Centre for Development Studies, Thiruvananthapuram.

Harilal, K.N. and K.J. Joseph (2000). "Stagnation and Revival of Kerala Economy: An Open Economy Perspective", *Working Paper* No. 305. Centre for Development Studies, Thiruvananthapuram.

Heller, Patrick (1999). *The Labor of Development: Workers and the Transformation of Capitalism in Kerala, India*. Ithaca: Cornell University Press.

Kannan, K.P. (2000). "People's Planning, Kerala's Dilemma", *Seminar* 485.

———. (2005). "Kerala's Turnaround in Growth: Role of Social Development, Remittances and Reform", *Economic and Political Weekly* 40(6): 548–554.

Kannan, K.P. and K. Pushpangadan (1988). "Agricultural Stagnation and Economic Growth in Kerala: An Exploratory Analysis", *Working Paper* No.227. Centre for Development Studies, Thiruvananthapuram.

———. (1990). "Dissecting Agricultural Stagnation in Kerala: An Analysis Across Crops, Seasons and Regions", *Economic and Political Weekly* 25(36): 1991–2004.

Kaumadi Online (2006). "Kerala Elderly to Get Benefits, December 20", 2006.

Kawashima, Koji (1998). *Missionaries and a Hindu State: Travancore 1858–1936*. New York: Oxford University Press.

Kerala Human Development Report (2006). State Planning Board, Government of Kerala, Thiruvananthapuram, pp.72-73.

Krishnan, T.N. (1999). "Access to Health and Burden of Treatment in India: An Inter-State Comparison", in Mohan Rao (ed) *Disinvesting in Health: The World Bank's Prescriptions for Health*. New Delhi: Sage. pp. 208-232.

Kunjaman, M. (2002). *Globalisation: A Subaltern Perspective*. Centre for Subaltern Studies, Thiruvananthapuram.

Kurien, John (1995). "The Kerala Model: Its Central Tendency and the Outlier", *Social Scientist* 23(1-3): 70-90.

Levesque, Jean-Frédéric., Slim, Haddad., Narayana, Delampady and Fournier, Pierre (2006). "Outpatient Care Utilization in Urban Kerala, India", *Health Policy and Planning* 21(4): 289-301.

MacDonald, Theodore L. (2005). *Third World Health: Hostage to First World Health*, Abingdon: Radcliffe.

Mishra, U.S. (2004). "Equity Implication of Health Sector Decentralization: The Case of Kerala State, India". Accessible from *http://www.yorku.ca/ishd/GrantWinners05/Mishra/Mishra.pdf*

National Sample Survey Organisation (2006). *Morbidity, Health Care and the Condition of the Aged*, National Sample Survey: Report No. 507, Ministry of Statistics and Programme Implementation, New Delhi.

Paleri, A. and M. Numpeli (2005). "The Evolution of Palliative Care Programmes in North Kerala", *Indian Journal of Palliative Care* 11(1): 15-18.

Pampallona, Sandro and Bollini, Paola (2004). "Palliative Care in Developing Countries: Why Research is Needed", *Journal of Pain & Palliative Care Pharmacotherapy* 17(¾): 171-182.

Panicker, P.G.K. (1992). "High Cost of Medical Care in Kerala Tentative Hypothesis", *Economic and Political Weekly* 27(23): 1179-1181.

Panicker, P.G.K. and C.R. Soman (1984). *Health Status of Kerala: The Paradox of Economic Backwardness and Health Development*, Centre for Development Studies, Thiruvananthapuram.

Prasad, Syam (2005). *A Crisis in Making: The Pension System in India with Special Reference to Kerala*, Thesis of M.phil 2003-2005, Centre for Development Studies, Thiruvananthapuram.

Rajagopal, M.R., Mazza, David and Lipman, Arthur G. (2003). *Pain and Palliative Care in the Developing World and Marginalized Populations: A Global Challenge*. Binghamton: Haworth Press Inc.

Rajagopal, M.R. and Gayatri Palat (2002). "Kerala, India—Status of Cancer Pain Relief and Palliative Care", *Journal of Pain and Symptom Management* 24(2): 191-193.

Rajan, S.I. (1989). "Aging in Kerala: One More Population Problem?", *Asia-Pacific Population Journal* 4(2): 19-48.

Raman Kutty, V. (2000). "Historical Analysis of the Development of Health Care Facilities in Kerala State, India", *Health Policy and Planning* 15(1): 103–109.

Reynolds, David and K.N. Harilal (2006). "Kerala: A Union Alternative to Corporate Globalization", *Working USA: The Journal of Labor and Society* 9(1): 29-39.

Sallnow, L. and S. Chenganakkattil (2005). "The Role of Religious, Social and Political Groups in Palliative Care in Northern Kerala", *Indian Journal of Palliative Care* 11(1): 10-14.

Sen, Amartya (1990). *Public Action to Remedy Hunger*, Arturo Tanco Memorial Lecture on August 2, 1990 at London. This lecture is accessible from *http://www.thp.org/reports/sen/sen890.htm#n1*

Singer, P.A. and K.W. Bowman (2002). "Quality Care at the End of Life: A Global Perspective", *BMC Palliative Care* 1(4): 1291-1292.

Stjernsward, Jan (2005). "Community Participation in Palliative Care", *Indian Journal of Palliative Care* 11(1): 22-27.

Subramanian, K.K. and Azeez, Abdul (2000). "Industrial Growth in Kerala:Trends and Explanations", *Working paper* No. 310, Centre for Development Studies, Thiruvananthapuram.

Suresh Kumar, K. (2006). "Neighborhood Networks in Palliative Care – A Social Experiment", Paper presented at UICC World Cancer Congress on July 8-12, 2006 at Washington DC, USA. Abstract of the paper is available at *http://2006.confex.com/uicc/uicc/techprogram/P3557.htm*

Tharamangalam, Joseph (1998). "The Perils of Social Development without Economic Growth: The Development Debacle of Kerala, India", *Bulletin of Concerned Asian Scholars* 30(1): 23-34.

Varatharajan, D. (2004). "Provision of Health Care by the Government", *Indian Journal of Medical Ethics* 2(4). Accessible from *http://www.ijme.in/124oa117.html*

Veron, R. (2001). "The "New" Kerala Model: Lessons for Sustainable Development", *World Development* 29(4): 601-617.

Vijaya Kumar, K., Y.S. Sivan, J.R. Reghu Ram Das, and V. Raman Kutty (1994). "Health of the Elderly in a Community in Transition: A Survey in Thiruvananthapuram City, Kerala, India", *Health Policy and Planning* 9(3): 331-336.

Vohra, U. (1999). "Family Planning Success Based on Equity: Human Development, Health and Governance in the Indian State of Kerala", *Health for the Millions* 25(2): 40-42.

Zachariah, K.C. and S. Irudaya Rajan (ed.) (1997). *Kerala's Demographic Transition: Determinants and Consequences*. New Delhi: Sage.

19

HIV in Kerala

K. AJITHKUMAR and RAKKEE THIMOTHY

Introduction

The deteriorating health status of people infected with Human Immunodeficiency Virus (HIV) challenges the world, even after 25 years of identification of the virus. As on 2006, there are 50.7 million people across the world infected with the virus (UNAIDS, 2006). The concerns regarding the lack of awareness and therapy to control the infection, during initial phase of the epidemic is at present replaced by unaffordability and inaccessibility of the antiretroviral drugs (ARVs) especially in the developing countries. Nevertheless, the public concern created by the association of individuals infected and affected with HIV and those concerned with the cause of the epidemic was something unmatched in the history of disease. To a large extent, this was instrumental in influencing the notions of the right to health and health care and redefined the role of the state and international community in some of these crucial issues.

The present chapter is an attempt to illustrate certain issues with respect to HIV prevention and control by analysing the experience from the state of Kerala. The chapter is divided into four sections. The second section presents a brief picture of the various dimensions of HIV infection and control activities in India. The third section situates the epidemic in Kerala, before attempting to do a critical evaluation of HIV programmes in the state in the fourth section.

HIV Infection in India

India, now has the largest number of HIV infected people in the world, with an estimated 5.7 million (UNAIDS, 2006). Though the total HIV infected forms only an insignificant percentage of total population, this poses a major risk, considering the large segment of sexually active age group of the country. The factors responsible for such rapid spread of the epidemic across the country includes labour migration in search of employment and low awareness about HIV among the potential high risk groups, to mention a few.

The initial response of government against the spread of HIV was that of denial and the first initiative for the HIV control was provided by the voluntary sector. Soon after, the HIV was identified among commercial sex workers in mid 1980s (Chatterjee and Sahgal, 2002). Later, the National AIDS Control Programme (NACP) was established in 1987 under the Ministry of Health and Family Welfare. In 1992, NACO, a semi-autonomous body was formed, with the primary objective of awareness creation and improving surveillance. Despite all its efforts, the awareness on HIV continues to be uneven among the general population varying from 12 per cent in Bihar to 93 per cent in Manipur and Mizoram (IIPS, 1998; Kore *et al.*, 2004). In 2004, there were 670 sentinel surveillance sites[1] established by NACO across the country. On the basis of HIV surveillance surveys, the NACO classifies the states according to the prevalence into high prevalence

Figure 19.1

Number of Sentinel Sites, 2004

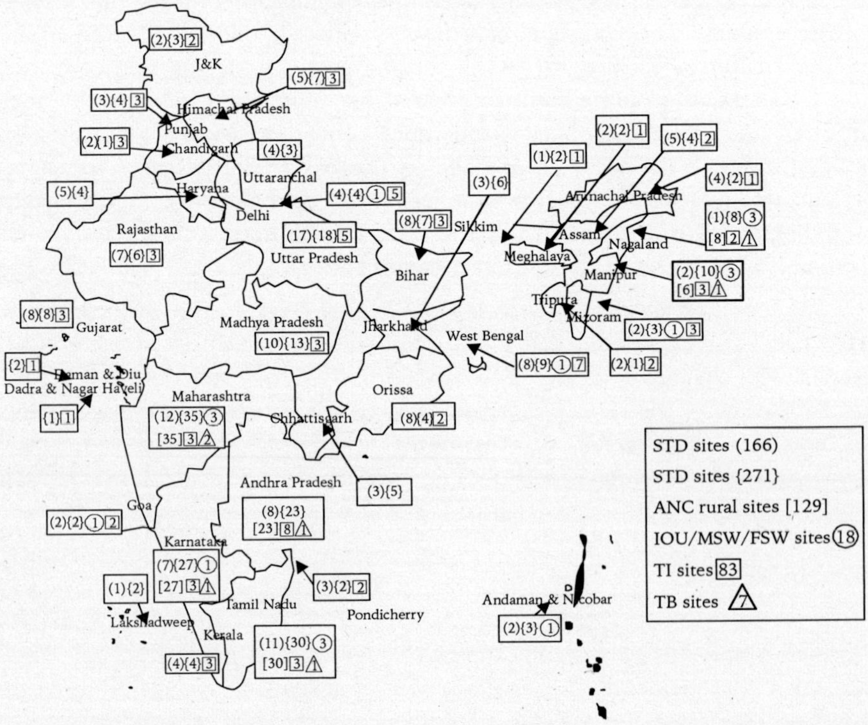

1. Of which sexually transmitted disease (STD) clinics consist of 166, antenatal clinics (ANC) consist of 396, 13 tuberculosis centres and the rest at locations to screen sex workers, homosexuals and drug users.

states (HPS)—HIV prevalence among antenatal women is 1 per cent or more, low prevalence states (LPS)—HIV prevalence in antenatal women is <1 per cent and among STD and other high risk groups are 5 per cent or more and medium prevalence states (MPS) where the HIV prevalence in antenatal women is <1 per cent and among STD and other high-risk groups <5 per cent. According to the above criterion, Maharashtra, Andhra Pradesh, Karnataka, Tamil Nadu, Manipur and Nagaland have been identified as HPS, Gujarat, Goa and Pondicherry are identified as MPS and the rest as LPS. Further, 45 districts in HPS and 4 districts from MPS have been identified as high prevalent districts, on the basis of consistent high prevalence levels reported in the three most recent rounds of HIV surveillance survey.

The pattern of HIV spread within India is diverse within its different regions, states and metropolitan areas. For instance, while heterosexual transmission predominates in Maharashtra and Tamil Nadu, infection

Figure 19.2

Adult HIV Prevalence, 2003

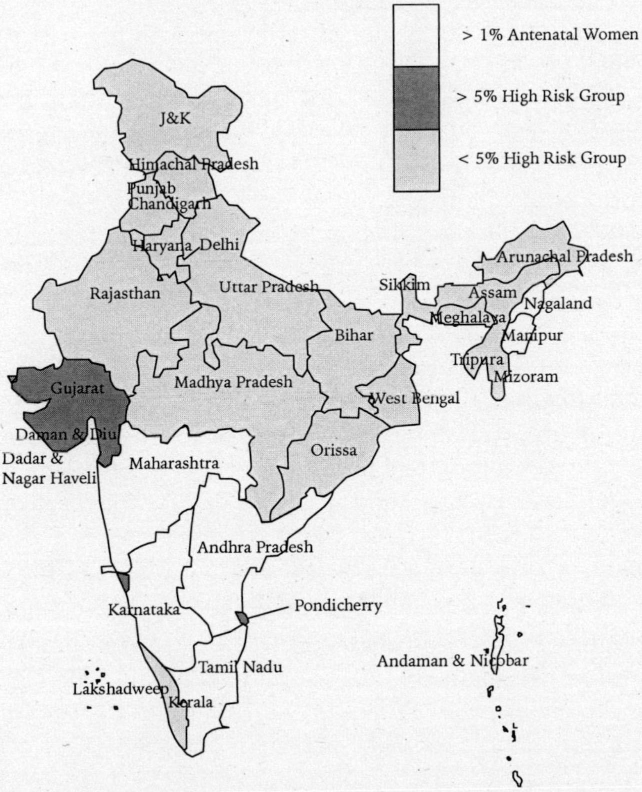

concentrating on injecting drug users (IDU) and their partners are predominant in Manipur. In Maharasthra, one of the worst affected states in India, the HIV prevalence is 54 per cent, 18 per cent and 1.25 per cent among commercial sex workers, those seeking treatment for sexually transmitted disease (STD) and antenatal attendees respectively as per the sentinel survey conducted in 2003. The other parts of the country, where there is severe localised epidemic is Namakkal in Tamil Nadu and Churachandpur in Manipur, where HIV prevalence among women attending antenatal clinics is over 3.3 per cent and 5.3 per cent, respectively. In Mumbai and Manipur, HIV infected accounts for 20-40 per cent of bed occupancy in referred hospitals.

The NACP Phase I was launched in 1992 with a soft loan from World Bank (WB) of US$ 84 million assistance and completed in 1999. By the end of the Phase I, a decentralised mechanism was established to facilitate effective state-level responses. But tremendous variation continues to exist in the level of commitment and capacity among states. For instance, while Tamil Nadu, Andhra Pradesh, Kerala and Manipur have demonstrated strong response and high level of political commitment, many states such as Bihar and Uttar Pradesh are yet to take the issue into serious consideration. The NACP Phase II (1999-2006) is almost completed with financial support from WB, Department for International Development (DFID), United States Agency for International Development (USAID) and Canadian International Development Agency (CIDA). In the first phase, the only initiative of the NACP was surveillance and controlling HIV spread. The low government priority to the epidemic in the initial years is reflected in weak technical capacity, delay in fund allocation and inadequate staffing, which seriously affected the control of the epidemic in the early years (Sethi, 2002). Further, the stigma and discrimination was flared up by the 'scare strategy' adopted in the awareness campaigns against HIV control and prevention in various media. Even though medical care for HIV infected could have provided within the existing medical system, only a hand full health care workers were ready to provide the care, due to the lack of awareness and stigmatisation of HIV in the society. In the second phase, during 1992-1999, there was a visible change in the strategies to control the epidemic, which an initiative to strengthen the capacity. There were steps to improve blood safety, establishment of state level structures, restructuring and introduction of awareness programmes like University Talk AIDS (UTA).

The priorities in different phases of HIV control and prevention in the country is evident in the pattern of budget allocation by the NACO. During the 1990s, the major expenditures of the HIV control programme were in promoting information, education and communication (IEC) activities and ensuring blood safety. The prevention and control of sexually transmitted infections (STIs) received only a small share of the total allocation for HIV control. Financial allocation for STI control declined from 12 per cent of the total financial outlay for HIV/AIDS control in the year 1992-93 to 4.6 per cent during the years 1994-1998. However, the year 1998-99 witnessed an increased financial allocation, perhaps, a reflection of the increased acknowledgement by policy makers of crucial links between STIs and HIV. It is worthwhile noting that the utilisation of funds allocated for HIV control has been sub optimal until very recently and only 50 per cent of the total allocation for HIV control was utilised during 1992-1995. Clinical management of people with HIV and surveillance of infection receive less than one-sixth of the AIDS control programme budget, however this is a substantial rise on the immediately preceding year's expenditure. The interim budget for the year 2004-05 indicates that care and support receives 30 per cent of the total allocation, which is a move in positive direction.

By the end of NACP Phase II, rapid changes occurred in the therapeutic scenario following the rapid reduction of the price of ART following the marketing of generic drugs from India, which changed the nature of HIV infection into a chronic manageable illness even in developing countries. With the funding received from World Health Organization under the 3 by 5 initiative which started in 2003, now ART is freely distributed through nearly 100 centres, catering 64000 infected. This initiative not only brings the infected back to life, but also reduces the stigma and discrimination against the disease. It is planned to have 100 ART centres by the end of 2006 and to enrol patients for free ART by the end of 2010.

Situating Challenges Created by HIV in Kerala

Kerala occupies a premier position among other Indian states in terms of social and demographic indicators, which is well documented in the development literature. The HIV infection in the state presents unique features differing from other southern states and remaining low prevalent region, despite having many features that would increase the risk of high HIV transmission rate. For instance, Kerala is geographically positioned near high HIV prevalent neighbouring states of Karnataka, Andhra Pradesh and Tamil Nadu. In addition, the state has high migration rate, and there is enough empirical evidence to point out that spread of HIV and migration is closely linked to it (Consultancy Group for Research and Forecasting, 2002; Thimothy, 2003). The highest rate of HIV infection is recorded in Thiruvananthapuram and Thrissur districts according to data published by Kerala AIDS Control Society, where migration rates are also the highest

(Zachariah *et al.*, 2003; Zachariah and Rajan, 2004). In this context, it would be appropriate to critically enquire the low HIV prevalence in Kerala.

Currently, it is estimated that Kerala have nearly 100,000 infected individuals, majority of them either infected outside Kerala or through their spouse or parents. In the year 2005, the prevalence of HIV in STD clinics of Kerala is 2.82 per cent, in antenatal clinic 0.25 per cent and among IDU 5.19 per cent, while the corresponding figures for Tamil Nadu are 9.2 per cent, 0.50 per cent and 18 per cent, respectively (NACO, 2006). From the available evidence at the micro level, we can conclude that though the state has high chances of becoming a high HIV prevalent state, the high literacy which resulted in better awareness in HIV control and prevention and the timely intervention of state along with active participation of various civil societies in empowering marginalised communities like commercial sex workers (CSWs) and homosexual individuals, has played a crucial role in controlling the epidemic. In addition, high treatment seeking behaviours and use of antibiotics has considerably reduced the prevalence of ulcerative sexually transmitted infections, which is a significant co-factor in the transmission of HIV.

Amidst these positive features, stigma and discrimination against HIV infected is very high in the state. In a way, this has led to the proliferation of quacks and miracle healers with the support of powerful lobbies. A much debated case of discrimination was the denial of education to children infected with HIV from Kollam district of the state. However, discussion provoked by such incidents was also helpful in dissemination of the correct message. At present, the HIV treatment scenario is better in the state compared to the rest of the country. Apart from the home based care, now there are few terminal care centres run by faith based organisation. Majority of HIV related activities in Kerala continues to be supported by NACO through Kerala State Aids Control Society. There are only very few projects or programmes which is independently funded. At the same time, prevention activities in the state were very effective in preventing the epidemic spreading inside the state. Targeted intervention projects implemented through various NGOs were effective in treating sexually transmitted diseases, empowering the commercial sex workers (CSWs), implementing harm reduction strategies among homosexuals and other high-risk population. For instance, the use of condom among CSWs is reported to be as high as 96 per cent in the state, which has reduced the incidence of HIV not only among CSWs but also in their clients as well (Jayasree, 2002). Even though there were attempts to introduce sexual health in school curriculum and introduce HIV-related issues in school level itself, the success of such programmes are yet to be evaluated. The first organisation of HIV positives, Council of People Living with HIV/

AIDS in Kerala (CPK+) was formed in 1999. Now there are a number of organisations for HIV infected people, which are involved in counseling, advocacy, social and financial support to affected individuals and families, treatment, education etc. At present, almost every district of the state has at least one network office. With the availability of treatment and widespread awareness programme and the changing perception about the disease, there is definite change in the attitude of the society.

State-sponsored Free ART Programme

As mentioned earlier, during the initial days of the epidemic there was very little treatment available for HIV. Few institutions especially the medical colleges provided the treatment for opportunistic infections. Even though antiretroviral were available in the state from early nineties, logistics to adequately monitor the treatment was limited in the state. Further, these drugs were unaffordable for the majority. The introduction of generic combination of antiretroviral initially by CIPLA and subsequently by many other Indian pharmaceuticals during late 1990s changed the scenario, making treatment affordable. In 2003, under the World Health Organization's 3 by 5 initiative, the Central government decided to introduce free ART in six high prevalent states and in New Delhi. As Kerala comes under LPS, the state did not figure in the Central government scheme. However, the state government initialised the treatment in the backdrop of pressure from various organisations of HIV infected people and public debate.

The free ART programme in Kerala, began functioning from November 2004 in the five medical colleges of the state. Each of the institutions identified space close to the out-patient department for situating the ART unit. The ARV drugs were initially purchased with state government funds. Prior to this, the following preparations were made for rolling out antiretroviral therapy. During February 2004, several brainstorming sessions were held with all stakeholders such as the faculty of medical colleges, doctors from health services, representatives of NGOs and PLWHAs on how to best conduct the ART programme. Training was given to the faculty of medical colleges and doctors from various specialties in the Health Department. Faculty from the Department of Infectious Diseases and Psychiatry from Christian Medical College, Vellore were the resource persons in these trainings. In addition, an elaborate manual was prepared by KSACS, resource materials provided by NACO were used for these trainings, covering all aspects of the ART programme. Fixed dose combination of ART first-line drugs in the NACO guidelines were purchased by the government. Stavudine containing drug regimens were preferred as recommended by NACO.

Efavirenz was also provided to those who required it. Only patients who had a CD4 count of less than 200 per cmm were enrolled in the programme. Any patient requiring ART, either because of a low CD4 count or on clinical grounds, was provided free ART. The NACO reporting formats and registers are being used throughout in the ART units. Currently, more than 2000 PLHA are being given ART from the five medical colleges. Recently, four of the ART centres were taken by NACO. There are three CD4 machines working in Kerala now. However, there are more institutions coming ready to start treatment.

In the context of Kerala, Thrissur model of HIV care also deserves special mention. This is a comprehensive HIV care model evolved in Thrissur medical college that provide integrated HIV care using existing infrastructure. This model worked on the concept of mainstreaming HIV care to the health care delivery system and do not require any extra financial support. And studies have proved that such arrangement resulted in direct improvement on the health and non-health functioning of the individuals attending the clinic (Thimothy *et al.*, 2006). This is unlike other models in India, which provides HIV care as a segregated component (e.g. GHTM Thambaram, YRG care are actually single disease hospitals). Established in an existing teaching hospital, HIV services are provided as part of general health care and the clinic is situated in the main out-patient area. Management of HIV care by a committed and trained multi-disciplinary team, including medical and other professionals with existing resources is one of the main concepts demonstrated by the care programme. A strong sense of commitment was developed among various team members so that the services are sustainable. Today, the entire hospital staff is involved in HIV care and staff capacity has increased. This centre has been able to garner support from the administration, KSACS, the government, the Positive Network, NGOs etc. HIV was used as an opportunity to improve other services like waste management and universal precautions as well as to strengthen the in-house training of the staff. An important achievement of the HIV care centre is in the way that HIV is no longer seen as an exotic disease to be managed by certain specialists alone, but as just another disease that any doctor or health care staff can attend to (Ajithkumar and Rajan, 2006). The most important aspect in initiating HIV care is the provision of a safe working environment for the health care staff along with imparting knowledge. This model proves that when it is impossible for individual specialists to manage an epidemic, it is possible to evolve models of integration and implement them. The HIV care centre at Thrissur has suitably demonstrated that teamwork and multi-disciplinary care can be replicated and is therefore, possible everywhere.

In the country, the prevailing stigma and discrimination against the HIV continues to push the epidemic invisible, which will further spread the infection. There requires mainstreaming of the HIV related services without losing the focus. The current attempt to reposition various HIV related services in government hospitals are a welcome step in this direction. There is an urgent need to redirect the discussions on sex and sexuality and introduce sex education in various curriculums. While Kerala continues to be a state of out-migrants, there is a steady increase in the migrants from other states including neighbouring high prevalent states.

Epidemic in Kerala continues to be one driven by migration; yet we do not have any programmes targeting the out-migrants or possible migrants. It is time to rethink our strategy and identify target groups from those who are likely to be migrants. We should have programmes addressing the needs of teenagers and young adults who are likely to migrate outside Kerala. About 50 per cent of our infected individuals are monogamous women who are infected by their spouses after marriages. It is important to address this issue and have a debate on provision of premarital counseling for youth. Though the state does not have a red street, the sex trade is booming in the state, which is evident in the numerous sex scandals and often commercial sexual activity flourishing in the background of tourism. In such a situation, there is a high chance of evading the people involving in high risk behaviour.

Experts in the field are of the opinion that there are pockets of high HIV prevalence within Kerala, especially in those regions where the state share border with high prevalent neighbouring states, which require specific strategies. With wider availability of ART, there is a definite chance of drug resistant strains circulating in the community. It is very important to have surveillance over the resistant strains in the community. If not properly monitored and corrected immediately, widespread occurrence of resistance and failure of treatment programmes may follow. And above all, there is a need to mainstream the treatment and prevention activities, absence of which will only catalyse stigma and discrimination.

Conclusion

Though Kerala continues to be a low prevalent state in the country, it has many features, which increase the risk of high HIV prevalence. Despite having better awareness and knowledge on HIV transmission and prevention, there exist intense stigma and discrimination against those infected and affected with HIV. These require increased attention to reach the general population and the high-risk population more effectively and to monitor the ART programme more closely.

References

Ajithkumar, K. and S. Irudaya Rajan (2006). "Medical Care for HIV: An Opportunity or Crisis?", *Economic and Political Weekly* XLI(15): 1428-30. April 15.

Chatterjee, Ashoke and Kusum Sahgal (2002). "The Role of the NGOs in India in HIV/AIDS Awareness and Control", in S. Panda, A. Chatterjee and A.S. Abdul-Quader (eds.). *Living with the AIDS Virus: The Epidemic and the Response in India*. New Delhi: Sage Publications India Pvt. Ltd. pp.62-76.

Consultancy Group for Research and Forecasting (2002). *Migration related HIV Infection in Kerala: A Case Control Study*. New Delhi: Submitted to UNDP.

HIV Sentinel Surveillance (2005). *Tamil Nadu Response to HIV AIDS 1986-2005.*

IIPS (1998). *National Family Health Survey (NFHS-2) India, 1998-99.* India.

Jayasree, A.K. (2002). "Issues of Sexual Identities of Sex Workers in Sex Health Intervention an Experience from Kerala". Retrieved from *http://www.thrani.com/*, on 1-10-06.

Kore, Shailesh J., Anahita Pandole, Yogini Nemade, Santosh Putharaya, V.R. Ambiye (2004). "Attitude, Knowledge, Beliefs about HIV/AIDS in College Going Adolescents", *Bombay Hospital Journal* 46(2), April (*www.bhj.org/journal/2004_4602_april/ html/attitude*)

Kurian, Thomas and S.P. Thyagarajan (eds.)(2006). *Conquering a Silent Epidemic.*

NACO (2006). *HIV/AIDS Epidemiological Surveillance and Estimation Report for the year 2005*, NACO, New Delhi.

Sethi, G. (2002). "AIDS in India: The Government's Response", in S. Panda, A. Chatterjee and A.S. Abdul-Quader (eds.). *Living with the AIDS Virus: The Epidemic and the Response in India.* New Delhi: Sage Publications India Pvt. Ltd.

Thimothy, Rakkee (2003). *The Economic Impact of HIV/AIDS in Kerala: An Analysis a Household Level.* M.Phil Dissertation submitted to the Jawaharlal Nehru University, New Delhi.

Thimothy, Rakkee, Ajithkumar, S. Irudaya Rajan (2006). "Viability of Providing HIV/AIDS Care in Public Sector: A Case Study from Kerala, India", *Journal of Health Management.*

UNAIDS (2004). *AIDS Epidemic Update.* UNAIDS: Geneva.

———. (2006). *AIDS Epidemic Update.* UNAIDS: Geneva.

Zachariah, K.C. and S. Irudaya Rajan (2004). "Gulf Revisited. Economic Consequences of Emigration from Kerala, Emigration and Unemployment", *Working Paper No. 363*, Centre for Development Studies, (Thiruvananthapuram). *www.cds.edu*

Zachariah, K.C., E.T. Mathew and S. Irudaya Rajan (2003). *Dynamics of Migration in Kerala. Dimensions, Determinants and Consequences.* London: Orient Longman Pvt. Limited.

20

Mental Health and Well-being

E. MOHAMED, S. IRUDAYA RAJAN, K. ANIL KUMAR
and P.M. SAIDU MOHAMMED

Introduction

Kerala ranks as the most literate among all states and union territories in India as per the 2001 census. The literacy rates for females and males in Kerala are 88 and 94 per cent respectively and the gender gap in literacy is just 6 per cent as against 22 per cent for the country (Banthia, 2001). The same census also reveals that Kerala is the only state in India where the sex ratio favours females. The sex ratio (females per 1000 males) in Kerala was 1058 as against 933 for India. In terms of reproductive behaviour, according to the Second National Family Health Survey, 1998-99, Keralite woman on an average end with 1.5 deliveries (International Institute for Population Sciences and ORC Macro, 2000). Indirect estimates based on the 2001 census show that Kerala as the leading state with below replacement level of fertility (Guilmoto and Rajan, 2002). The Human Development Index (HDI) prepared by the Indian Planning Commission ranks Kerala as first throughout the last 20 years. Kerala's HDI for 2001 was 0.638 as against the all-India index of 0.472 (Planning Commission, 2002). Evidently, all the conventional indicators rank Kerala as the top most. Even the Gender Empowerment Measure (GEM) developed by the United Nations Development Programme and the alternative measures developed by Hirway and Mahadevia also accord Kerala the leading position (UNDP, 1995; Hirway and Mahadevia, 1996).

However, it seems that the status of Kerala women in respect of non conventional indicators presents a dismal picture. In an earlier study, Eapen and Kodoth (2002) concluded that Kerala women did not fare well in terms of non-conventional indicators (Sonpar and Kapur, 2003) such as gender-based violence, mental ill-health, incidence of suicide and growth and spread of dowry and related crimes (Eapen and Kodoth, 2002; Eapen, 2002).

What are the ills of Kerala society? They consist of high incidence of suicides and accidents, cancer, widespread alcoholism, mental disorders, high rates of divorce and separation, HIV and AIDS, growing individualism and decline of family support networks partly due to internal as well as international migration. Let us assess the status of Kerala women in terms of some non-conventional indicators in detail.

The major mode of contraception in India is the high acceptance of female sterilisation. Direct involvement of men in the family planning programme is dismally low. Kerala is not an exception in this respect. Almost half of the women in Kerala undergo sterilisation whereas the percentage for India is only 34 (International Institute for Population Sciences and ORC Macro, 2001). Though the Sample Registration System (SRS) of India puts the infant mortality rate in Kerala as 14, other indirect estimates put Kerala's infant mortality rate at almost 37 (Rajan and Mohanachandran, 1999a; 1999b). Surprisingly, the same SRS places Kerala as having the highest still birth rate (around 10 per thousand live births). In Kerala, the number of deaths before birth is almost equal to the number of deaths during the first week of their life (Rajan and Mohanachandran, 1999b).

Though excess females are reported at all ages in Kerala (partly due to international migration), the sex ratio among children indicates to the possibility of sex selective abortions of female babies in Kerala. In other words, the birth of some female children is aborted in Kerala partly due to the prevalence of dowry (Rajan, Sudha and Mohanachandran, 2000). Dowry is often cited as one of the major uses to which remittances from abroad are put, apart from the construction of houses, repayment of debts, education of children and consumption expenditure (Zachariah *et al.*, 2001a; 2001b; 2003).

Though Kerala death rate is the lowest, it has the highest suicide rate in India—three times more than the national average—and 50 per cent more than Karnataka, the state with the second highest rate (Halliburton, 1998); According to the data released from the crime branch of the police department of Kerala, there were 9304 suicides in Kerala in 2000 as against 8389 in 1995. Family problems (22 per cent) are cited as the most important reason for suicide, followed by bankruptcy (14 per cent), prolonged illness (14 per cent) and mental illness (9 per cent). The other major causes reported include unemployment, professional problem, love affairs, fall in social esteem and the incidence of cancer. Dowry disputes and the resulting divorces are also reported as reasons for suicide (only in 34 instances in 2000). According to official sources, the dowry system results in the suicide or killing of 16 women everyday in India while the unofficial estimates put the figure at 68. According to the National Bureau of Investigation, 2000 women commit suicide as a direct consequence of dowry (National Bureau of Investigation, 2000). The proportion of suicides in Kerala among people in the range of '30-50 years' (39.2 per cent) and '50 years and above' (24.4 per cent) are greater than the national average of 32.3 per cent and 12.8 per cent respectively (Rajan, 2003; Halliburton, 1998). Suicide thus ranks as the second major cause of death in Kerala. It is estimated that while the annual suicide rate in Kerala was 31 per lakh population in 2000 (15 in 1970s), the national average was just 8 per lakh population. Another disturbing dimension of suicides in Kerala is family suicide. Still worse, it is on the increase. For instance, out of a total of 154 family suicides reported for India in 1999, Kerala accounted for 59, followed by Andhra Pradesh (42) and Tamil Nadu (34). It seems that family suicide is uncommon in the rest of India compared to southern region.

According to Government of Kerala's Mental Health Policy document, around 3-5 lakh citizens of Kerala have serious mental disorders. The same report also points out that there exist 238 psychiatric units in the state (both in private and public sectors). The perceived high rate of psychopathology may relate to the fact that Kerala has the highest number of psychiatric centres in India. While Kerala has around 4 per cent of India's population, about one third of institutions dealing with mental illness and related disorders in public and private sectors are located in Kerala (Franke and Chasin, 1994).

According to the unpublished information collected by the authors from five family courts of Kerala, while the number of cases registered in 1997 came to 2364, it increased to 4628 in 2001—a 50 per cent increase in 5 years. Incidentally, among the cases filed in the family courts for divorce, 60 per cent of cases were filed by women—among them 70 per cent of them stated cruelty by husbands (domestic violence) as the main reason.

Violence against women is a reflection of unequal gender relations in the society which perpetuate exploitation, discrimination, marginalisation and exclusion of women. According to the data provided by the crime branch of Police Department of Kerala, crimes against women increased from 1967 in 1990 to 7568 in 2001—four-fold increase in a decade. Over 25 per cent of these crimes consisted of either molestation or rape. According to the Planning Commission, while crime against women numbered 135 per million population in India, the rate for Kerala was as high as 151 per million population. According to 'Sakhi', the State Women's Commission received about 15,000 complaints within its two years of inception and 80 per cent of them related to sexual and domestic violence (Sakhi, 2002). With respect to domestic violence, Kerala is well ahead of other states. Thiruvananthapuram, the capital city of Kerala is ranked first among five cities in India in the prevalence of domestic violence, both physical and psychological (INCLEN/ICRW, 2000). However, there has been no systematic study in Kerala to assess the well-being, mental health in Kerala. The present chapter addresses this issue.

Objectives

The objectives of the present chapter are: (a) to assess the subjective well being, mental health and their determinants and (b) to examine mental distress experienced by men and women of Kerala.

Data Sources

The Kerala Migration Survey (KMS) conducted at the Centre for Development Studies (CDS), Thiruvananthapuram, attempted to portray the migrant profile of Kerala and also to critically examine the trends, differentials and determinant of migration from Kerala (for more details, see Zachariah *et al.*, 2001a; 2001b) The study covered all the 14 districts of the state. Within a district, the locality (*panchayat* or municipal ward) was used as the first stage of sampling unit. The list of sample localities was selected at random with probability proportional to the number of households in the locality. From each selected locality, one ward was chosen at random and from each selected ward, 50 households were chosen to form the sample of households. On the basis of the expected variation in the proportion of migrants in a household, the total sample size for the state as a whole was fixed at 10,000 households (Table 20.1 for details). Household was the ultimate sampling unit for all the questionnaires.

The sample for this study 'Gender and Mental Health, Kerala' (GMHK) is a sub-sample of households taken from the larger sample of KMS. In KMS, 200 localities were surveyed with 50 households each based on random sampling. The first step for GMHK was to select 100 localities from 200 localities of KMS. The following sampling method has been used for selecting the sample of 1000 households from 14 districts of Kerala.

(i) Hundred *panchayat*/municipal wards were selected by systematic random sampling method. The localities with numbers 1, 3, 5, 7, ... 199 were selected as the first stage sampling units.

(ii) In each of the 100 selected localities, 10 households were selected systematically with random start to get 10 from each of the localities which finally added up to 1000 households (see Table 20.1 for details).

Table 20.1

Sample Size by District: KMS and GMHK

District	*No. of Households*	*KMS (1998)*	*GMHK (2002)*
Kasaragod	181,667	330	30
Kannur	371,221	673	72
Wayanad	134,654	244	30
Kozhikode	456,673	828	79
Malappuram	477,292	866	90
Palakkad	444,998	897	80
Thrissur	522,159	947	99
Ernakulam	555,657	1008	96
Idukki	232,995	423	40
Kottayam	361,813	656	64
Alappuzha	405,210	735	70
Pathanamthitta	259,629	471	50
Kollam	489,774	888	90
Thiruvananthapuram	619,558	1,124	110
Kerala	5,513,300	10,000	1000

Source: Zachariah *et al.*, 2003.

Measures

The Subjective Well-being Inventory (SUBI)

SUBI was developed by Sell and Nagpal (1992). The original version consists of a 40-item questionnaire. For each item, there are three response options. It yields a total score as well as subscores for the positive (well-being) and negative aspects (ill-being). This is validated through factor analysis. Eleven factors are identified from which a short version consisting of three very sensitive factors are taken for the purpose of the study. This short version is a 9-item questionnaire and the factors are general well being-positive affect, expectation achievement congruence and confidence in coping.

General Health Questionnaire (GHQ)

Developed by Goldberg (1972), GHQ has found application in a variety of psychiatric and non-psychiatric contexts and has been translated, revalidated and used in many countries including India. It has been used in many studies related to the economic situation, occupation and unemployment (Strandh, 2000; Warr *et al.*, 1988; Banks *et al.*, 1983). The GHQ is available in several versions of varying length. The 12-item GHQ has the advantage of brevity and hence, convenience of administration and scoring. It is also as sensitive and valid as are the longer versions. It consists of the 12 "best items" of the original 60-item questionnaire, that is, those items that were most discriminating in determining clinical status and were not endorsed by a physically ill control group. In India, the 12-item GHQ has been validated against the Indian Psychiatric Survey Schedule and has been found to demonstrate excellent sensitivity and specificity, that is, it is able to accurately identify the presence of psychological disturbance with few false negatives and false positives (Shamsunder *et al.*, 1986). Each of the 12 items of the questionnaire has four possible response choices. The scoring is simple, the total score being a summation of the score on each item. In surveys, the GHQ can be used as a dimensional measure of psychological disturbance and can also be used to identify a "case". In the former situation, the total score is used to indicate the degree of psychological distress. In the latter situation, a threshold score is used so that persons scoring above the threshold are identified as potential psychiatric cases.

Stress

A questionnaire was prepared by the research team for eliciting specific stress factors experienced by both men and women. It consists of 10 sub sections with separate questions to elicit information on stress in the areas of finance, health, workload, occupation, future, addictions, relationships, violence, decision-making and migration respectively.

Results and Discussion: Subjective Well-being

As stated earlier, the household survey was conducted among males and females of age group between 15-59 and responsive ones between 60-69 years in the selected 1000 households from Kerala. In total, we have responses from 1308 males and 1477 females. Human well-being is measured on the basis of 9 questions with 3 multiple choices and the scores are based on the chosen answer. The lower the score, the better is the well being of individuals and vice versa. Keralite men report comparatively higher levels of well-being than women. The mean score for men (17.35) is significantly lower than that for women (17.9). The difference is statistically significant (Table 20.2).

It was also found that male members of female-headed households have significantly higher well-being than female members of female-headed households. No significant gender difference exists between members of male-headed families in this respect. Men of the female-headed households reported higher well-being than men of male-headed households. On the other hand, women of female-headed families are worse than the females of male-headed households (Table 20.3).

Table 20.2

Index of Subjective Well-being by Sex in Kerala, 2002

Gender	*Total Numbers*	*Score Mean*	*t value*	*Significance*
Male	1308	17.35	-3.509*	.006
Female	1477	17.90		

Note: * Significant at 1% level.
Source: Field Survey, 2002.

Table 20.3

Index of Subjective Well-being by Head of the Household, 2002

Household Head	*Total Families*	*Total Members*	*Mean of the Scores*		*t value*	*Significance*
			Male	*Female*		
Male	757	2174	17.75	17.63	0.384	.701
Female	243	611	17.57	18.92	-3.333*	.001

Note: * Significant at 1% level.
Source: Field Survey, 2002.

Well-being diminishes as age advances in both men and women. However, among women a sudden decline is observed in well-being between the ages of 25 and 34 (when the student status of the women ends and they get married or enter into workforce); of course, well-being improves later and then to decline again beyond the age of 55. This pattern is not true for men whose well-being improves marginally after 55. Though the difference between men and women is important in all age groups, the difference gains statistical significance only among those who are above the age of 55 (Table 20.4). Gender disparity is more marked in older persons and this could be an indication that there is a positive impact of social change in the direction of gender equality in the younger cohorts. Well-being of the elderly females is also affected by their widowhood status in old age.

Men reported higher levels of well-being irrespective of whether they were single, married or widowed. Though not statistically significant, a reverse trend was noticed among divorced men and women where women reported relatively higher well-being. Marriage seems to cause a negative impact on the well-being of both men and women of Kerala. Again, the condition gets much worse, if they become widowed or divorced.

Table 20.4

Index of Subjective Well-being by Age and Sex in Kerala, 2002

			Mean of the Scores			
Age	*Male*	*Female*	*Male*	*Female*	*t value*	*Significance*
15-24	344	343	16.41	16.88	-1.639	.102
25-34	269	313	17.21	19.75	-1.507	.133
35-44	237	313	17.63	18.13	-2.285	.200
45-54	233	277	18.19	18.54	-.885	.377
55+	225	231	17.80	19.64	-4.955*	.000

Note: * Highly significant.
Source: Field Survey, 2002.

Table 20.5

Index of Subjective Well-being by Sex and Marital Status in Kerala, 2002

			Mean of the Scores			
Marital Status	*Male*	*Female*	*Male*	*Female*	*t value*	*Significance*
Unmarried	99	79	15.52	16.82	-2.272**	.026
Married	1086	1117	17.33	17.89	-3.286*	.001
Widowed	98	220	18.75	19.81	-1.715***	.090
Divorced	10	24	19.40	17.90	1.123	.290

Note: * Significant at 1% level; ** Significant at 5 % level; *** Significant at 10% level.
Source: Field Survey, 2002.

As one would expect, education has a positive influence on the well-being of both men and women. Our data support this; the higher the level of educational attainment, the higher is the sense of well-being. However, gender difference is found to be significant only among literates and those with primary and secondary levels of education. Interestingly, illiterates and degree holders have shown no significant gender differences. Does it confirm the old saying, "a little knowledge is dangerous"? Though the total number of men and women of the sample were comparable, illiterate women were three times more than illiterate men and the sample size is also low for both sexes among the literates (Table 20.6). It also indicates that there was a gender difference in the schooling of the older generation although currently enrolment among boys and girls are around 100 per cent.

Labourers showed the highest gender disparity in well-being, followed by government employees, farmers and self-employed persons. Though the number of men and women with secondary and college education were equal in our sample, women's representation in employment—government, private or self-employment—was found to be much lower (one-fourth of men). In other words, three-fourths of the women who were eligible to seek employment were not actually employed unlike their male counterparts. Though gender disparity is high among women working in government sector, their well-being is higher compared to women who work as farmers, labourers or household workers. Among men, farmers have the lowest level of well-being (Table 20.7).

Table 20.6

Index of Subjective Well-being by Educational Attainment and Sex, 2002

Educational Attainment	*Male*	*Female*	*Mean of the Scores*		*t value*	*Significance*
			Male	*Female*		
Illiterate	42	123	19.57	20.07	-.523	.604
Literate	34	33	19.12	20.91	-1.717***	.096
Primary	188	246	17.74	19.55	-1.935***	.054
Middle	598	658	17.70	17.86	-.714	.476
Secondary	330	321	16.21	16.79	-2.007**	.046
Degree	116	94	15.35	15.77	-.825	.411

Note: ** Significant at 5% level; *** Significant at 10% level.
Source: Field Survey, 2002.

Table 20.7

Index of Subjective Well-being by Work Status and Sex in Kerala, 2002

Work Status	*Male*	*Female*	*Mean of the Scores*		*t value*	*Significance*
			Male	*Female*		
Government	80	30	14.57	16.80	-2.082***	.046
Private	86	32	16.59	17.84	-1.323	.196
Self-employed	261	42	17.67	19.40	-2.289***	.027
Farmers	121	53	18.51	20.51	-2.792**	.007
Labourers	374	77	17.10	20.55	-5.324*	.000
Unemployed	186	81	17.80	17.84	-.220	.826
Student	171	146	15.61	16.16	-1.494	.137
House work	18	1012	17.83	18.17	-.198	.845

Note: * Highly significant; ** Significant at 1% level; *** Significant at 5% level.
Source: Field Survey, 2002.

Syrian Christians and Nair men report the highest well-being whereas the same communities also score high on gender differences. It seems that men's well-being is maintained at the cost of women. Surprisingly, we did not find gender disparity among Muslims, Ezhavas, and Scheduled Castes and Tribes of Kerala, though they are far behind in their well-being compared to the more advanced communities consisting of Syrian Christians and Nairs (Table 20.8).

Table 20.8

Index of Subjective Well-being by Religion and Caste in Kerala, 2002

Religion/Caste	Male	Female	Mean of the Scores Male	Mean of the Scores Female	t value	Significance
SC/ST	94	109	18.27	18.76	-.931	.354
Nair	133	143	16.68	17.86	-2.43**	.016
Ezhava	292	322	17.95	18.07	-.354	.723
Syrian Christians	138	135	16.57	17.71	-2.531**	.013
Other Christians	151	180	17.20	18.48	-2.835*	.005
Muslims	258	335	17.35	17.62	-.720	.472
Others	173	173	17.35	17.84	-1.200	.232

Note: * Significant at 1% level; ** Significant at 5% level.
Source: Field Survey, 2002.

Gender difference in well-being is very high in southern Kerala and the difference narrows down as we move to central Kerala. In north Kerala, women are slightly better in terms of well-being compared to men though this difference is not statistically significant. Among men, well-being declines as we move from south to north whereas the reverse is experienced in the case of women (Table 20.9).

Table 20.9

Index of Subjective Well-being by Region and Sex in Kerala, 2002

Region	Male	Female	Mean of the Scores Male	Mean of the Scores Female	t value	Significance
South	417	442	17.10	18.10	-3.809*	.000
Central	490	541	17.25	17.92	-2.592**	.010
North	400	494	17.74	17.63	.384	.701

Note: * Highly significant; ** Significant at 1% level.
Source: Field Survey, 2002.

Irrespective of gender, well-being is the highest among emigrant households (households with at least one emigrant member) and lowest among non-migrant households. It is possible that economic benefits derived through remittances have added to their well-being among internal and international migrant families. Gender difference is the highest among non migrant households. On the other hand, families of returned emigrants and out-migrants reported a decline in well-being. These groups have significant gender disparities (Table 20.10).

Table 20.10

Index of Subjective Well-being by Migration Status of the Household, 2002

Migration Status	*Male*	*Female*	*Mean of the Scores* *Male*	*Female*	*t value*	*Significance*
REM	125	144	17.06	18.02	-1.901**	.060
EMI	161	231	16.94	16.55	.897	.371
ROM	172	181	17.28	17.81	-1.273	.205
OMI	114	123	17.37	17.87	-1.041	.300
No migration	811	900	17.48	18.22	-3.584*	.000

Note: REM = Return emigrants in the households; EMI: Emigrant in the households; ROM= Return out-migrant in the households; OMI = Out-migrant in the households.
* Highly Significant; ** Significant at 10% level.

Source: Field Survey, 2002.

Well-being has a positive association with the quality of housing including the availability of electricity (Table 20.11). The gender difference is not much among members sharing decent housing whereas the difference is significant in the case of residents who have poor housing. Probably, in poor households women have to work extra hours to run the household.

Table 20.11

Index of Subjective Well-being by Household Characteristics, 2002

Housing Quality	*Total*	*Mean of the Scores* *Male*	*Female*	*t value*	*Significance*
Very good	423	16.11	16.62	-1.340	.182
Good	1491	17.49	17.58	-.411	.681
Poor	721	17.90	19.48	-5.335*	.000
Electricity in the household					
Yes	1858	17.11	17.39	-1.503	.133
No	778	18.06	19.17	-3.966*	.000

Note: * Highly significant.

Source: Field Survey, 2002.

Table 20.12

Determinants of Subjective Well-being

Model Summary

R	*R Square*	*Adjusted R Square*	*Std. Error of the Estimate*
.359	.129	.126	3.84

ANOVA

	Sum of Squares	*Df*	*Mean Square*	*F*	*Sig.*
Regression	5716.056	9	635.117	42.999	.000
Residual	38757.559	2624	14.770		
Total	44473.615	2633			

Coefficients

	Unstandardised Coefficients		*Standardised Coefficients*	*t*	*Sig.*
	B	*Std. Error*	*Beta*		
(Constant)	14.577	.858		16.986	.000
Educational attainment	-.687	.076	-.192	-8.979	.000
Marital status	.613	.134	.092	4.572	.000
Housing quality	.731	.139	.115	5.248	.000
Gender	.581	.155	.071	3.759	.000
Age	2.519E-02	.006	.093	4.133	.000
Electricity in the house	.467	.192	.052	2.439	.015
Region	.285	.102	.055	2.788	.005
Employment status	9.513E-02	.044	.043	2.154	.031
Religion	-7.815E-02	.037	-.039	-2.105	.035

Excluded Variables

	Beta	*t*	*Sig.*	*Partial Correlation*	*Collinearity Statistics Tolerance*
Return emigrant	.011	.585	.558	.011	.960
Emigrant	-.012	-.620	.535	-.012	.962
Return out-migrant	-.009	-.484	.628	-.009	.964
Out-migrant	.010	.537	.592	.010	.980
No migrant	.000	.004	.997	.000	.915

Source: Field Survey, 2002.

To identify the determinants of well-being, we have done multiple regression analysis using all the relevant variables collected from the households. The findings are as follows: educational attainment of the individual, marital status, quality of housing, availability of electricity, gender, age, religion, region of the state where the person lives and employment status are found to be significant factors which affect well-being of the individuals (Table 20.12). However, migration status of the households has no significant impact on well-being.

Mental Health

In this section, we analyse 12 questions canvassed among the individuals to assess the level of mental health in Kerala. All questions had 4 possible response choices and the individuals were requested to select one choice for all 12 questions. The higher the score, the lower is the mental health. Keralites show significant gender disparity in mental health. Females are lower in scale compared to men in mental health (Table 20.13).

Table 20.13

Index of Mental Health in Kerala by Sex, 2002

Gender	*Total*	*Score Mean*	*t value*	*Significance*
Male	1308	1.81	-4.518*	.000
Female	1477	2.33		

Note: * Highly significant.
Source: Field Survey, 2002.

Women of female-headed households are the lowest in mental health compared to either males of female-headed households or males or females of the male-headed households. Not much gender disparity in mental health was observed in male-headed households. Men are not affected by the gender of the head of the household (Table 20.14).

Table 20.14

Index of Mental Health in Kerala by Head of the Household, 2002

Gender	*Total Families*	*Total Members*	*Mean of the Scores*		*t value*	*Significance*
			Male	*Female*		
Male	757	2174	1.90	1.98	-.388	.698
Female	243	611	1.99	3.03	-3.219*	.001

Note: * Significant at 1% level.
Source: Field Survey, 2002.

Females have lower mental health irrespective of their age; this disparity is particularly significant in two broad age groups namely 25-34 and above 55 (elderly). In the case of other age groups, of course differences exist but they are not statistically significant. As age advances, mental health declines for both men and women. However, while for men this is a more or less linear movement, in respect of women there seems to be a sudden leap in the case of two age groups. This may be associated with changes in life stages. (Table 20.15).

Table 20.15

Index of Mental Health in Kerala by Age and Sex, 2002

Age	Male	Female	Mean of the Scores Male	Mean of the Scores Female	t value	Significance
15-24	344	343	1.04	1.36	-1.903**	.058
25-34	269	313	1.49	2.36	-3.581*	.000
35-44	237	313	1.90	2.11	-.750	.454
45-54	233	277	2.31	2.71	-1.245	.214
55+	225	231	2.79	4.09	-3.714*	.000

Note: * Highly significant; ** Significant at 10% level.
Source: Field Survey, 2002.

As reported in the earlier section on well-being, a similar and perhaps related trend is also seen in mental heath. After marriage, distress increases for both men and women but more so among women (twice as much). Gender difference in mental distress is highly significant in married groups. Death of spouse also seems to affect women's mental health more than that of men (Table 20.16).

Table 20.16

Index of Mental Health in Kerala by Marital Status, 2002

Marital Status	Male	Female	Mean of the Scores Male	Mean of the Scores Female	t value	Significance
Unmarried	99	79	1.22	1.35	-.354	.724
Married	1086	1117	1.78	2.28	-3.966*	.000
Widowed	98	220	2.50	3.62	-2.332**	.022
Divorced	10	24	1.90	2.70	-.897	.393

Note: * Highly significant; ** Significant at 5% level.
Source: Field Survey, 2002.

Mental distress comes down as the level of education goes up for both men and women. But gender difference is more significant among those with primary, upper primary, middle and secondary education. For those with education upto and above degree level, gender difference is negligible. In respect of illiterates and literates with the minimum education, women seem to be less distressed than men though this difference is not statistically significant. Remaining uneducated may be more distressing for a man in our society than it is for a woman (Table 20.17). The gender related influence of education on mental health seems to follow something like 'Dodson's inverted U curve'.

Table 20.17

Index of Mental Health in Kerala by Educational Attainment, 2002

Educational Attainment	Male	Female	Mean of the Scores		t value	Significance
			Male	Female		
Illiterate	42	123	3.88	3.30	.652	.518
Literate	34	33	3.45	3.21	.291	.773
Primary	188	246	2.3	3.48	-2.023**	.045
Middle	598	658	1.83	2.32	-2.851*	.005
Secondary	330	321	1.14	1.56	-2.253**	.025
Degree	116	94	0.84	1.38	-1.613	.110

Note: * Significant at 1% level; ** Significant at 5% level.
Source: Field Survey, 2002.

Except for those engaged in household work (domestic chores), women experience more distress than men. Gender difference is significant for labourers and those who are self-employed including farmers, people holding salaried jobs in the public or private sector and those who are unemployed. For the average Keralite, it seems to be less mentally distressing to remain unemployed than to be a farmer. The mental distress experienced by a female labourer is three times more than that of male counterparts. Students have minimal distress irrespective of gender. But men in government service are similar to students in this respect but for women in government service, mental distress increases three-fold compared to female students (Table 20.18).

Nair men and Muslim women have better mental health compared to others. But gender difference is significantly high within Nair community whereas it is minimal among Muslims. Both men and women of Scheduled Castes/Tribes report mental distress. Gender difference is also high among them. Ezhavas and Syrian Christians also show gender differences in mental health (Table 20.19).

Table 20.18

Index of Mental Health in Kerala by Work Status, 2002

Employment Status	Male	Female	Mean of the Scores Male	Mean of the Scores Female	t value	Significance
Government	80	30	0.700	2.30	-2.227***	.034
Private	86	32	1.06	2.78	-2.768**	.009
Self-employed	261	42	1.02	3.33	-4.175 *	.000
Farmers	121	53	2.13	3.51	-1.917****	.061
Labourers	374	77	1.05	3.96	-5.629*	.000
Unemployed	186	81	1.82	3.13	-2.60**	.011
Student	171	146	.88	.91	-.135	.893
House work	18	1012	4.50	2.5	1.635	.120

Note: * Highly significant; ** Significant at 1% level; *** Significant at 5% level; * *** Significant at 10% level.

Source: Field Survey, 2002.

Table 20.19

Index of Mental Health in Kerala by Religion/Caste, 2002

Religion/Caste	Male	Female	Mean of the Scores Male	Mean of the Scores Female	t value	Significance
SC/ST	94	109	2.17	2.82	-1.667***	.099
Nair	133	143	1.43	2.23	-2.350**	.020
Ezhava	292	322	2.10	2.53	-1.720***	.087
Syrian Christians	138	135	1.58	2.55	-2.753*	.007
Other Christians	151	180	2.02	2.45	-1.338	.183
Muslims	258	335	1.78	1.98	-.773	.440
Others	173	173	1.46	2.49	-3.158*	.002

Note: * Significant at 1% level; ** Significant at 5% level; *** Significant at 10% level.

Source: Field Survey, 2002.

Mental health declines for men as one moves from south to north Kerala but the reverse is true for women (Table 20.20). Gender disparity in mental health is highest in south Kerala; it is relatively less in central Kerala and negligible in north.

Gender differences in mental health are the highest among non-migrant households. Members of out-migrant and returned out-migrant households also report significant gender differences in mental health (Table 20.21). Women of emigrant and returned emigrant families have relatively better mental health and the gender differences also are low for those households. On the other hand, men of migrant and out-migrant families have relatively more mental distress. Men belonging to non-migrant households have the highest level of mental health in spite of the fact that the same people reported lowest well-being. These findings substantiate once again that psychological distress and well-being are two separate dimensions and not two poles of the same dimension.

Table 20.20

Index of Mental Health in Kerala by Region, 2002

			Mean of the Scores			
Region	*Male*	*Female*	*Male*	*Female*	*t value*	*Significance*
South	417	442	1.75	2.74	-4.918*	.000
Central	490	541	1.81	2.33	-2.753**	.006
North	400	494	1.90	1.98	-.388	.698

Note: * Highly significant; ** Significant at 1% level.
Source: Field Survey, 2002.

Table 20.21

Index of Mental Health in Kerala by Migration Status of the Household, 2002

			Mean of the Scores			
Migration Status	*Male*	*Female*	*Male*	*Female*	*t value*	*Significance*
REM	125	144	1.99	2.08	-.282	.778
EMI	161	231	2.07	2.08	-0.036	.972
ROM	172	181	1.87	2.85	-2.991**	.003
OMI	114	123	2.08	2.75	-1.737***	.085
No migration	811	900	1.76	2.27	-3.548*	.000

Note: * Highly significant; ** Significant at 1% level; *** Significant at 10% level.
Source: Field Survey, 2002.

As the quality of housing improves, mental distress comes down for both sexes. But gender difference in mental health is present in all types of households irrespective of housing quality (Table 20.22).

We also ran multiple regressions to ascertain the determinants of mental health in Kerala (Table 20.23). The factors affecting the mental health are educational attainment, age, gender, marital status, housing, availability of electricity and households with no migrant. On the other hand, migration status, geographical region, religion and employment status do not seem to influence mental health in any significant manner.

Table 20.22

Index of Mental Health in Kerala by Household Characteristics, 2002

		Mean of the Scores			
Housing Quality	*Total*	*Male*	*Female*	*t value*	*Significance*
Very good	423	1.31	1.88	-2.122***	0.035
Good	1491	1.75	2.22	-3.164**	0.002
Poor	721	2.21	2.96	-2.917**	0.004
Electricity in the household					
Yes	1858	1.61	2.15	-4.069*	.000
No	778	2.48	2.77	-2.084**	.038

Note: * Highly significant; ** Significant at 1% level; *** Significant at 5% level.
Source: Field Survey, 2002.

Table 20.23

Determinants of Index of Mental Health

Model Summary

R	*R Square*	*Adjusted R Square*	*Std. Error of the Estimate*
.332	.110	.108	2.97

ANOVA

	Sum of Squares	*Df*	*Mean Square*	*F*	*Sig.*
Regression	2869.204	7	409.886	46.366	.000
Residual	23214.485	2626	8.840		
Total	26083.689	2633			

Coefficients

	Unstandardised Coefficients		*Standardised Coefficients*	*t*	*Sig.*
	B	*Std. Error*	*Beta*		
(Constant)	-.211	.524		-.402	.688
Educational attainment	-.420	.058	-.153	-7.250	.000
Age	2.818E-02	.004	.135	6.324	.000
Gender	.597	.118	.095	5.056	.000
Marital status	.435	.103	.085	4.212	.000
Electricity in the household	.409	.148	.059	2.770	.006
House quality	.283	.104	.058	2.725	.006
No migrant	.138	.057	.047	2.438	.015

contd...

...contd...

Excluded Variables					
	Beta	*t*	*Sig.*	*Partial Correlation*	*Collinearity Statistics Tolerance*
REM	-.006(g)	-.321	.748	-.006	.846
EMI	.010(g)	.486	.627	.009	.756
ROM	-.001(g)	-.028	.978	-.001	.709
OMI	-.004(g)	-.171	.864	-.003	.619
Region	-.004(g)	-.185	.853	-.004	.895
Religion	-.033(g)	-1.769	.077	-.035	.982
Employment status	.034(g)	1.691	.091	.033	.846

Source: Field Survey, 2002.

Stress among Keralites

Current financial worries, insecurities of the future, poor health and heavy burden of work are the major causes of stress among both men and women of Kerala. Stress related to aggression, violence and threat of violence are much more relevant for women compared to men. Addiction in the members of the family causes twice as much stress for women as for men. However, if men happen to be addicts, they tend to undergo much stress in their occupation. The same is true for financial stress (Table 20.24). But general impression derived from the study is that women in Kerala are under greater stress compared to their male counterparts.

Table 20.24

Stress among Keralites, 2002

Characteristics	*Male*	*Rank*	*Female*	*Rank*
Financial	75.31	1	69.19	1
Anxiety	61.31	2	62.49	2
Health	35.40	3	44.21	3
Workload	19.95	4	28.44	4
Interpersonal relationship	17.20	5	19.03	7
Aggression and violence	14.45	6	20.51	6
Stress yourself	13.69	7	01.96	10
Stress in family	09.33	8	20.99	5
Occupational	07.42	9	03.11	9
Threat of aggression and violence	01.76	10	18.89	8

Source: Field Survey, 2002.

Regarding stress arising from anxiety about the future, generally men are mainly concerned with only income security. On the other hand, women bother more about health, ageing, children's education and the future of every body else in the household.

Examining the reasons for financial stress, it is seen that inadequate income is the foremost cause for both sexes (Table 20.25). Next come burden of debt, illness, the need to have one's own house and education of children, in that order. Financial stress arising from one's job or business is reported more by men while various stress related to marriage are more common among women.

Table 20.25

Reasons for Financial Stress, 2002

	Male	*Rank*	*Females*	*Rank*
Insufficient income	74.42	1	70.25	1
Debt	58.07	2	63.31	2
Illness	32.79	3	39.04	3
House construction	20.41	4	21.04	4
Education of children	14.31	5	17.12	5
Employment or business	12.39	6	07.24	7
Marriage and dowry	11.98	7	13.99	6
Others	04.57	8	06.36	8

Source: Field Survey, 2002.

Men report stress caused by excessive (non-domestic) workload as of prime importance (79 per cent). Routine household work (domestic chores) is a stress factor for only 21 per cent of men compared to 86 per cent for women (Table 20.26). Stress associated with managing household work and work outside home, burden of caring for the sick or the elderly in the household and supervision of children is felt more by women. This confirms to the traditional gender role of man as the breadwinner and woman as the homemaker.

When we examine relationship-related stress, it matters with whom a stressful relationship exists. For about 54 per cent of married women, the relationship with the husband is the most stressful. Only 19 per cent of married men have the same complaint about their wives (Table 20.27). In other words, women are more stressed in married life compared to men. Also, 28 per cent of married women experience stress in their relationship with the husband's family (parents, sisters and brothers) compared to 6 per cent among men. For men, relationship with siblings, neighbours and colleagues is more stressful.

Table 20.26

Reasons for Work Load Stress, 2002

Reasons	*Male*	*Rank*	*Female*	*Rank*
Excessive (non-domestic) work load	78.93	1	19.05	3
House and outside work	28.74	2	40.95	2
Routine house work	21.07	3	85.48	1
Burden of caring for sick or elderly	12.26	4	15.71	4
Supervision of children	08.05	5	14.52	5
Others	05.75	6	01.90	6

Source: Field Survey, 2002.

Table 20.27

Reasons for Stress on Future, 2002

Reasons	*Male*	*Rank*	*Female*	*Rank*
Income security	85.04	1	72.37	1
Health	35.16	2	43.66	2
Son's future	29.30(34.97)	3	41.17(56.55)	3
Daughter's future	25.81(30.80)	4	34.13(45.45)	4
Children education	16.08(19.20)	5	17.77(23.67)	7
Other	15.71	6	10.94	8
Spouse future	16.21(19.34)	7	29.90(39.83)	5
Ageing	13.59	8	(19.61	6

Note: Percentages in the brackets are percentages from the married people, who answered for this question.

Source: Field Survey, 2002.

Women tend to experience more stress at home or in intimate circles whereas for men, it is mostly outside home. Females report stress arising from physical or mental violence more than males (Tables 20.28 and 20.29). For men, actual violence or threat of violence from neighbours form the highest source of stress (29 per cent) but for married women, female-in-laws are a source of much stress (48 per cent).

Do Keralite women suffer violence and aggression within home more than outside? It seems Keralite women are more subjected to violence in intimate personal circles either at home or outside home. But for men, non-relatives/ or distantly related persons constitute the major source of violence with an exception of brothers (19 per cent).

Table 20.28

Stress on Relationship, 2002

By Whom	*Male*	*Rank*	*Female*	*Rank*
Sibling	28.44	1	24.56	3
Neighbours	26.67	2	22.78	4
Other	18.22	3	27.05	2
Extended kin	16.89	4	19.93	5
Spouse	16.44(19.37)	5	37.22(53.81)	1
Work colleagues	14.22	6	02.85	8
Mother-in-law and daughter-in-law	04.89(05.76)	7	19.57(27.91)	6
Parent-child	02.67(03.14)	8	13.17(17.78)	7

Note: Percentages in the brackets are percentages from the married people, who answered for this question.

Source: Field Survey, 2002.

Table 20.29

Stress on Physical or Mental Violence, 2002

By Whom	*Male*	*Rank*	*Female*	*Rank*
Neighbours	28.57	1	20.13	2
Brother	19.05	2	13.20	5
Extended kin	16.40	3	19.47	4
Other	15.34	4	05.28	8
Work colleagues	13.23	5	03.96	9
Spouse	12.70(14.37)	6	19.47(29.06)	3
Father	07.94	7	02.97	10
Mother	06.35	8	02.31	11
Son	04.76(05.38)	9	(06.60(09.85)	7
Female-in-law	04.23(04.79)	10	32.34(48.28)	1
Male-in-law	04.23(04.79)	11	11.22)(17.75)	6

Note: Percentages in the brackets are percentages from the married people, who answered for this question.

Source: Field Survey, 2002.

If we examine causes for violence, financial matters constitute the foremost for both sexes; however, for men it is twice as much as it is for women. Next come disputes over property which is of the same magnitudes for both sexes (Table 20.30). But when it comes to dowry, alcohol-related problems, insubordination to spouse, infidelity real or imagined, sexual discord, sloppy performance of household chores, more women suffer violence.

Table 20.30

Reasons for Violence, 2002

Reasons	*Male*	*Rank*	*Female*	*Rank*
Money matters	60.85	1	32.28	1
Property dispute	21.69	2	22.44	2
Other	20.11	3	16.17	5
Alcohol	16.40	4	21.78	3
Disobedience or disrespect to spouse	10.58(11.97)	5	09.57(14.29)	8
Suspicious and infidelity	03.17	6	19.80	4
Not doing household work properly	02.65	7	11.88	6
Dowry	00.00	8	09.57(14.29)	7
Refusing to have sex	00.00	9	03.63(5.41)	9

Note: Percentages in the brackets are percentages from the married people, who answered for this question.

Source: Field Survey, 2002.

Table 20.31

Reasons for Stress on Decision-making, 2002

Reasons	*Male*	*Female*
Property matters	06.57	13.61
Community activities	01.68	06.30
Decisions on how many children	00.84	04.87

Source: Field Survey, 2002.

Table 20.32

Reasons for Stress due to Migration

Reasons	*Total*	
	Male	*Female*
Feeling lonely	0.00	9.88
No adult male in the house	1.00	5.55
Having to make decisions	0.60	7.10
Many tasks and responsibilities	1.20	5.72
Controlled too much by in-laws	0.00	3.64
Vulnerable to gossip	0.20	2.95
Improper advances of men	0.40	1.21
Separation from parents	1.20	4.15
Jealousy	0.20	3.29
Handling large money	0.20	1.73

Source: Field Survey, 2002.

Emigrant status of households is not seen as much stressful by men in emigrant households. On the other hand, women report much more stress associated with Gulf migration. Loneliness is the top most stress factor for women (10 per cent). An earlier study conducted by Zachariah and Rajan (2001) also reports similar findings about Gulf wives whose husbands were away. Exclusive responsibility for decision-making, undue control of in-laws, having too many responsibilities to shoulder, absence of an adult male at home, separation from parents and envy of others are all viewed as stress factors by women of migrant households (Table 20.32).

Summary and Conclusions

A household survey was conducted among all members of age group 15-59 years and among responsive persons between 60-69 years in a randomly selected sample of 1000 households in Kerala. The major aim was to elucidate gender-related issues in mental health, human well-being, stress experience of the Kerala population. Men in general were found to have relatively better sense of well-being and mental health. Women reported more stress than men in most of the areas concerned. However, there is indication that gender differences are converging over the generations and especially women seem to be changing more in a positive direction in most of the selected indices. The overall impact of a woman being head of the family is positive on men living in the same household. But the same is not true in the case of women. The younger generation, the better educated ones and the unmarried score better on most of the indices irrespective of gender. Marriage seems to have a negative impact in terms of both well-being and mental health of persons. Migration status exerts a positive influence on well being of people but not necessarily on mental health. Working in the public sector is good for men and women on all counts but men are definitely better off than women in public sector jobs. Farmers in Kerala suffer the most compared to those in other walks of life. Well-being and mental health of men steadily increase as we move from north to southern region of Kerala while the reverse is true for women.

References

Banks, Michael H., Paul R. Jackson, Elizabeth M. Stafford and Peter B. Warr (1983). "Unemployment and Psychological Distress in Young People: The Moderating Role of Employment Commitment", *Journal of Applied Psychology* 68(3): 525-535.

Banthia, (2001). "Census of India 2001, Series 1, India, Provisional Population Totals", Paper 1 of 2001. Registrar General and Census Commissioner of India.

Eapen, Mridul (2002). "Mental Health of Women in Kerala: The Need for a Gender Perspective", *Samyukta—A Journal of Women's Studies* 2(2): 25-36.

Eapen, Mridul and Praveena Kodoth (2002). "Family Structure, Women's Education and Work: Re-examining the High Status of Women in Kerala", *Working Paper* No. 341, November. Thiruvananthapuram: Centre for Development Studies.

Franke, Richard W. and Barbara H. Chasin (1994). *Kerala: Radical Reform as Development in an Indian State.* Oakland, California: Institute for Food and Development Policy.

Goldberg, D.P. (1972). *The Detecting of Psychiatric Illness by Questionnaire: A Technique for the Identification and Assessment of Non-Psychotic Psychiatric Disease.* Oxford: Oxford University Press.

Guilmoto, Christophe Z. and S. Irudaya Rajan (2002). "District Level Estimates of Fertility from India's 2001 Census", *Economic and Political Weekly* XXXVII(7): 665-672.

Halliburton, Murphy (1998). "Suicide: A Paradox of Development in Kerala", *Economic and Political Weekly* 33(36&37): 2341-2345.

Hirway, Indira and Darshini Mahadevia (1996). "Critique of Gender Development Index: Towards an Alternative", *Economic and Political Weekly* 31(43): WS 87-96.

Hochschild, A.R. (1997). *The Time Bind when Work Becomes Home and Home Becomes Work.* Metropolitan Books.

INCLEN/ICRW (2000). *Indiasafe: Studies of Abuse in the Family Environment in India: A Summary Report.* International Clinical Epidemiologists Network, India.

International Institute for Population Sciences (IIPS) and ORC Macro (2000). *National Family Health Survey (NFHS-2), 1998-99.* Mumbai: IIPS. (*www.nfhsindia.org*)

Irudaya Rajan, S. (2006). *Suicides among Elderly in Kerala.* (paper under preparation).

Irudaya Rajan S. and P. Mohanachandran (1999a). "Is the IMR in Kerala as low as 12? Beginning an Exploration", *Demography India* 28(1): 131-144.

———. (1999b). "Estimating Infant Mortality in Kerala", *Economic and Political Weekly* XXXIV(12): 713-716. March 20-26.

Irudaya Rajan, S., S. Sudha and P. Mohanachandran (2000). "Fertility Decline and Worsening Gender Bias in India: Is Kerala no Longer an Exception?", *Development and Change* 31(4): 1085-92.

Planning Commission (2002). *National Human Development Report (2001).* Government of India. March.

Rosenfield and Sarah (1989). "The Effect of Women's Employment: Personal Control and Sex Difference in Mental Health", *Journal of Health and Social Behaviour* 30: 77-91.

Ross, C.E. and J. Mirowisky (2002). *Social Psychology Quarterly* 65(2): 125-145.

Sakhi (2002). *Support Services to Counter Violence against Women in Kerala: A Resource Directory.* Trivandrum: SAKHI Resource Centre for Women.

Sell, H. and R. Nagpal (1992). "Assessment of Subjective Well-Being", *SEARO Regional Health Paper* No. 24.

Shamsunder, C., T.G. Sriram, S.G. Muraliraj and V. Shanmughan (1986). "Validity of a Short 5-Items Version of the General Health Questionnaire", *Indian Journal of Psychiatry* 28:217-19.

Sonpar, S. and R.L. Kapur (2003). "Non-conventional Indicators of Gender Disparities under Structural Reforms", in Mukhopadhyay and Sudarshan (eds.), *Tracking Gender Equity under the Economic Reforms.* New Delhi: Kali for Women.

Strandh, M. (2000). "Different Exit Routes from Unemployment and their Impact on Mental Well-Being", *Work, Employment & Society* 14(3): 459-479.

United Nations Development Programme (1995). *Human Development Report 1995.* New Delhi: Oxford University Press.

Warr, P., P. Jackson and M. Banks (1988). "Unemployment and Mental Health: Some British Studies", *Journal of Social Issues* 44(4): 47-68.

Zachariah, K.C. and E.T. Mathew and Irudaya Rajan (2003). *Dynamics of Migration in Kerala: Dimensions, Differentials and Consequences*. Hyderabad: Orient Longman Private Limited.

Zachariah, K.C. and S. Irudaya Rajan (2001a). "Gender Dimensions of Migration in Kerala: Macro and Micro Evidences", *Asia Pacific Population Journal* 16(3): 47-70.

———. (2001b). "Migration Mosaic in Kerala: Trends and Determinants", *Demography India* 30(1): 137-165.

Zachariah, K.C., B.A. Prakash and S. Irudaya Rajan (2002). "Gulf Migration Study: Employment, Wages and Working Conditions of Kerala Emigrants in the United Arab Emirates", *Working Paper* No. 326. Centre for Development Studies.

Zachariah, K.C., E.T. Mathew and S. Irudaya Rajan (2001a). "Impact of Migration on Kerala's Economy and Society", *International Migration* 39(1): 63-88. (First published as a CDS *Working Paper* no. 297)

———. (2001b). "Social, Economic and Demographic Consequences of Migration on Kerala", *International Migration* 39(2): 43-71. (First published as a CDS *Working Paper* no. 303)

Zachariah, K.C., P.R. Gopinathan Nair and S. Irudaya Rajan (2001). "Return Emigrants in Kerala: Rehabilitation Problems and Development Potential", Centre for Development Studies, *Working Paper* No.319.

21

The Emerging Demographic Situation in Kerala

M. VIJAYANUNNI

As per the 2001 census age data, the proportion of population in the working age group 15-59 in Kerala was 63.4 per cent as against the all-India figure of 56.9 per cent in the same age group. The corresponding figures for Kerala in 1991 was 61.2 per cent as against the all-India figure of 55.4 per cent. Thus, the working age population in Kerala has been on the rise in the recent decades.

When a country has more people in the working age group, it is supposed to generate higher GDP growth. GDP is produced by labour and capital. Working age population provides labour and also saves for investment. Hence, at this stage of the demographic transition, the country is expected to enjoy the double benefit of more people in the labour market and more savings in the capital market. This has been the recent experience of other fast-growing Asian economies.

When the proportion of working age population decreases due to low fertility rates, it will adversely affect economic growth. For example, the 15 to 64 age group population in Japan, which was 70 per cent in 1990 has now dropped to 66 per cent and will further drop to 56 per cent by 2035. This would mean that Japan would require an annual migrant infusion of 600,000 workers to sustain its economy in the coming years.

India, and particularly Kerala, is now supposed to be at an advantageous position in this regard with a growing young population. Has Kerala been able to translate this strength into economic growth? The economic growth figures of the state during the last four years, sector-wise, tell their own story.

Year	*Growth Rate (per cent)*			
	Primary	*Secondary*	*Tertiary*	*Overall*
2001-02	-0.06	-0.84	2.84	1.50
2002-03	1.47	5.81	8.55	6.63
2003-04	-2.01	6.02	8.88	6.31
2004-05	-2.88	5.56	8.76	6.15

Source: State Planning Board (2005). *Economic Review 2004*. Thiruvananthapuram: Govt. of Kerala.

Thus, the growth figures of the state during the last four years do not seem to commensurate with the existence of the growing young population, which is quite obvious from the high unemployment burden of nearly 40 lakh registered in the Employment Exchanges which is 10 per cent of the all-India figure of 410 lakh (2003), as compared to Kerala's share of population of 3.1 per cent. Kerala's economic growth rates in all the sectors are actually lower than those of all-India despite the higher proportion of working age population.

Kerala's economic growth has been particularly affected adversely by a crisis in the primary sector marked by negative growth. While the state was characterised b a primarily rural agrarian economy in the last century, the agricultural sector has witnessed a steep drop in the percentage of cultivators plus agricultural labour which has come down from 48 per cent in 1971 to 40 per cent in 1991 and further down to 22.8 per cent in 2001. The percentage of cultivators fell from 13.2 per cent in 1991 to 7 per cent in 2001, while the percentage of landless agricultural labourers also fell drastically from 26.8 per cent in 1991 to 15.8 per cent in 2001. Thus, agriculture as a source of subsistence and employment is fast shrinking in importance in the state, accentuated by the continuing spectra of farmer suicides, rising debt burden and falling returns of most farm produce.

The number of operational holdings in the state has increased from 25 lakh in 1966-67 to 38 lakh in 1980-81, 49 lakh in 1985-86, 54 lakh in 1990-1991 and to 65 lakh by 1998-99. Fifty lakh of these holdings were less than one hectare in size and 45 lakh were less than half hectare. Seventy-seven per cent of paddy field holdings are less than one hectare and 87 per cent of cultivators come in this category. This shows the inviability of the holdings.

The average size of homestead in the state is less than 0.44 hectare in 70 per cent of the homesteads and a majority of the homesteads fall into either overcrowding or under-utilisation resulting in low system productivity. The reason for this were many like pests and diseases, unfavourable market conditions, absence of family labour consequent to the migration of males, the unavailability and high cost of hired labour and lack of government support to the homesteads.

That takes us to the concept of 'ecological footprint', which is the land needed to maintain a population at its present level of consumption. This differs from country to country. The world average figure at present is 2 hectares per inhabitant. The current population of the world of 630 crore is already 'over the limit' and hence, the present level of consumption cannot expect to be sustained.

Each US citizen requires 10 hectares to sustain his consumption at the present level. Just to cite a few statistics to illustrate this: The US uses twice as much energy per capita as Europeans, 10 times more than Asians and 20 times more than Africans. The US uses more than one-fourth of the world's oil. The average American in a lifetime consumes 62,000 pounds of animal products, 55,000 pounds of plant foods, 770 tonnes of minerals and the energy equivalent of 4000 barrels of petroleum.

An Indian, at the present level of consumption, requires one hectare per head, and India's present population size of 105 crores is three times over the limit, while Kerala's population of 330 lakh is already 10 times over the limit.

That Kerala's ecosystem and natural resources are put to the severest test due to the high levels of population density will be obvious from some representative statistics given in the following paragraphs.

Kerala produces 6000 tonnes of waste per day, which is more than double the national average in India. The per capita annual consumption of plastic is 6 kg in Kerala against 1.8 kg in India, pointing to the higher levels of population in the state. According to the WHO norms, garbage landfills should be located at least 50 km away from inhabited areas. But with its high levels of population density and land utilisation for human habitators, no vacant land fulfilling this criterion can be easily located in the state and disposal of urban solid waste is a constant and daily source of friction and conflict between municipal bodies and local people all across the state.

The deteriorating air quality and increasing levels of air and noise pollution in the state are also causing serious concern. The number of vehicles has increased 20 times during the last three decades causing increasing levels of air pollution. The Eloor industrial area has the dubious distinction of being the first inhabited area in the world where the presence of the most toxic substance dioxane in the form of hexachlorobutadiene has been detected with a presence of 655 times the safe level. Chloroform at 85 times the safe level have also been detected there.

Across the world, at the current level of CO_2 omissions, the concentrations in the atmosphere will double by 2100, resulting in a rise in the global temperature of one degree celsius over this country. But in Kerala, the maximum, minimum and average temperature have already registered a growth of 0.8, 0.2 and 0.5 degree celsius since 1961 due to omission of greenhouse gases, increase in population and changes in land use pattern, contributing to climate change.

All rivers in the state are polluted by human waste. Even the holy river of Pamba was found to carry 200 times the permitted level of coliform bacteria originating from human excreta, with 100 millilitres of water containing 95,000 bacteria as against the WHO norm which allows only a maximum of 500 even in water of bathing. One litre of water from the river was found to contain 2 milligram of ammonia which is 40 times the allowed limit. The dissolved oxygen content was found to be only 0.73 milligram whereas at least 4 milligram is required for fish to survive, thus making the river uninhabitable even for fish.

Kerala is already facing acute water shortage despite 300 cm of rainfall annually, which is two and a half times the national average. The state was having an excellent water storage system with 50 lakh open wells and innumerable ponds and tanks dotting the entire length and breadth of the countryside and supplying the required water round the year for a sustainable population in the past. But now with an unsustainable level of human habitation and continuing wetland reclamation, water is fast becoming a scarce commodity in this state.

There was a devastating flood in the year 1924 and another similar one recently in the year 2001. Though the flood waters of 1924 reached a height of one and a half meters higher than those of 2001, the waters flowed out completely within 24 hours whereas in 2001, it took 48 hours for the flood water to recede fully. This shows how much the ecosystem of the state has been adversely affected due to uncontrolled land reclamation during the recent past.

Despite the definite progress achieved by the state in socio-economic parameters during the past decades, there is no gainsaying the fact that social tensions are an inescapable part of the present demographic situation in the state. This is manifest in the fact that Kerala's suicide rate is among the highest in the world for the last many years and has been further rising from year to year. The suicide rate in the state which was 24.5 in 1989 as against the national average of 8.5, rose to 25.9 in 1995, 28.5 in 1997 and further to 31.5 in 2000 as against the national average of 11.2.

There is urgent need to adopt a new and innovation development paradigm, which will address and take care of the emerging demographic problems of the state of Kerala, which are entirely different from those of the other parts of Inida. The supposed 'Kerala model of development' has failed to redeem and vindicate itself.

References

Director of Census Operation, Kerala (2004). *Final Population Totals, Kerala*, Census of India 2001, Controller of Publications, Delhi.

———. (2005). *Primary Census Abstract, Kerala*, Census of India 2001, Controller of Publications, Delhi.

Registrar General and Census Commissioner, India (2004). *Primary Census Abstract, India*, Census of India 2001, Controller of Publications, Delhi.

———. (2004). *Report and Tables on Age, India*, Census of India 2001, Controller of Publications, Delhi.

State Planning Board (2005). *Economic Review 2004*, Government of Kerala, Trivandrum.